LET'S SHAKE HANDS

AT KORAKUEN AMUSEMENT PARK.

ROAR

Takeshi Obata

We've reached volume six. We've been serialized for more than a year now. I have an expensive Go board and Go bowls at work, and I even have a mountain of books about Go. Sigh... It's about time I learned to play.

—Takeshi Obata

It all began when Yumi Hotta played a pick-up game of Go with her father-in-law. As she was learning how to play, Ms. Hotta thought it might be fun to create a story around the traditional board game. More confident in her storytelling abilities than her drawing skills, she submitted the beginnings of **Hikaru no Go** to **Weekly Shonen Jump**'s Story King Award. The Story King Award is an award that picks the best story, manga, character design and youth (under 15) manga submissions every year in Japan. As fate would have it, Ms. Hotta's story (originally named, "*Kokonotsu no Hoshi*"), was a runner-up in the "Story" category of the Story King Award. Many years earlier, Takeshi Obata was a runner-up for the Tezuka Award, another Japanese manga contest sponsored by **Weekly Shonen Jump** and **Monthly Shonen Jump**. An editor assigned to Mr. Obata's artwork came upon Ms. Hotta's story and paired the two for a full-fledged manga about Go. The rest is modern Go history.

HIKARU NO GO VOL. 6
The SHONEN JUMP Manga Edition

This manga contains material that was originally published in English from
SHONEN JUMP #33 to #37.

STORY BY YUMI HOTTA
ART BY TAKESHI OBATA
Supervised by YUKARI UMEZAWA (5 Dan)

Translation & English Adaptation/Andy Nakatani
English Script Consultant/Janice Kim (3 Dan)
Touch-up Art & Lettering/Adam Symons
Design/Courtney Utt
Additional Touch-up/Josh Simpson
Editor/Yuki Takagaki

Managing Editor/Elizabeth Kawasaki
Director of Production/Noboru Watanabe
Vice President of Publishing/Alvin Lu
Vice President & Editor in Chief/Yumi Hoashi
Sr. Director of Acquisitions/Rika Inouye
Vice President of Sales & Marketing/Liza Coppola
Publisher/Hyoe Narita

Printed in the U.S.A.

Published by VIZ Media, LLC
P.O. Box 77010
San Francisco, CA 94107

SHONEN JUMP Manga Edition
10 9 8 7 6 5 4 3 2 1
First printing, January 2006

www.viz.com

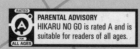

PARENTAL ADVISORY
HIKARU NO GO is rated A and is
suitable for readers of all ages.

THE WORLD'S
MOST POPULAR MANGA

www.shonenjump.com

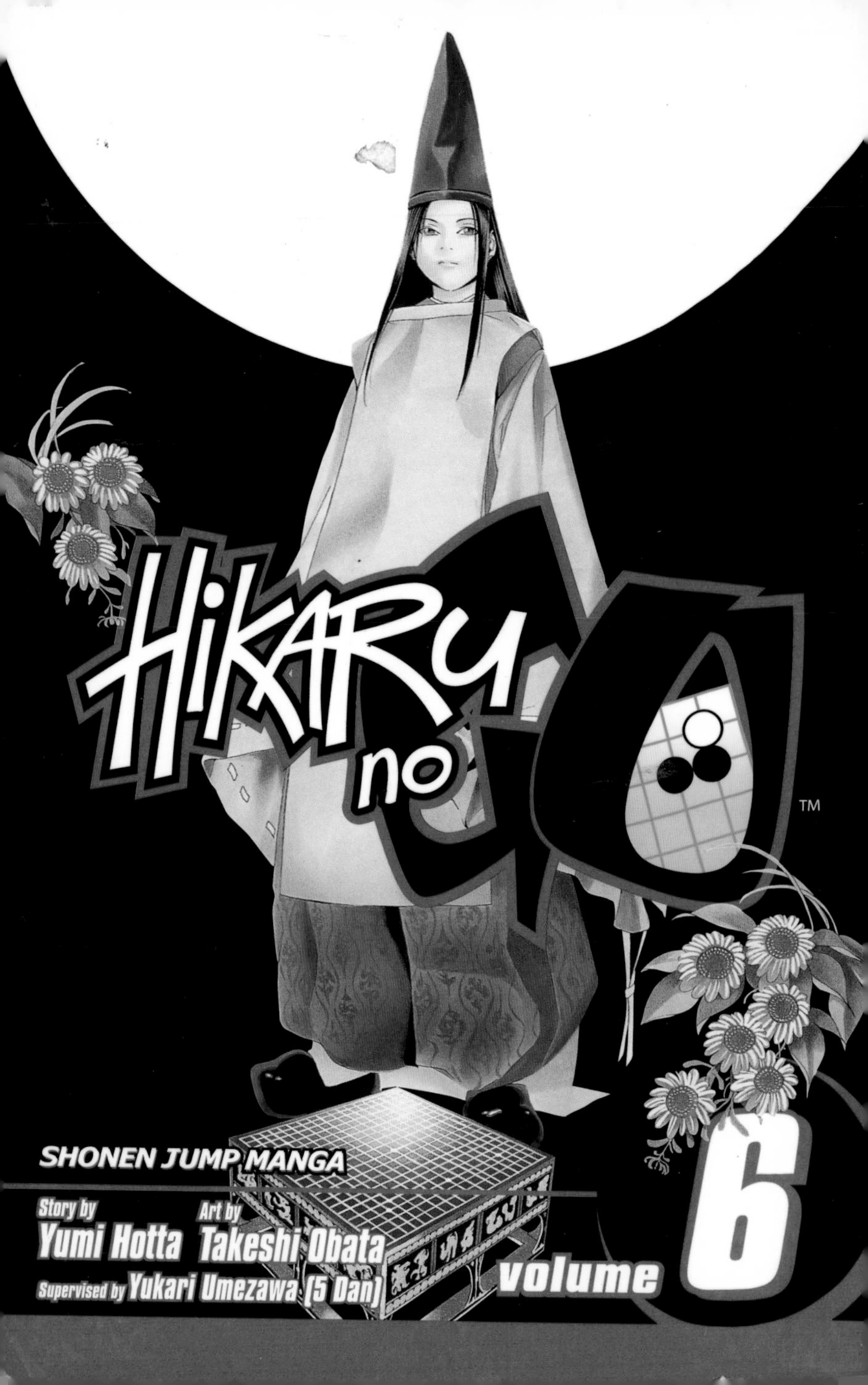
HIKARU no GO™
SHONEN JUMP MANGA
Story by
Yumi Hotta
Art by
Takeshi Obata
Supervised by Yukari Umezawa (5 Dan)
volume 6

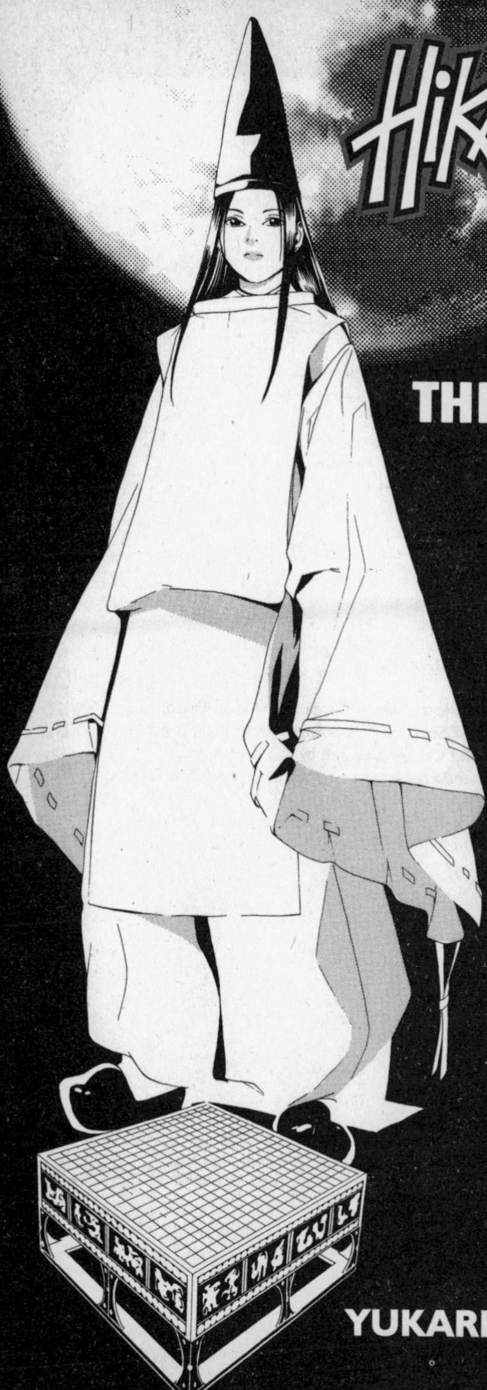

Hikaru no Go™

THE INSEI EXAM

6

STORY BY
YUMI HOTTA

ART BY
TAKESHI OBATA

Supervised by
YUKARI UMEZAWA (5 Dan)

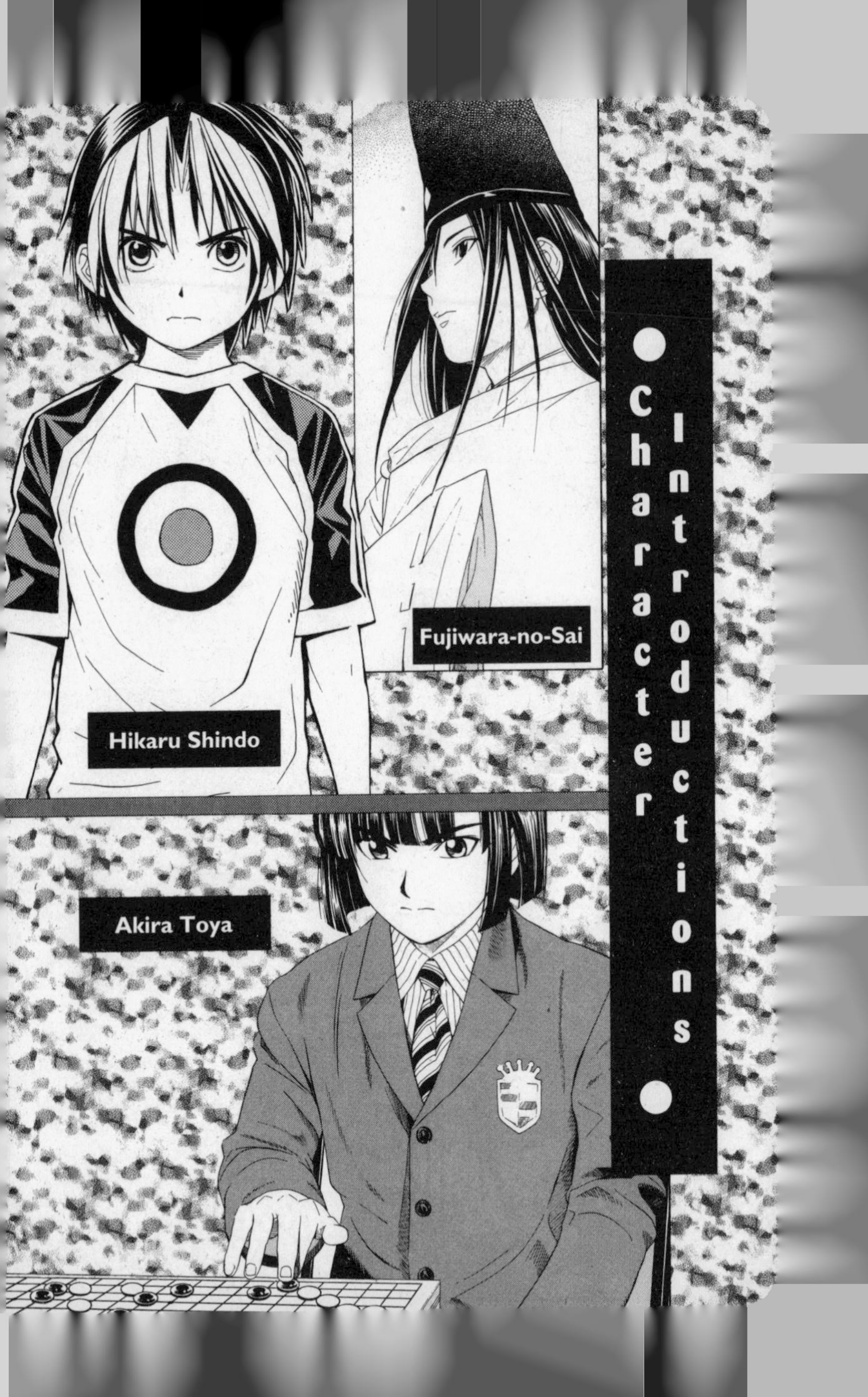
Character Introductions
Fujiwara-no-Sai
Hikaru Shindo
Akira Toya

Yoshitaka Waya
Yuki Mitani
Kimihiro Tsutsui
Shinichiro Isumi
Akari Fujisaki
Tetsuo Kaga

Story Thus Far

One day, sixth-grader Hikaru discovers an old Go board in his grandfather's storage room. The instant he touches the board, the spirit of a genius Go player from the Heian Era, Fujiwara-no-Sai, enters Hikaru's consciousness. Sai's love of Go, and a chance encounter with the child prodigy Akira Toya (son of Go master Toya Meijin), inspire Hikaru, and he slowly becomes interested in Go.

Hikaru uses the screen name "sai"to play online Go with Akira, but Akira quits the game out of the blue and asks for a rematch on another day. He skips the first day of his pro test for the rematch, but still loses to "sai." Meanwhile, Hikaru has been steadily improving his game. One day, he runs into Kaoru Kishimoto of Kaio's Go club, who mentions that Akira has passed the pro test. It dawns on Hikaru that he may never catch up to Akira, and he decides to take the *insei* exam. But he forgets that *insei* aren't allowed to play in amateur tournaments and fights with Yuki over quitting the school Go club. In the end, Hikaru proves himself to the club by playing simultaneous games against Kimihiro, Yuki, and Kaga. Now, the day of Hikaru's insei exam has finally arrived.

CONTENTS

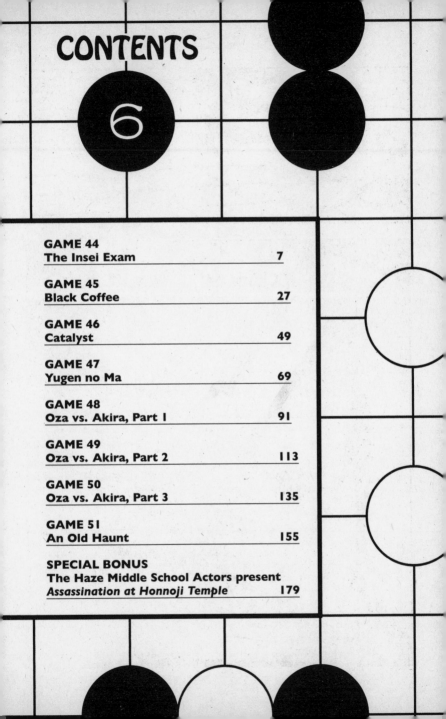

6

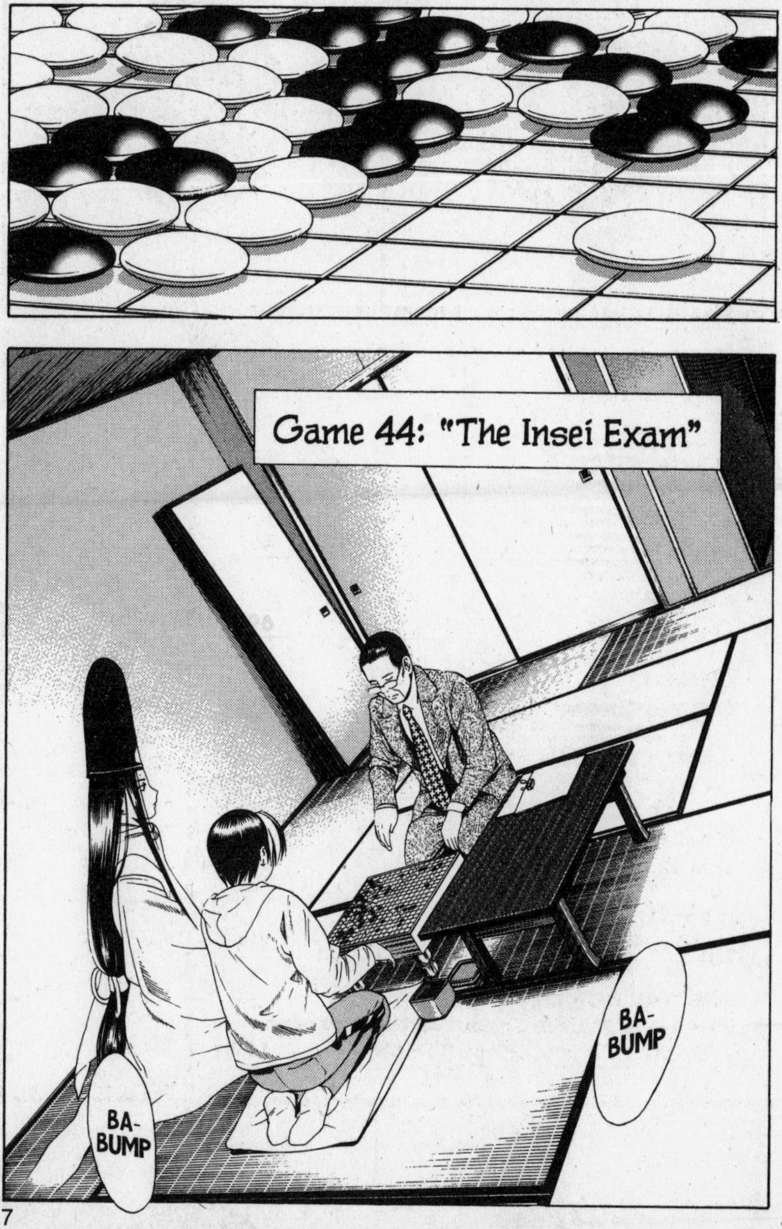
Game 44: "The Insei Exam"
BA-
BUMP
BA-
BUMP

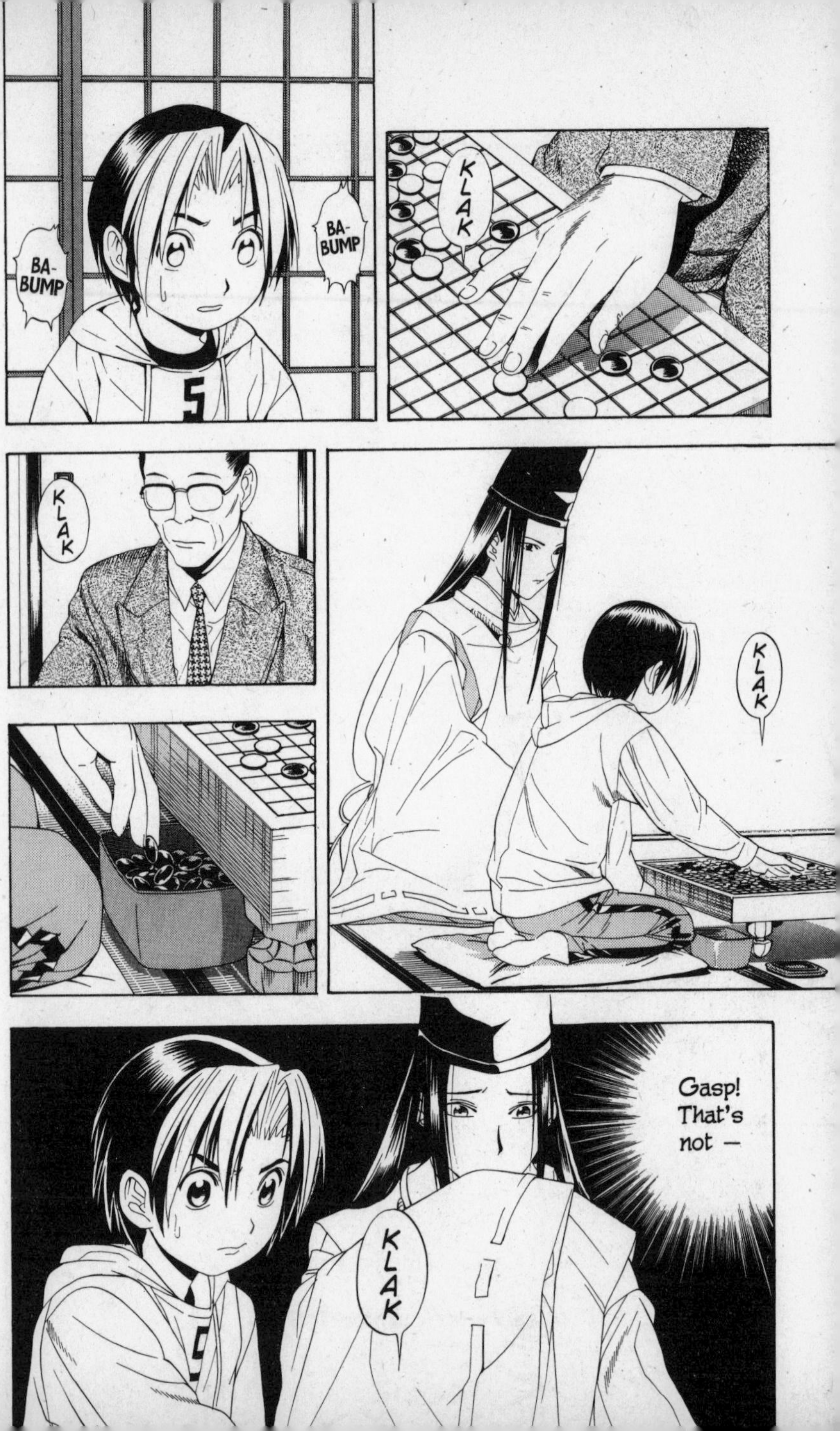
KLAK
BA-BUMP
BA-BUMP
KLAK
KLAK
Gasp! That's not —
KLAK

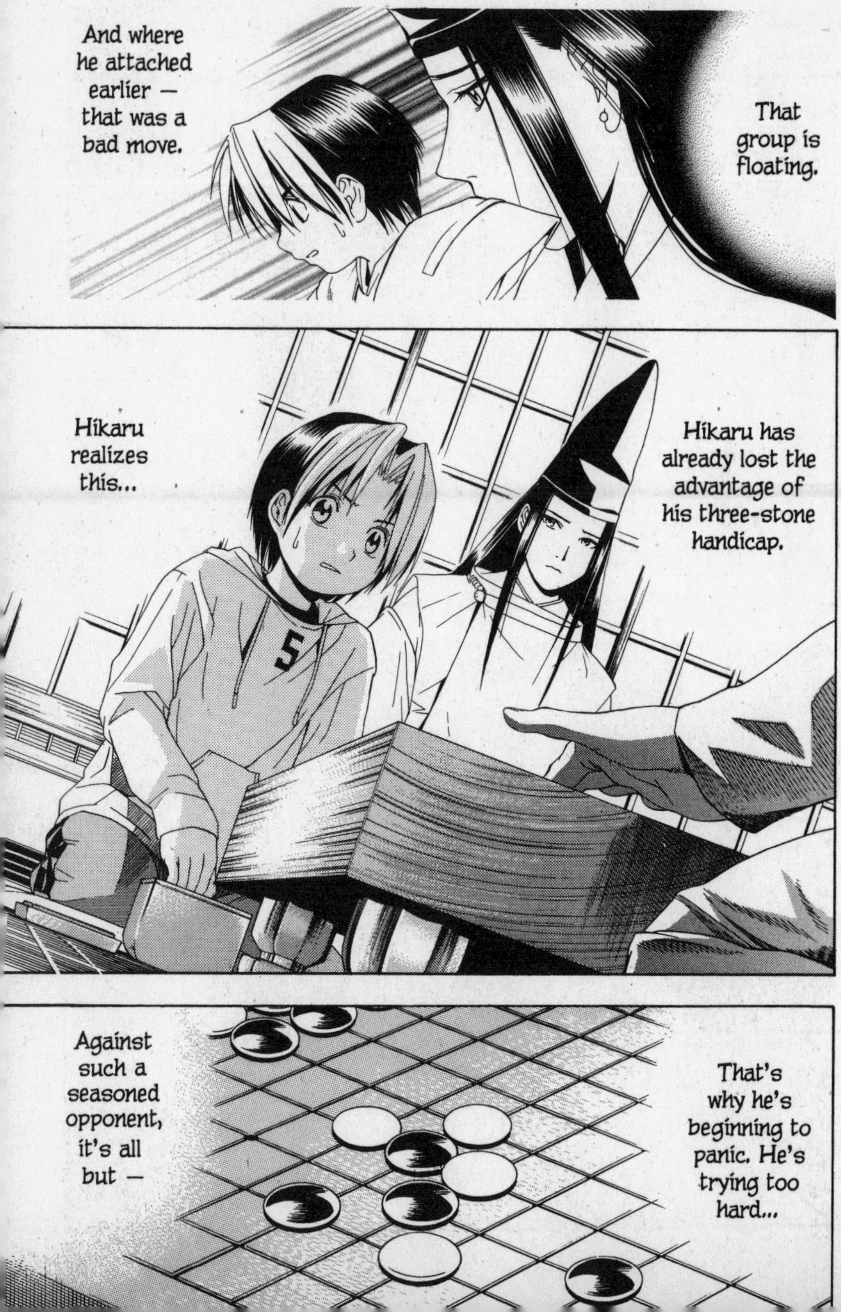
That group is floating.
And where he attached earlier — that was a bad move.
Hikaru has already lost the advantage of his three-stone handicap.
Hikaru realizes this...
Against such a seasoned opponent, it's all but —
That's why he's beginning to panic. He's trying too hard...

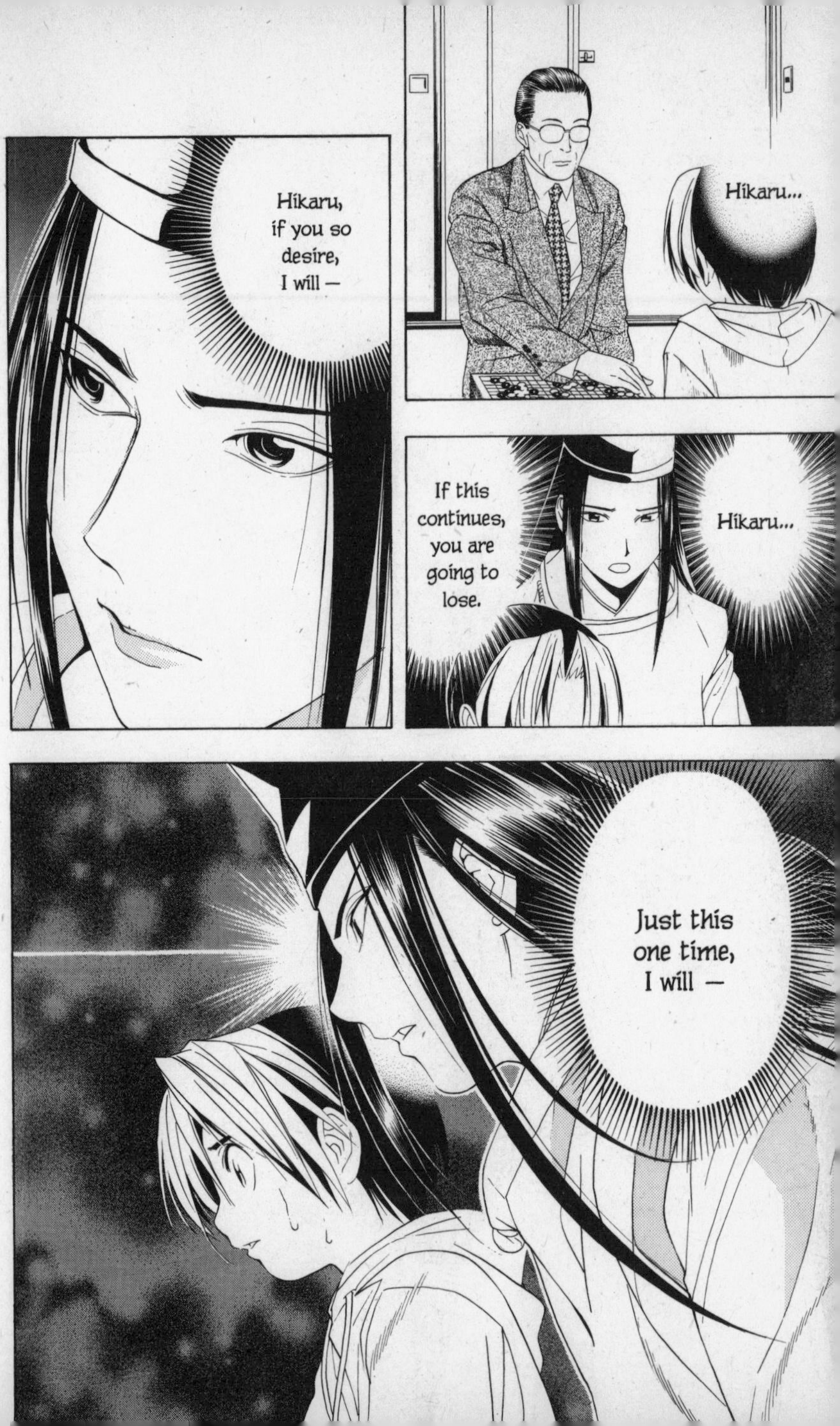
Hikaru...
Hikaru...
If this continues, you are going to lose.
Hikaru, if you so desire, I will —
Just this one time, I will —

READ THIS WAY

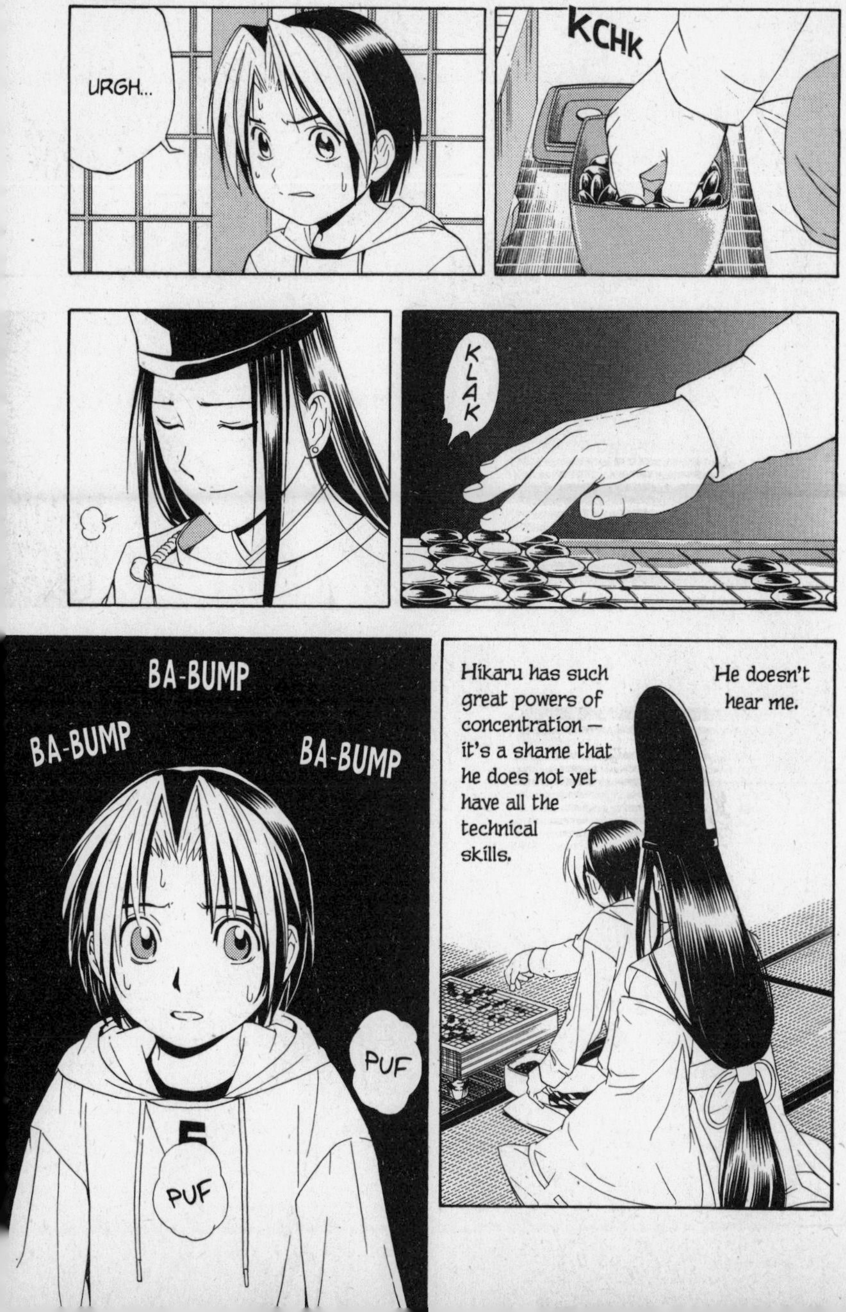
KCHK
URGH...
KLAK
He doesn't hear me.
Hikaru has such great powers of concentration – it's a shame that he does not yet have all the technical skills.
BA-BUMP
BA-BUMP
BA-BUMP
PUF
PUF

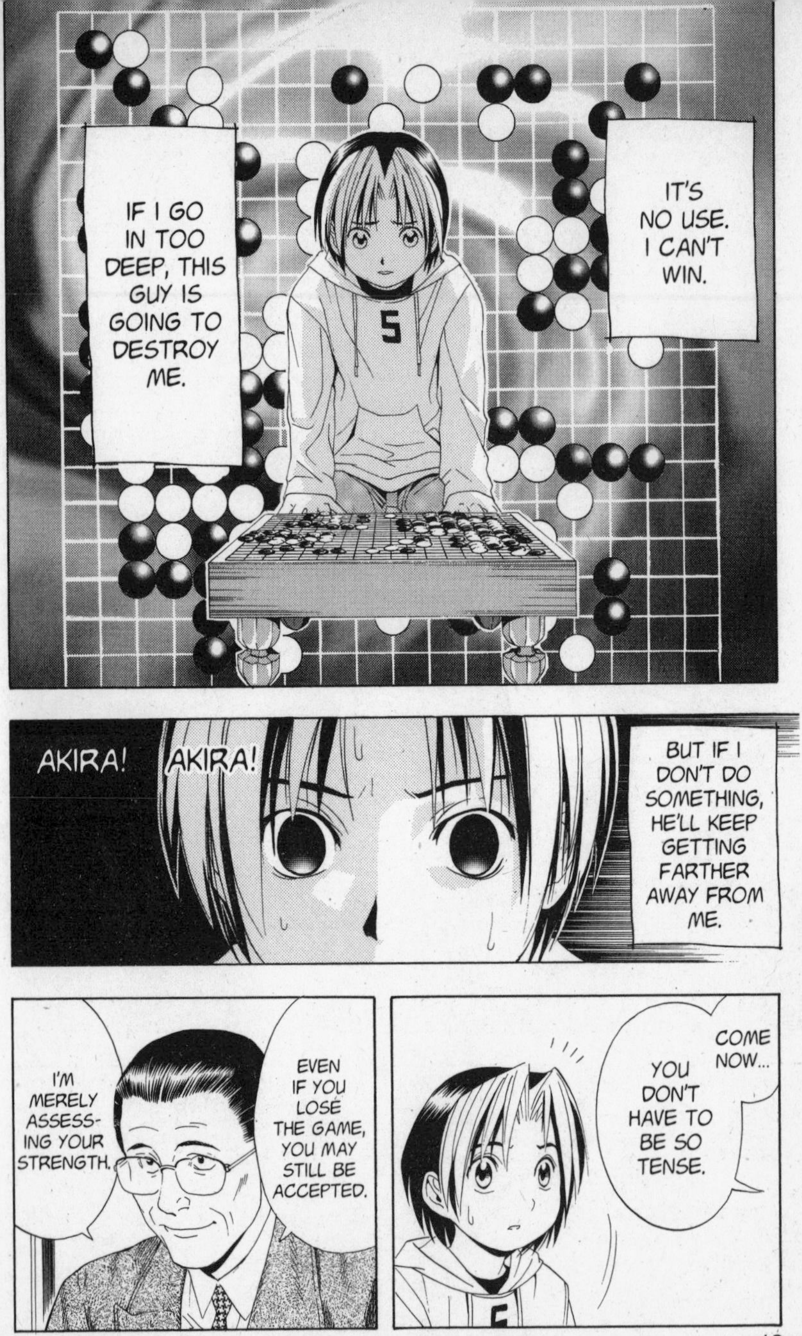
IT'S NO USE. I CAN'T WIN.
IF I GO IN TOO DEEP, THIS GUY IS GOING TO DESTROY ME.
BUT IF I DON'T DO SOMETHING, HE'LL KEEP GETTING FARTHER AWAY FROM ME.
AKIRA!
AKIRA!
COME NOW...
YOU DON'T HAVE TO BE SO TENSE.
EVEN IF YOU LOSE THE GAME, YOU MAY STILL BE ACCEPTED.
I'M MERELY ASSESS-ING YOUR STRENGTH.

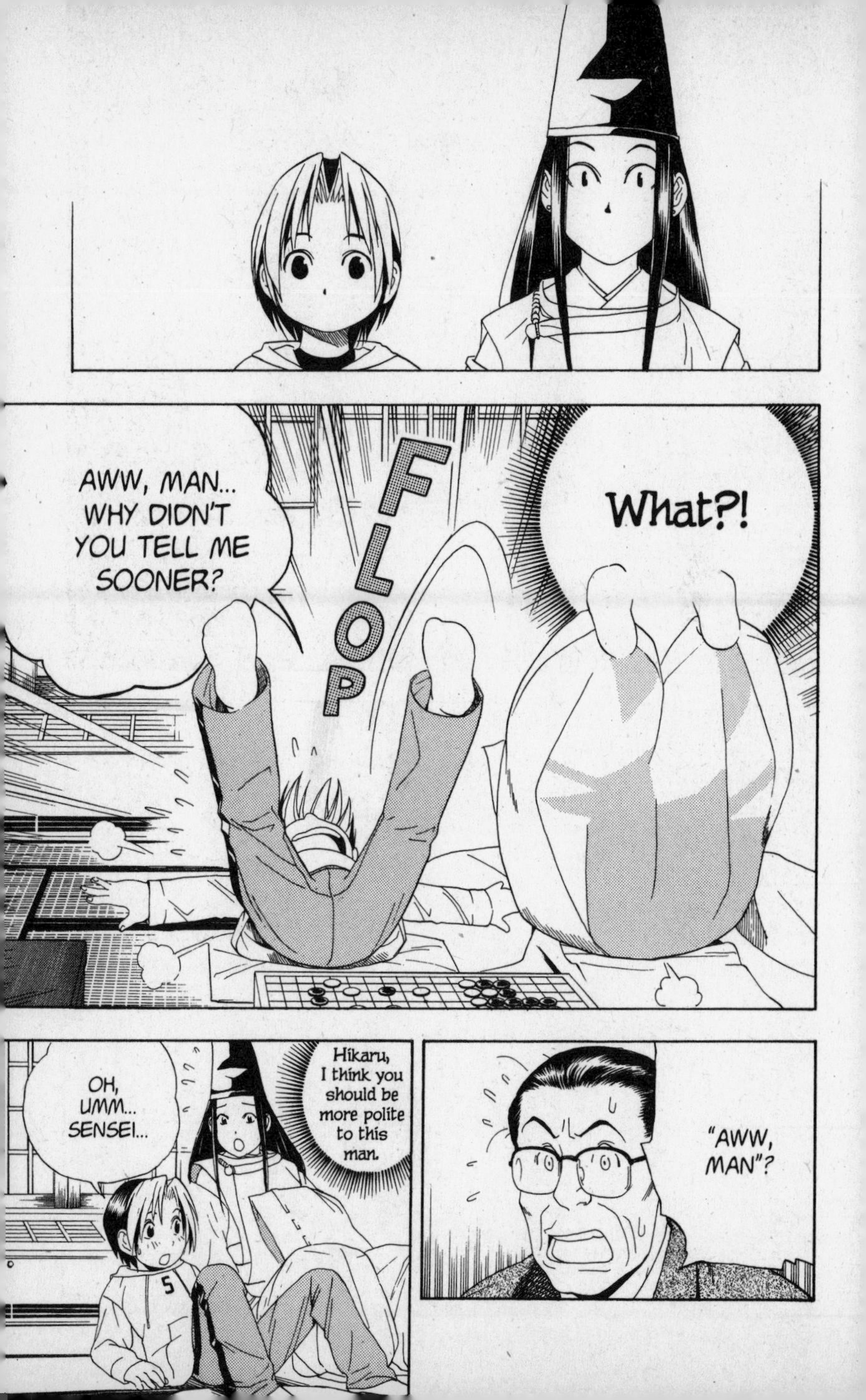
What?!
FLOP
AWW, MAN... WHY DIDN'T YOU TELL ME SOONER?
"AWW, MAN"?
Hikaru, I think you should be more polite to this man.
OH, UMM... SENSEI...

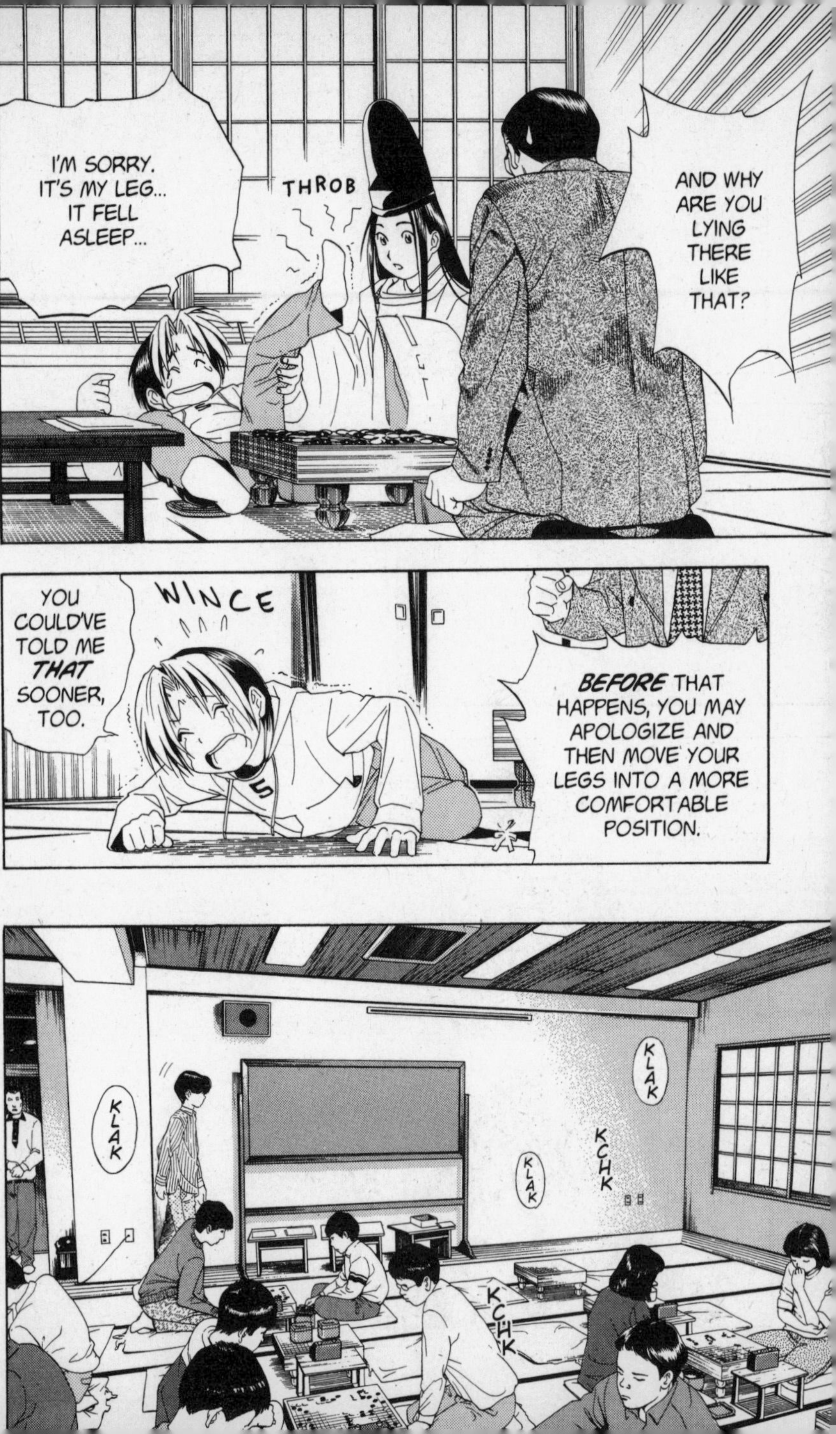
AND WHY ARE YOU LYING THERE LIKE THAT?
THROB
I'M SORRY. IT'S MY LEG... IT FELL ASLEEP...
BEFORE THAT HAPPENS, YOU MAY APOLOGIZE AND THEN MOVE YOUR LEGS INTO A MORE COMFORTABLE POSITION.
WINCE
YOU COULD'VE TOLD ME **THAT** SOONER, TOO.
KLAK
KCHK
KLAK
KCHK
KLAK

READ THIS WAY

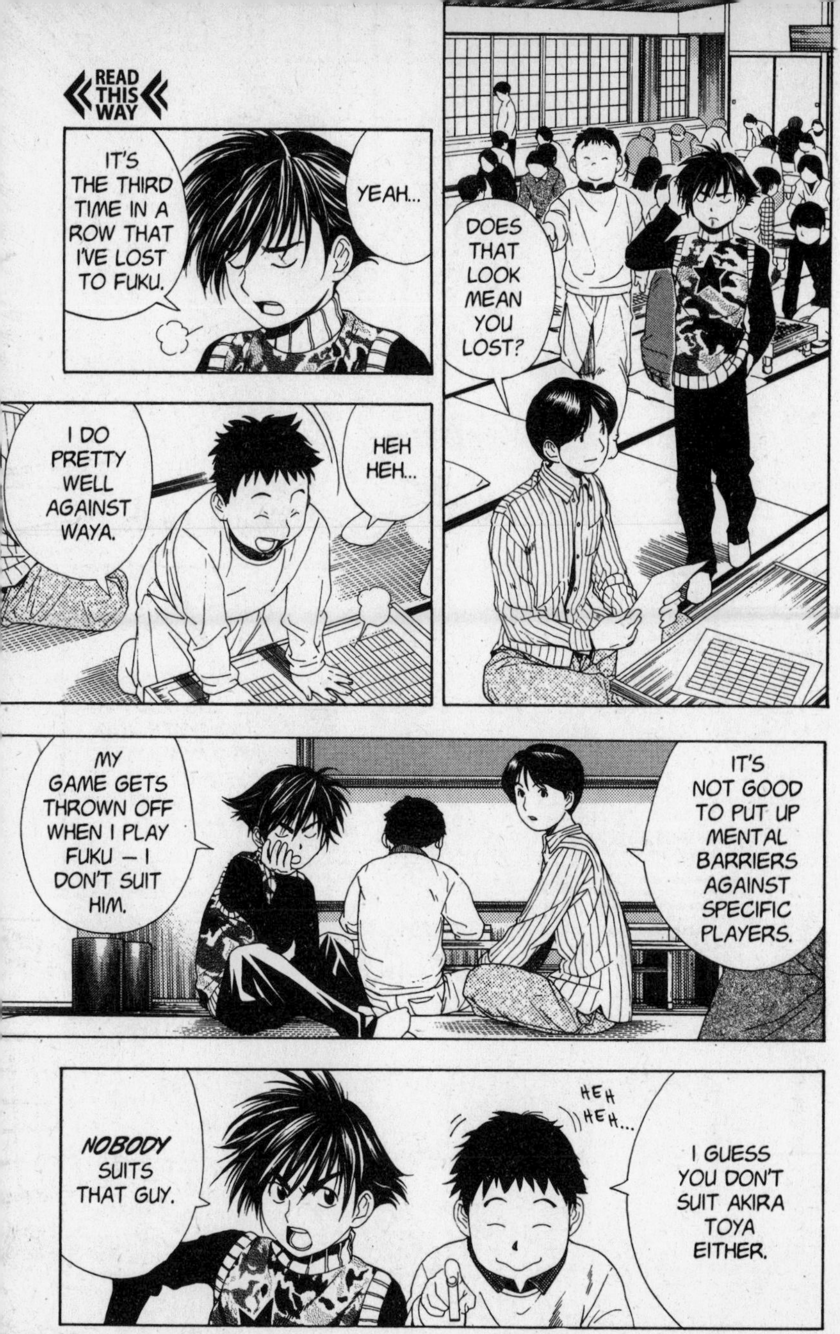

DOES THAT LOOK MEAN YOU LOST?
YEAH...
IT'S THE THIRD TIME IN A ROW THAT I'VE LOST TO FUKU.
HEH HEH...
I DO PRETTY WELL AGAINST WAYA.
IT'S NOT GOOD TO PUT UP MENTAL BARRIERS AGAINST SPECIFIC PLAYERS.
MY GAME GETS THROWN OFF WHEN I PLAY FUKU – I DON'T SUIT HIM.
I GUESS YOU DON'T SUIT AKIRA TOYA EITHER.
HEH HEH...
NOBODY SUITS THAT GUY.

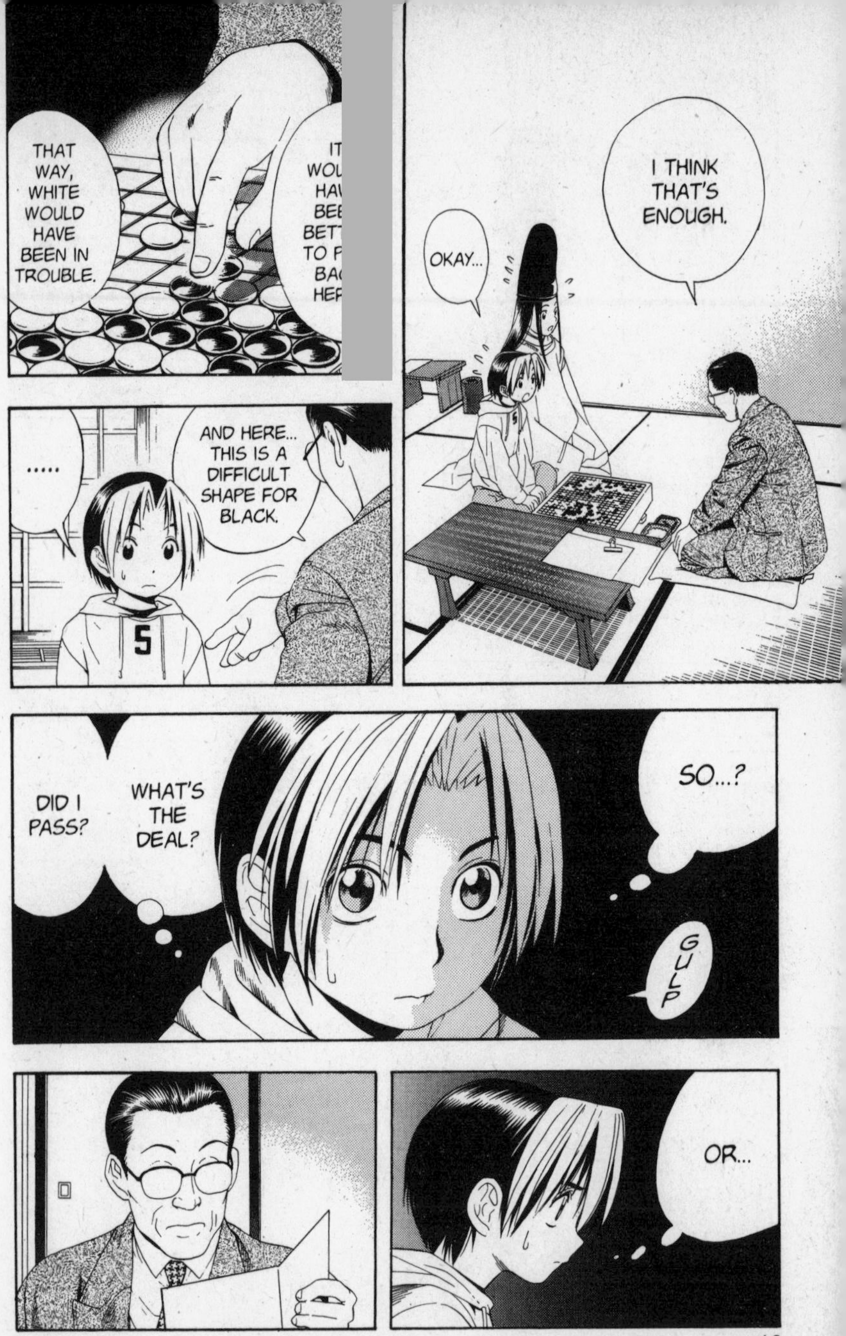
I THINK THAT'S ENOUGH.
OKAY...
THAT WAY, WHITE WOULD HAVE BEEN IN TROUBLE.
AND HERE... THIS IS A DIFFICULT SHAPE FOR BLACK.
.....
SO...?
GULP
WHAT'S THE DEAL?
DID I PASS?
OR...

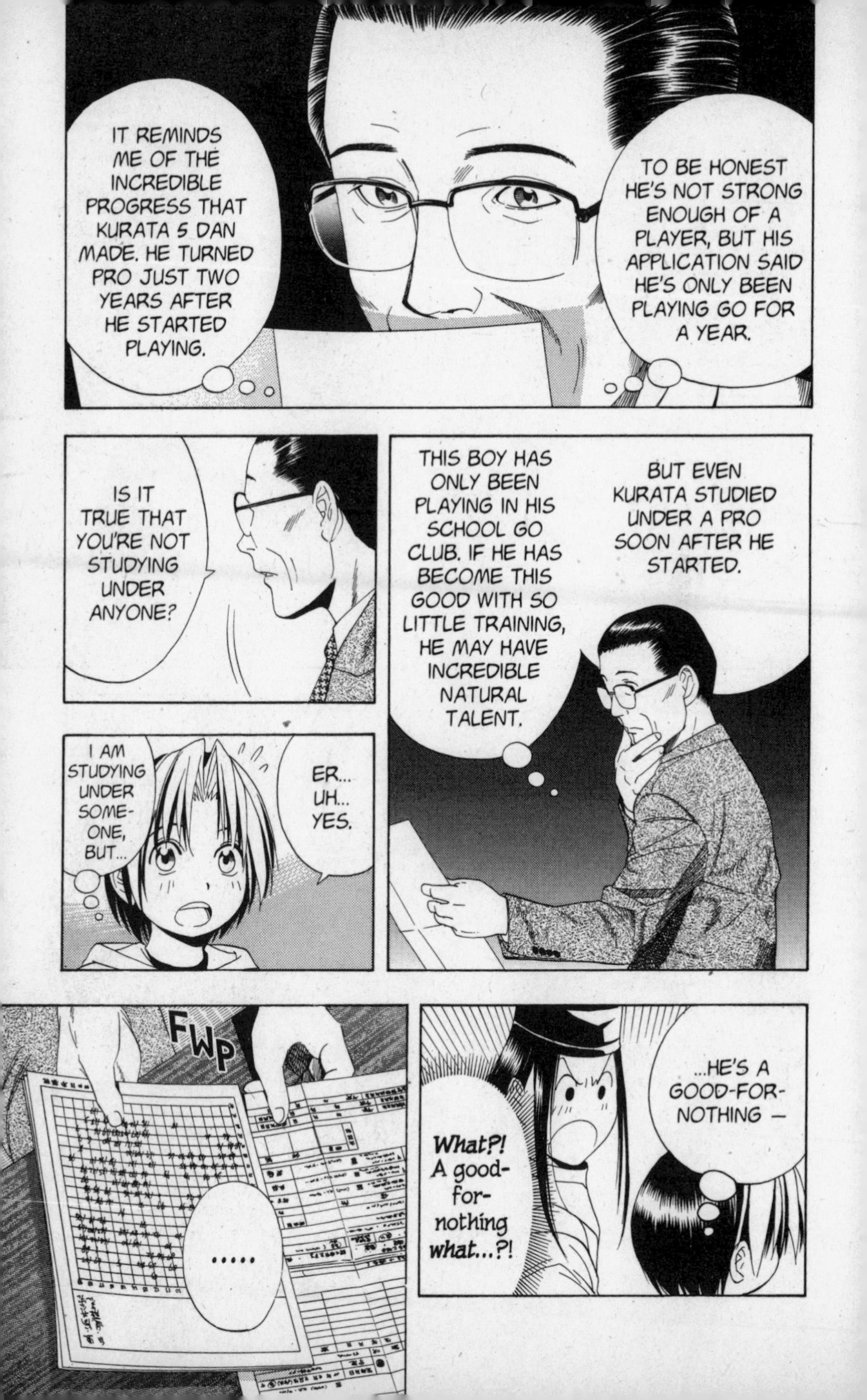
TO BE HONEST HE'S NOT STRONG ENOUGH OF A PLAYER, BUT HIS APPLICATION SAID HE'S ONLY BEEN PLAYING GO FOR A YEAR.
IT REMINDS ME OF THE INCREDIBLE PROGRESS THAT KURATA 5 DAN MADE. HE TURNED PRO JUST TWO YEARS AFTER HE STARTED PLAYING.
THIS BOY HAS ONLY BEEN PLAYING IN HIS SCHOOL GO CLUB. IF HE HAS BECOME THIS GOOD WITH SO LITTLE TRAINING, HE MAY HAVE INCREDIBLE NATURAL TALENT.
BUT EVEN KURATA STUDIED UNDER A PRO SOON AFTER HE STARTED.
IS IT TRUE THAT YOU'RE NOT STUDYING UNDER ANYONE?
ER... UH... YES.
I AM STUDYING UNDER SOME-ONE, BUT...
...HE'S A GOOD-FOR-NOTHING —
What?! A good-for-nothing what...?!
FWP
.....

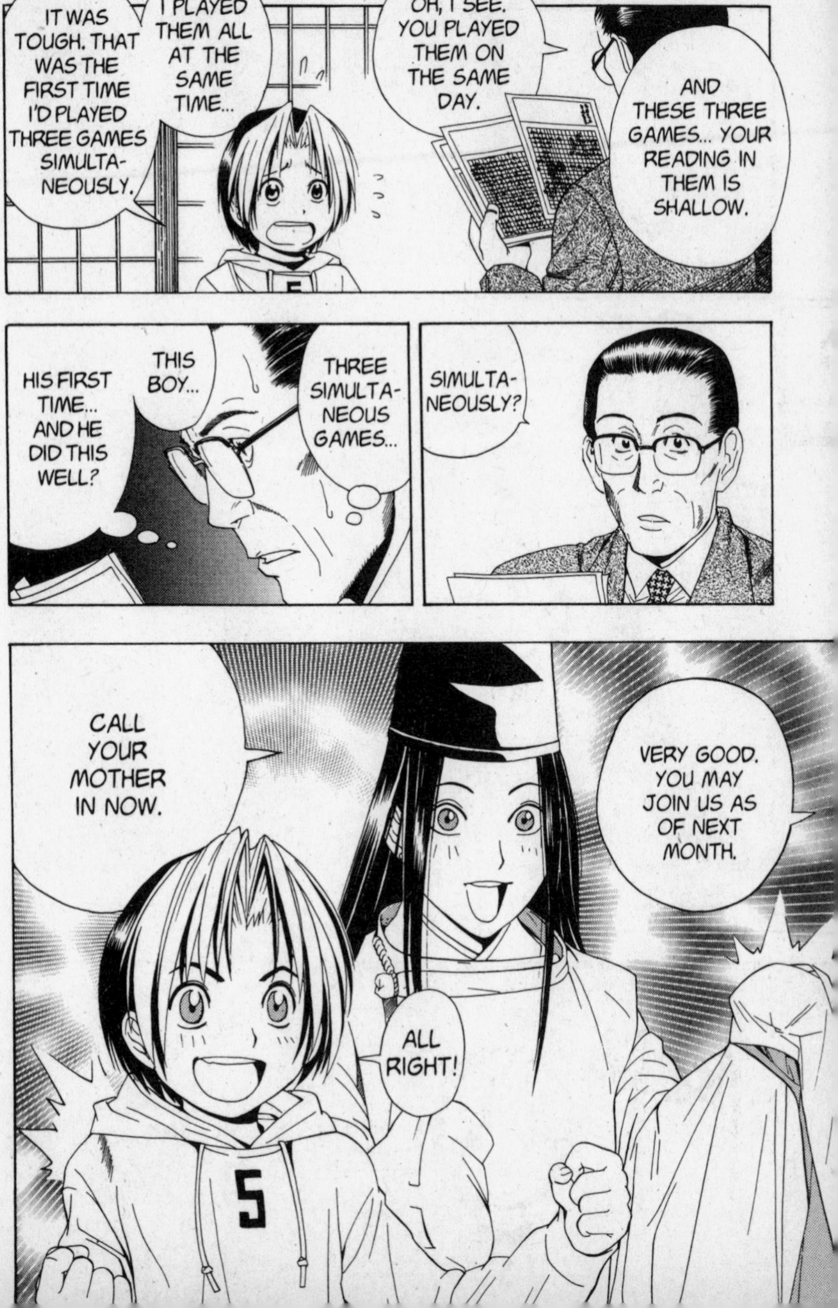
AND THESE THREE GAMES... YOUR READING IN THEM IS SHALLOW.
OH, I SEE. YOU PLAYED THEM ON THE SAME DAY.
I PLAYED THEM ALL AT THE SAME TIME...
IT WAS TOUGH. THAT WAS THE FIRST TIME I'D PLAYED THREE GAMES SIMULTANEOUSLY.
SIMULTANEOUSLY?
THREE SIMULTANEOUS GAMES...
THIS BOY...
HIS FIRST TIME... AND HE DID THIS WELL?
VERY GOOD. YOU MAY JOIN US AS OF NEXT MONTH.
CALL YOUR MOTHER IN NOW.
ALL RIGHT!

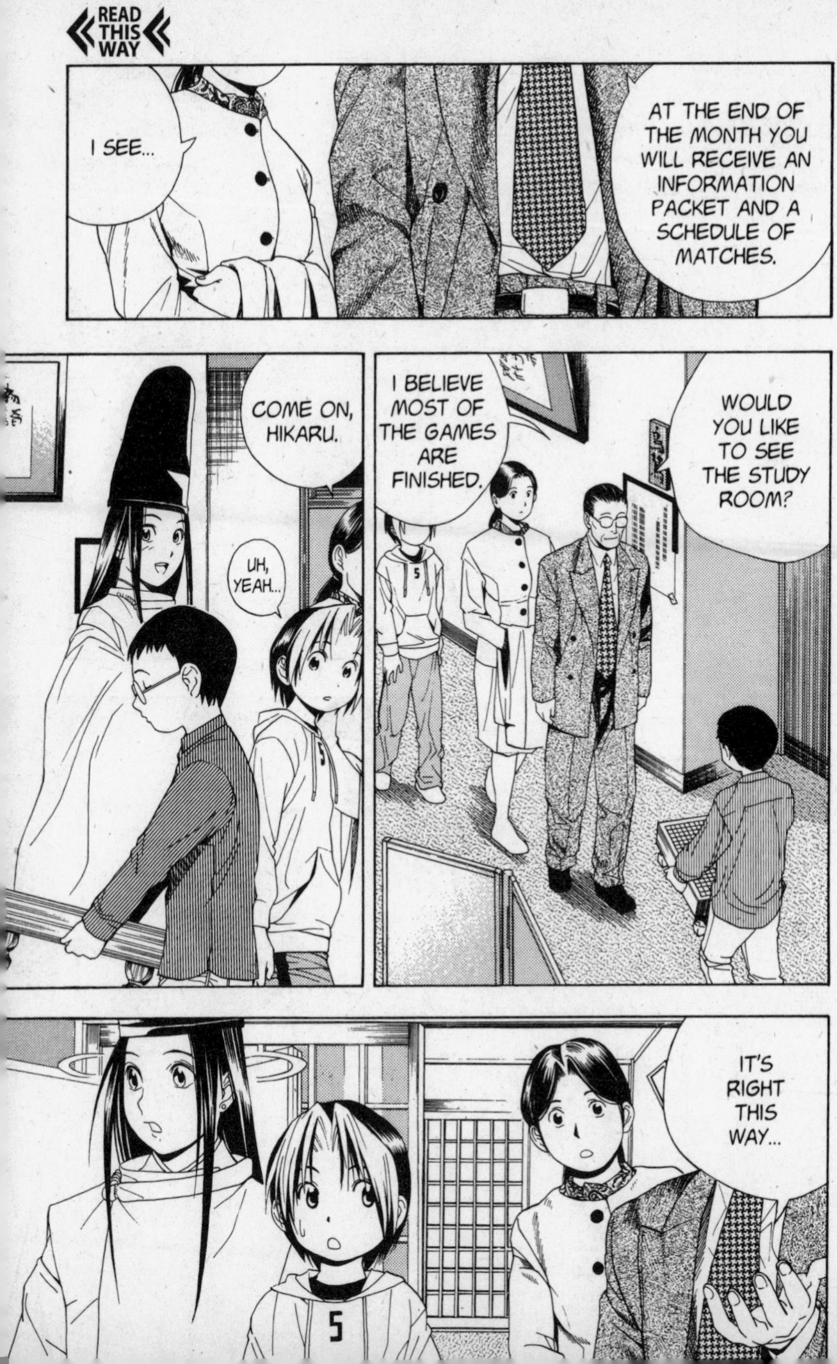
READ THIS WAY
AT THE END OF THE MONTH YOU WILL RECEIVE AN INFORMATION PACKET AND A SCHEDULE OF MATCHES.
I SEE...
WOULD YOU LIKE TO SEE THE STUDY ROOM?
I BELIEVE MOST OF THE GAMES ARE FINISHED.
COME ON, HIKARU.
UH, YEAH...
IT'S RIGHT THIS WAY...

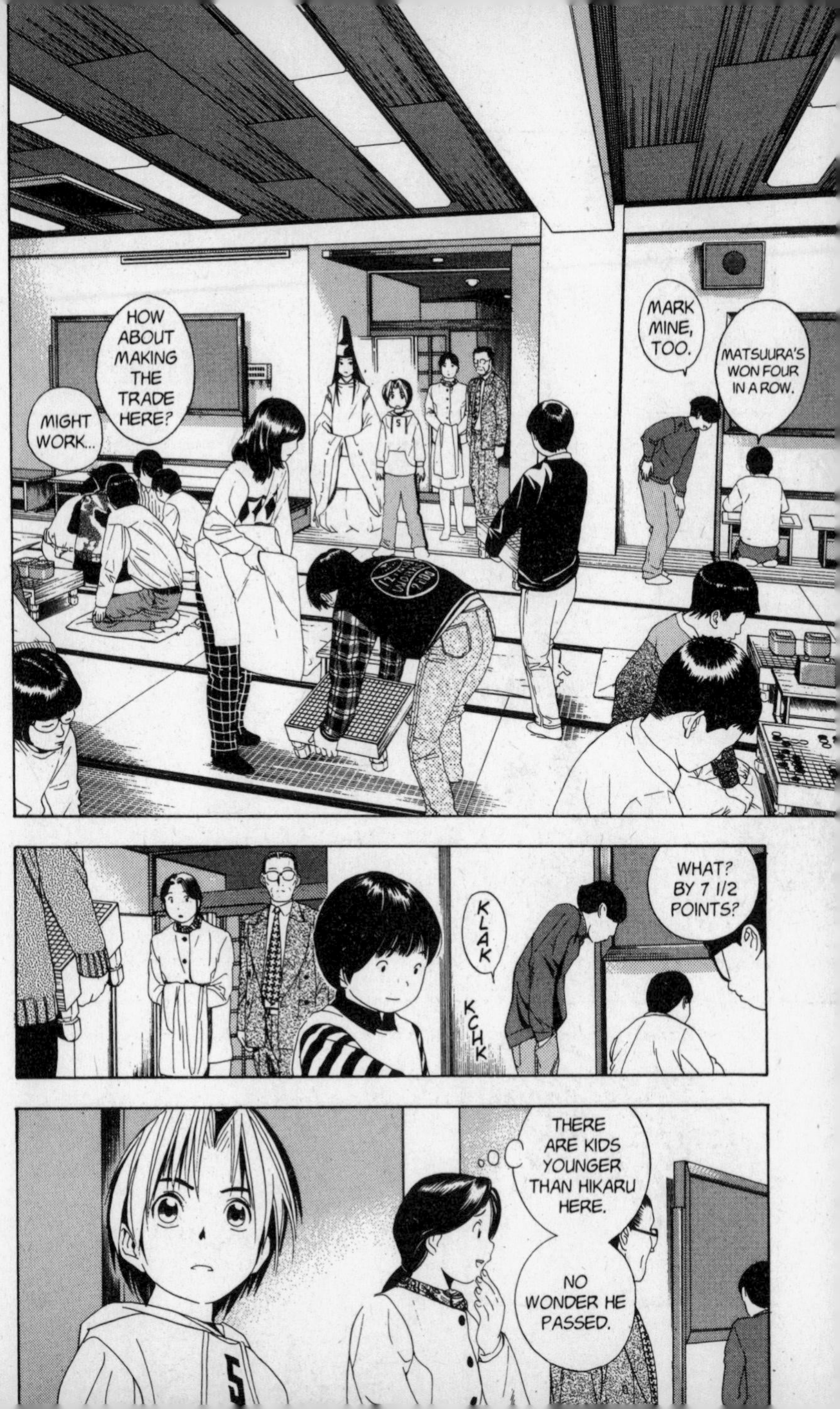
MATSUURA'S WON FOUR IN A ROW.
MARK MINE, TOO.
HOW ABOUT MAKING THE TRADE HERE?
MIGHT WORK...
WHAT? BY 7 1/2 POINTS?
KLAK
KCHK
THERE ARE KIDS YOUNGER THAN HIKARU HERE.
NO WONDER HE PASSED.

READ THIS WAY

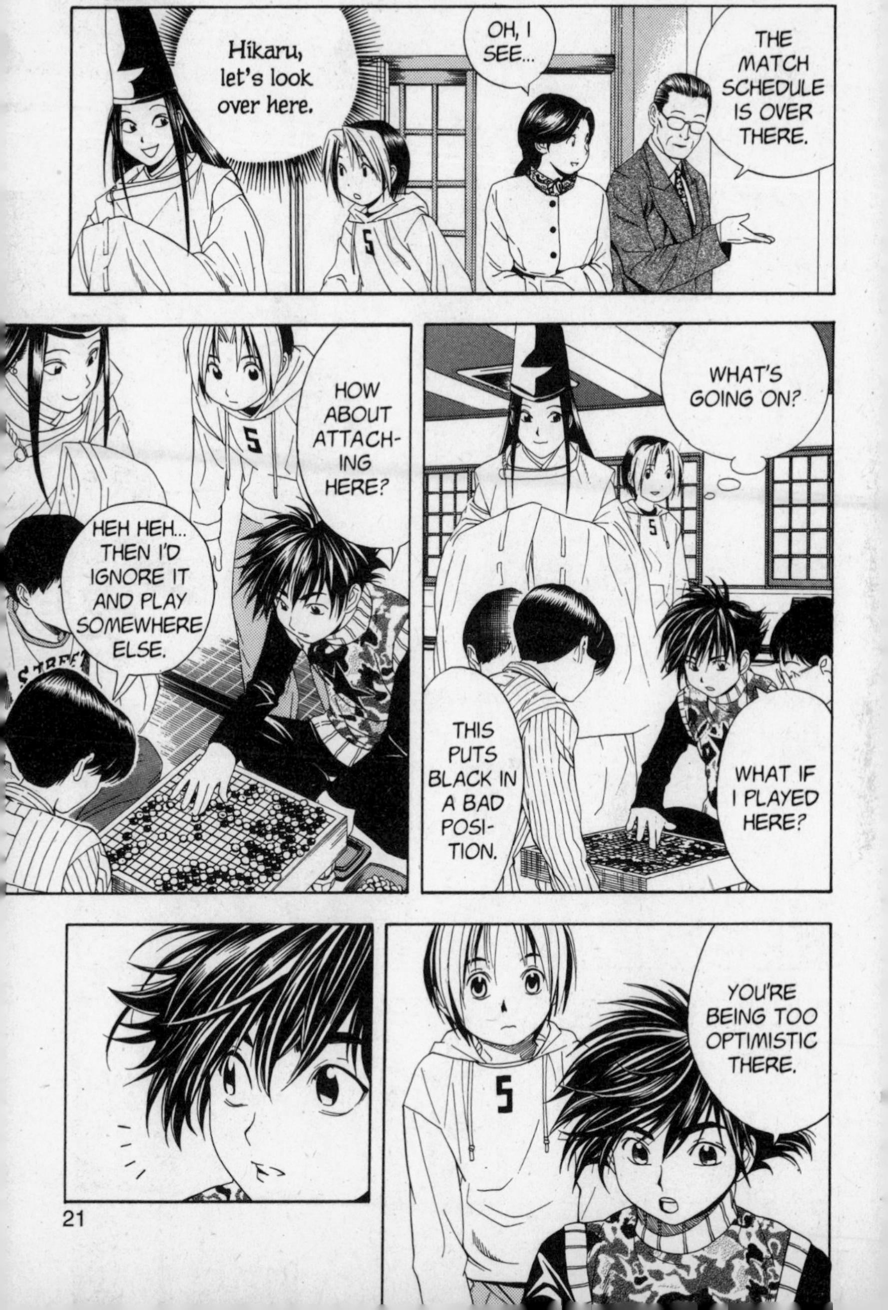
THE MATCH SCHEDULE IS OVER THERE.
OH, I SEE...
Hikaru, let's look over here.
WHAT'S GOING ON?
WHAT IF I PLAYED HERE?
THIS PUTS BLACK IN A BAD POSI-TION.
HOW ABOUT ATTACH-ING HERE?
HEH HEH... THEN I'D IGNORE IT AND PLAY SOMEWHERE ELSE.
YOU'RE BEING TOO OPTIMISTIC THERE.

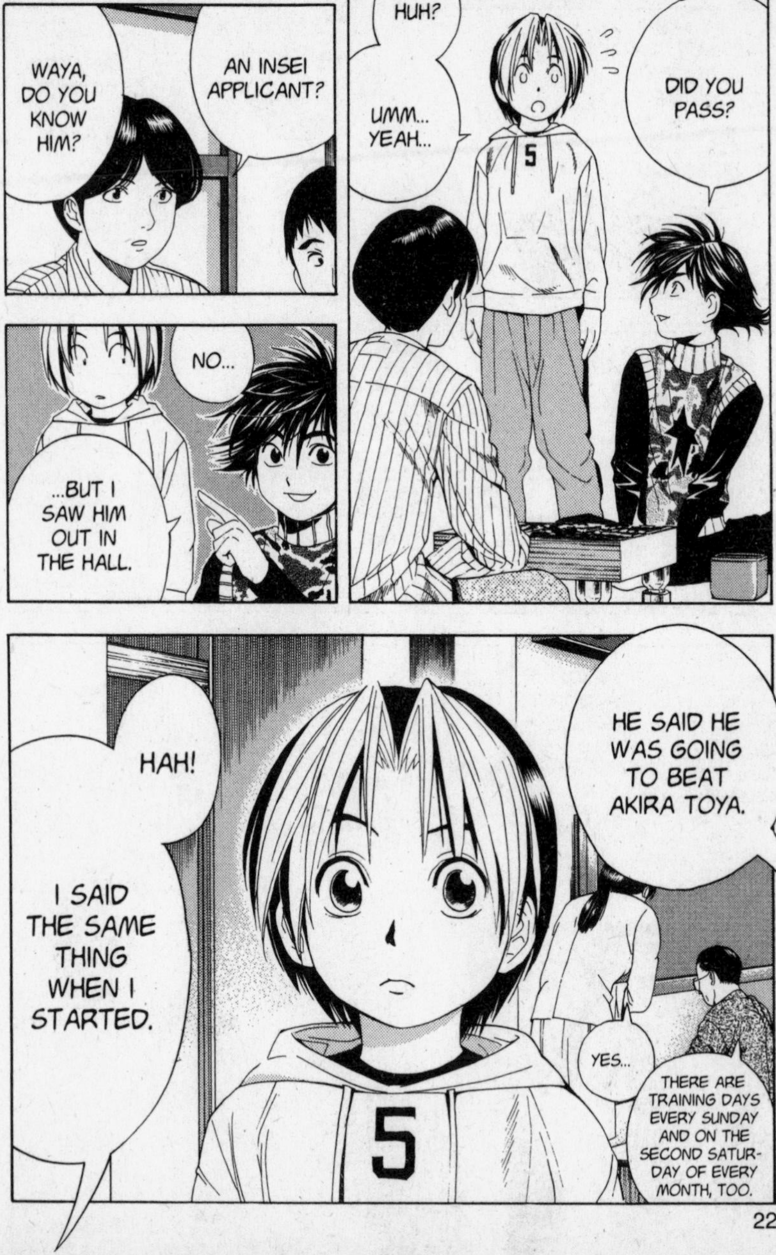
DID YOU PASS?
HUH?
UMM... YEAH...
AN INSEI APPLICANT?
WAYA, DO YOU KNOW HIM?
NO...
...BUT I SAW HIM OUT IN THE HALL.
HE SAID HE WAS GOING TO BEAT AKIRA TOYA.
HAH!
I SAID THE SAME THING WHEN I STARTED.
THERE ARE TRAINING DAYS EVERY SUNDAY AND ON THE SECOND SATURDAY OF EVERY MONTH, TOO.
YES...

READ THIS WAY

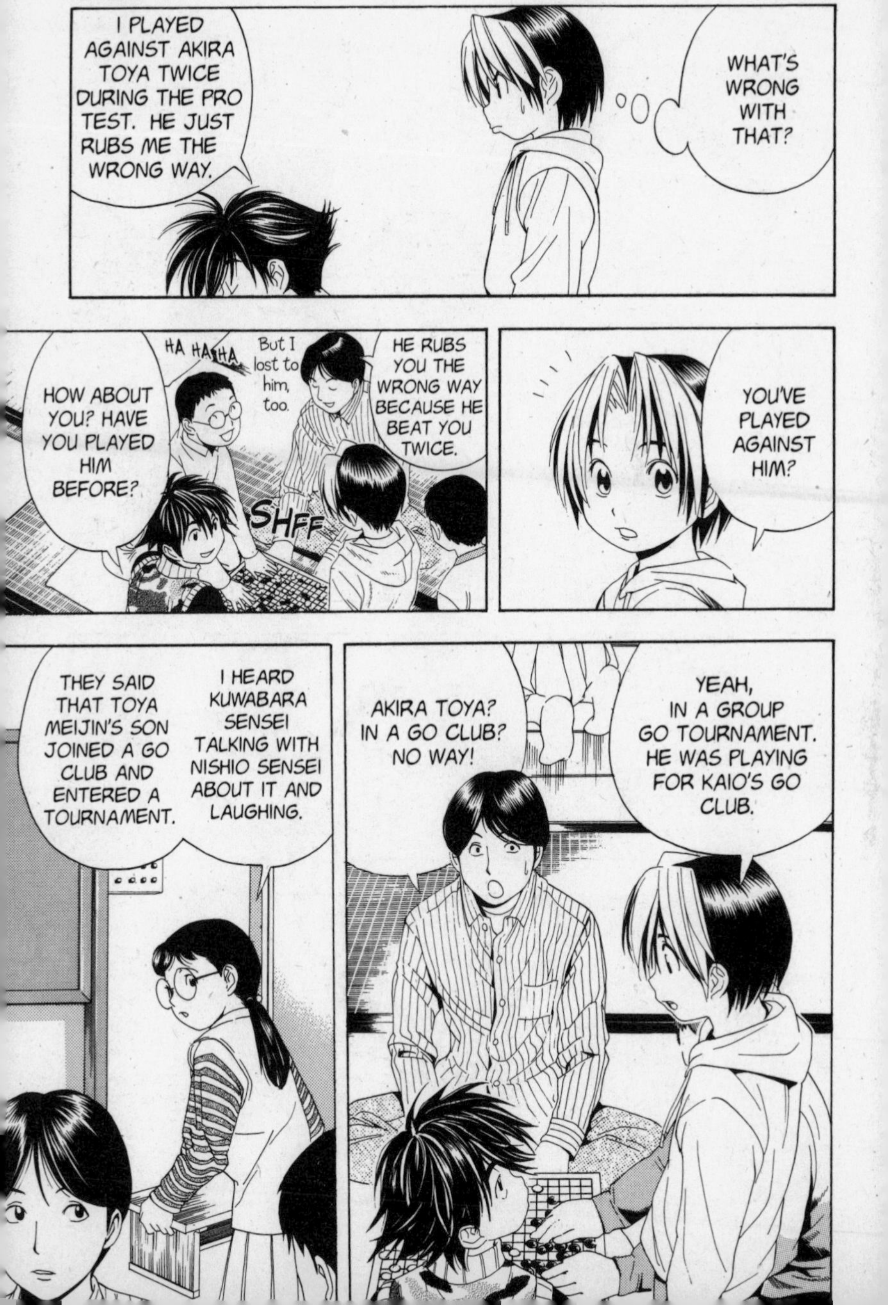
WHAT'S WRONG WITH THAT?
I PLAYED AGAINST AKIRA TOYA TWICE DURING THE PRO TEST. HE JUST RUBS ME THE WRONG WAY.
YOU'VE PLAYED AGAINST HIM?
HE RUBS YOU THE WRONG WAY BECAUSE HE BEAT YOU TWICE.
But I lost to him, too.
HA HA HA
HOW ABOUT YOU? HAVE YOU PLAYED HIM BEFORE?
SHFF
YEAH, IN A GROUP GO TOURNAMENT. HE WAS PLAYING FOR KAIO'S GO CLUB.
AKIRA TOYA? IN A GO CLUB? NO WAY!
I HEARD KUWABARA SENSEI TALKING WITH NISHIO SENSEI ABOUT IT AND LAUGHING.
THEY SAID THAT TOYA MEIJIN'S SON JOINED A GO CLUB AND ENTERED A TOURNAMENT.

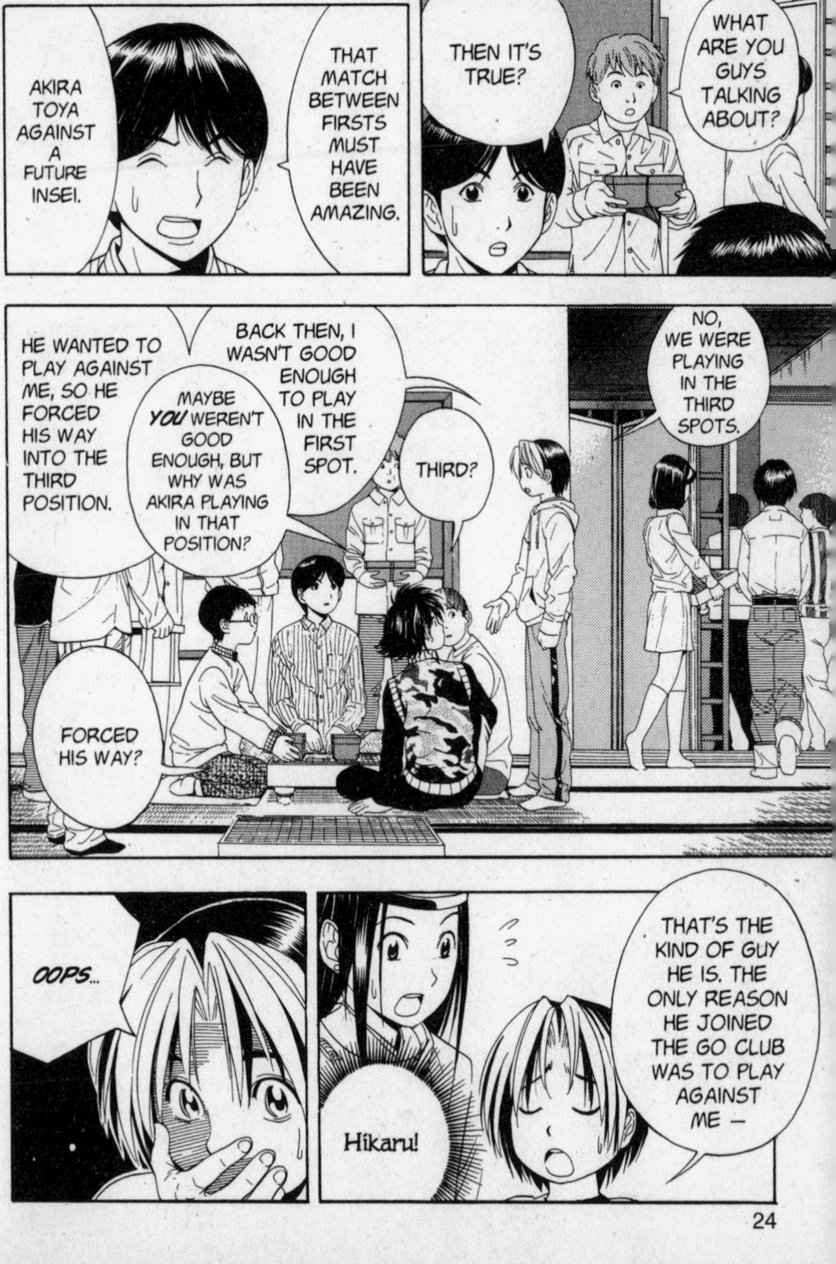

WHAT ARE YOU GUYS TALKING ABOUT?
THEN IT'S TRUE?
THAT MATCH BETWEEN FIRSTS MUST HAVE BEEN AMAZING.
AKIRA TOYA AGAINST A FUTURE INSEI.
NO, WE WERE PLAYING IN THE THIRD SPOTS.
THIRD?
BACK THEN, I WASN'T GOOD ENOUGH TO PLAY IN THE FIRST SPOT.
MAYBE *YOU* WEREN'T GOOD ENOUGH, BUT WHY WAS AKIRA PLAYING IN THAT POSITION?
HE WANTED TO PLAY AGAINST ME, SO HE FORCED HIS WAY INTO THE THIRD POSITION.
FORCED HIS WAY?
THAT'S THE KIND OF GUY HE IS. THE ONLY REASON HE JOINED THE GO CLUB WAS TO PLAY AGAINST ME —
Hikaru!
OOPS...

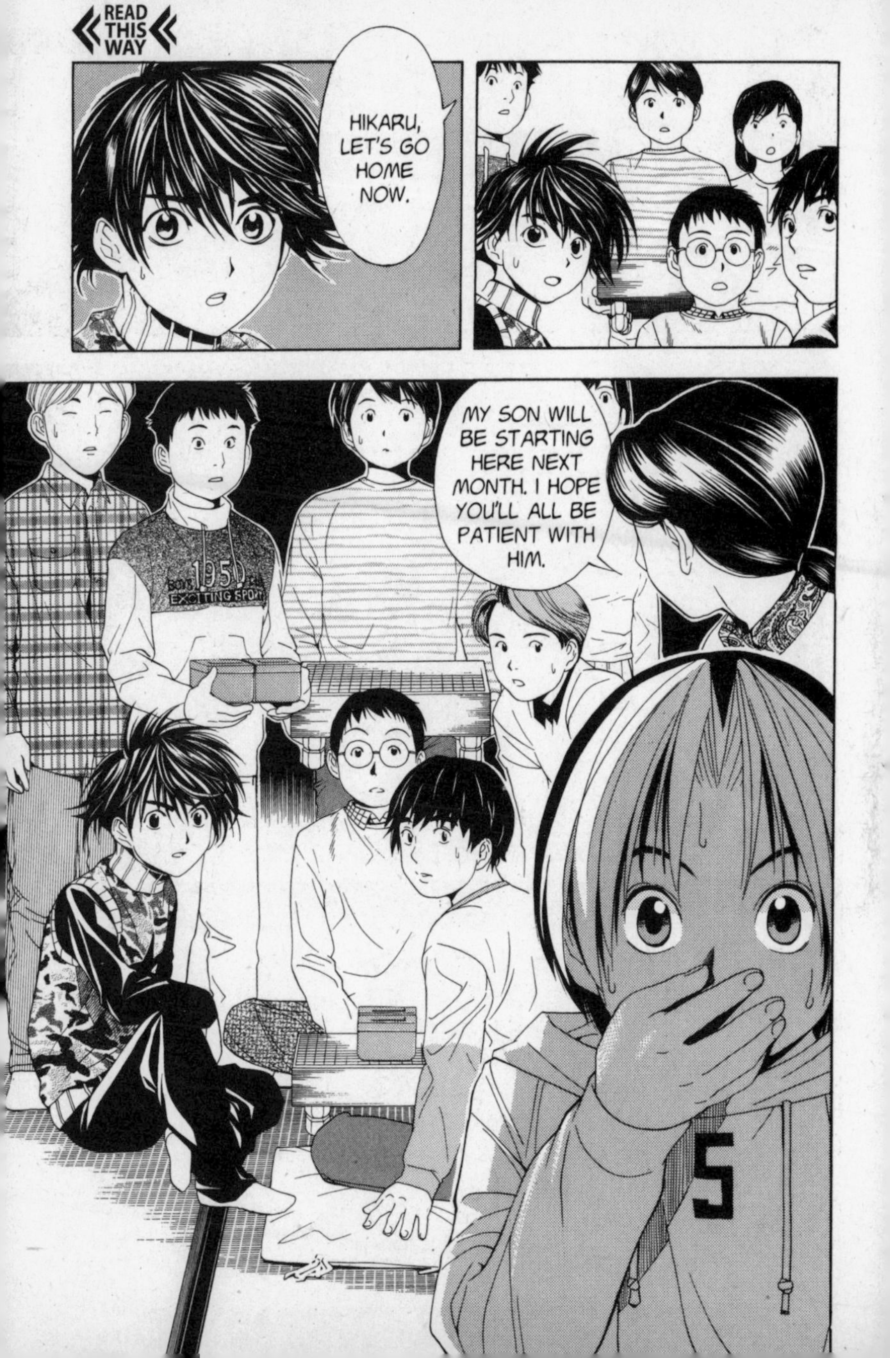
READ THIS WAY
HIKARU, LET'S GO HOME NOW.
MY SON WILL BE STARTING HERE NEXT MONTH. I HOPE YOU'LL ALL BE PATIENT WITH HIM.

A WORD ABOUT HIKARU NO GO

HIKARU'S SHOES

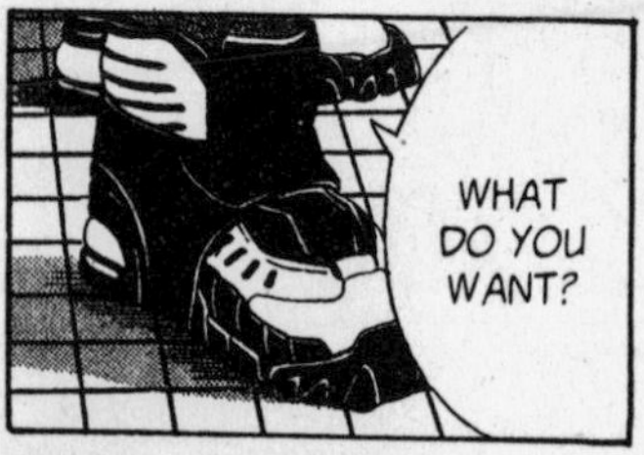
WHAT DO YOU WANT?

HIKARU'S SHOES ARE EXACTLY LIKE TAKESHI OBATA'S FAVORITE PAIR. AND OGATA 9 DAN'S CHAIR IS TAKESHI OBATA'S FAVORITE CHAIR.

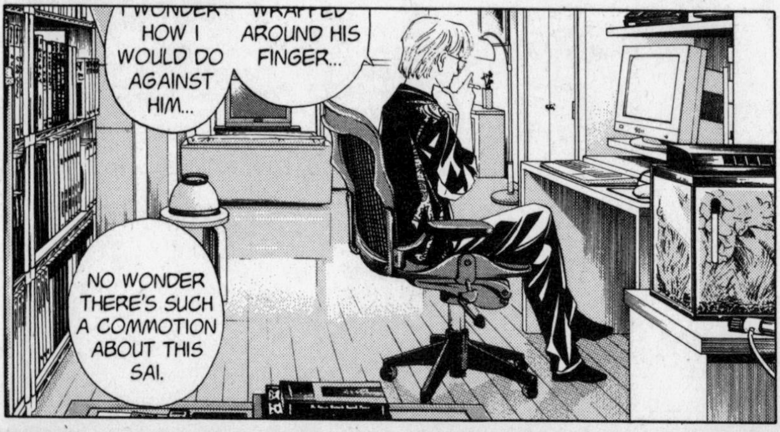
AROUND HIS FINGER...
HOW I WOULD DO AGAINST HIM...
NO WONDER THERE'S SUCH A COMMOTION ABOUT THIS SAI.

THIS KIND OF THING HAPPENS OFTEN IN THE ARTWORK. I WONDER IF THAT'S ALSO THE CASE IN GAME 38 WITH THE GAMERA* THAT APPEARS IN HIKARU'S ROOM. AND ARE THOSE TAKESHI OBATA'S FAVORITE DUMBBELLS?

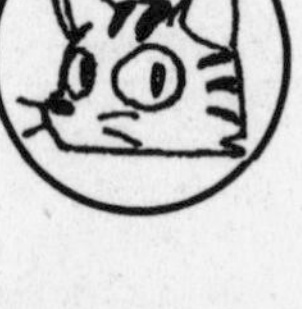

*GAMERA IS A GIANT MONSTER FROM THE MOVIES, SIMILAR TO GODZILLA.

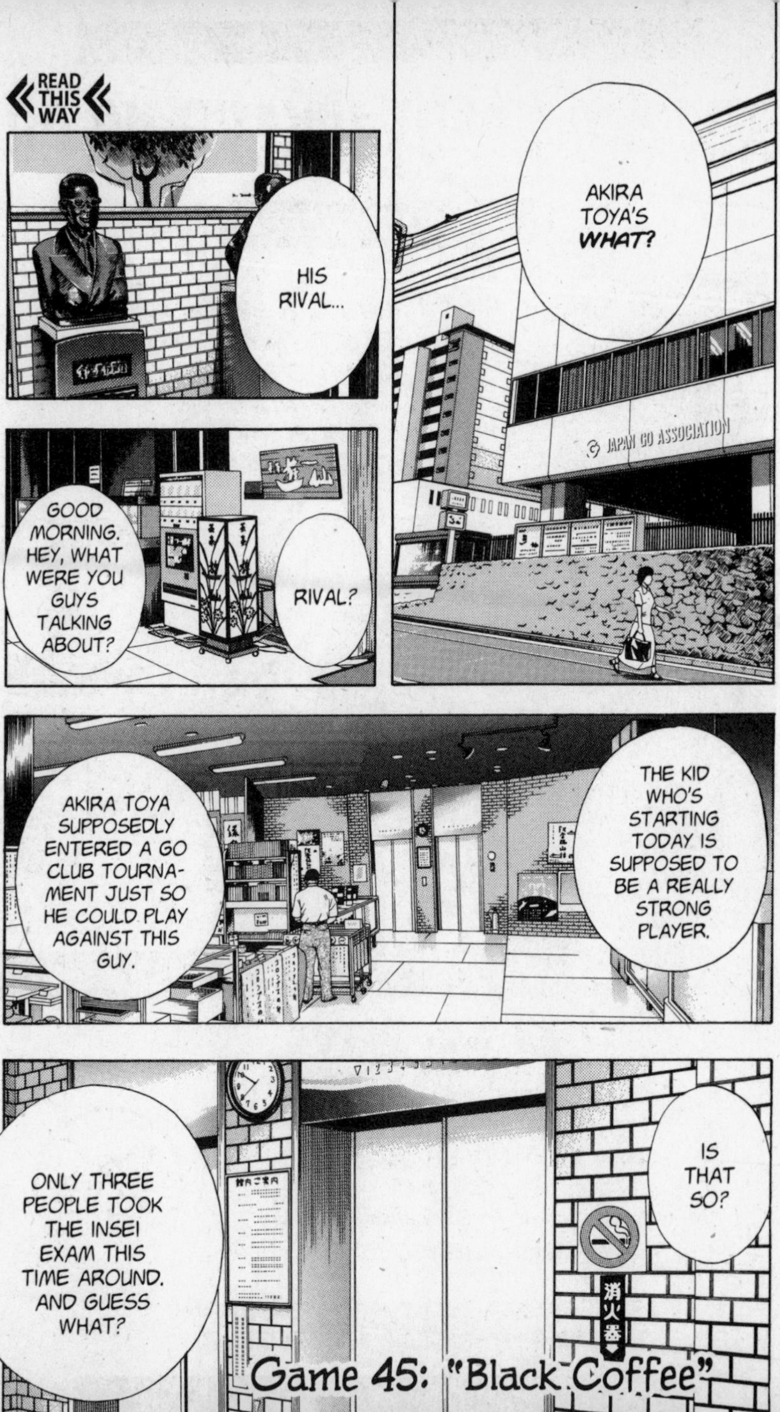
READ THIS WAY
AKIRA TOYA'S **WHAT?**
JAPAN GO ASSOCIATION
HIS RIVAL...
RIVAL?
GOOD MORNING. HEY, WHAT WERE YOU GUYS TALKING ABOUT?
THE KID WHO'S STARTING TODAY IS SUPPOSED TO BE A REALLY STRONG PLAYER.
AKIRA TOYA SUPPOSEDLY ENTERED A GO CLUB TOURNAMENT JUST SO HE COULD PLAY AGAINST THIS GUY.
IS THAT SO?
ONLY THREE PEOPLE TOOK THE INSEI EXAM THIS TIME AROUND. AND GUESS WHAT?
消火器
Game 45: "Black Coffee"

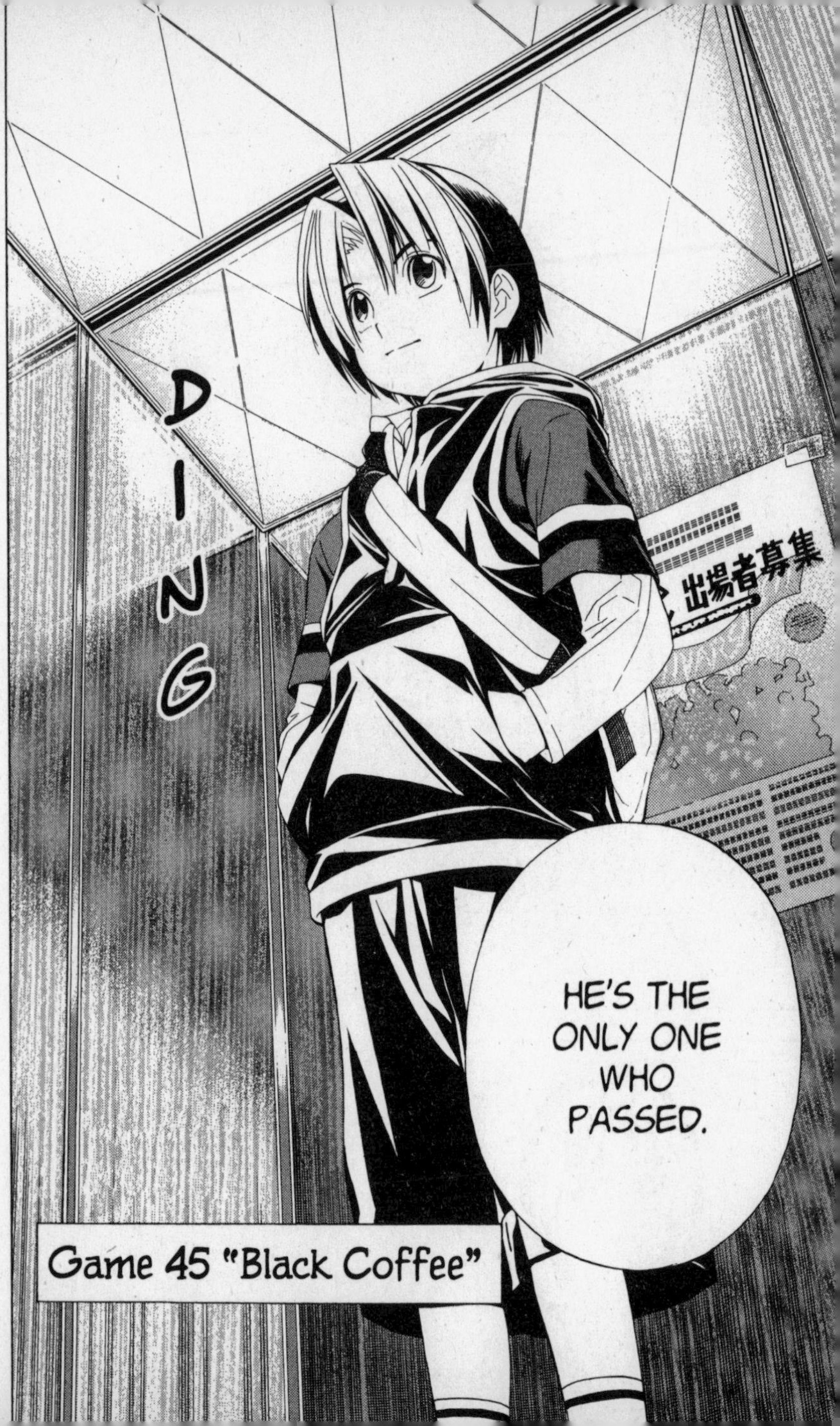
DING
出場者募集
HE'S THE ONLY ONE WHO PASSED.
Game 45 "Black Coffee"

READ THIS WAY

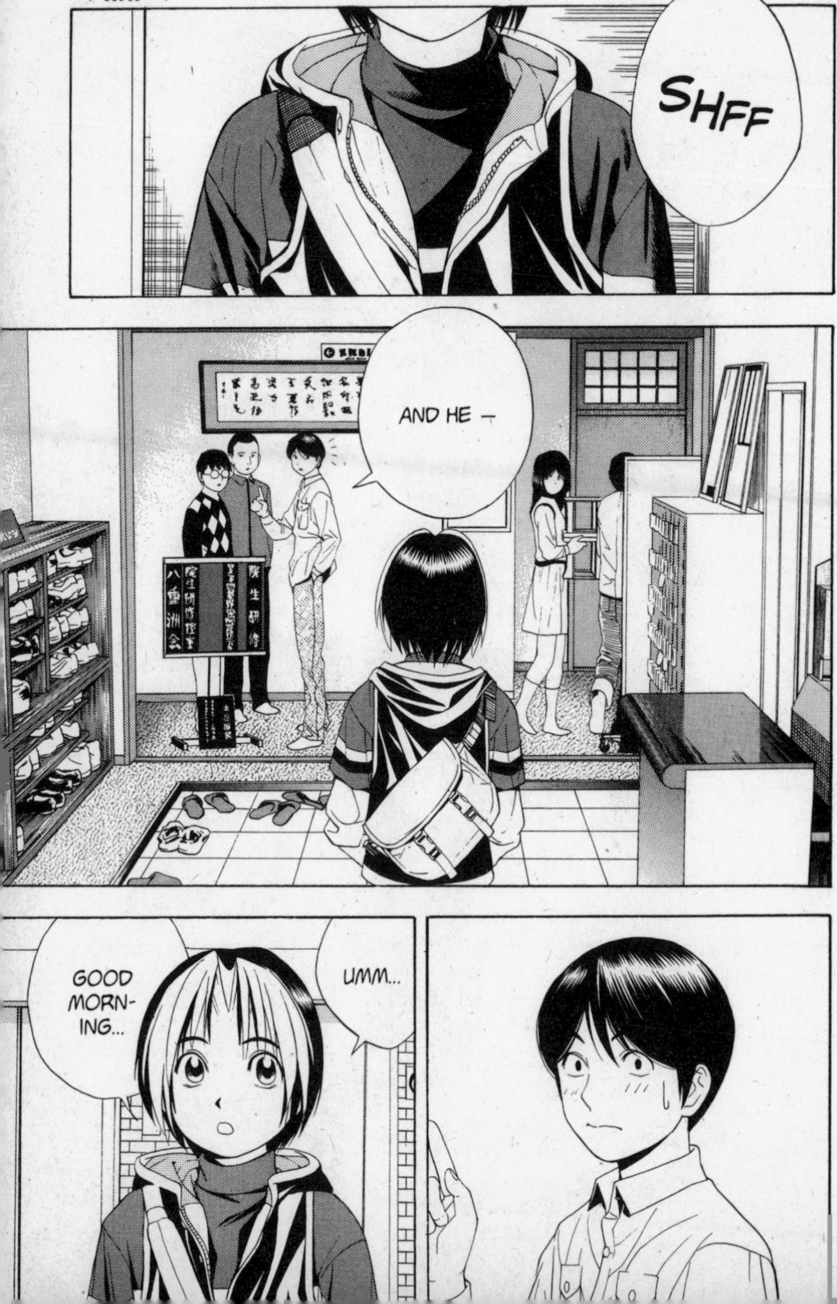
SHFF
AND HE —
UMM...
GOOD MORNING-ING...

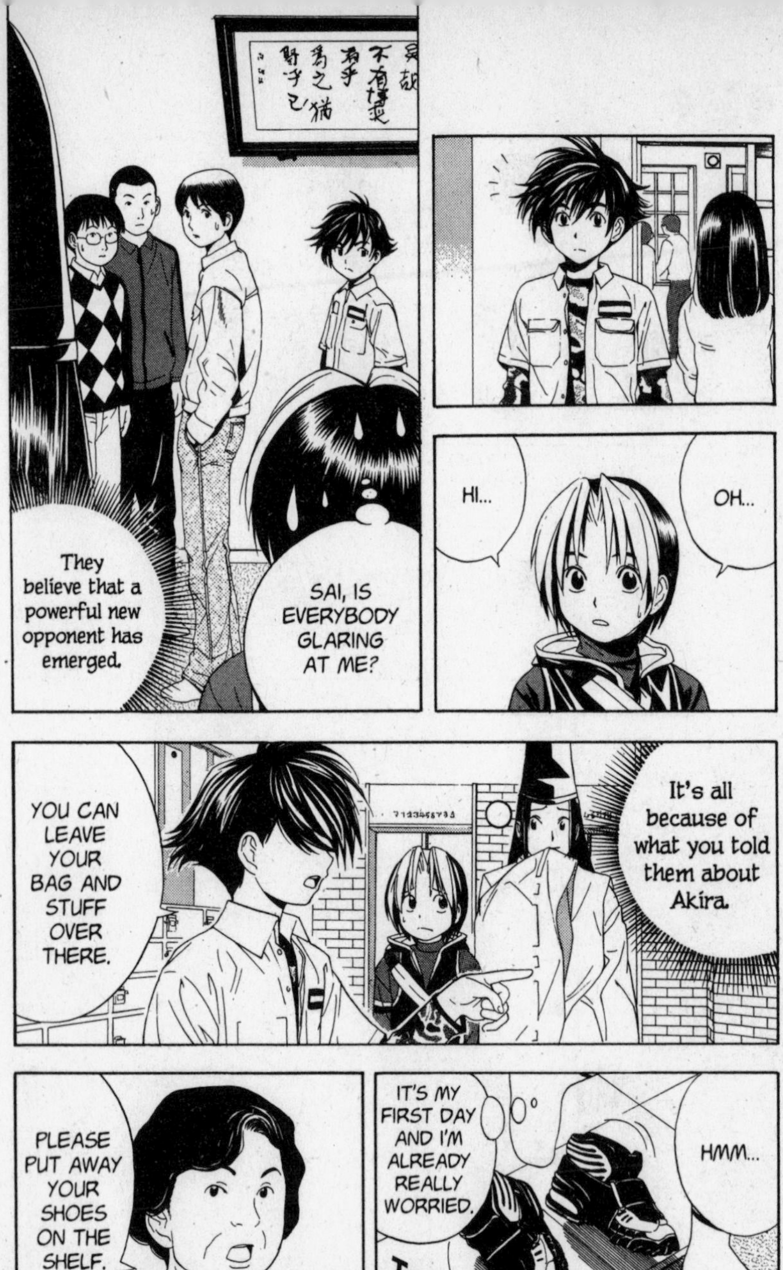
OH...
HI...
SAI, IS EVERYBODY GLARING AT ME?
They believe that a powerful new opponent has emerged.
It's all because of what you told them about Akira.
YOU CAN LEAVE YOUR BAG AND STUFF OVER THERE.
HMM...
IT'S MY FIRST DAY AND I'M ALREADY REALLY WORRIED.
TMP
PLEASE PUT AWAY YOUR SHOES ON THE SHELF.

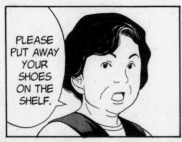

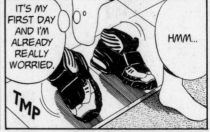

READ THIS WAY

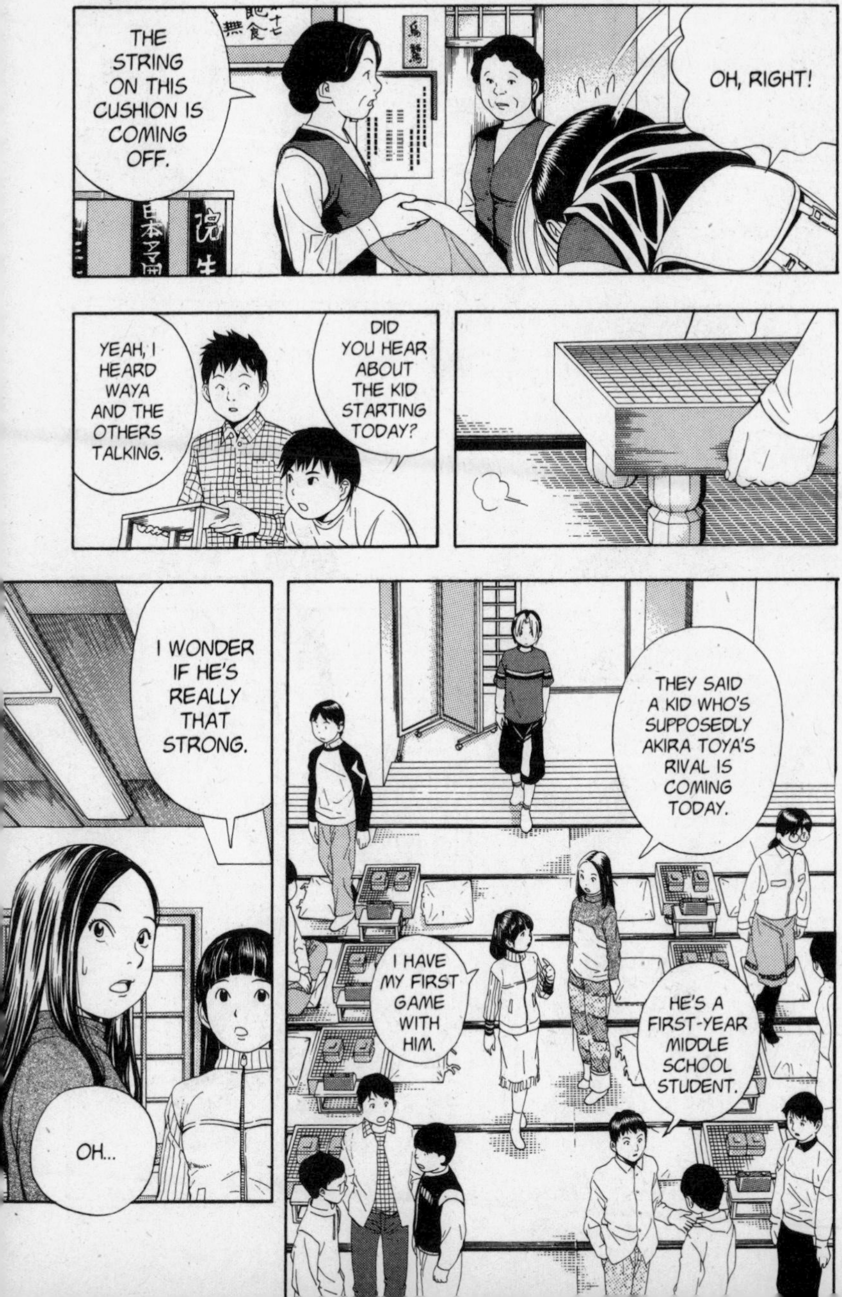
OH, RIGHT!
THE STRING ON THIS CUSHION IS COMING OFF.
DID YOU HEAR ABOUT THE KID STARTING TODAY?
YEAH, I HEARD WAYA AND THE OTHERS TALKING.
THEY SAID A KID WHO'S SUPPOSEDLY AKIRA TOYA'S RIVAL IS COMING TODAY.
HE'S A FIRST-YEAR MIDDLE SCHOOL STUDENT.
I HAVE MY FIRST GAME WITH HIM.
I WONDER IF HE'S REALLY THAT STRONG.
OH...

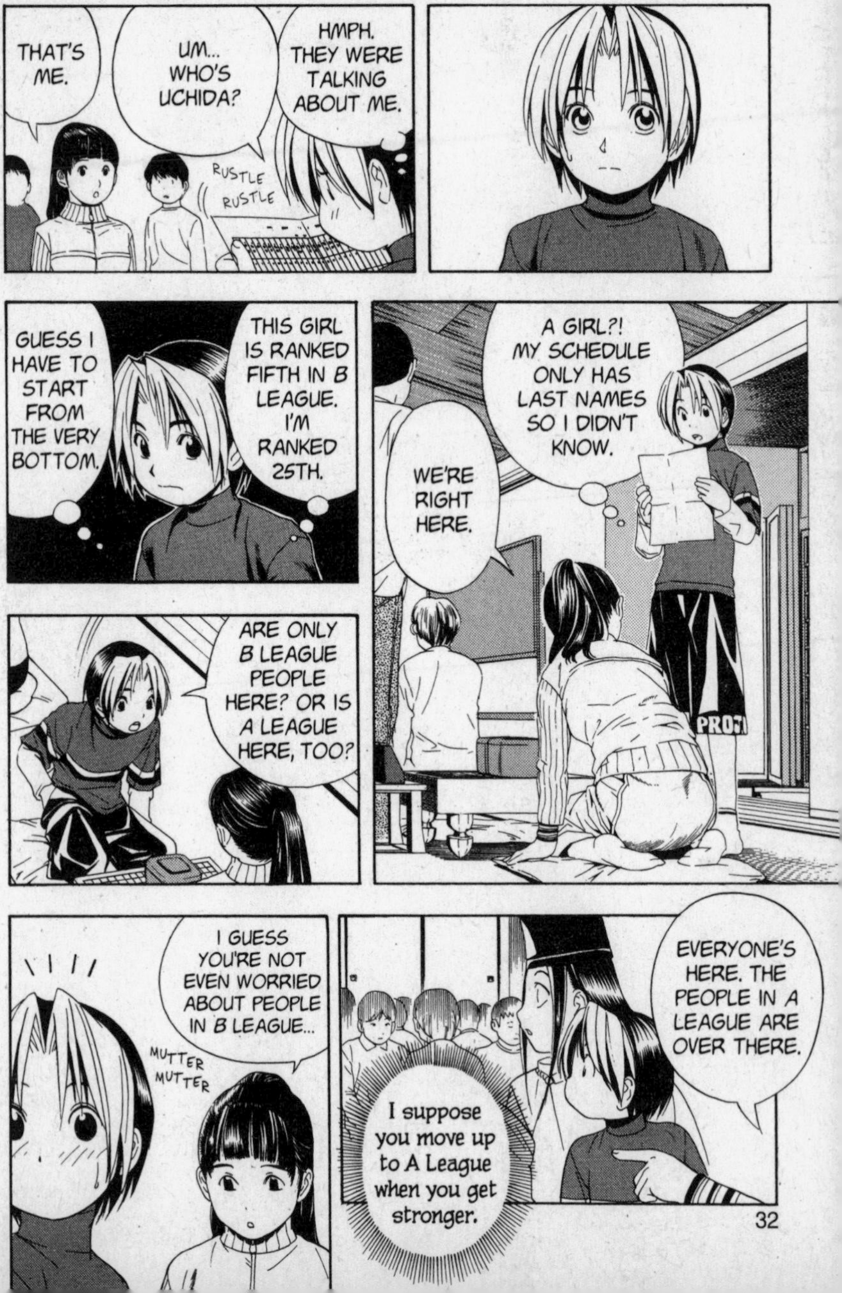
HMPH. THEY WERE TALKING ABOUT ME.
UM... WHO'S UCHIDA?
THAT'S ME.
RUSTLE RUSTLE
A GIRL?! MY SCHEDULE ONLY HAS LAST NAMES SO I DIDN'T KNOW.
WE'RE RIGHT HERE.
PROJ
THIS GIRL IS RANKED FIFTH IN B LEAGUE. I'M RANKED 25TH.
GUESS I HAVE TO START FROM THE VERY BOTTOM.
ARE ONLY B LEAGUE PEOPLE HERE? OR IS A LEAGUE HERE, TOO?
EVERYONE'S HERE. THE PEOPLE IN A LEAGUE ARE OVER THERE.
I suppose you move up to A League when you get stronger.
I GUESS YOU'RE NOT EVEN WORRIED ABOUT PEOPLE IN B LEAGUE...
MUTTER MUTTER

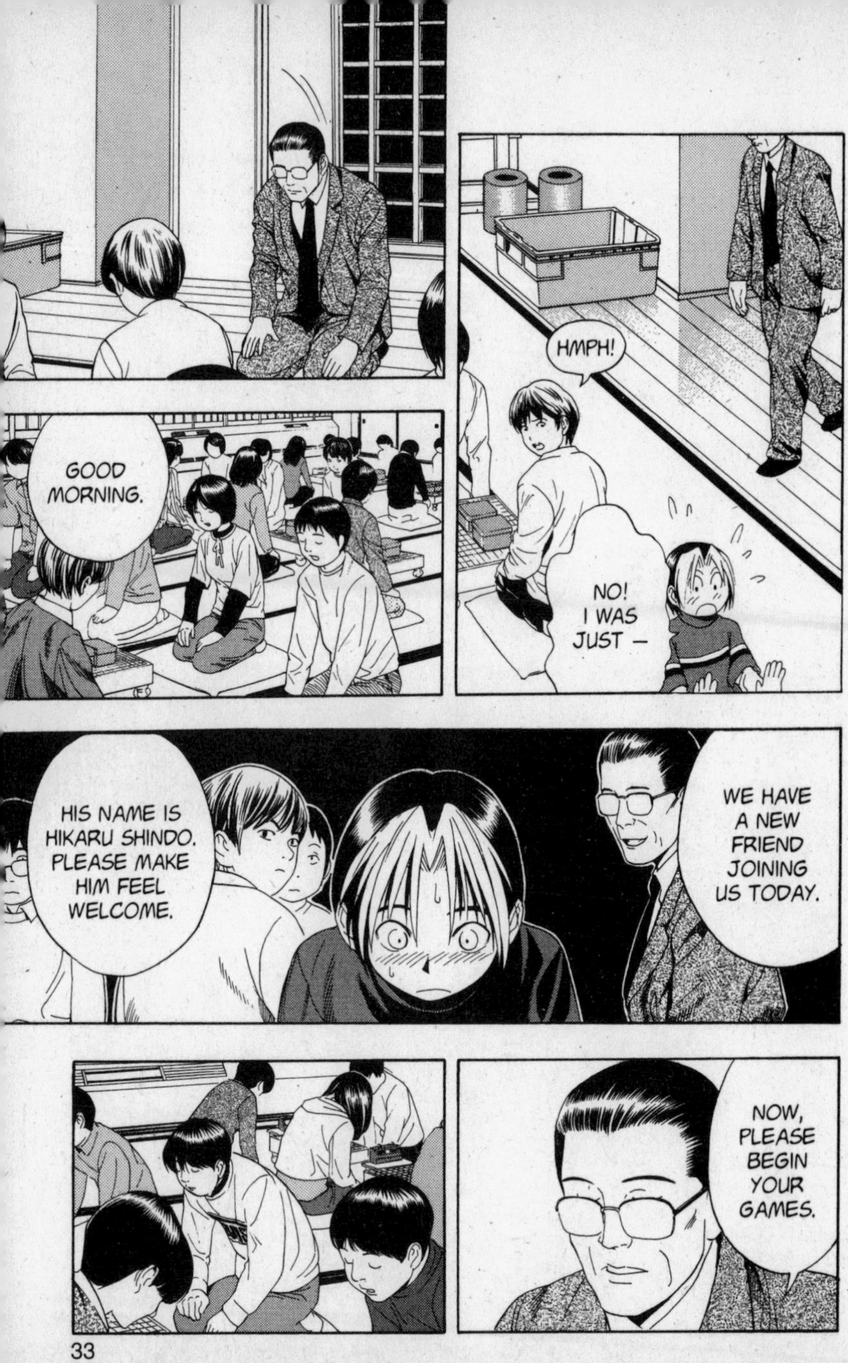
HMPH!
NO! I WAS JUST —
GOOD MORNING.
WE HAVE A NEW FRIEND JOINING US TODAY.
HIS NAME IS HIKARU SHINDO. PLEASE MAKE HIM FEEL WELCOME.
NOW, PLEASE BEGIN YOUR GAMES.

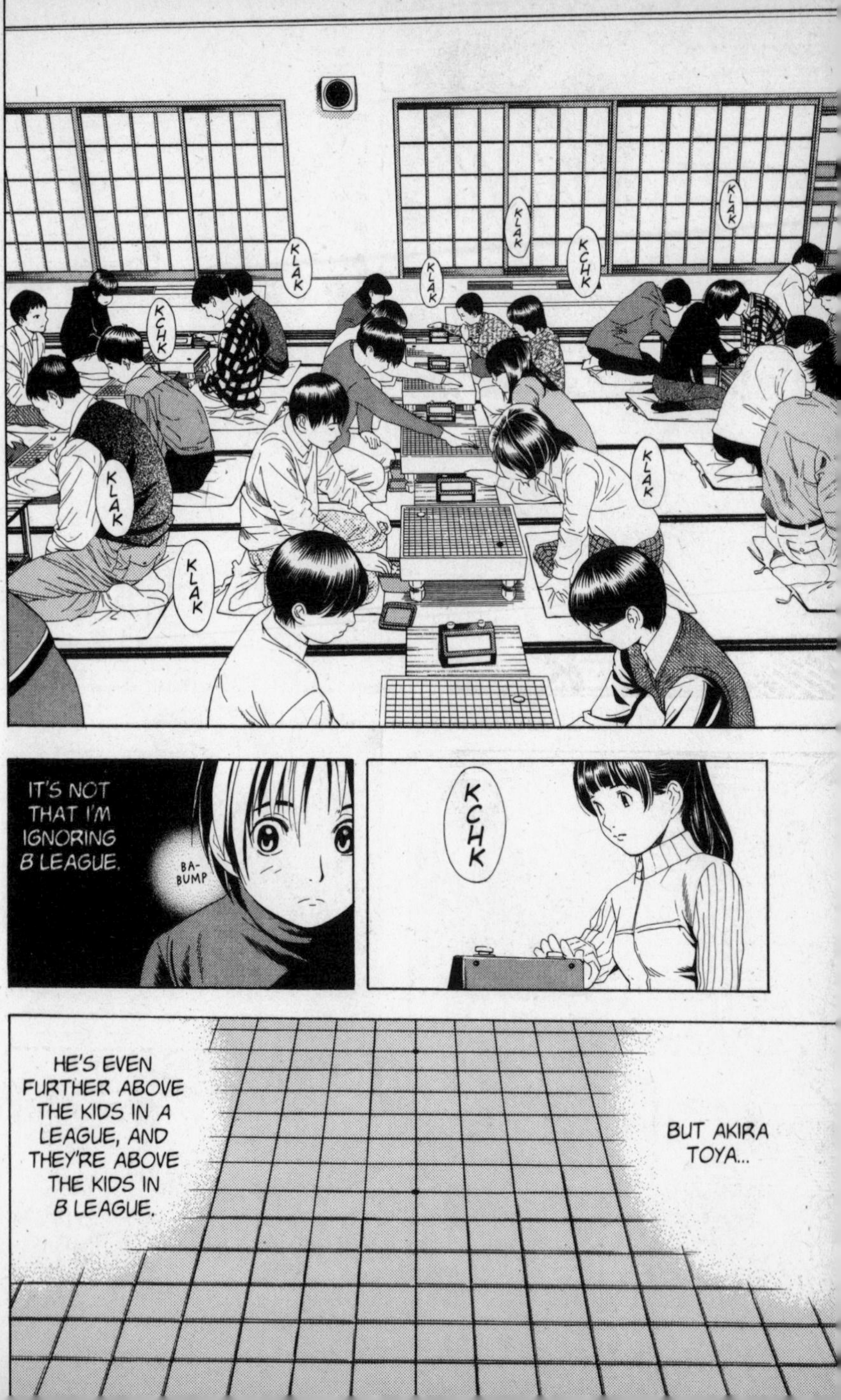
KLAK
KCHK
KLAK
KLAK
KLAK
KLAK
KCHK
KLAK
KLAK
KCHK
IT'S NOT THAT I'M IGNORING B LEAGUE.
BA-BUMP
BUT AKIRA TOYA...
HE'S EVEN FURTHER ABOVE THE KIDS IN A LEAGUE, AND THEY'RE ABOVE THE KIDS IN B LEAGUE.

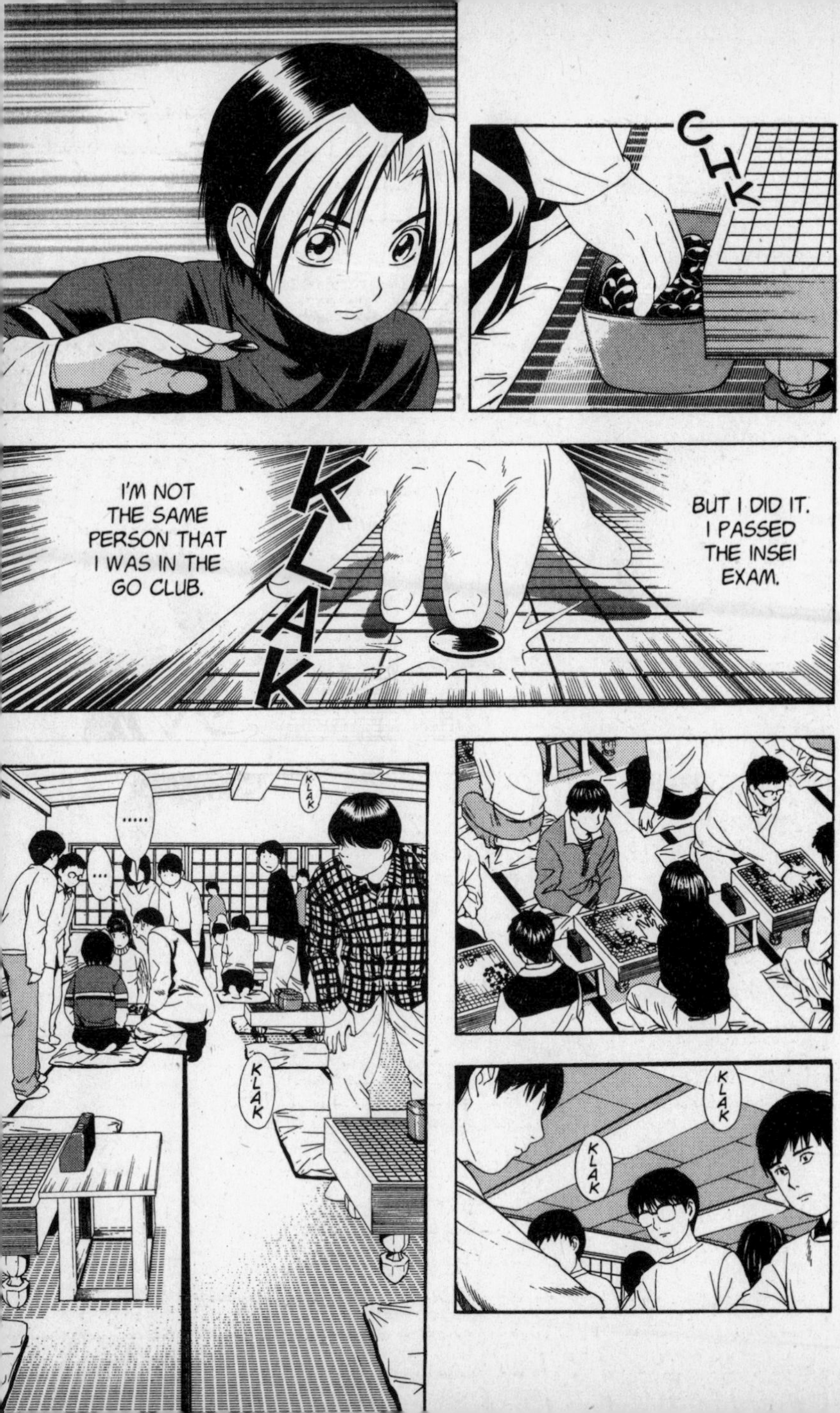
CHK
BUT I DID IT. I PASSED THE INSEI EXAM.
KLAK
I'M NOT THE SAME PERSON THAT I WAS IN THE GO CLUB.
KLAK
KLAK
KLAK
......
...
KLAK

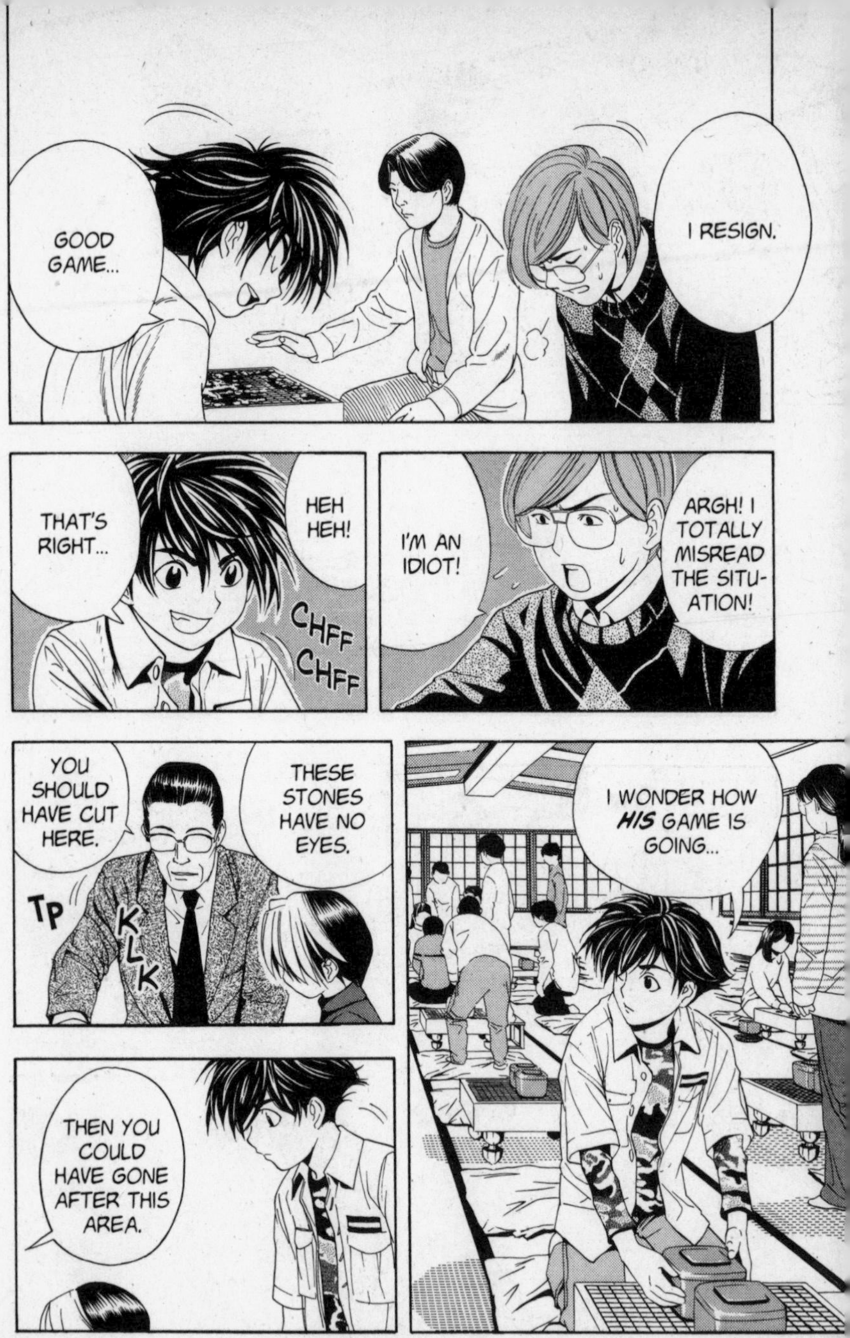
I RESIGN.
GOOD GAME...
ARGH! I TOTALLY MISREAD THE SITUATION!
I'M AN IDIOT!
HEH HEH!
CHFF CHFF
THAT'S RIGHT...
I WONDER HOW *HIS* GAME IS GOING...
THESE STONES HAVE NO EYES.
YOU SHOULD HAVE CUT HERE.
TP
KLK
THEN YOU COULD HAVE GONE AFTER THIS AREA.

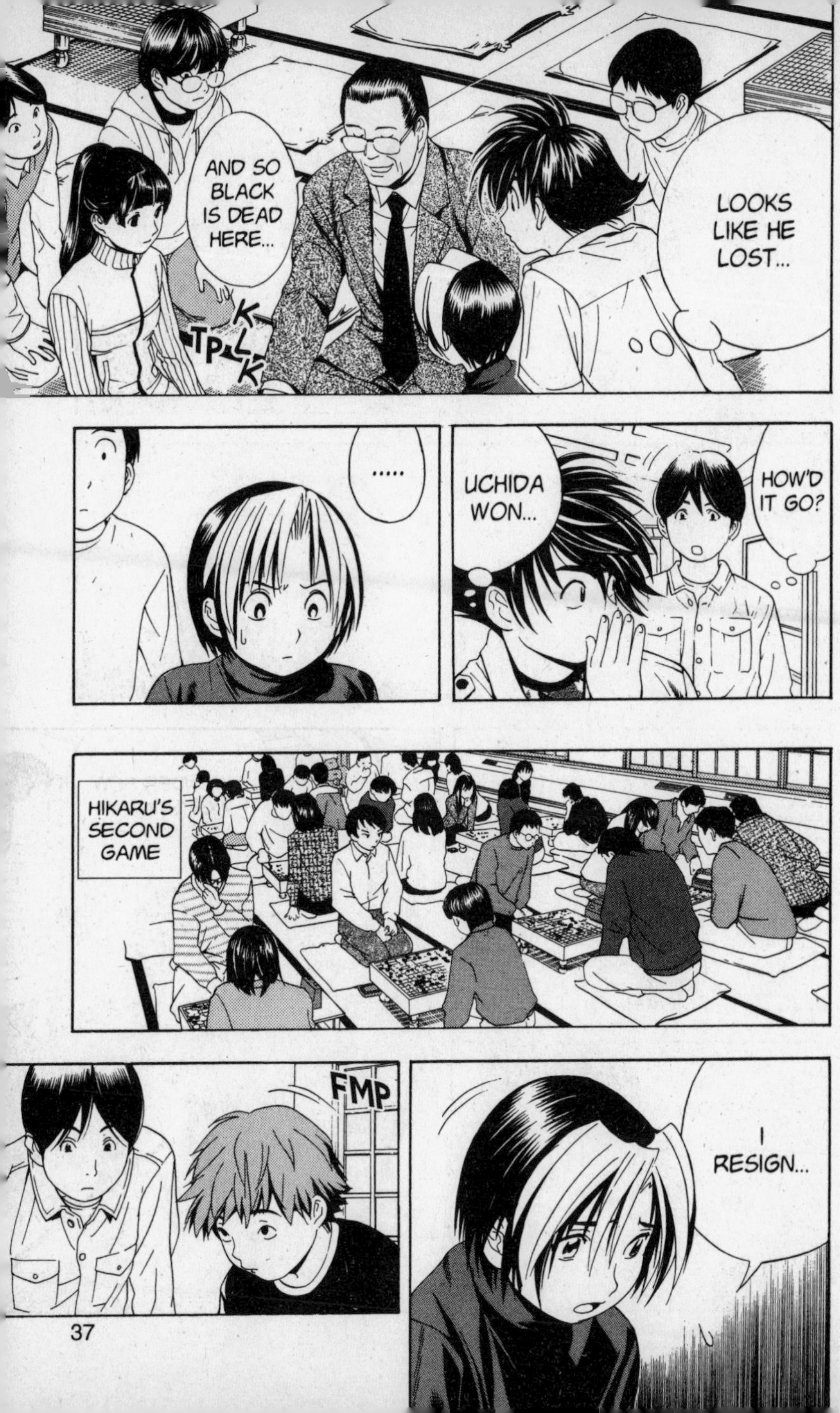
LOOKS LIKE HE LOST...
AND SO BLACK IS DEAD HERE...
TP KLK
HOW'D IT GO?
UCHIDA WON...
.....
HIKARU'S SECOND GAME
I RESIGN...
FMP

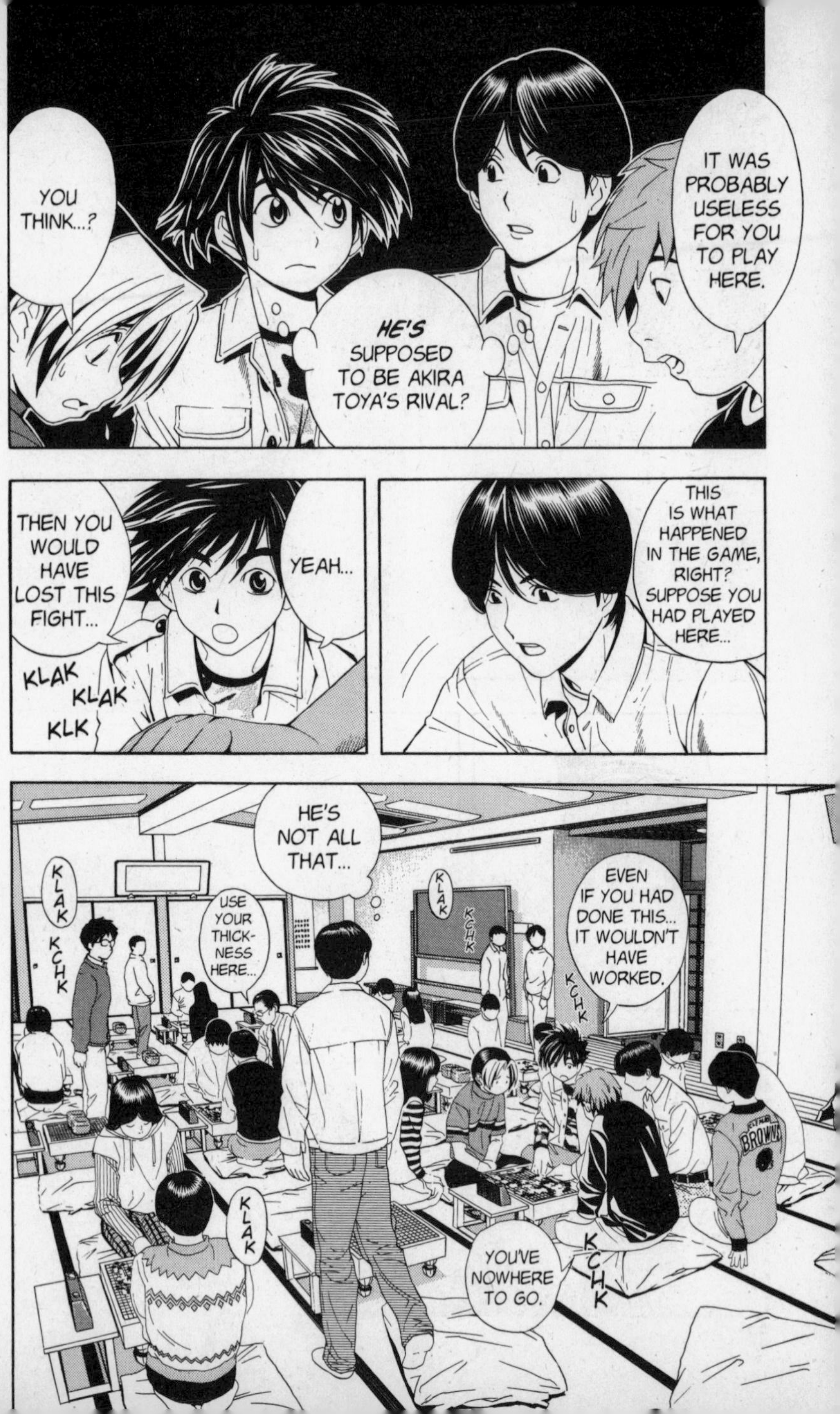
IT WAS PROBABLY USELESS FOR YOU TO PLAY HERE.
HE'S SUPPOSED TO BE AKIRA TOYA'S RIVAL?
YOU THINK...?
THIS IS WHAT HAPPENED IN THE GAME, RIGHT? SUPPOSE YOU HAD PLAYED HERE...
YEAH...
THEN YOU WOULD HAVE LOST THIS FIGHT...
KLAK KLAK KLK
EVEN IF YOU HAD DONE THIS... IT WOULDN'T HAVE WORKED.
KCHK
KLAK
KCHK
HE'S NOT ALL THAT...
USE YOUR THICK-NESS HERE...
KLAK
KCHK
YOU'VE NOWHERE TO GO.
KCHK
KLAK

READ THIS WAY

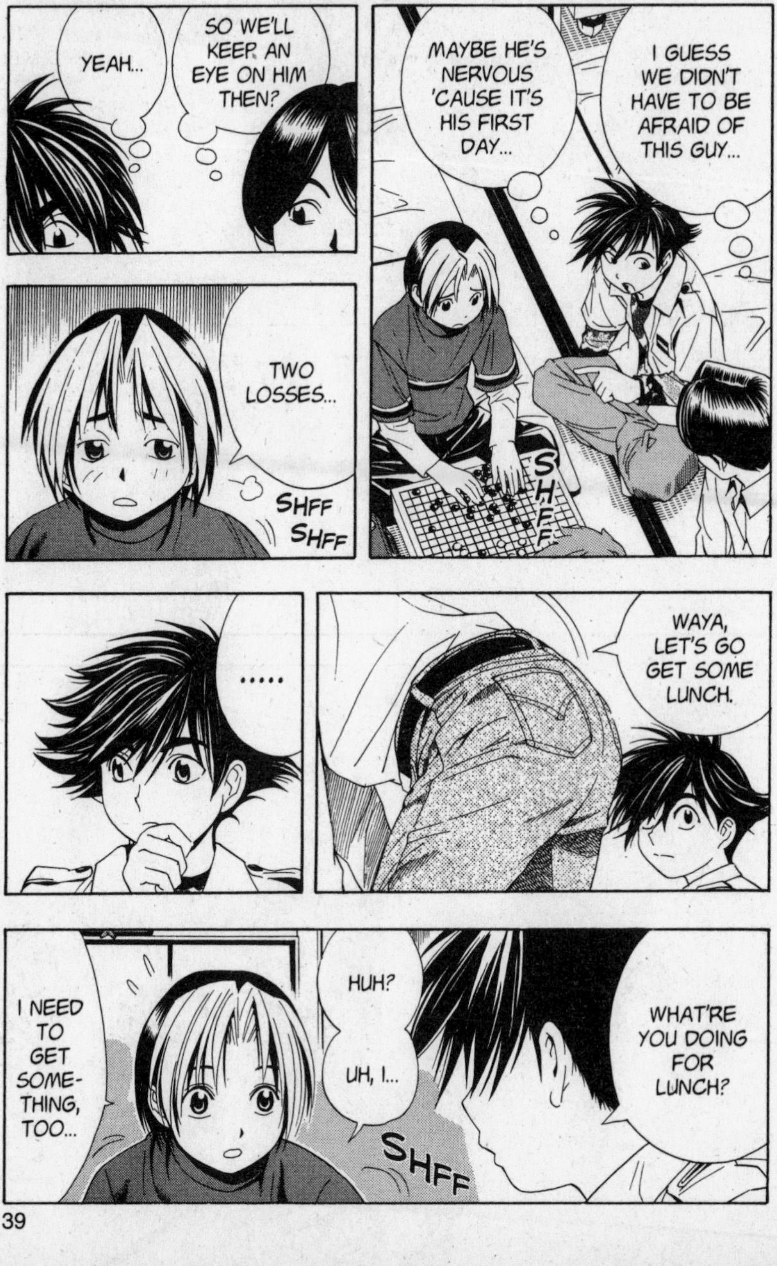

I GUESS WE DIDN'T HAVE TO BE AFRAID OF THIS GUY...
MAYBE HE'S NERVOUS 'CAUSE IT'S HIS FIRST DAY...
SHFF
SO WE'LL KEEP AN EYE ON HIM THEN?
YEAH...
TWO LOSSES...
SHFF SHFF
WAYA, LET'S GO GET SOME LUNCH.
.....
WHAT'RE YOU DOING FOR LUNCH?
HUH?
UH, I...
SHFF
I NEED TO GET SOME-THING, TOO...

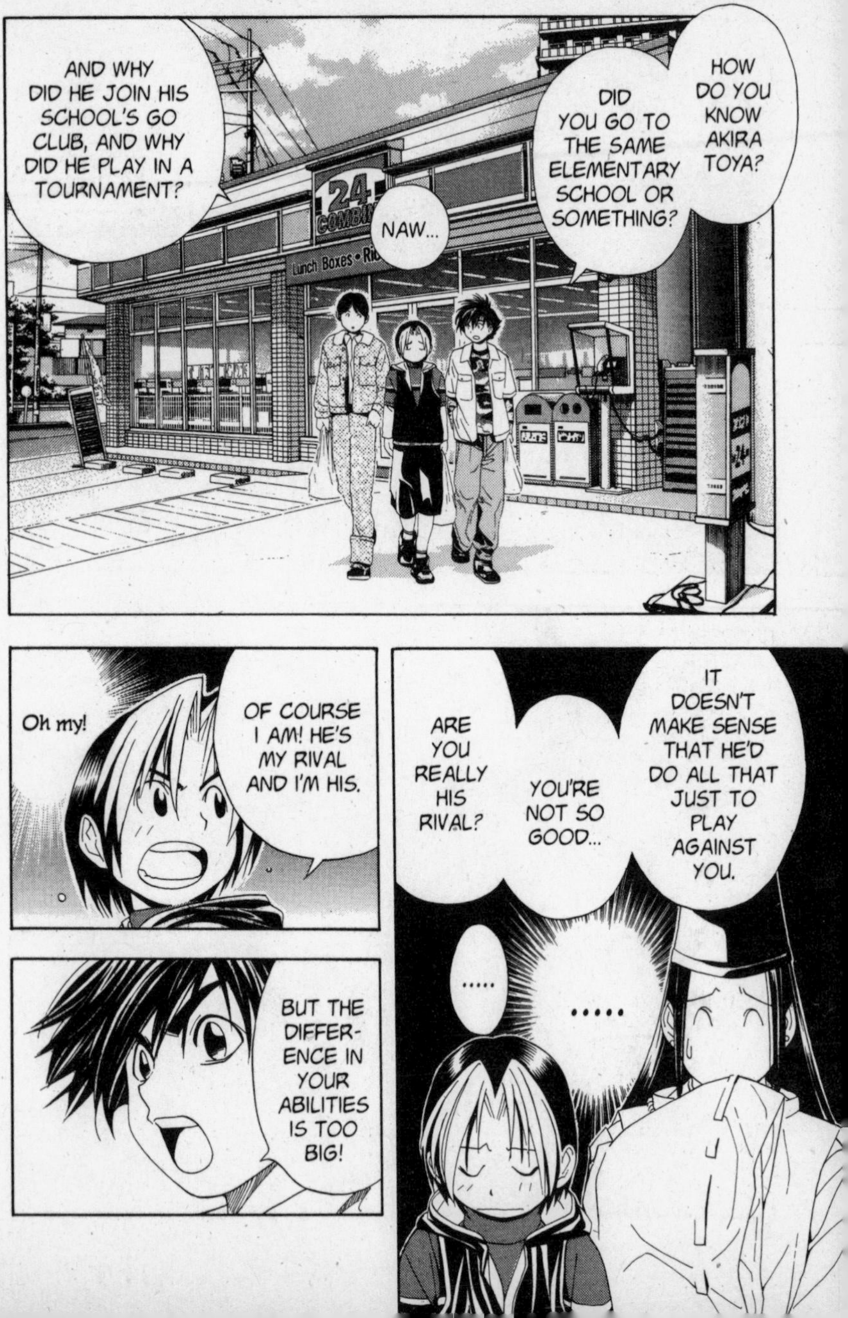
HOW DO YOU KNOW AKIRA TOYA?
DID YOU GO TO THE SAME ELEMENTARY SCHOOL OR SOMETHING?
NAW...
AND WHY DID HE JOIN HIS SCHOOL'S GO CLUB, AND WHY DID HE PLAY IN A TOURNAMENT?
Lunch Boxes
IT DOESN'T MAKE SENSE THAT HE'D DO ALL THAT JUST TO PLAY AGAINST YOU.
YOU'RE NOT SO GOOD...
ARE YOU REALLY HIS RIVAL?
.....
.....
OF COURSE I AM! HE'S MY RIVAL AND I'M HIS.
Oh my!
BUT THE DIFFER-ENCE IN YOUR ABILITIES IS TOO BIG!

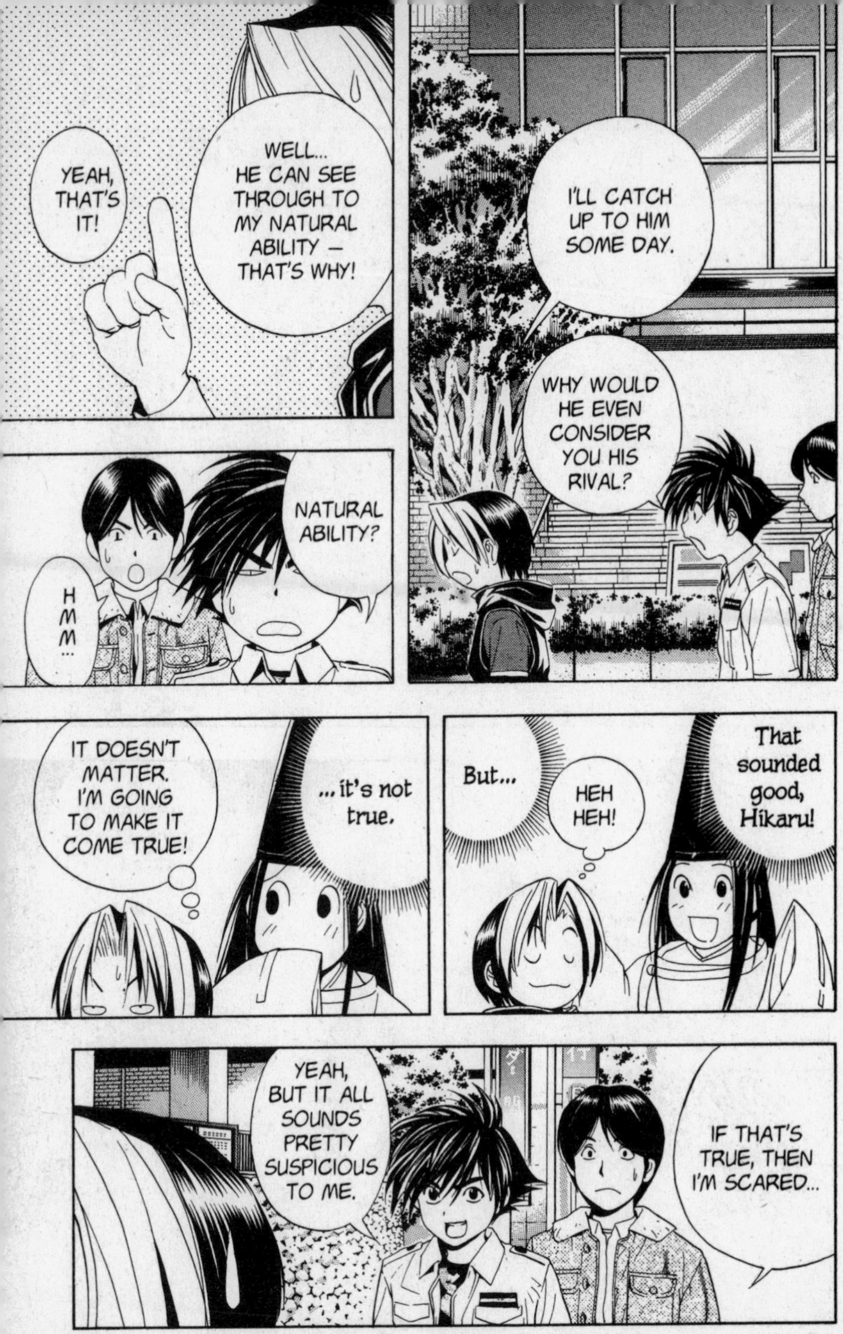

I'LL CATCH UP TO HIM SOME DAY.
WHY WOULD HE EVEN CONSIDER YOU HIS RIVAL?
WELL... HE CAN SEE THROUGH TO MY NATURAL ABILITY – THAT'S WHY!
YEAH, THAT'S IT!
NATURAL ABILITY?
HMM...
That sounded good, Hikaru!
HEH HEH!
But...
...it's not true.
IT DOESN'T MATTER. I'M GOING TO MAKE IT COME TRUE!
IF THAT'S TRUE, THEN I'M SCARED...
YEAH, BUT IT ALL SOUNDS PRETTY SUSPICIOUS TO ME.

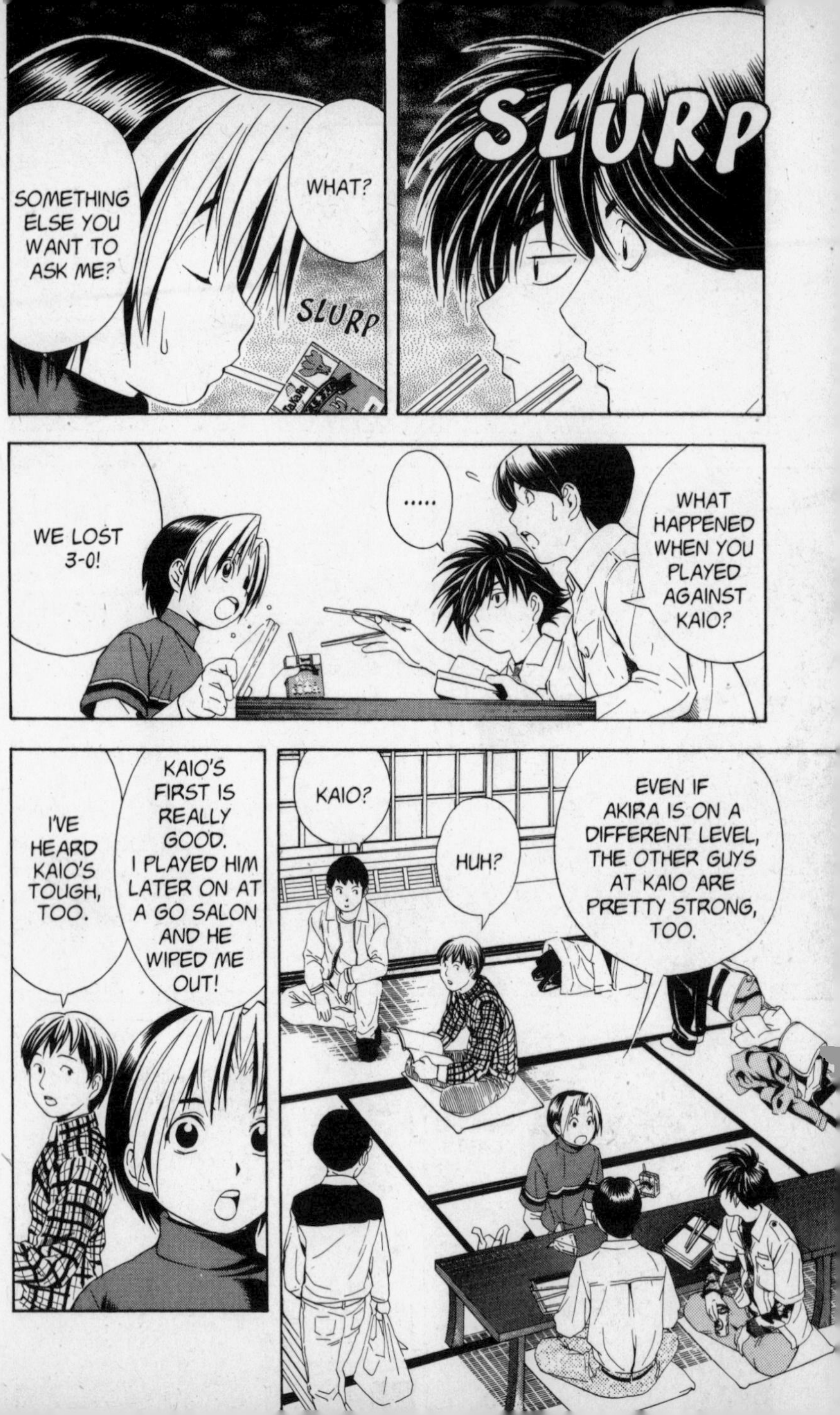
SLURP
WHAT?
SOMETHING ELSE YOU WANT TO ASK ME?
SLURP
WHAT HAPPENED WHEN YOU PLAYED AGAINST KAIO?
......
WE LOST 3-0!
EVEN IF AKIRA IS ON A DIFFERENT LEVEL, THE OTHER GUYS AT KAIO ARE PRETTY STRONG, TOO.
HUH?
KAIO?
KAIO'S FIRST IS REALLY GOOD. I PLAYED HIM LATER ON AT A GO SALON AND HE WIPED ME OUT!
I'VE HEARD KAIO'S TOUGH, TOO.

READ THIS WAY

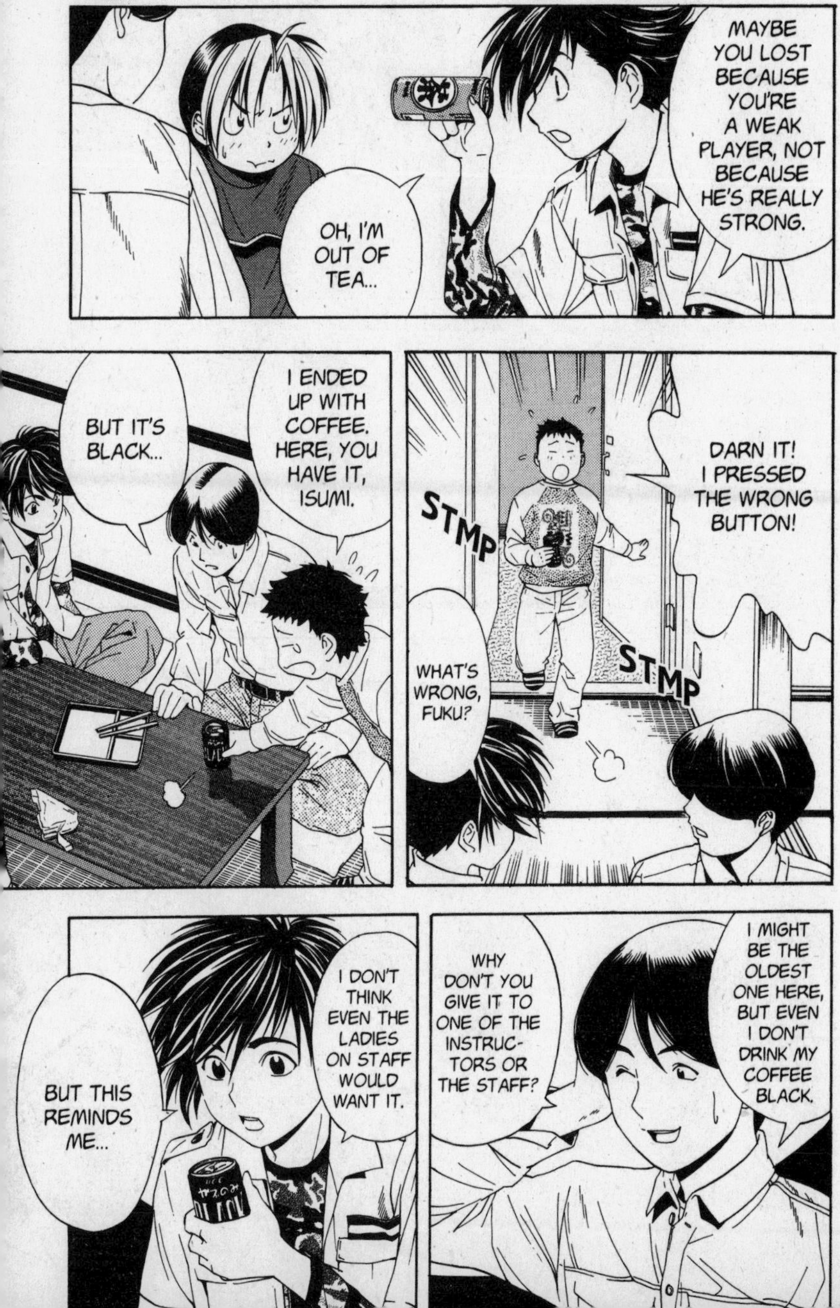
MAYBE YOU LOST BECAUSE YOU'RE A WEAK PLAYER, NOT BECAUSE HE'S REALLY STRONG.
OH, I'M OUT OF TEA...
DARN IT! I PRESSED THE WRONG BUTTON!
STMP
STMP
WHAT'S WRONG, FUKU?
I ENDED UP WITH COFFEE. HERE, YOU HAVE IT, ISUMI.
BUT IT'S BLACK...
I MIGHT BE THE OLDEST ONE HERE, BUT EVEN I DON'T DRINK MY COFFEE BLACK.
WHY DON'T YOU GIVE IT TO ONE OF THE INSTRUC-TORS OR THE STAFF?
I DON'T THINK EVEN THE LADIES ON STAFF WOULD WANT IT.
BUT THIS REMINDS ME...

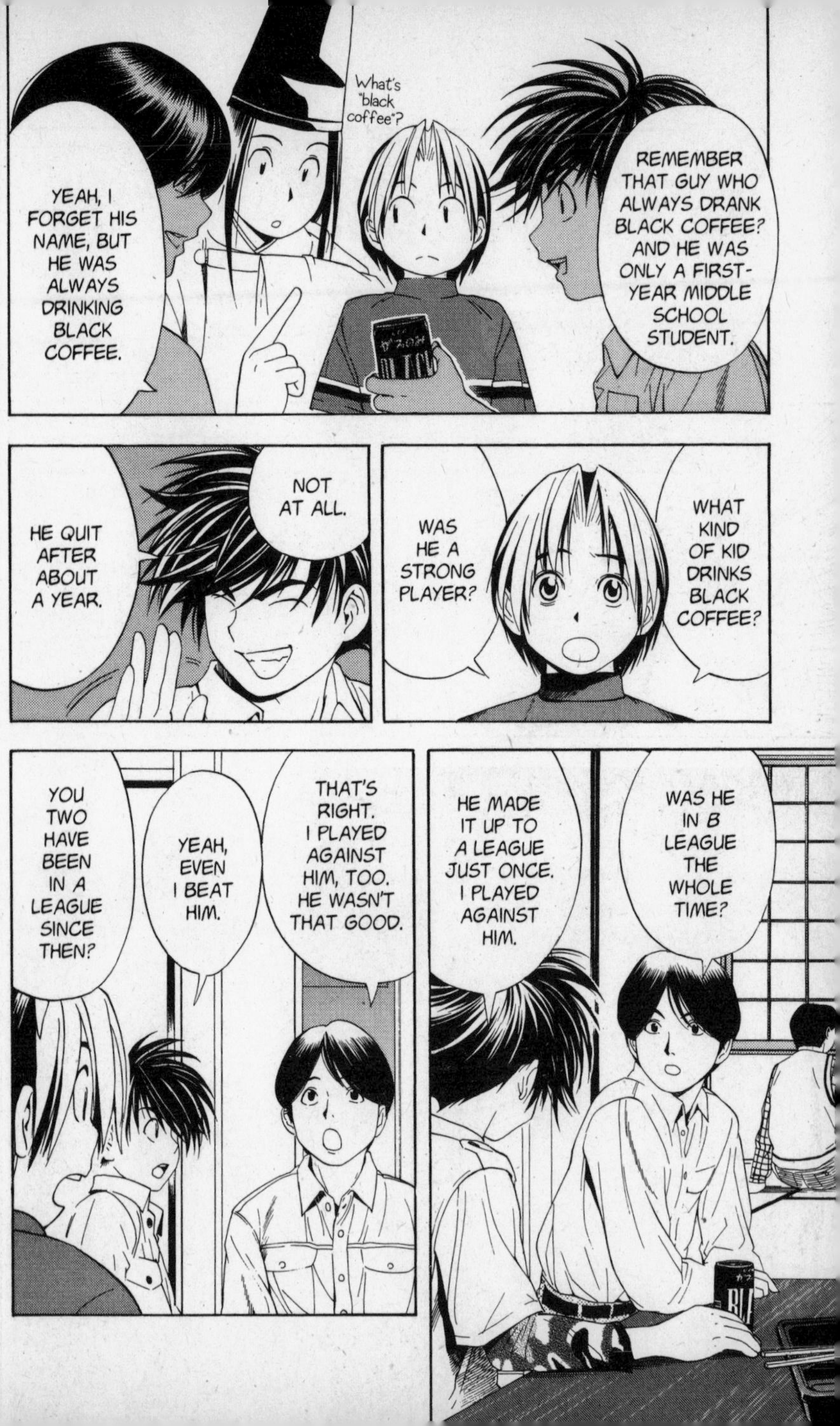
REMEMBER THAT GUY WHO ALWAYS DRANK BLACK COFFEE? AND HE WAS ONLY A FIRST-YEAR MIDDLE SCHOOL STUDENT.
What's "black coffee"?
YEAH, I FORGET HIS NAME, BUT HE WAS ALWAYS DRINKING BLACK COFFEE.
WHAT KIND OF KID DRINKS BLACK COFFEE?
WAS HE A STRONG PLAYER?
NOT AT ALL.
HE QUIT AFTER ABOUT A YEAR.
WAS HE IN *B* LEAGUE THE WHOLE TIME?
HE MADE IT UP TO A LEAGUE JUST ONCE. I PLAYED AGAINST HIM.
THAT'S RIGHT. I PLAYED AGAINST HIM, TOO. HE WASN'T THAT GOOD.
YEAH, EVEN I BEAT HIM.
YOU TWO HAVE BEEN IN A LEAGUE SINCE THEN?

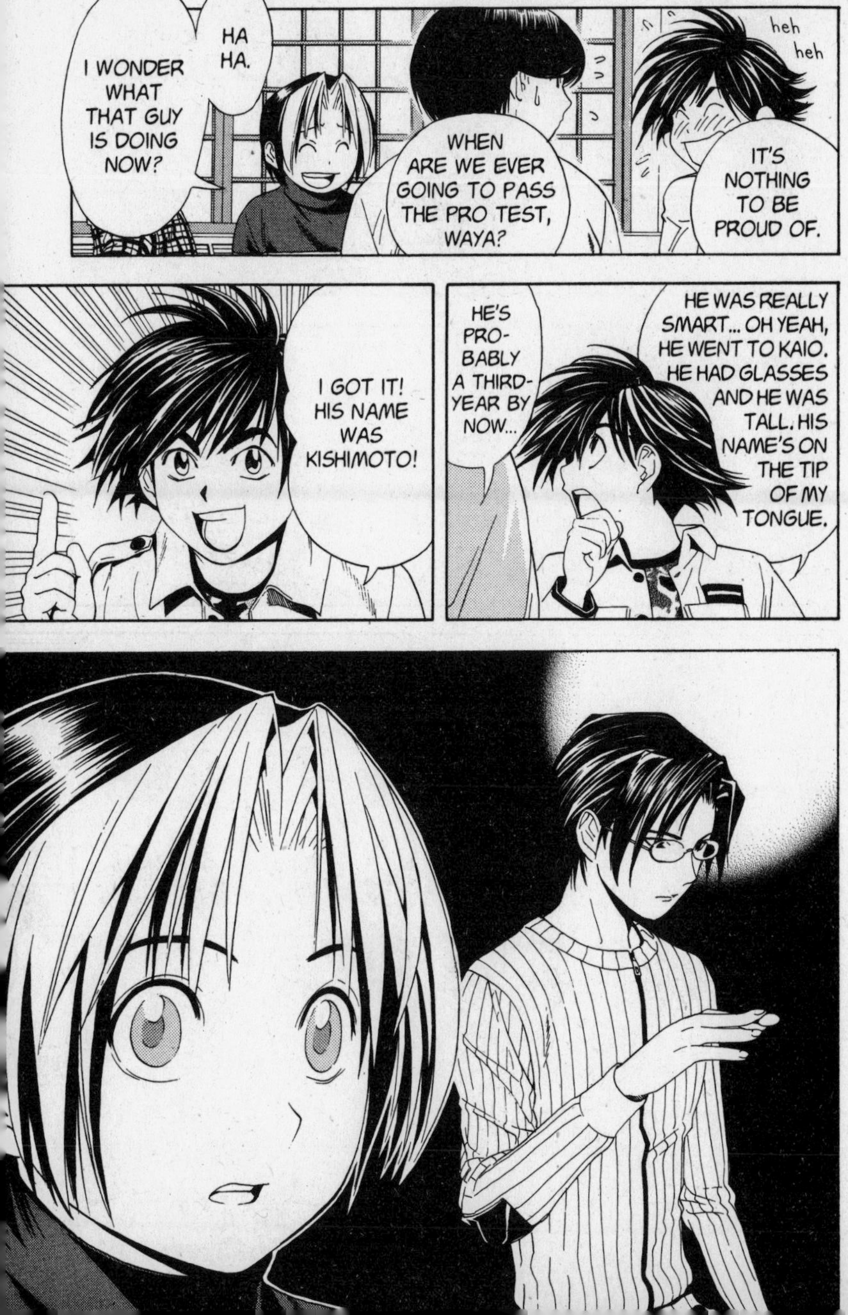
heh heh
IT'S NOTHING TO BE PROUD OF.
WHEN ARE WE EVER GOING TO PASS THE PRO TEST, WAYA?
HA HA.
I WONDER WHAT THAT GUY IS DOING NOW?
HE WAS REALLY SMART... OH YEAH, HE WENT TO KAIO. HE HAD GLASSES AND HE WAS TALL. HIS NAME'S ON THE TIP OF MY TONGUE.
HE'S PRO-BABLY A THIRD-YEAR BY NOW...
I GOT IT! HIS NAME WAS KISHIMOTO!

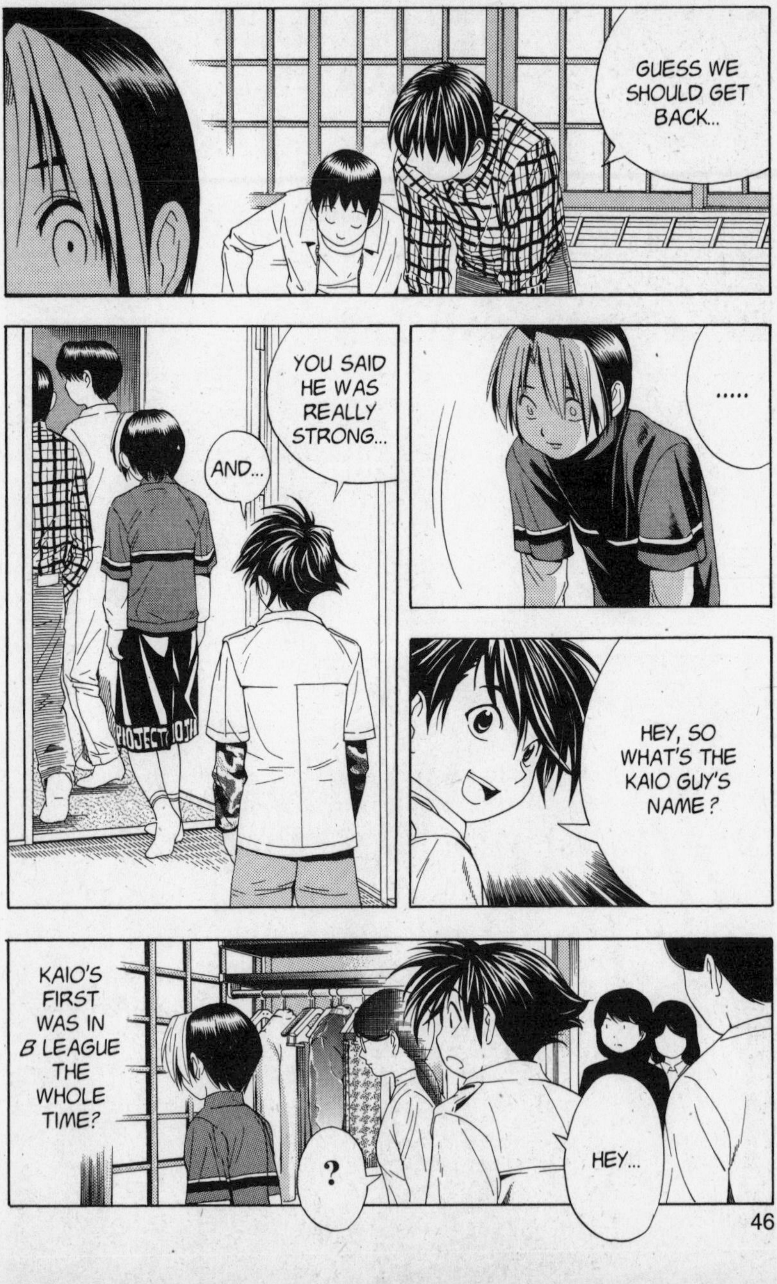
GUESS WE SHOULD GET BACK...
.....
HEY, SO WHAT'S THE KAIO GUY'S NAME?
YOU SAID HE WAS REALLY STRONG...
AND...
HEY...
?
KAIO'S FIRST WAS IN B LEAGUE THE WHOLE TIME?

READ THIS WAY

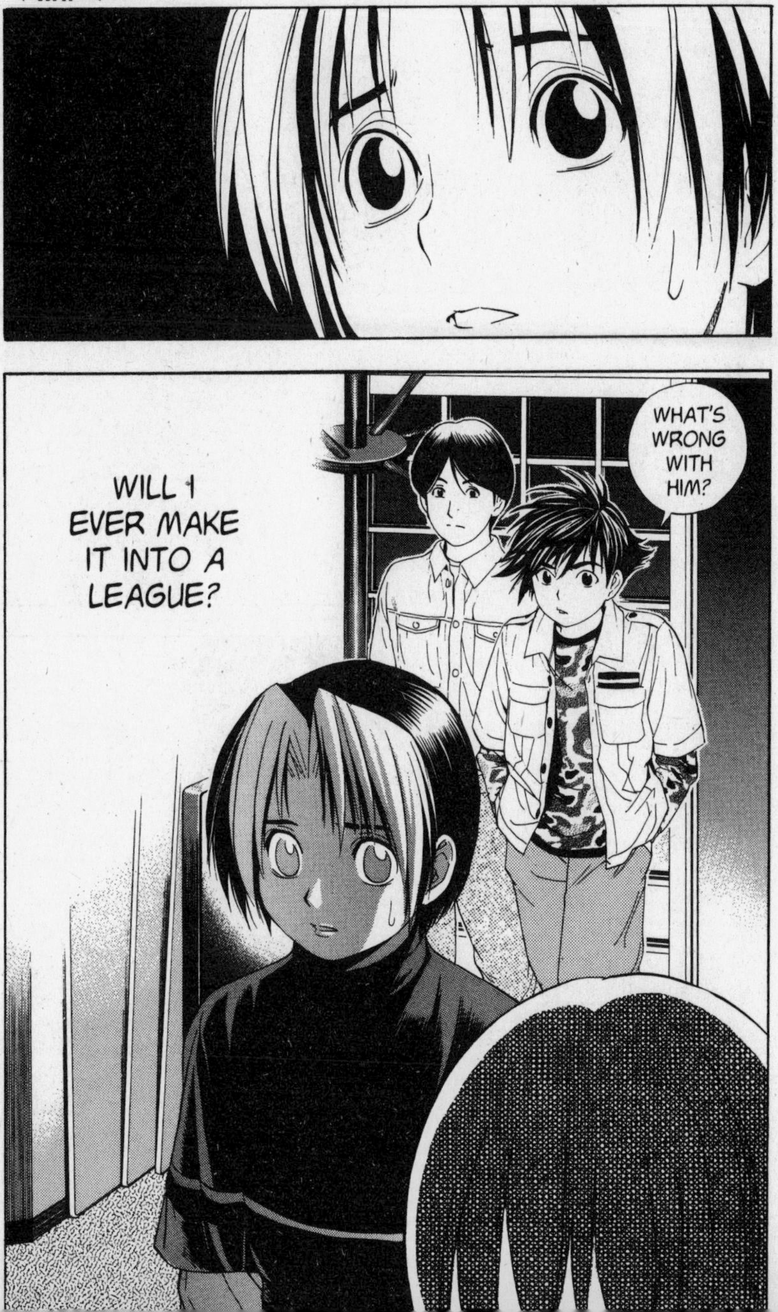
WHAT'S WRONG WITH HIM?
WILL I EVER MAKE IT INTO A LEAGUE?

HIKARU NO GO STORYBOARDS ⑮

YUMI HOTTA

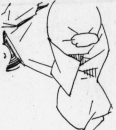

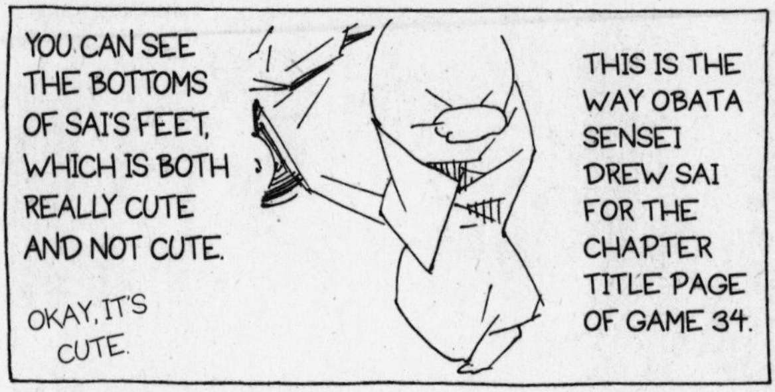

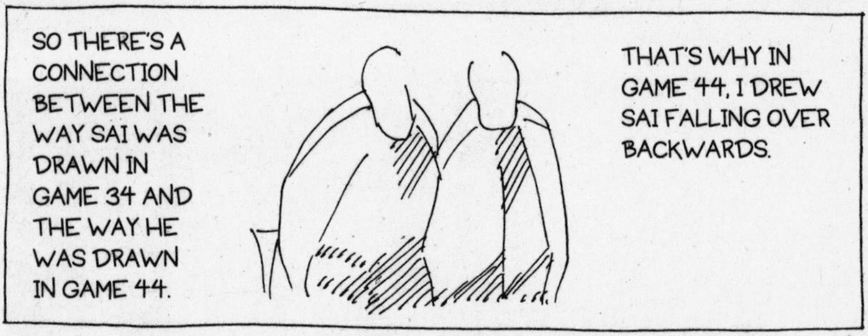

THIS IS THE WAY OBATA SENSEI DREW SAI FOR THE CHAPTER TITLE PAGE OF GAME 34.
YOU CAN SEE THE BOTTOMS OF SAI'S FEET, WHICH IS BOTH REALLY CUTE AND NOT CUTE.
OKAY, IT'S CUTE.

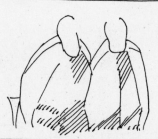

THAT'S WHY IN GAME 44, I DREW SAI FALLING OVER BACKWARDS.
SO THERE'S A CONNECTION BETWEEN THE WAY SAI WAS DRAWN IN GAME 34 AND THE WAY HE WAS DRAWN IN GAME 44.

AND THEN IN GAME 48, THERE'S THE IMAGE OF SAI CRYING BEHIND AN INSEI INSTRUCTOR.

THIS TURNED OUT TEN TIMES CUTER THAN MY STORYBOARD DRAWING.

I SAW THAT, AND IT JUST MADE ME WANT TO DRAW SAI EVEN CUTER.

AND THEN OBATA SENSEI TURNS IT AROUND AND DRAWS SAI EVEN CUTER.

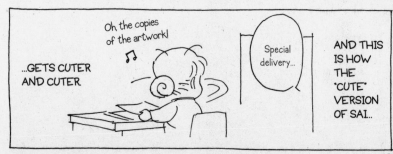

AND THIS IS HOW THE "CUTE" VERSION OF SAI...
Special delivery...
Oh, the copies of the artwork! ♫
...GETS CUTER AND CUTER.

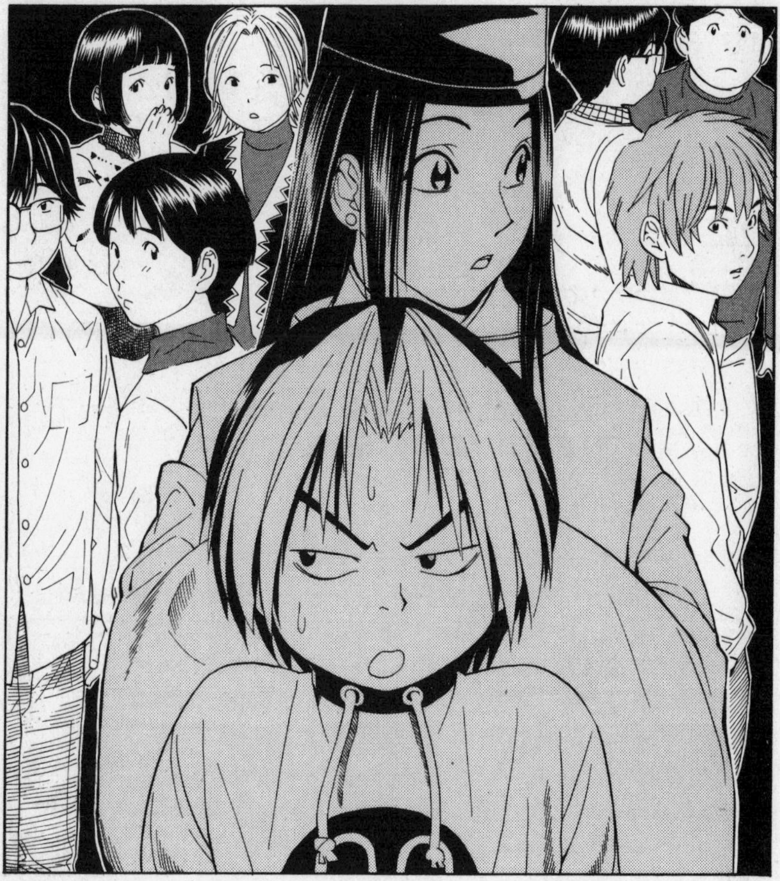

Game 46 "Catalyst"

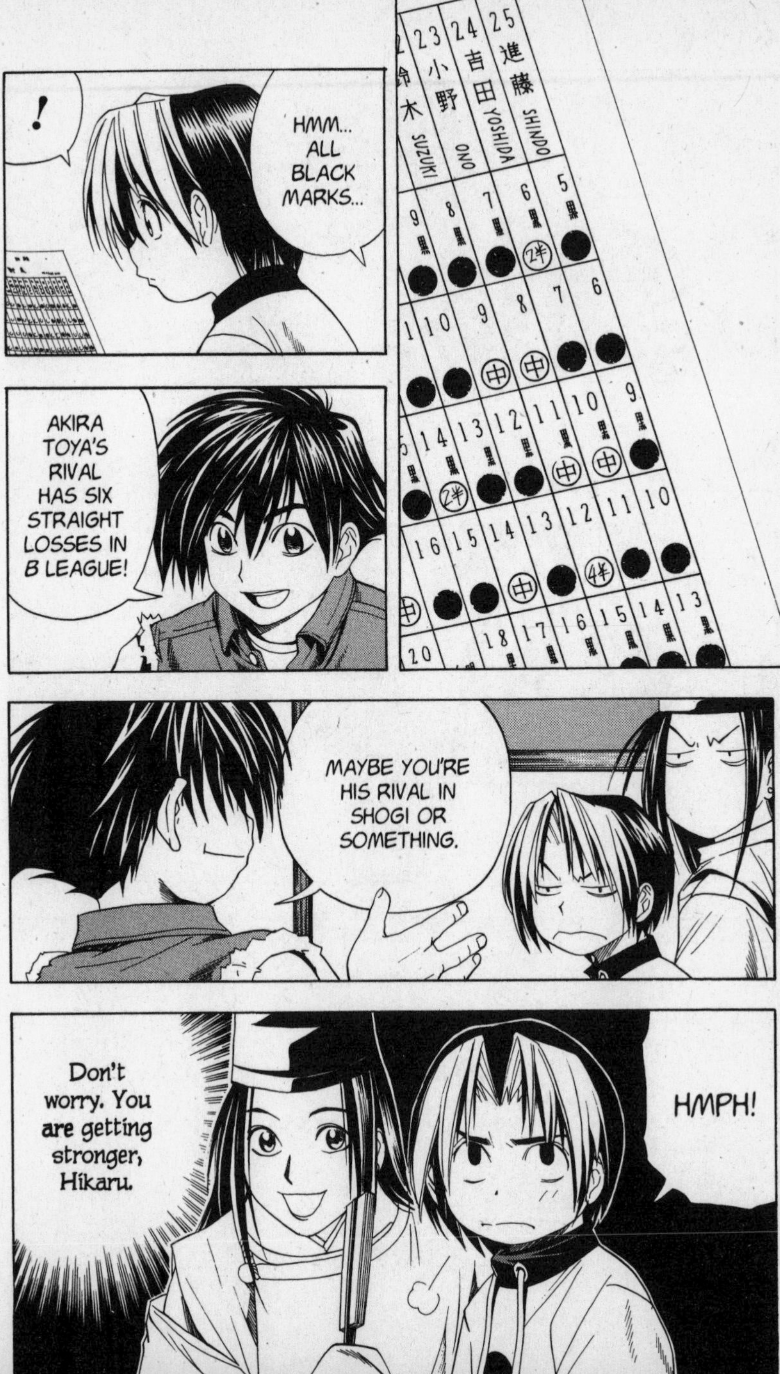

23 小野 ONO
24 吉田 YOSHIDA
25 進藤 SHINDO
鈴木 SUZUKI
HMM... ALL BLACK MARKS...
!
AKIRA TOYA'S RIVAL HAS SIX STRAIGHT LOSSES IN B LEAGUE!
MAYBE YOU'RE HIS RIVAL IN SHOGI OR SOMETHING.
HMPH!
Don't worry. You are getting stronger, Hikaru.

READ THIS WAY

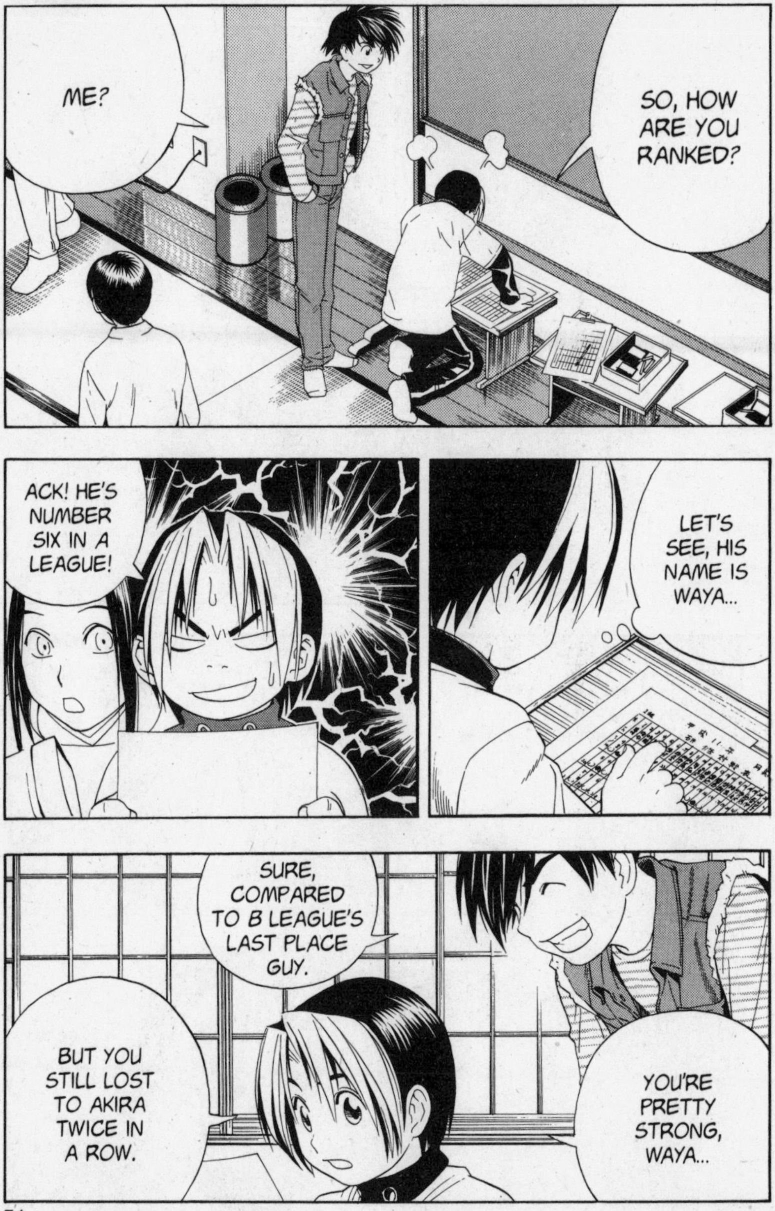
SO, HOW ARE YOU RANKED?
ME?
LET'S SEE, HIS NAME IS WAYA...
ACK! HE'S NUMBER SIX IN A LEAGUE!
YOU'RE PRETTY STRONG, WAYA...
SURE, COMPARED TO B LEAGUE'S LAST PLACE GUY.
BUT YOU STILL LOST TO AKIRA TWICE IN A ROW.

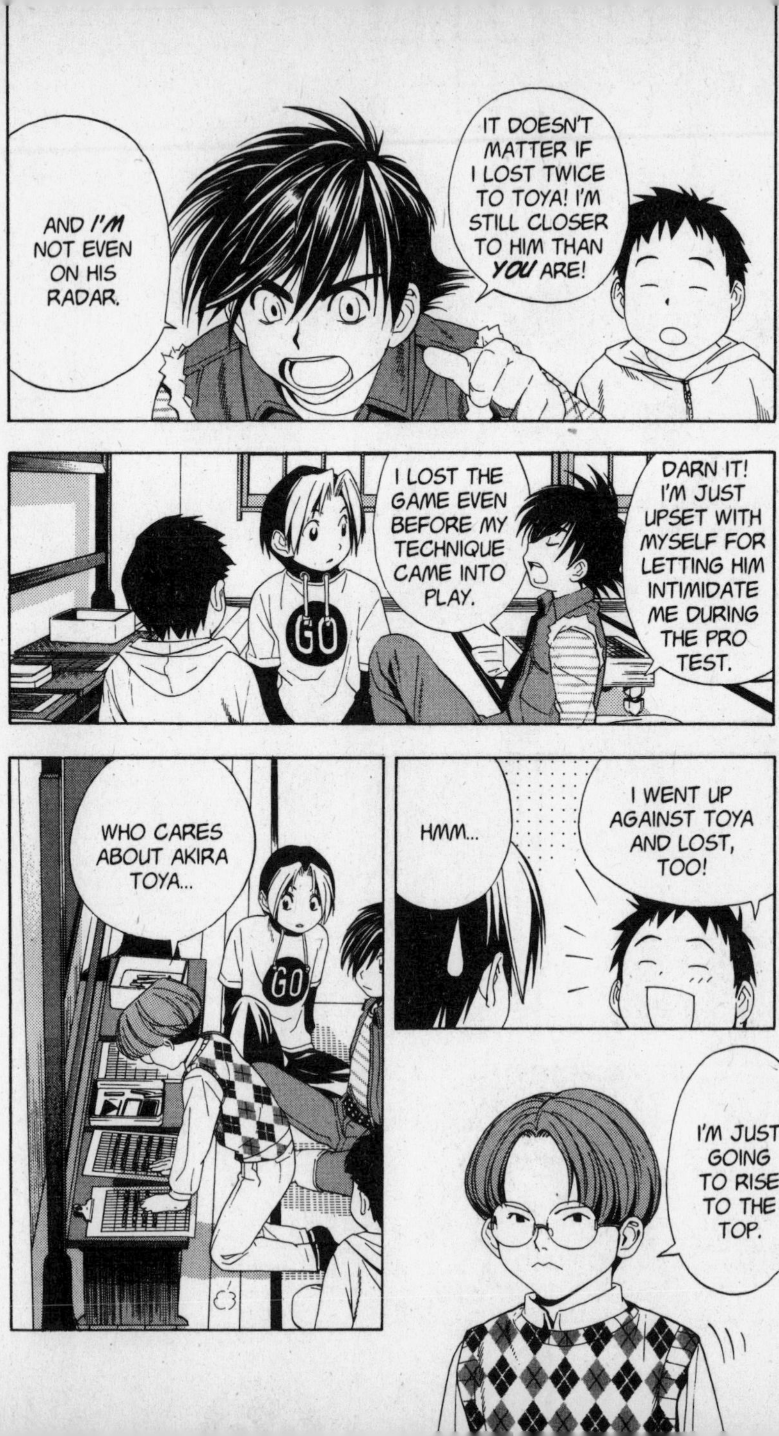
IT DOESN'T MATTER IF I LOST TWICE TO TOYA! I'M STILL CLOSER TO HIM THAN YOU ARE!
AND I'M NOT EVEN ON HIS RADAR.
DARN IT! I'M JUST UPSET WITH MYSELF FOR LETTING HIM INTIMIDATE ME DURING THE PRO TEST.
I LOST THE GAME EVEN BEFORE MY TECHNIQUE CAME INTO PLAY.
I WENT UP AGAINST TOYA AND LOST, TOO!
HMM...
I'M JUST GOING TO RISE TO THE TOP.
WHO CARES ABOUT AKIRA TOYA...

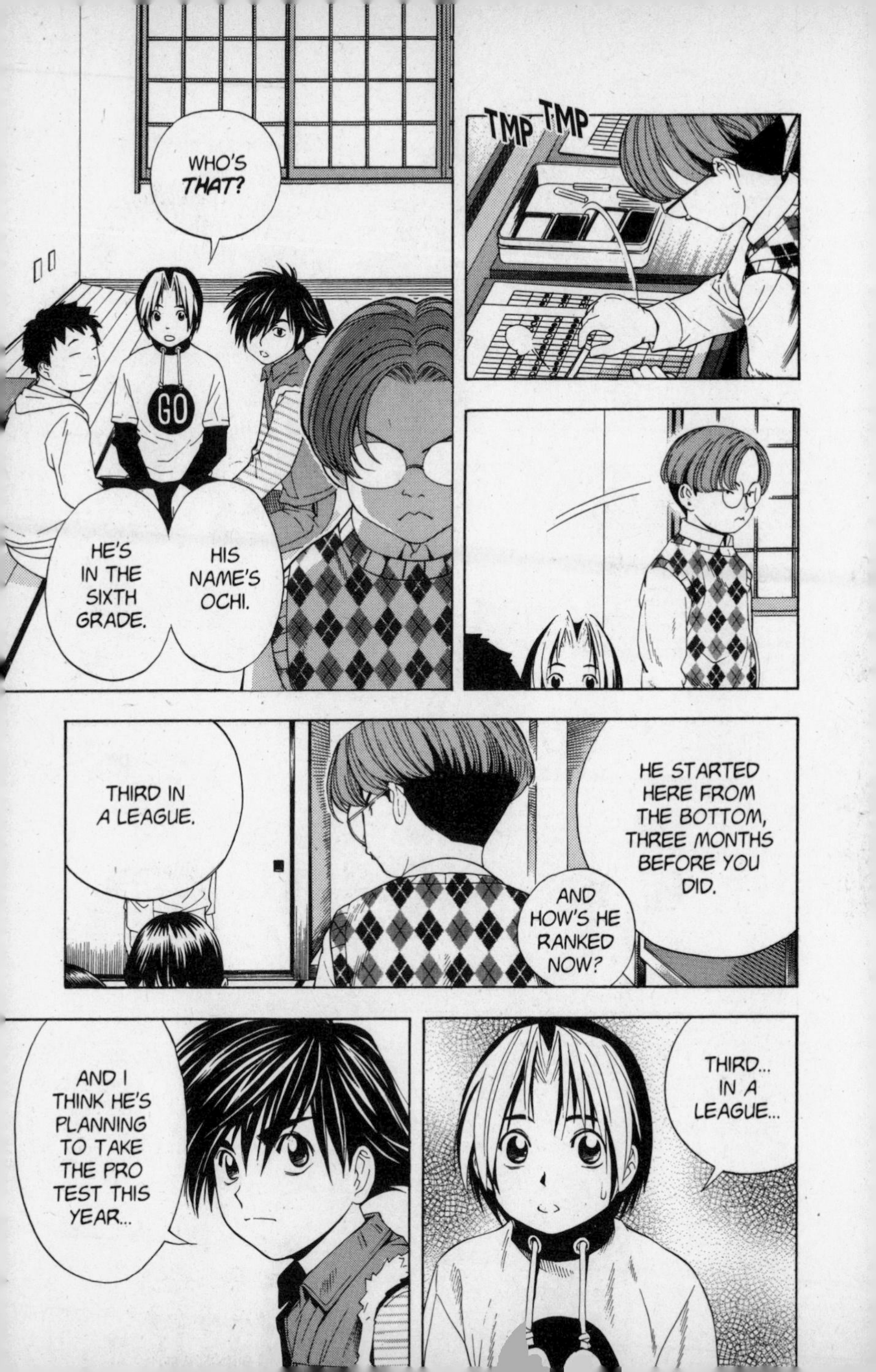
TMP TMP
WHO'S THAT?
HIS NAME'S OCHI.
HE'S IN THE SIXTH GRADE.
HE STARTED HERE FROM THE BOTTOM, THREE MONTHS BEFORE YOU DID.
AND HOW'S HE RANKED NOW?
THIRD IN A LEAGUE.
THIRD... IN A LEAGUE...
AND I THINK HE'S PLANNING TO TAKE THE PRO TEST THIS YEAR...

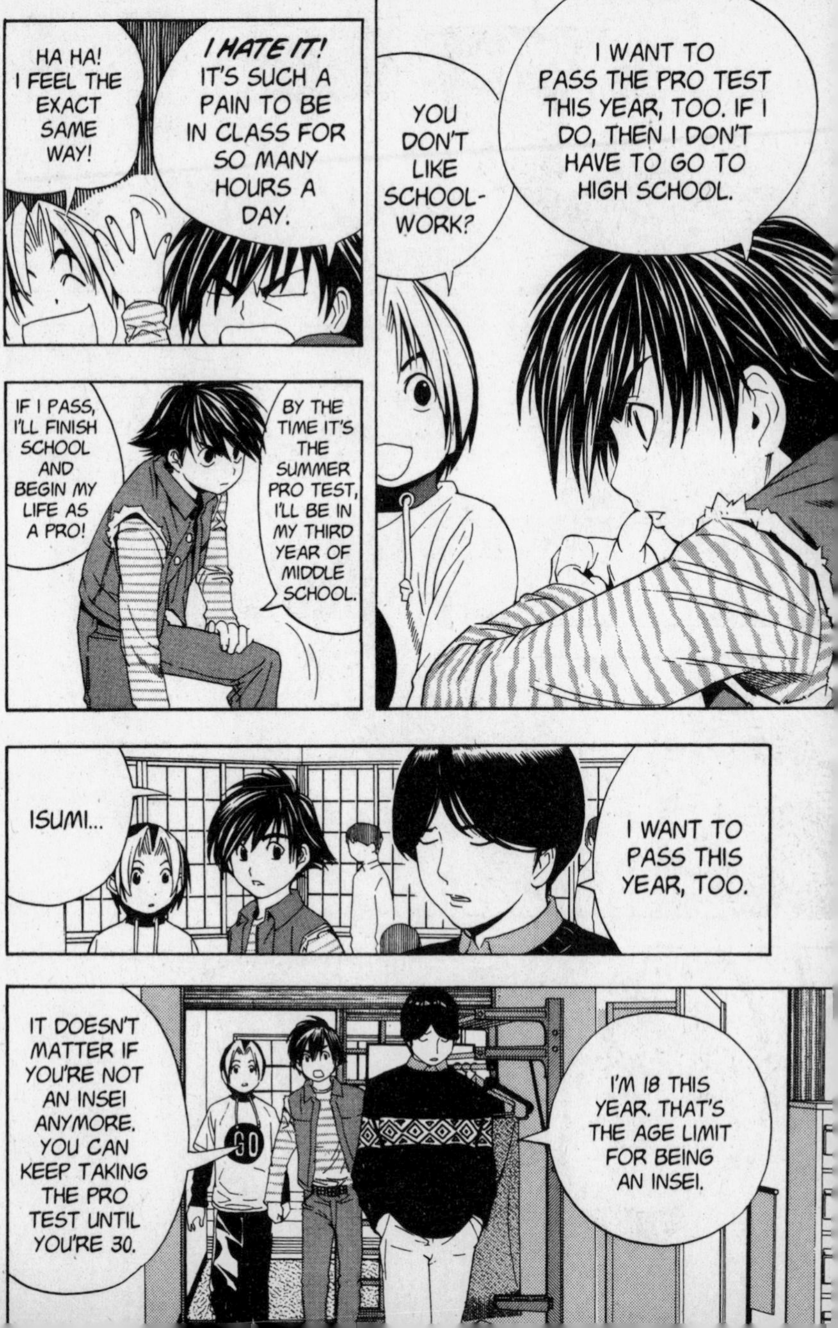
I WANT TO PASS THE PRO TEST THIS YEAR, TOO. IF I DO, THEN I DON'T HAVE TO GO TO HIGH SCHOOL.
YOU DON'T LIKE SCHOOL-WORK?
I HATE IT! IT'S SUCH A PAIN TO BE IN CLASS FOR SO MANY HOURS A DAY.
HA HA! I FEEL THE EXACT SAME WAY!
BY THE TIME IT'S THE SUMMER PRO TEST, I'LL BE IN MY THIRD YEAR OF MIDDLE SCHOOL.
IF I PASS, I'LL FINISH SCHOOL AND BEGIN MY LIFE AS A PRO!
I WANT TO PASS THIS YEAR, TOO.
ISUMI...
I'M 18 THIS YEAR. THAT'S THE AGE LIMIT FOR BEING AN INSEI.
GO
IT DOESN'T MATTER IF YOU'RE NOT AN INSEI ANYMORE. YOU CAN KEEP TAKING THE PRO TEST UNTIL YOU'RE 30.

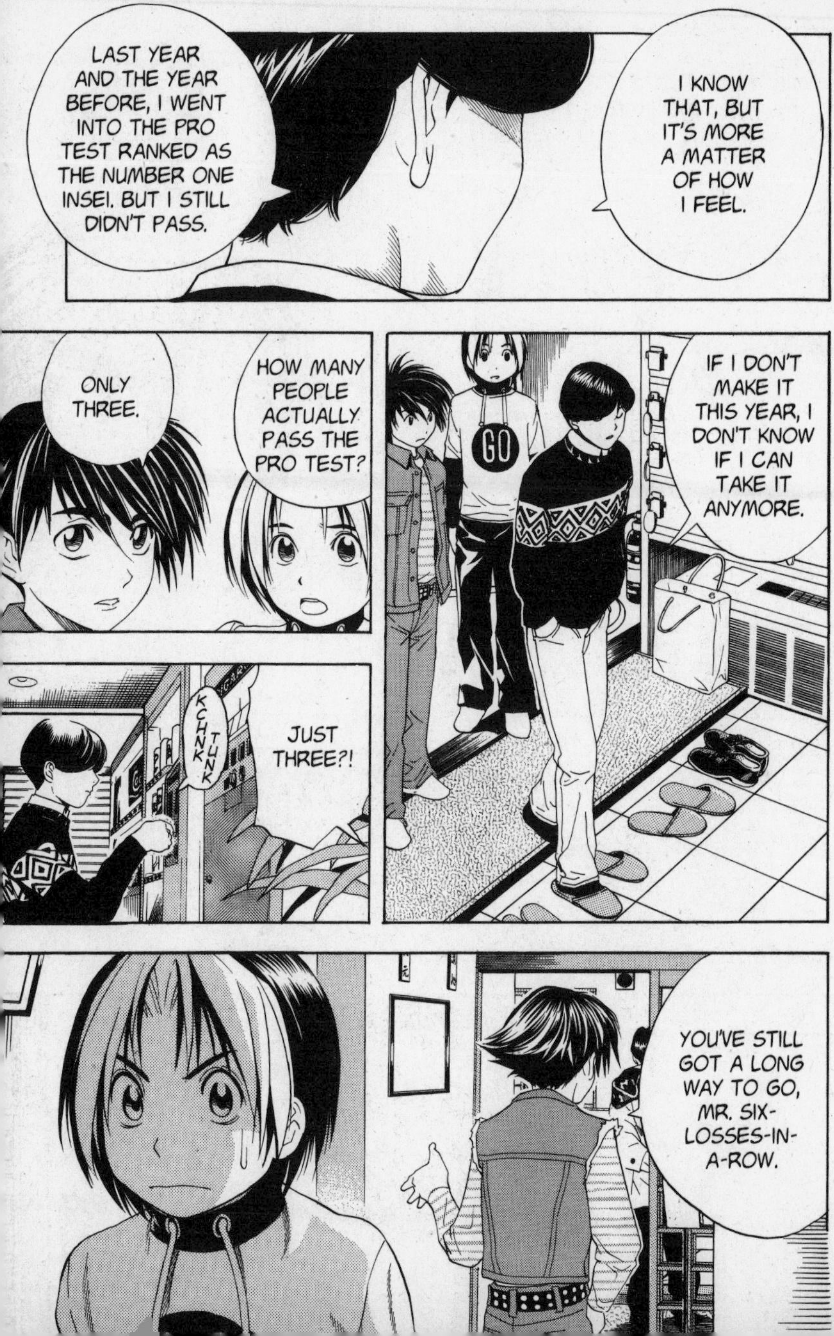
I KNOW THAT, BUT IT'S MORE A MATTER OF HOW I FEEL.
LAST YEAR AND THE YEAR BEFORE, I WENT INTO THE PRO TEST RANKED AS THE NUMBER ONE INSEI. BUT I STILL DIDN'T PASS.
IF I DON'T MAKE IT THIS YEAR, I DON'T KNOW IF I CAN TAKE IT ANYMORE.
HOW MANY PEOPLE ACTUALLY PASS THE PRO TEST?
ONLY THREE.
JUST THREE?!
KCHNK THUNK
YOU'VE STILL GOT A LONG WAY TO GO, MR. SIX-LOSSES-IN-A-ROW.

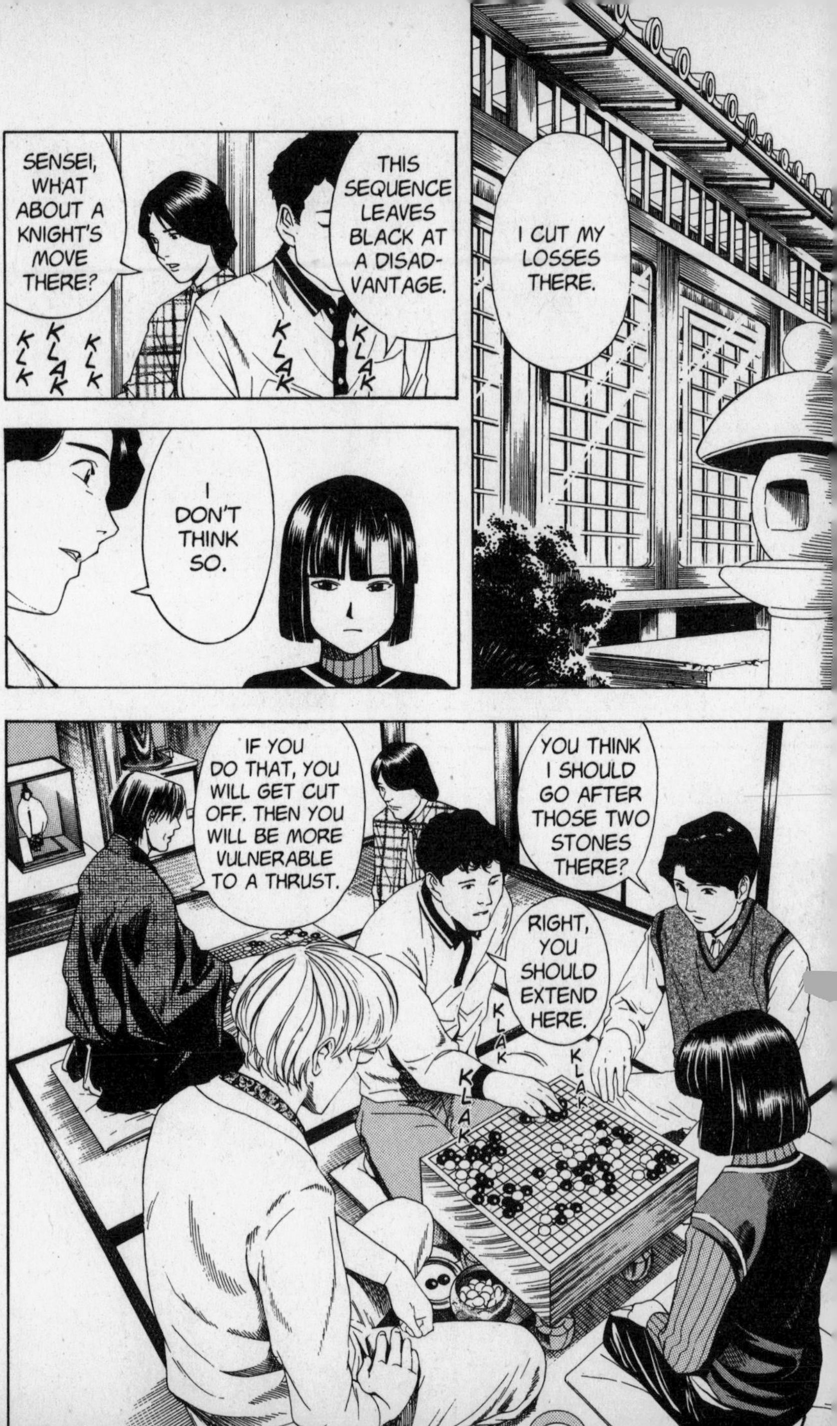
I CUT MY LOSSES THERE.
THIS SEQUENCE LEAVES BLACK AT A DISADVANTAGE.
KLAK
KLAK
SENSEI, WHAT ABOUT A KNIGHT'S MOVE THERE?
KLK
KLAK
KLK
I DON'T THINK SO.
YOU THINK I SHOULD GO AFTER THOSE TWO STONES THERE?
IF YOU DO THAT, YOU WILL GET CUT OFF. THEN YOU WILL BE MORE VULNERABLE TO A THRUST.
RIGHT, YOU SHOULD EXTEND HERE.
KLAK
KLAK
KLAK

READ THIS WAY

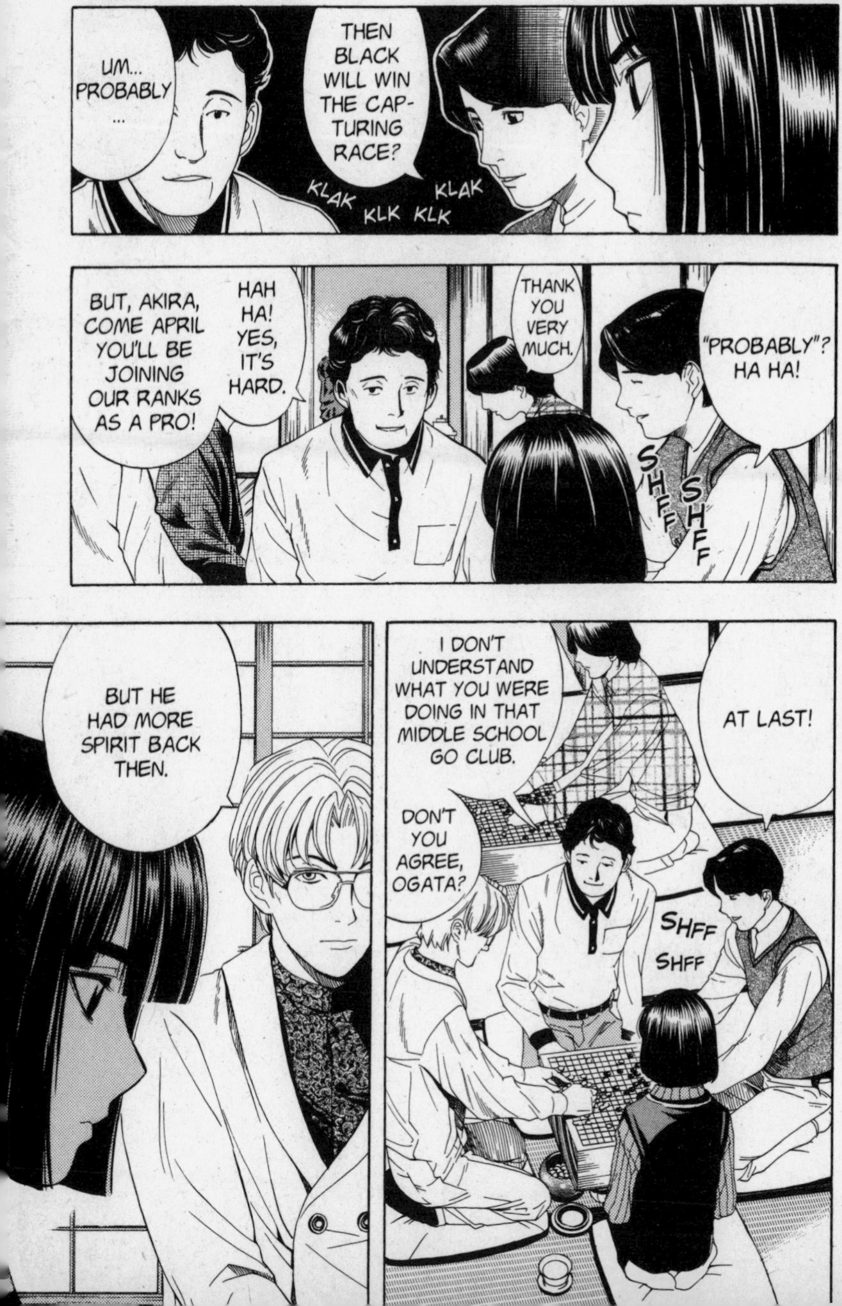
THEN BLACK WILL WIN THE CAP-TURING RACE?
KLAK KLK KLK KLAK
UM... PROBABLY ...
"PROBABLY"? HA HA!
THANK YOU VERY MUCH.
SHFF SHFF
HAH HA! YES, IT'S HARD.
BUT, AKIRA, COME APRIL YOU'LL BE JOINING OUR RANKS AS A PRO!
AT LAST!
I DON'T UNDERSTAND WHAT YOU WERE DOING IN THAT MIDDLE SCHOOL GO CLUB.
DON'T YOU AGREE, OGATA?
SHFF SHFF
BUT HE HAD MORE SPIRIT BACK THEN.

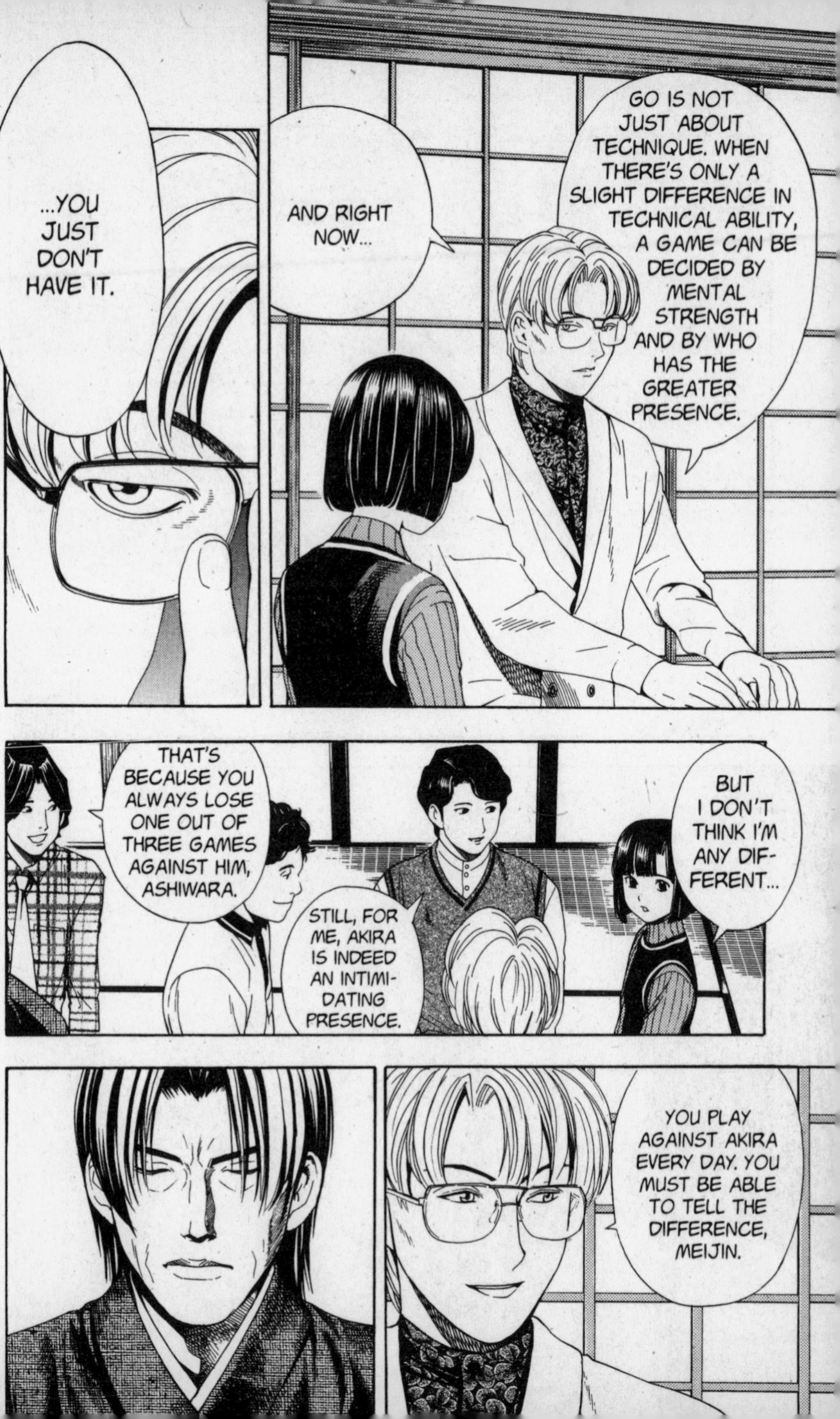
GO IS NOT JUST ABOUT TECHNIQUE. WHEN THERE'S ONLY A SLIGHT DIFFERENCE IN TECHNICAL ABILITY, A GAME CAN BE DECIDED BY MENTAL STRENGTH AND BY WHO HAS THE GREATER PRESENCE.
AND RIGHT NOW...
...YOU JUST DON'T HAVE IT.
BUT I DON'T THINK I'M ANY DIF-FERENT...
STILL, FOR ME, AKIRA IS INDEED AN INTIMI-DATING PRESENCE.
THAT'S BECAUSE YOU ALWAYS LOSE ONE OUT OF THREE GAMES AGAINST HIM, ASHIWARA.
YOU PLAY AGAINST AKIRA EVERY DAY. YOU MUST BE ABLE TO TELL THE DIFFERENCE, MEIJIN.

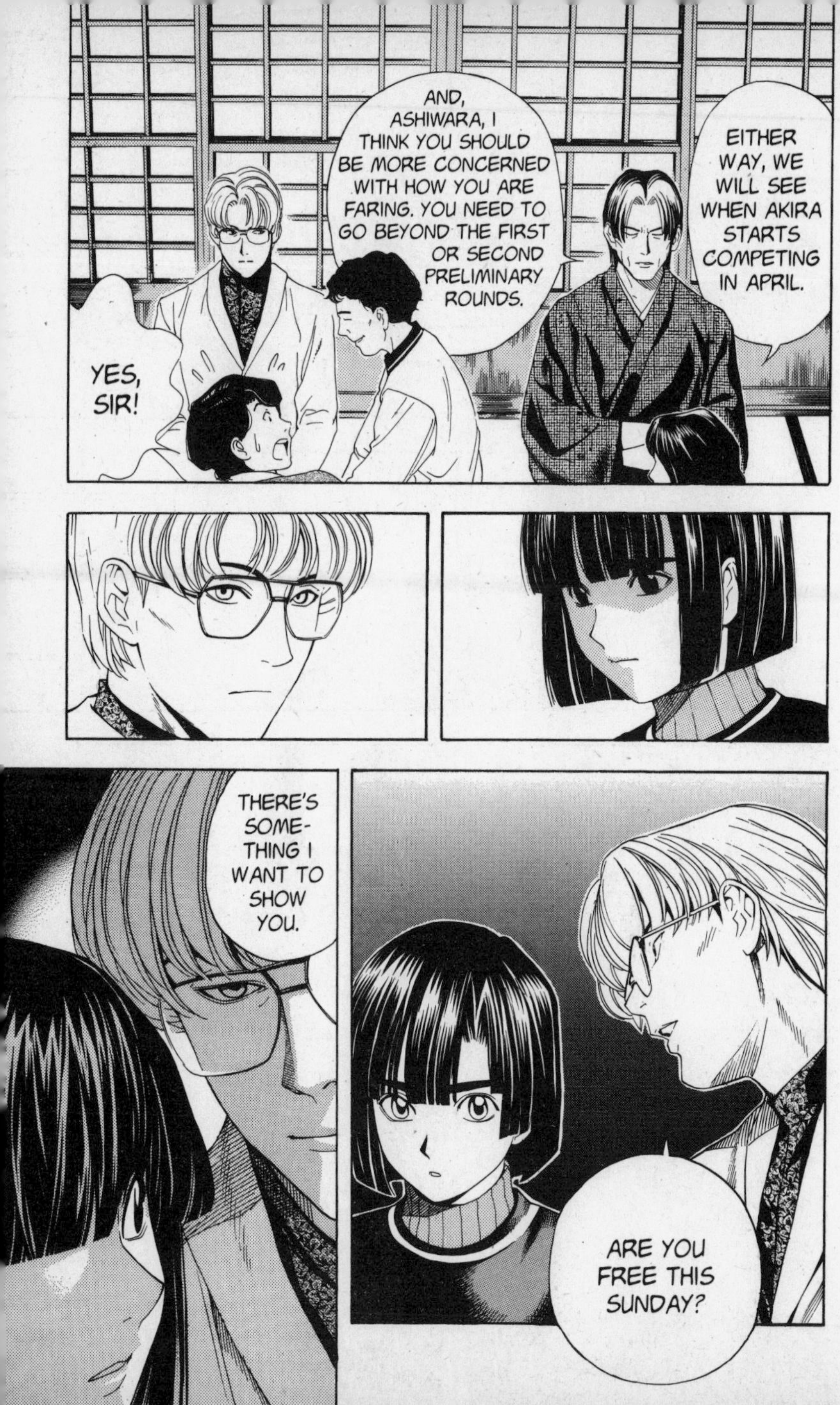
EITHER WAY, WE WILL SEE WHEN AKIRA STARTS COMPETING IN APRIL.
AND, ASHIWARA, I THINK YOU SHOULD BE MORE CONCERNED WITH HOW YOU ARE FARING. YOU NEED TO GO BEYOND THE FIRST OR SECOND PRELIMINARY ROUNDS.
YES, SIR!
ARE YOU FREE THIS SUNDAY?
THERE'S SOME-THING I WANT TO SHOW YOU.

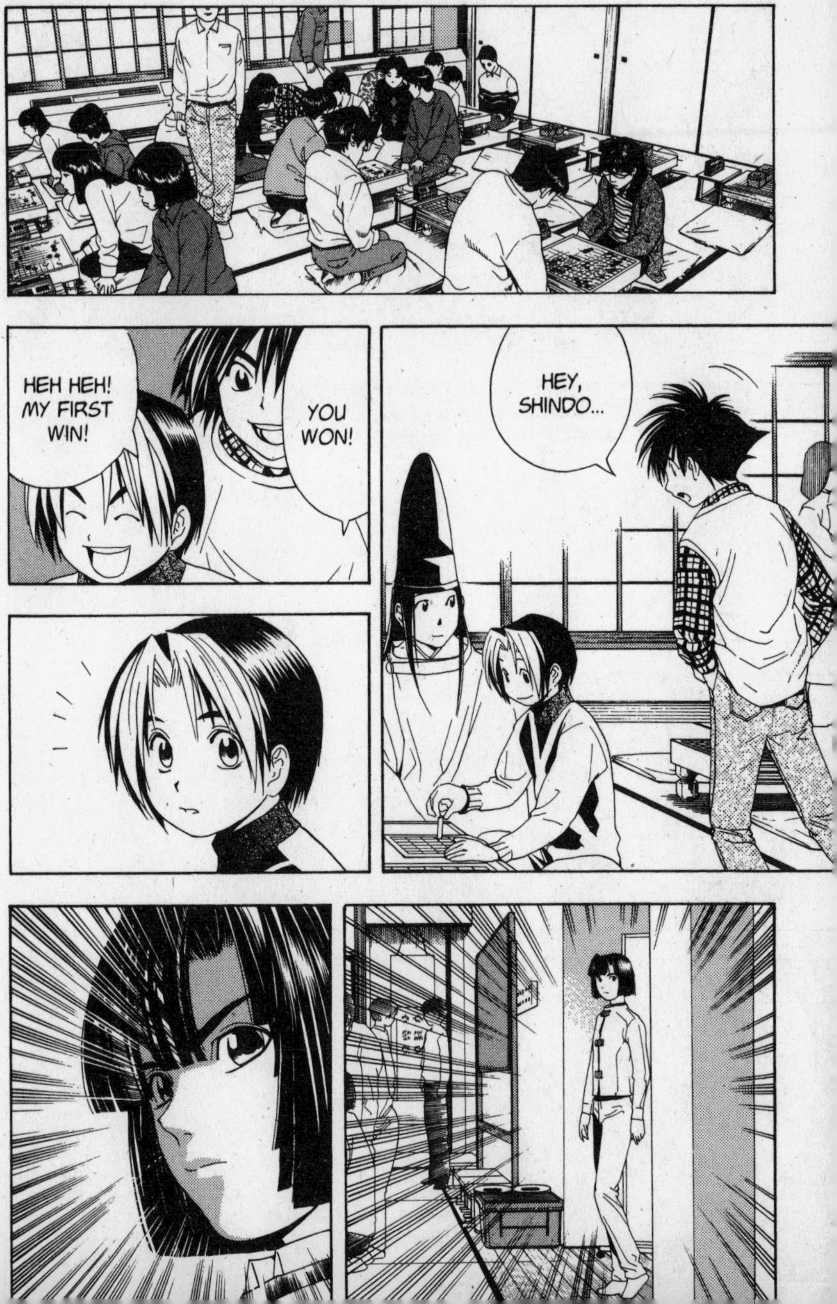
HEY, SHINDO...
YOU WON!
HEH HEH! MY FIRST WIN!

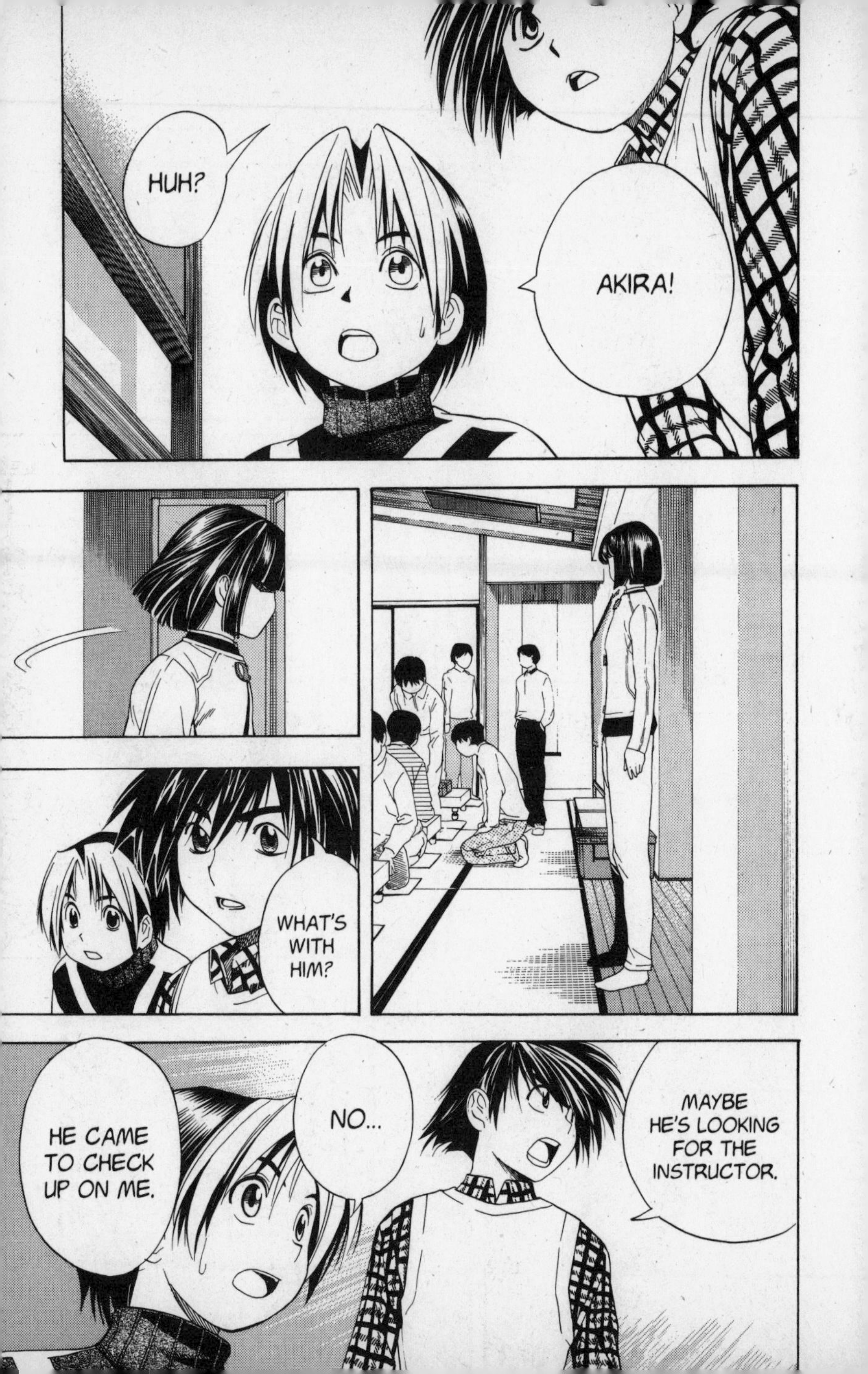
AKIRA!
HUH?
WHAT'S WITH HIM?
MAYBE HE'S LOOKING FOR THE INSTRUCTOR.
NO...
HE CAME TO CHECK UP ON ME.

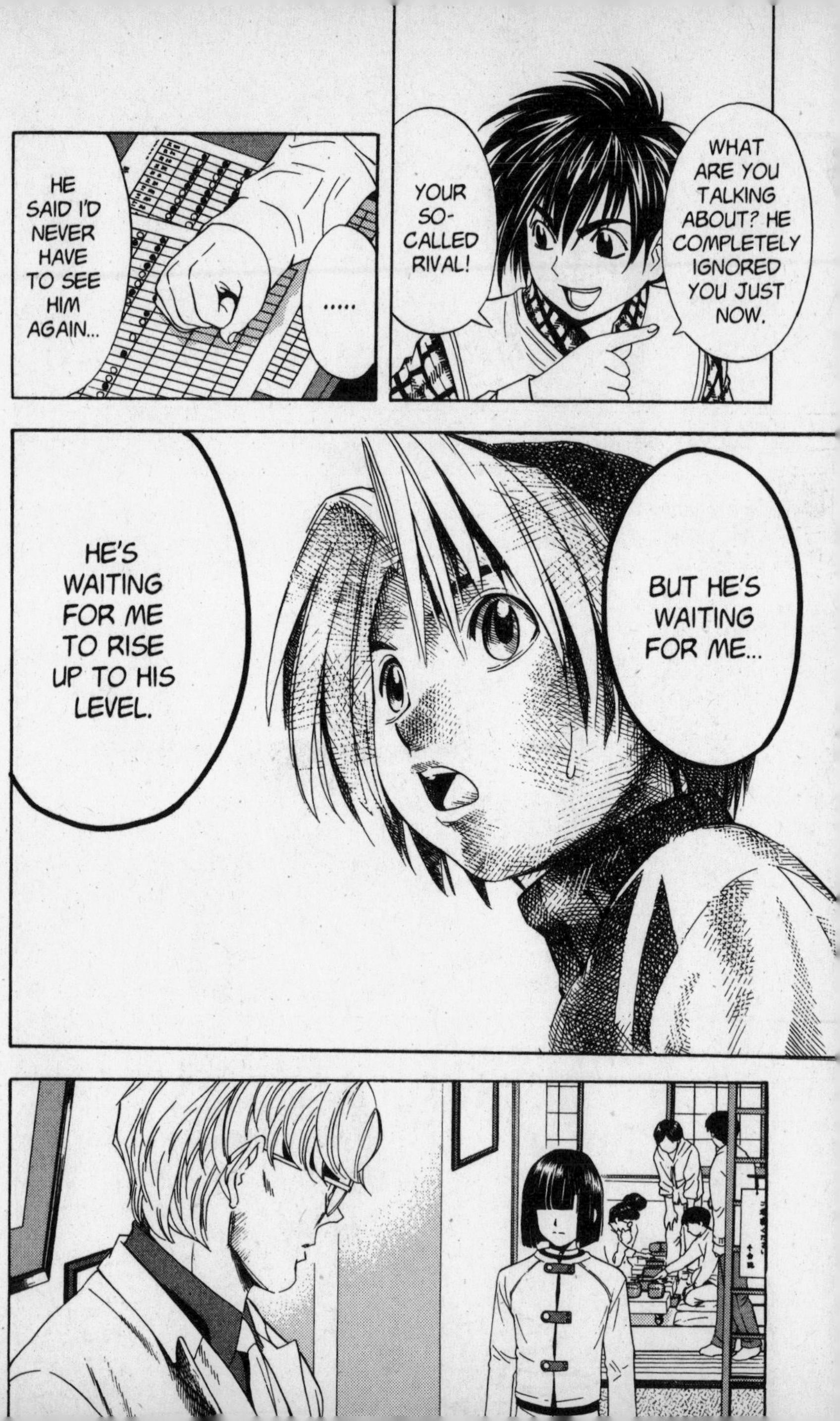
WHAT ARE YOU TALKING ABOUT? HE COMPLETELY IGNORED YOU JUST NOW.
YOUR SO-CALLED RIVAL!
.....
HE SAID I'D NEVER HAVE TO SEE HIM AGAIN...
BUT HE'S WAITING FOR ME...
HE'S WAITING FOR ME TO RISE UP TO HIS LEVEL.

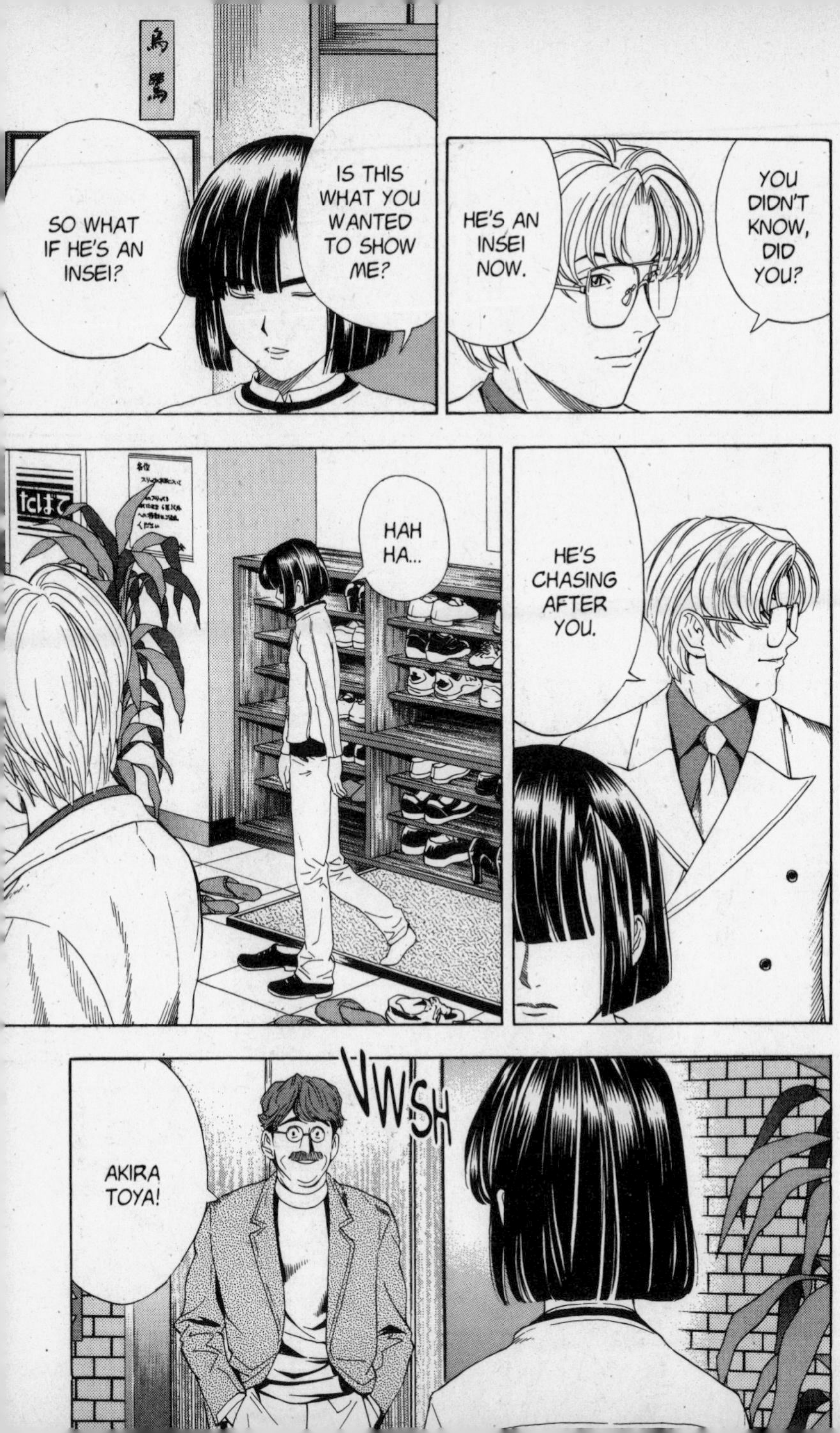
YOU DIDN'T KNOW, DID YOU?
HE'S AN INSEI NOW.
IS THIS WHAT YOU WANTED TO SHOW ME?
SO WHAT IF HE'S AN INSEI?
HE'S CHASING AFTER YOU.
HAH HA...
VWSH
AKIRA TOYA!

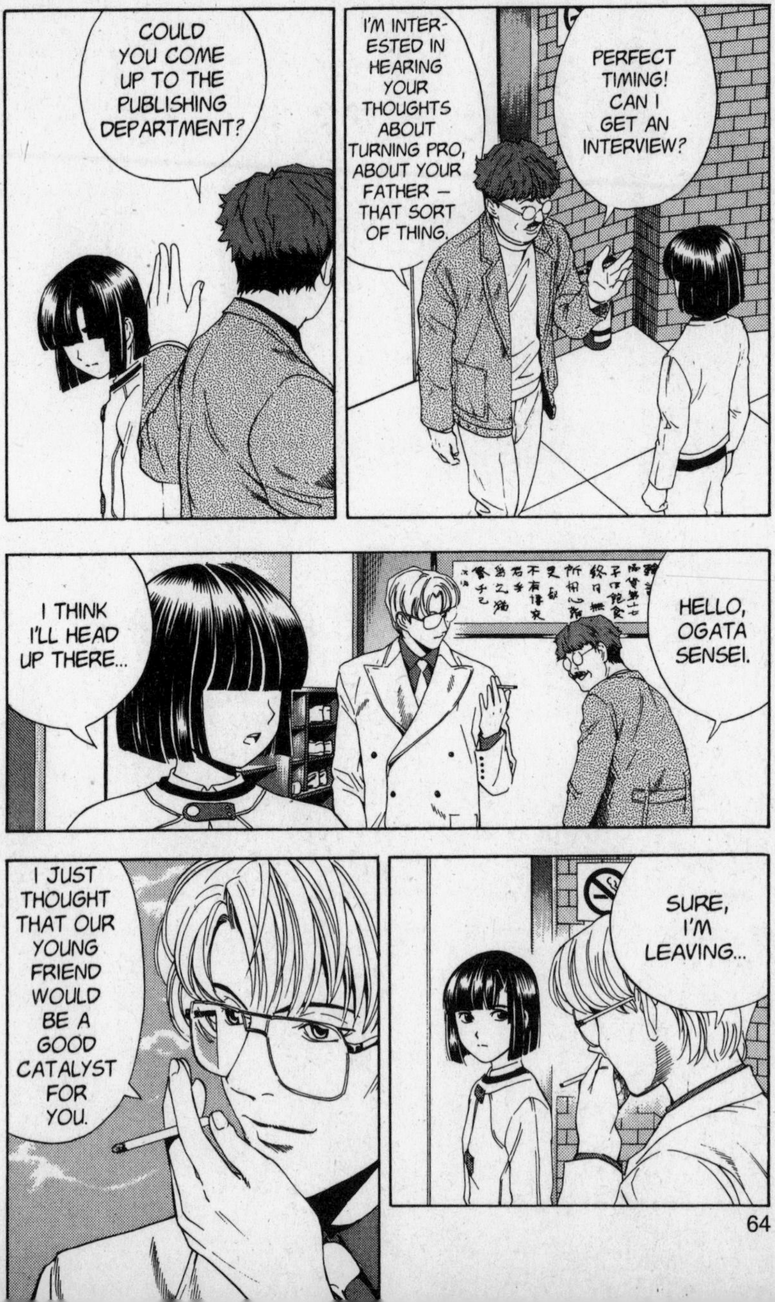
PERFECT TIMING! CAN I GET AN INTERVIEW?
I'M INTERESTED IN HEARING YOUR THOUGHTS ABOUT TURNING PRO, ABOUT YOUR FATHER — THAT SORT OF THING.
COULD YOU COME UP TO THE PUBLISHING DEPARTMENT?
HELLO, OGATA SENSEI.
I THINK I'LL HEAD UP THERE...
SURE, I'M LEAVING...
I JUST THOUGHT THAT OUR YOUNG FRIEND WOULD BE A GOOD CATALYST FOR YOU.

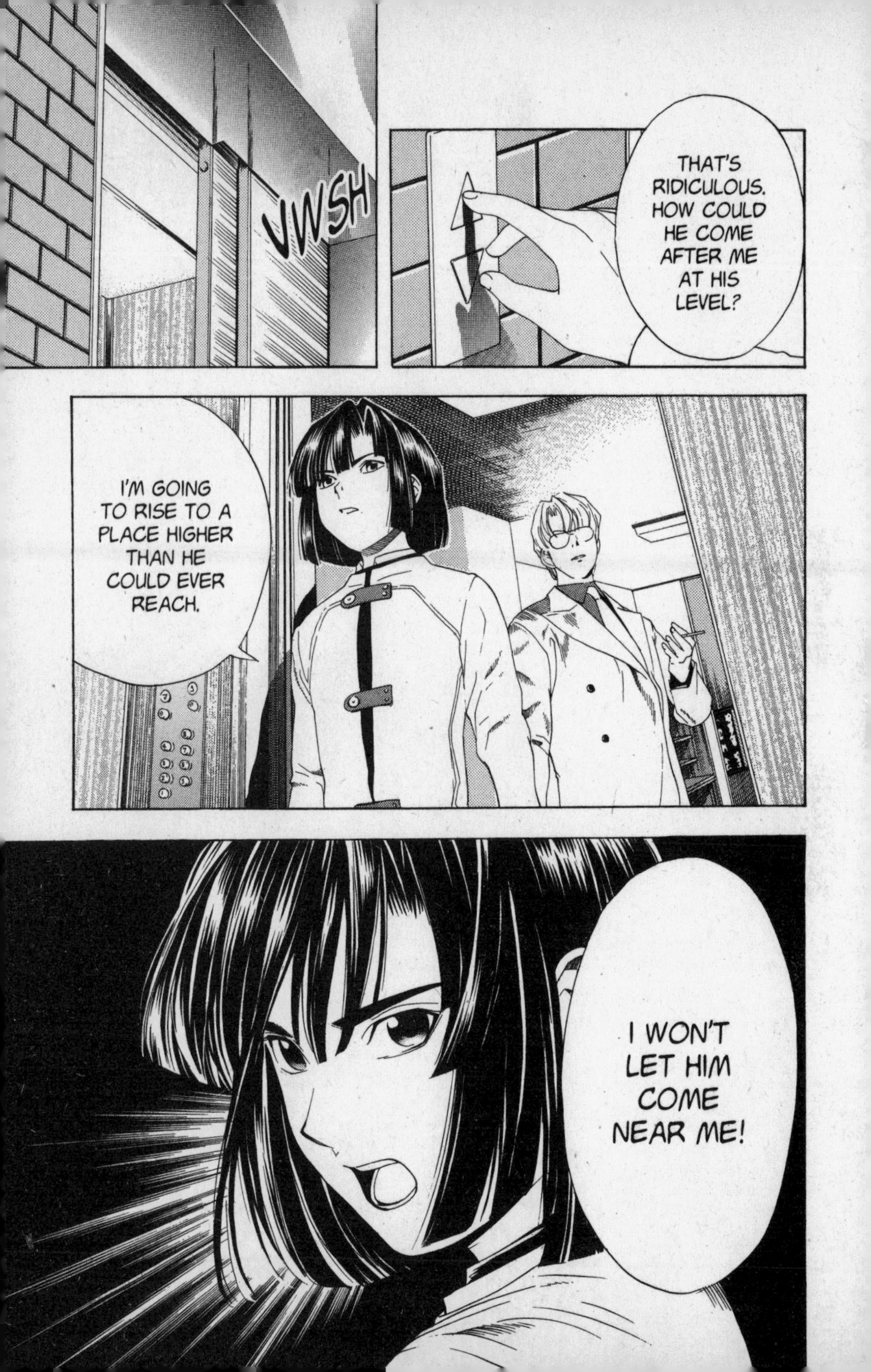
THAT'S RIDICULOUS. HOW COULD HE COME AFTER ME AT HIS LEVEL?
VWSH
I'M GOING TO RISE TO A PLACE HIGHER THAN HE COULD EVER REACH.
I WON'T LET HIM COME NEAR ME!

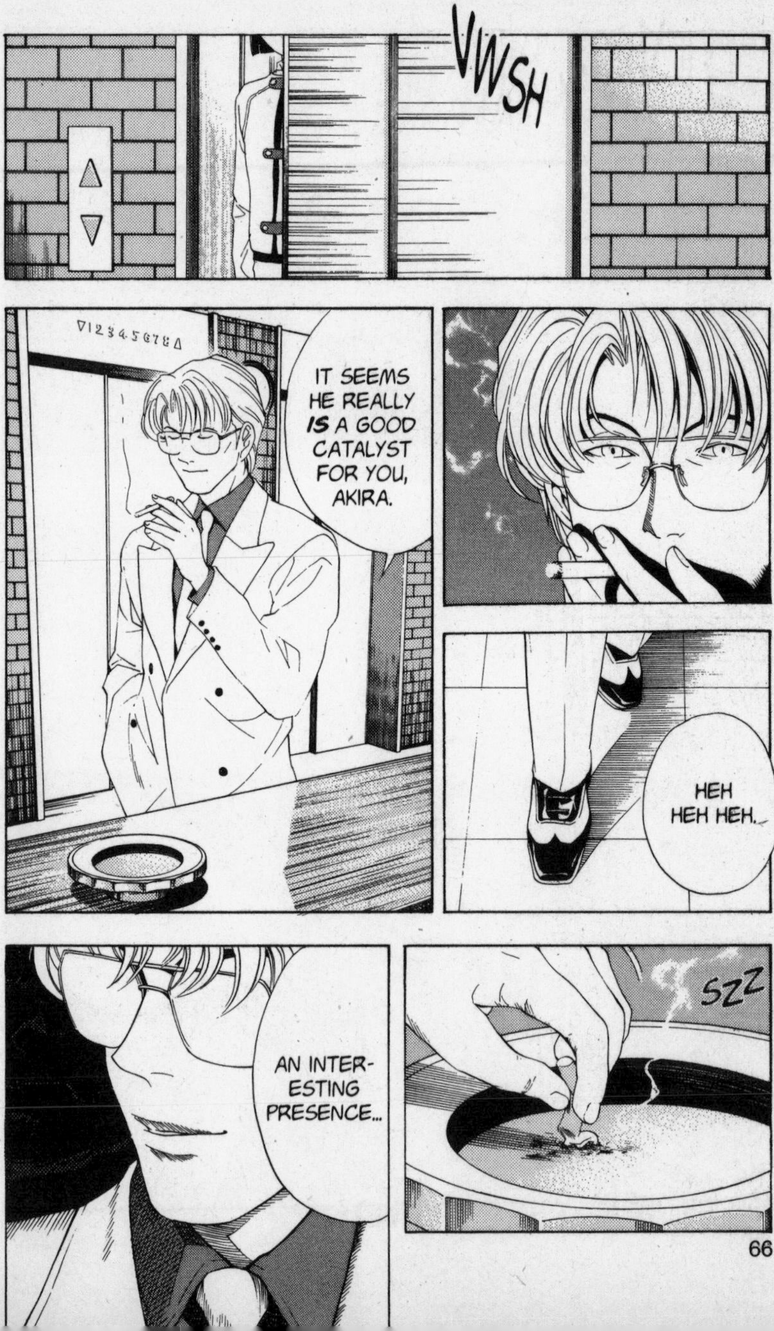
VWSH
HEH HEH HEH.
IT SEEMS HE REALLY **IS** A GOOD CATALYST FOR YOU, AKIRA.
SZZ
AN INTER-ESTING PRESENCE...

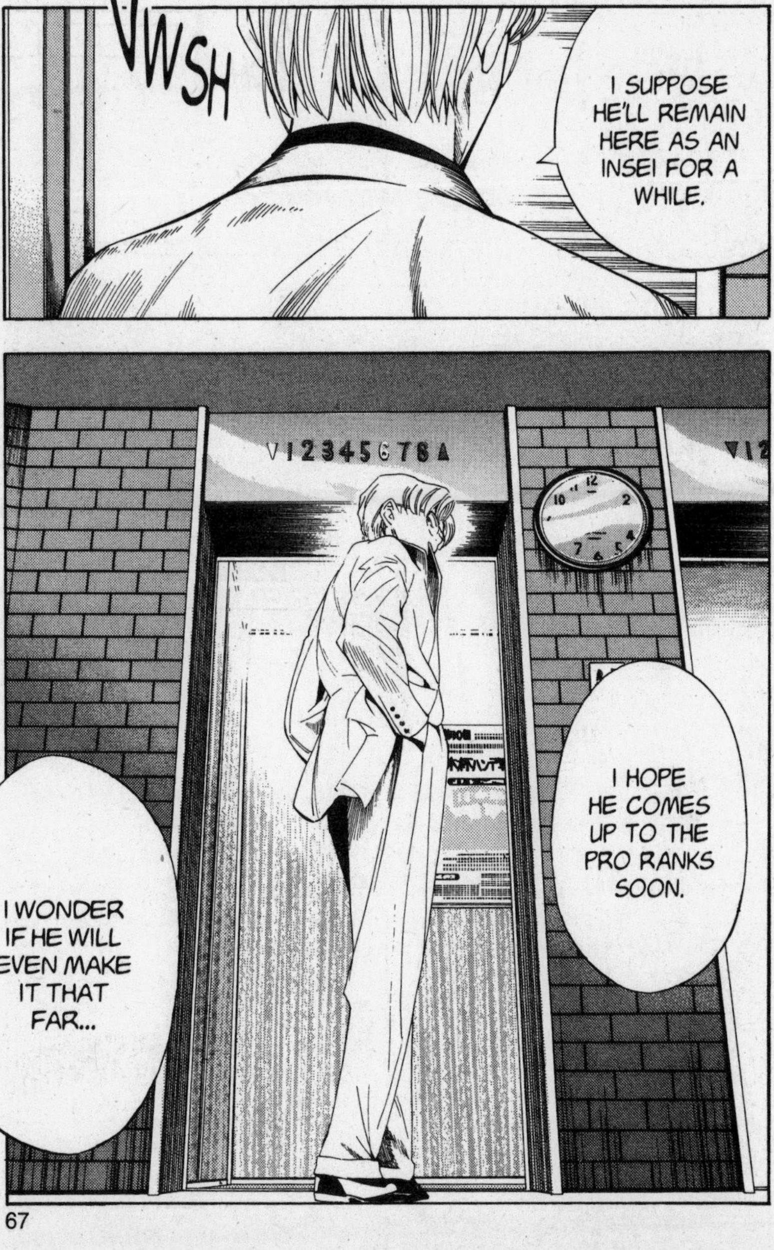
I SUPPOSE HE'LL REMAIN HERE AS AN INSEI FOR A WHILE.
VWSH
I HOPE HE COMES UP TO THE PRO RANKS SOON.
I WONDER IF HE WILL EVEN MAKE IT THAT FAR...

A WORD ABOUT HIKARU NO GO

PRO RANKINGS

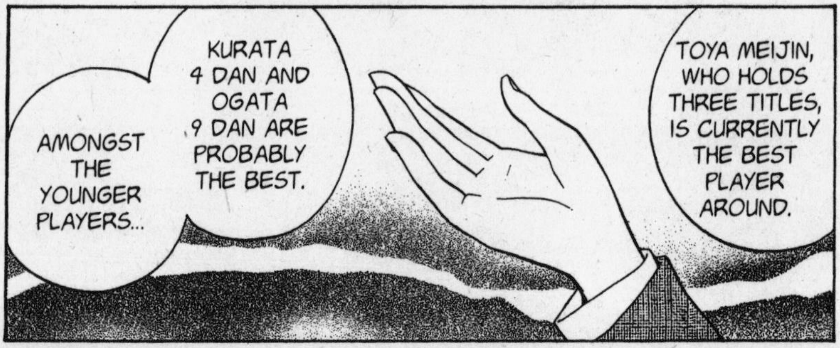
TOYA MEIJIN, WHO HOLDS THREE TITLES, IS CURRENTLY THE BEST PLAYER AROUND.
AMONGST THE YOUNGER PLAYERS...
KURATA 4 DAN AND OGATA 9 DAN ARE PROBABLY THE BEST.

PRO RANKINGS RANGE FROM 1 DAN UP TO 9 DAN. AND BELOW THE PRO RANKINGS, THERE ARE AMATEUR DAN RANKINGS. THE HIGHEST AMATEUR RANKING IS 7 DAN. BELOW THAT IS 6 DAN, 5 DAN, ALL THE WAY DOWN TO 1 DAN. BELOW THE 1 DAN AMATEUR RANKING IS 1 KYU, AND BELOW THAT IS 2 KYU, 3 KYU AND SO ON. THE KYU RANKINGS GO ALL THE WAY DOWN TO INFINITY.

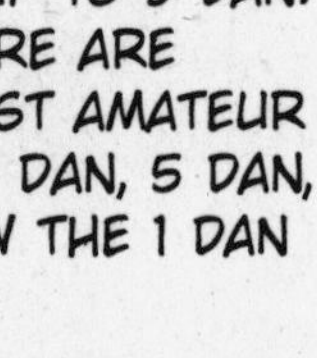

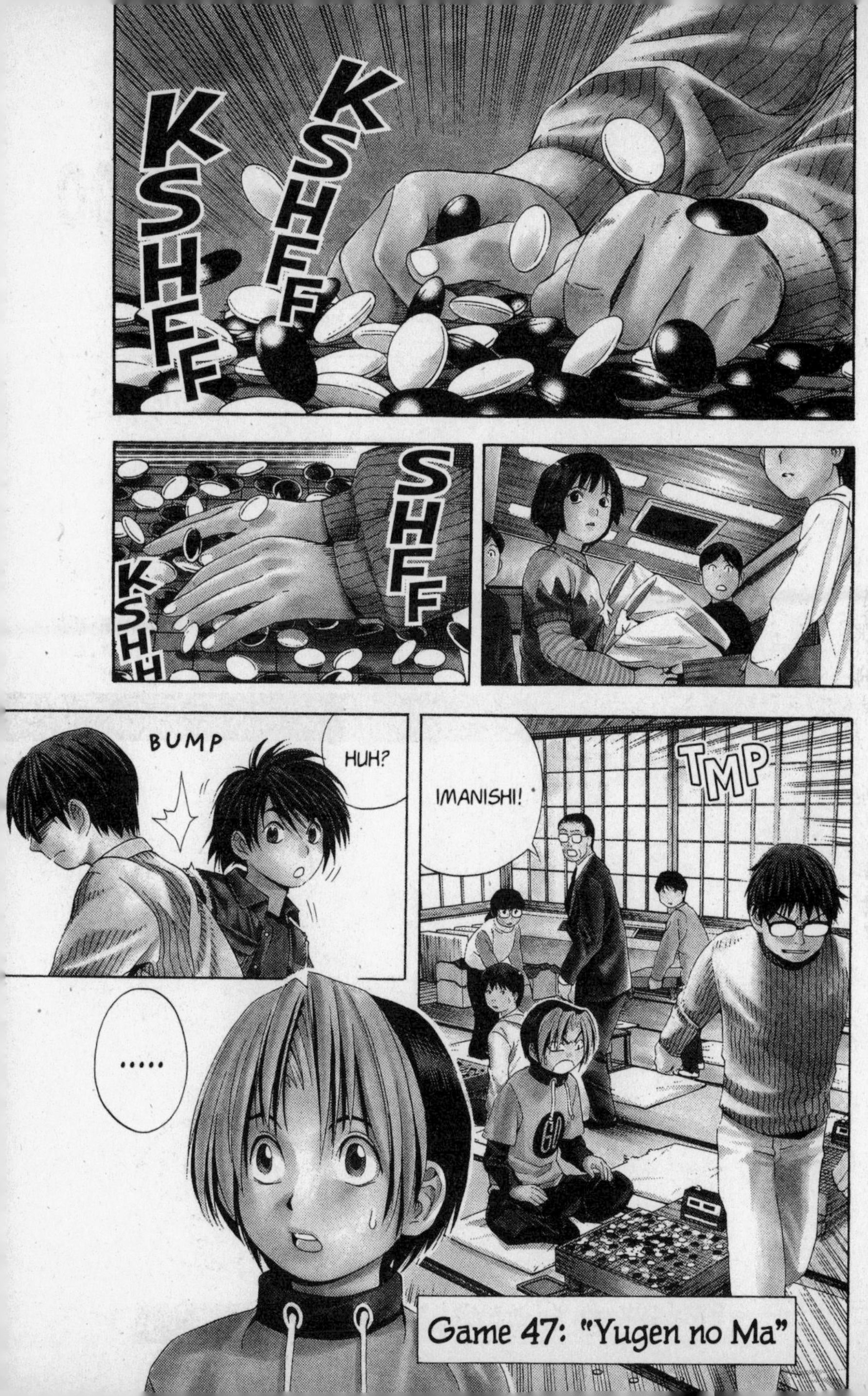
KSHFF
KSHFF
SHFF
KSHH
TMP
IMANISHI!
HUH?
BUMP
......
Game 47: "Yugen no Ma"

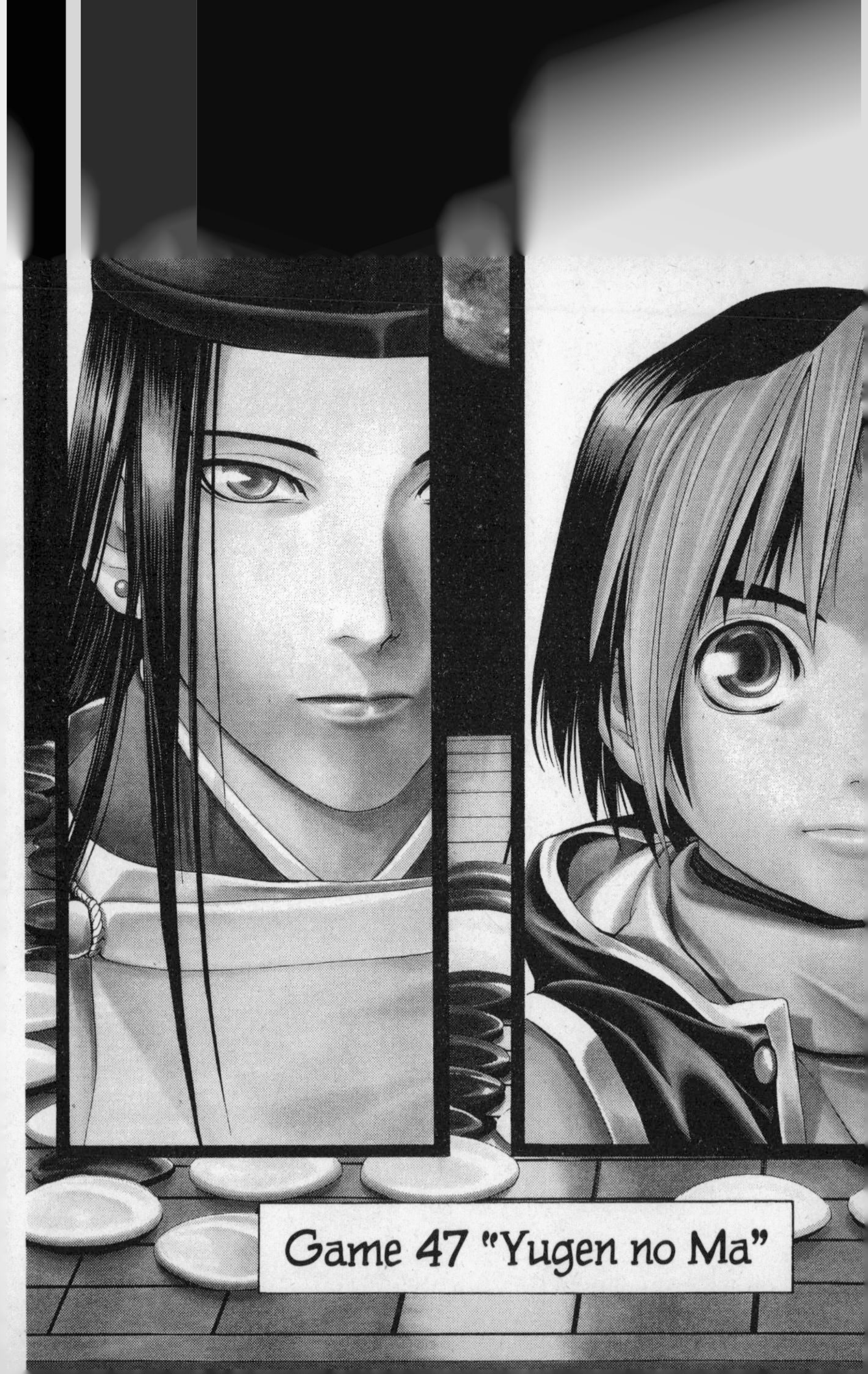
Game 47 "Yugen no Ma"

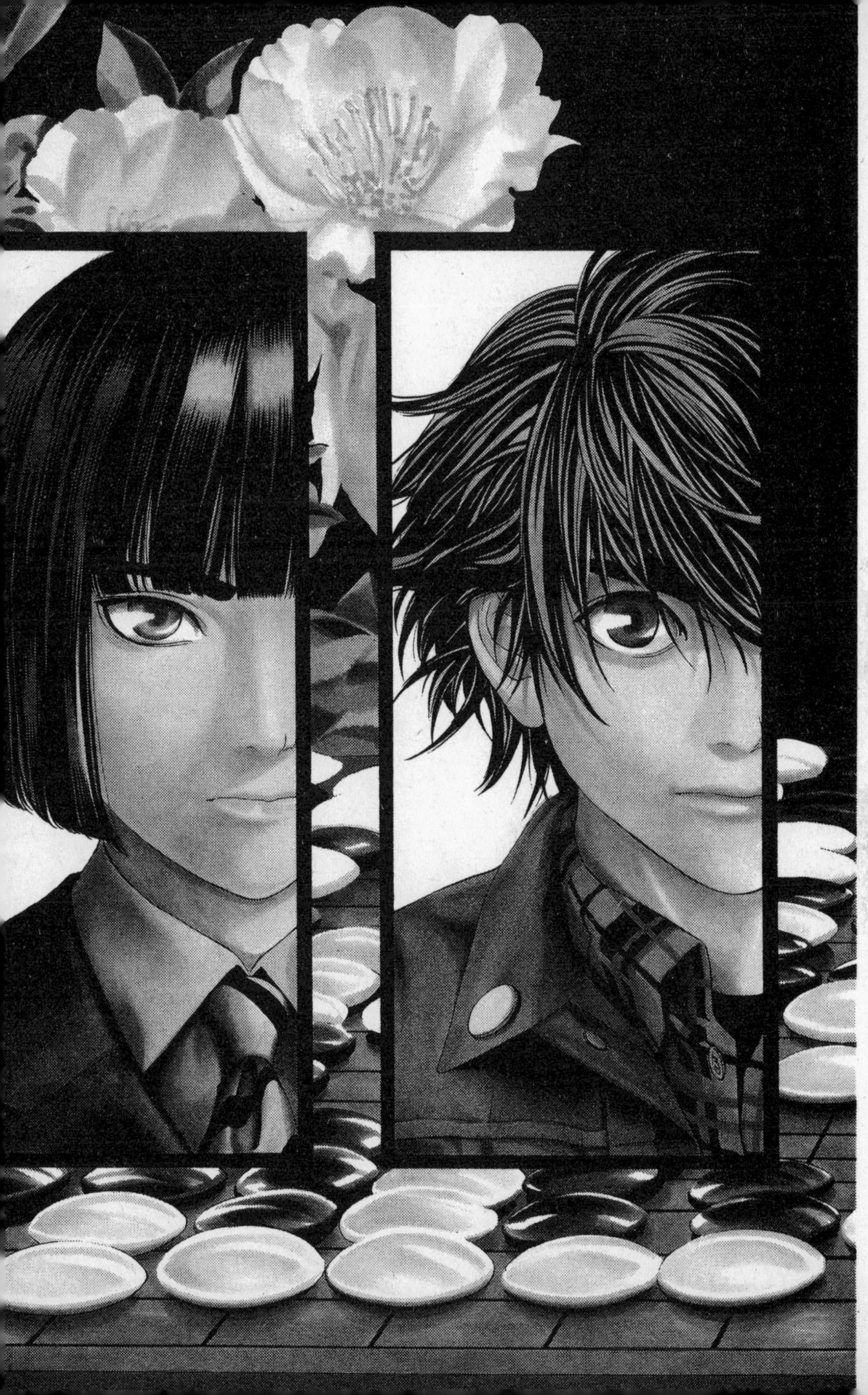

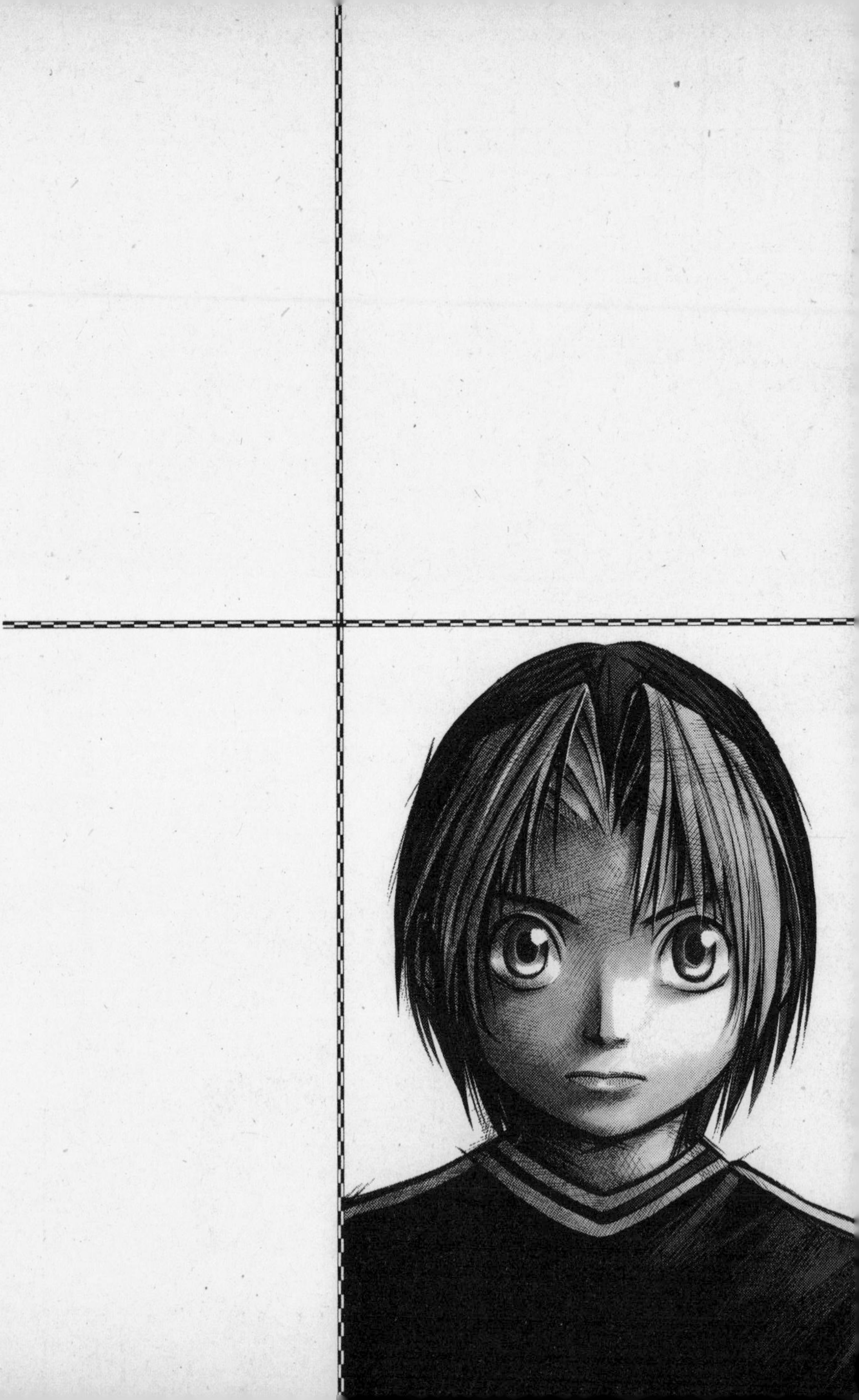

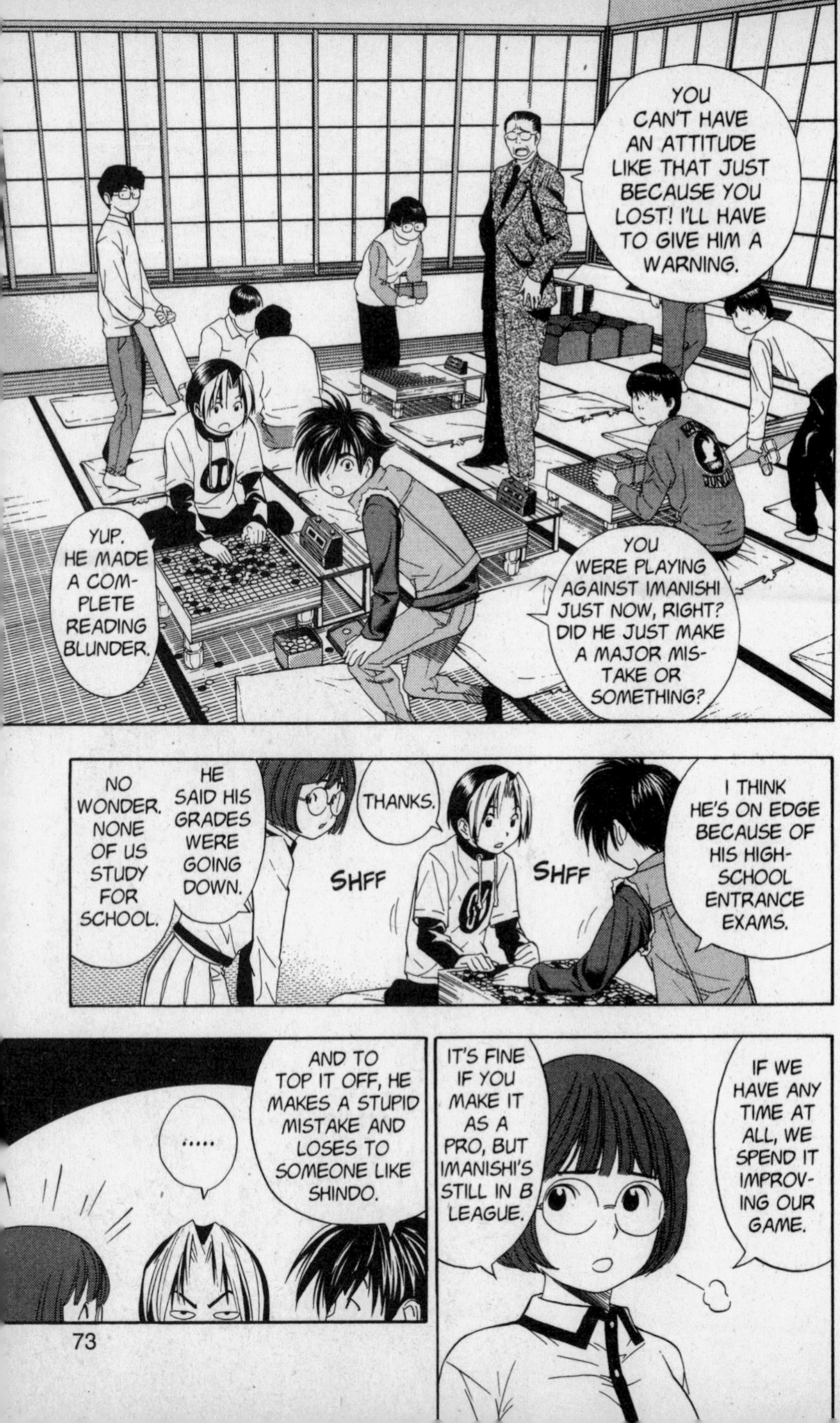
YOU CAN'T HAVE AN ATTITUDE LIKE THAT JUST BECAUSE YOU LOST! I'LL HAVE TO GIVE HIM A WARNING.
YOU WERE PLAYING AGAINST IMANISHI JUST NOW, RIGHT? DID HE JUST MAKE A MAJOR MIS-TAKE OR SOMETHING?
YUP. HE MADE A COM-PLETE READING BLUNDER.
I THINK HE'S ON EDGE BECAUSE OF HIS HIGH-SCHOOL ENTRANCE EXAMS.
SHFF
THANKS.
SHFF
HE SAID HIS GRADES WERE GOING DOWN.
NO WONDER. NONE OF US STUDY FOR SCHOOL.
IF WE HAVE ANY TIME AT ALL, WE SPEND IT IMPROV-ING OUR GAME.
IT'S FINE IF YOU MAKE IT AS A PRO, BUT IMANISHI'S STILL IN B LEAGUE.
AND TO TOP IT OFF, HE MAKES A STUPID MISTAKE AND LOSES TO SOMEONE LIKE SHINDO.
.....

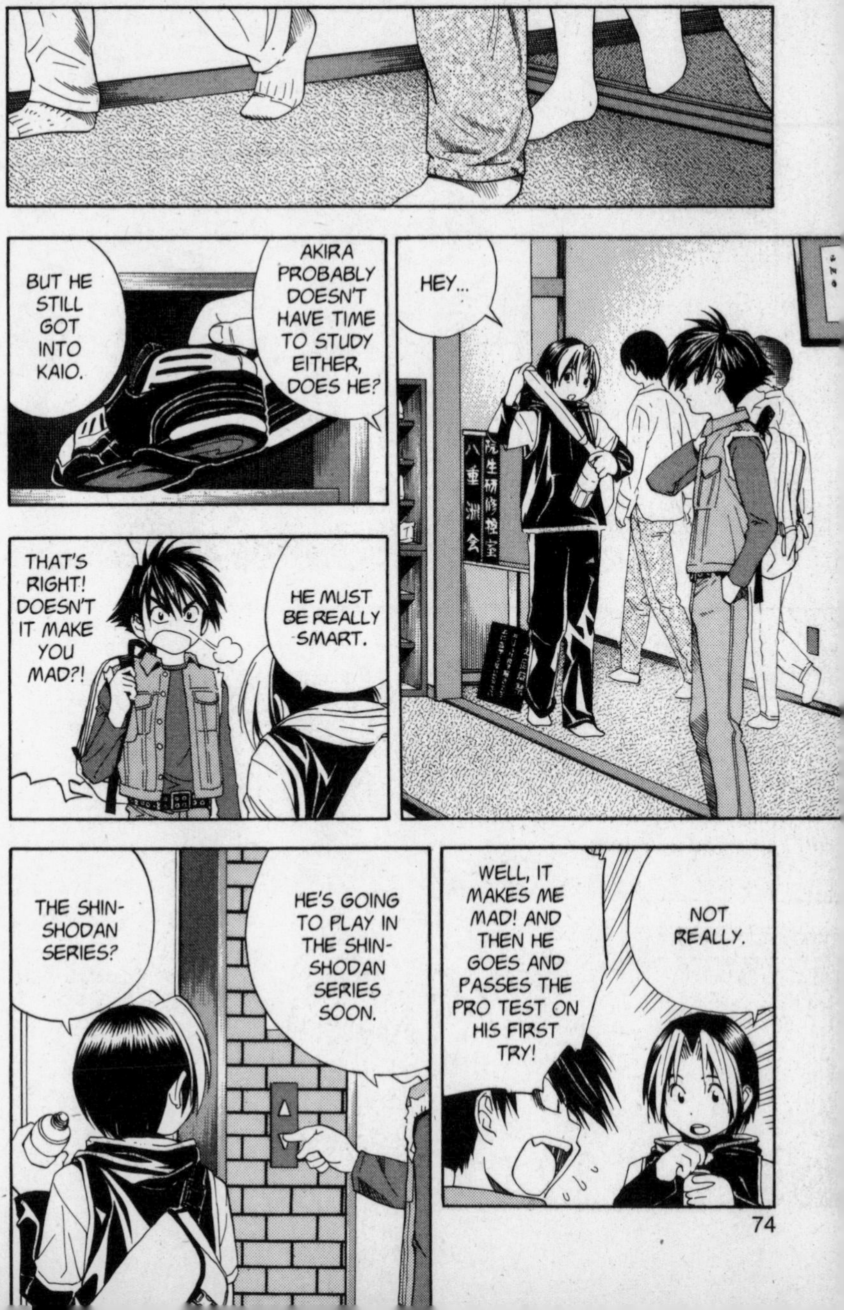
HEY...
院生研修控室
八重洲会
AKIRA PROBABLY DOESN'T HAVE TIME TO STUDY EITHER, DOES HE?
BUT HE STILL GOT INTO KAIO.
HE MUST BE REALLY SMART.
THAT'S RIGHT! DOESN'T IT MAKE YOU MAD?!
NOT REALLY.
WELL, IT MAKES ME MAD! AND THEN HE GOES AND PASSES THE PRO TEST ON HIS FIRST TRY!
HE'S GOING TO PLAY IN THE SHIN-SHODAN SERIES SOON.
THE SHIN-SHODAN SERIES?

READ THIS WAY

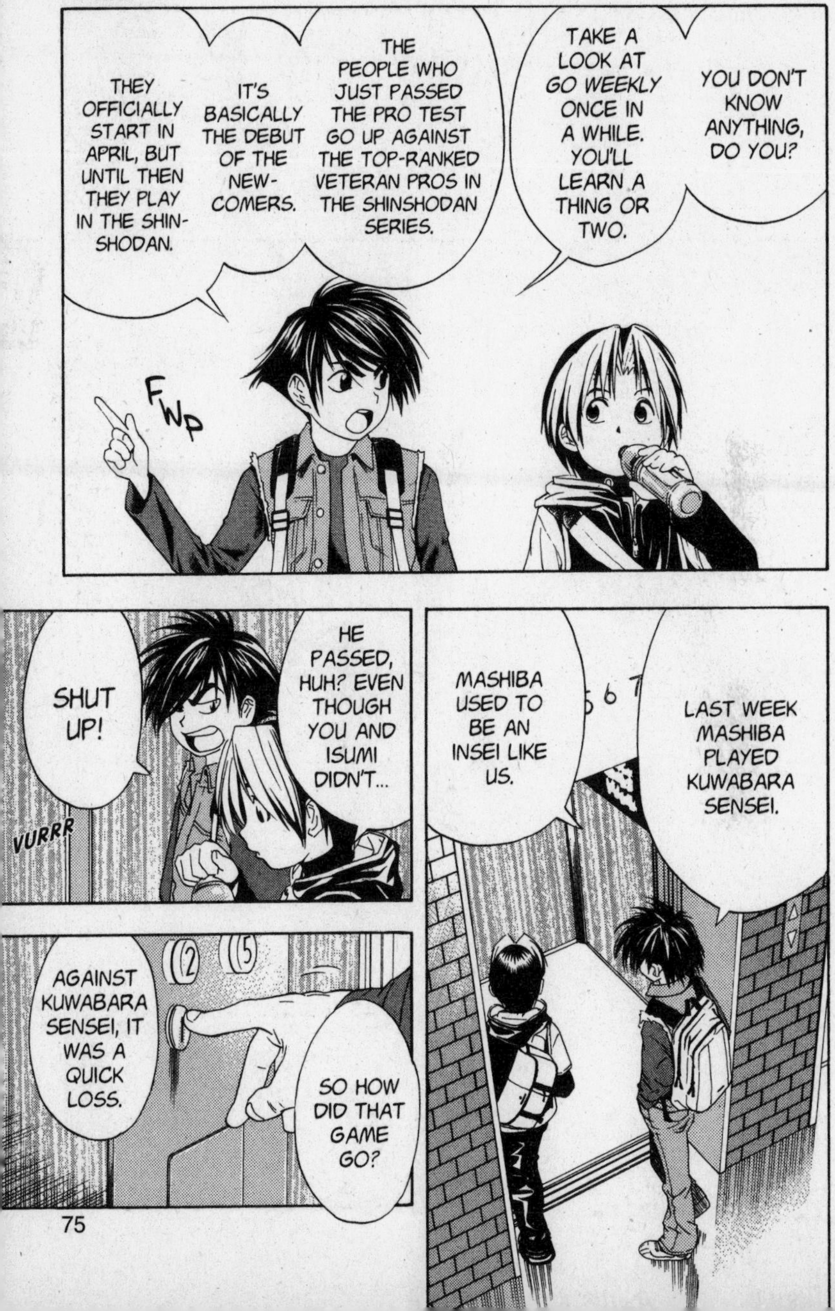
YOU DON'T KNOW ANYTHING, DO YOU?
TAKE A LOOK AT GO WEEKLY ONCE IN A WHILE. YOU'LL LEARN A THING OR TWO.
THE PEOPLE WHO JUST PASSED THE PRO TEST GO UP AGAINST THE TOP-RANKED VETERAN PROS IN THE SHINSHODAN SERIES.
IT'S BASICALLY THE DEBUT OF THE NEW-COMERS.
THEY OFFICIALLY START IN APRIL, BUT UNTIL THEN THEY PLAY IN THE SHIN-SHODAN.
FWP
LAST WEEK MASHIBA PLAYED KUWABARA SENSEI.
MASHIBA USED TO BE AN INSEI LIKE US.
HE PASSED, HUH? EVEN THOUGH YOU AND ISUMI DIDN'T...
SHUT UP!
VURRR
SO HOW DID THAT GAME GO?
AGAINST KUWABARA SENSEI, IT WAS A QUICK LOSS.

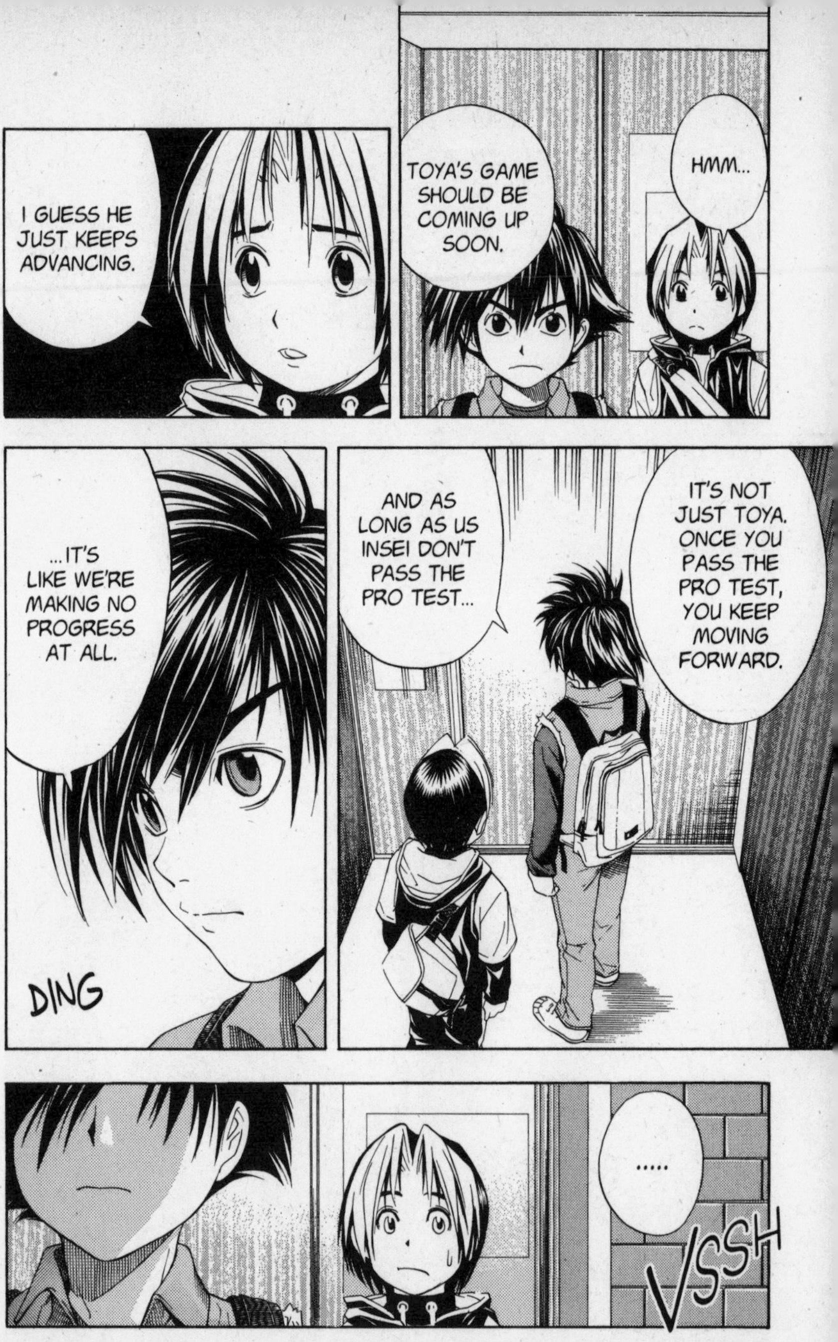
HMM...
TOYA'S GAME SHOULD BE COMING UP SOON.
I GUESS HE JUST KEEPS ADVANCING.
IT'S NOT JUST TOYA. ONCE YOU PASS THE PRO TEST, YOU KEEP MOVING FORWARD.
AND AS LONG AS US INSEI DON'T PASS THE PRO TEST...
...IT'S LIKE WE'RE MAKING NO PROGRESS AT ALL.
DING
.....
VSSH

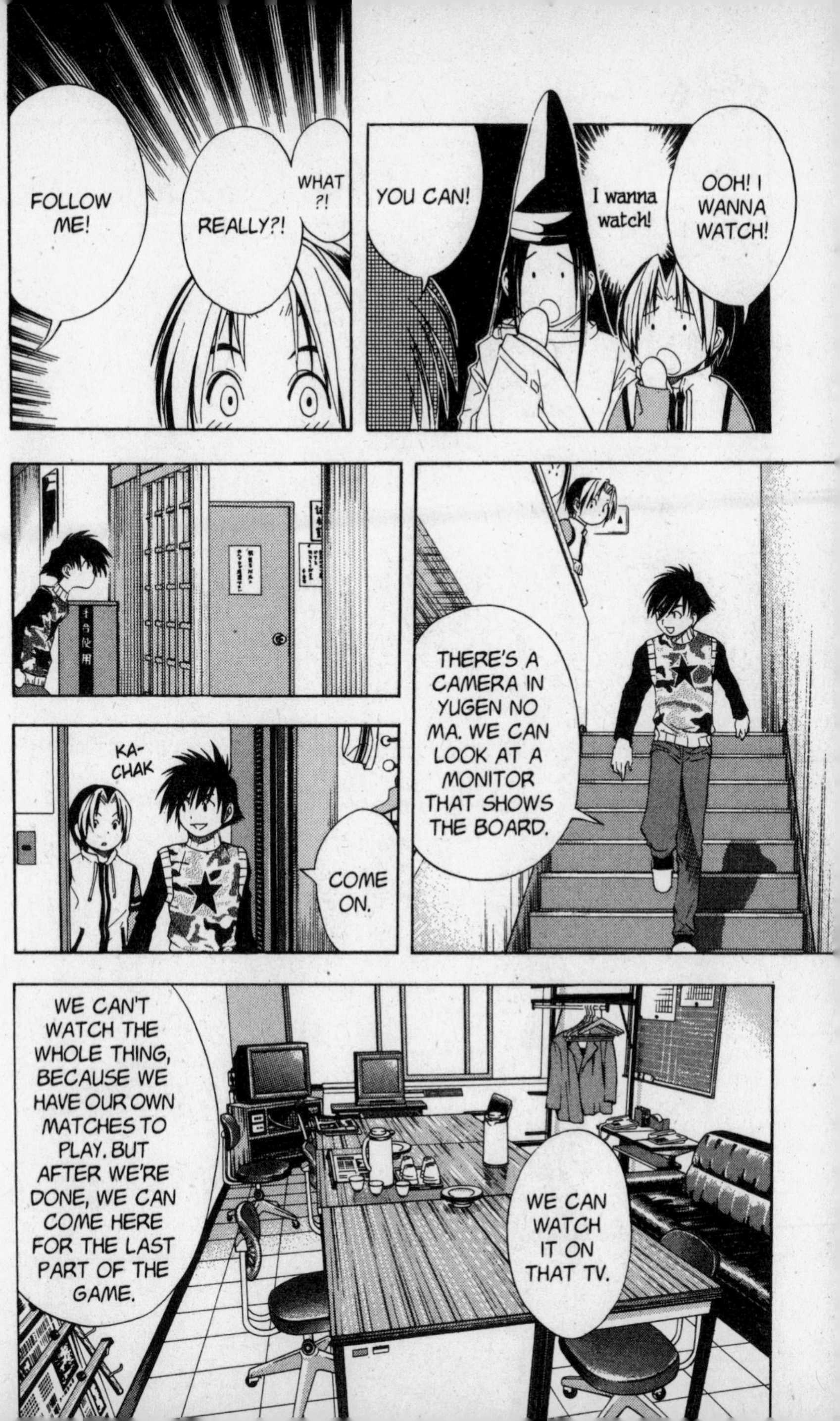
OOH! I WANNA WATCH!
I wanna watch!
YOU CAN!
WHAT?!
REALLY?!
FOLLOW ME!
THERE'S A CAMERA IN YUGEN NO MA. WE CAN LOOK AT A MONITOR THAT SHOWS THE BOARD.
KA-CHAK
COME ON.
WE CAN WATCH IT ON THAT TV.
WE CAN'T WATCH THE WHOLE THING, BECAUSE WE HAVE OUR OWN MATCHES TO PLAY. BUT AFTER WE'RE DONE, WE CAN COME HERE FOR THE LAST PART OF THE GAME.

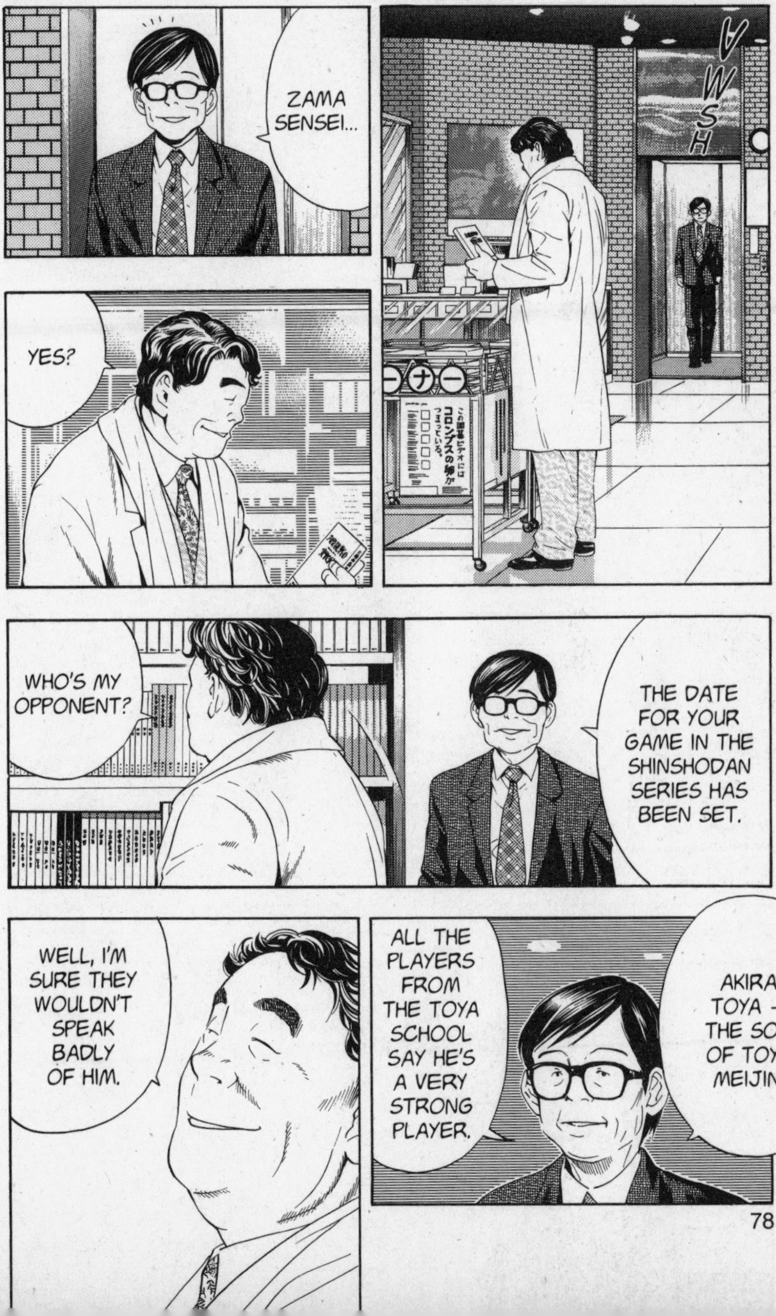
VWSH
ZAMA SENSEI...
YES?
THE DATE FOR YOUR GAME IN THE SHINSHODAN SERIES HAS BEEN SET.
WHO'S MY OPPONENT?
AKIRA TOYA — THE SON OF TOYA MEIJIN.
ALL THE PLAYERS FROM THE TOYA SCHOOL SAY HE'S A VERY STRONG PLAYER.
WELL, I'M SURE THEY WOULDN'T SPEAK BADLY OF HIM.

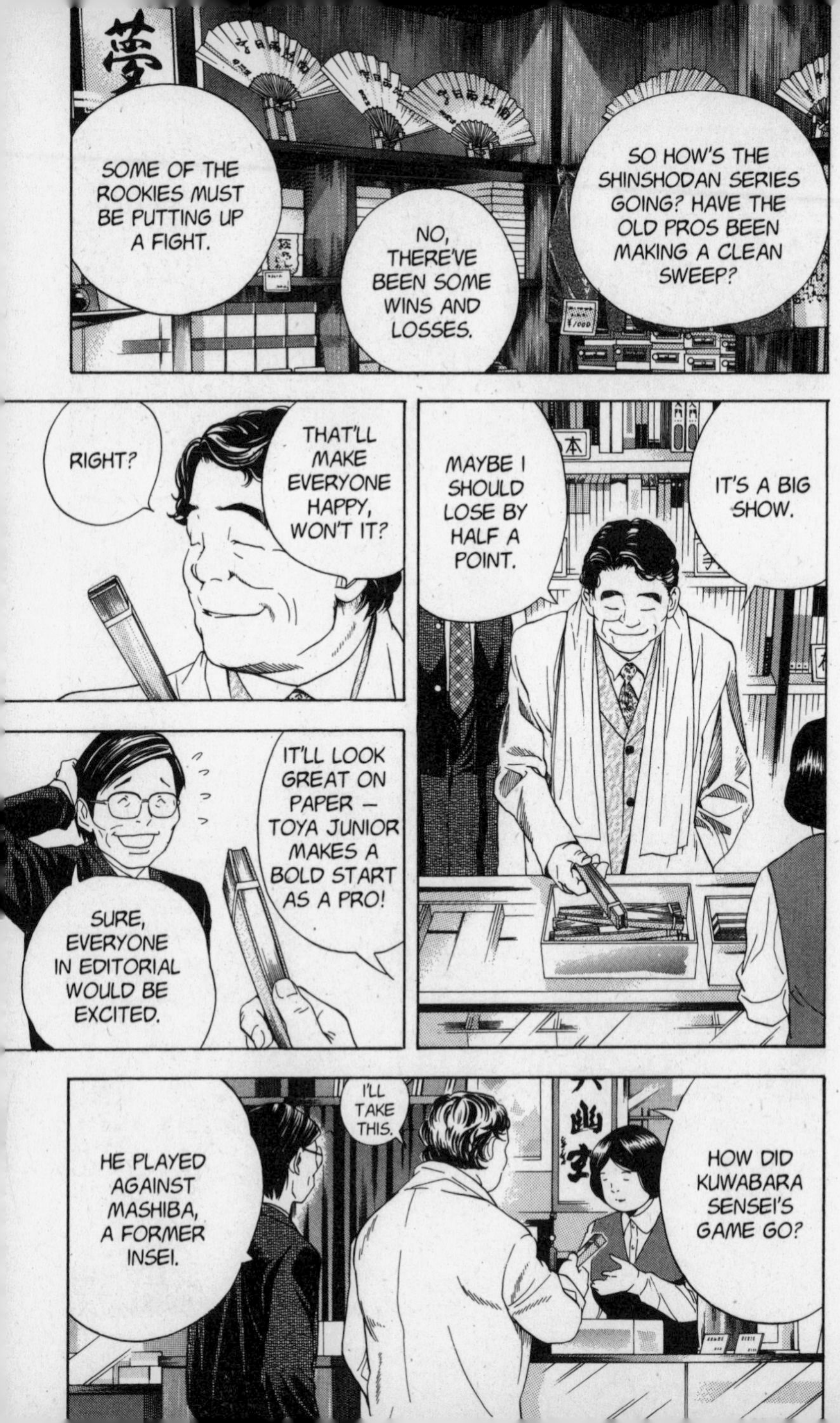
SO HOW'S THE SHINSHODAN SERIES GOING? HAVE THE OLD PROS BEEN MAKING A CLEAN SWEEP?
NO, THERE'VE BEEN SOME WINS AND LOSSES.
SOME OF THE ROOKIES MUST BE PUTTING UP A FIGHT.
IT'S A BIG SHOW.
MAYBE I SHOULD LOSE BY HALF A POINT.
THAT'LL MAKE EVERYONE HAPPY, WON'T IT?
RIGHT?
IT'LL LOOK GREAT ON PAPER — TOYA JUNIOR MAKES A BOLD START AS A PRO!
SURE, EVERYONE IN EDITORIAL WOULD BE EXCITED.
HOW DID KUWABARA SENSEI'S GAME GO?
I'LL TAKE THIS.
HE PLAYED AGAINST MASHIBA, A FORMER INSEI.

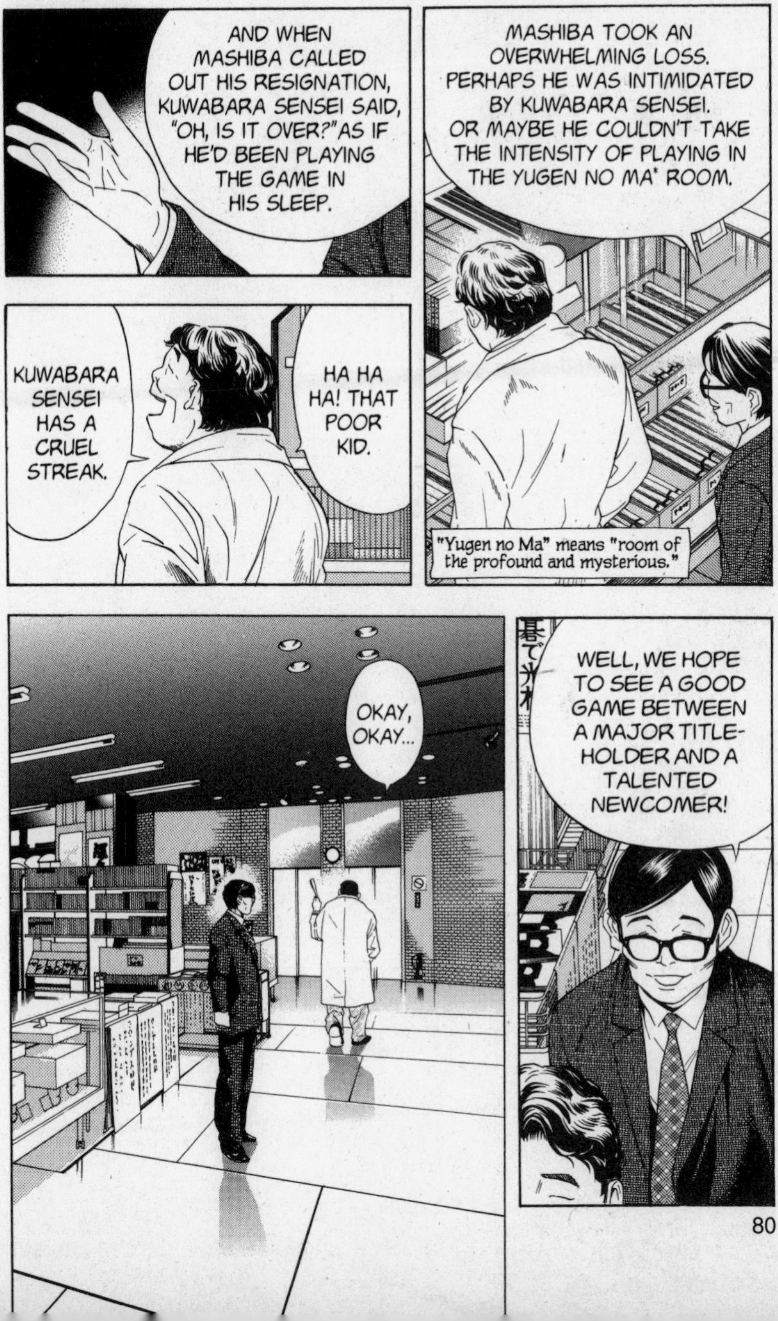
MASHIBA TOOK AN OVERWHELMING LOSS. PERHAPS HE WAS INTIMIDATED BY KUWABARA SENSEI. OR MAYBE HE COULDN'T TAKE THE INTENSITY OF PLAYING IN THE YUGEN NO MA* ROOM.
"Yugen no Ma" means "room of the profound and mysterious."
AND WHEN MASHIBA CALLED OUT HIS RESIGNATION, KUWABARA SENSEI SAID, "OH, IS IT OVER?" AS IF HE'D BEEN PLAYING THE GAME IN HIS SLEEP.
HA HA HA! THAT POOR KID.
KUWABARA SENSEI HAS A CRUEL STREAK.
WELL, WE HOPE TO SEE A GOOD GAME BETWEEN A MAJOR TITLE-HOLDER AND A TALENTED NEWCOMER!
OKAY, OKAY...

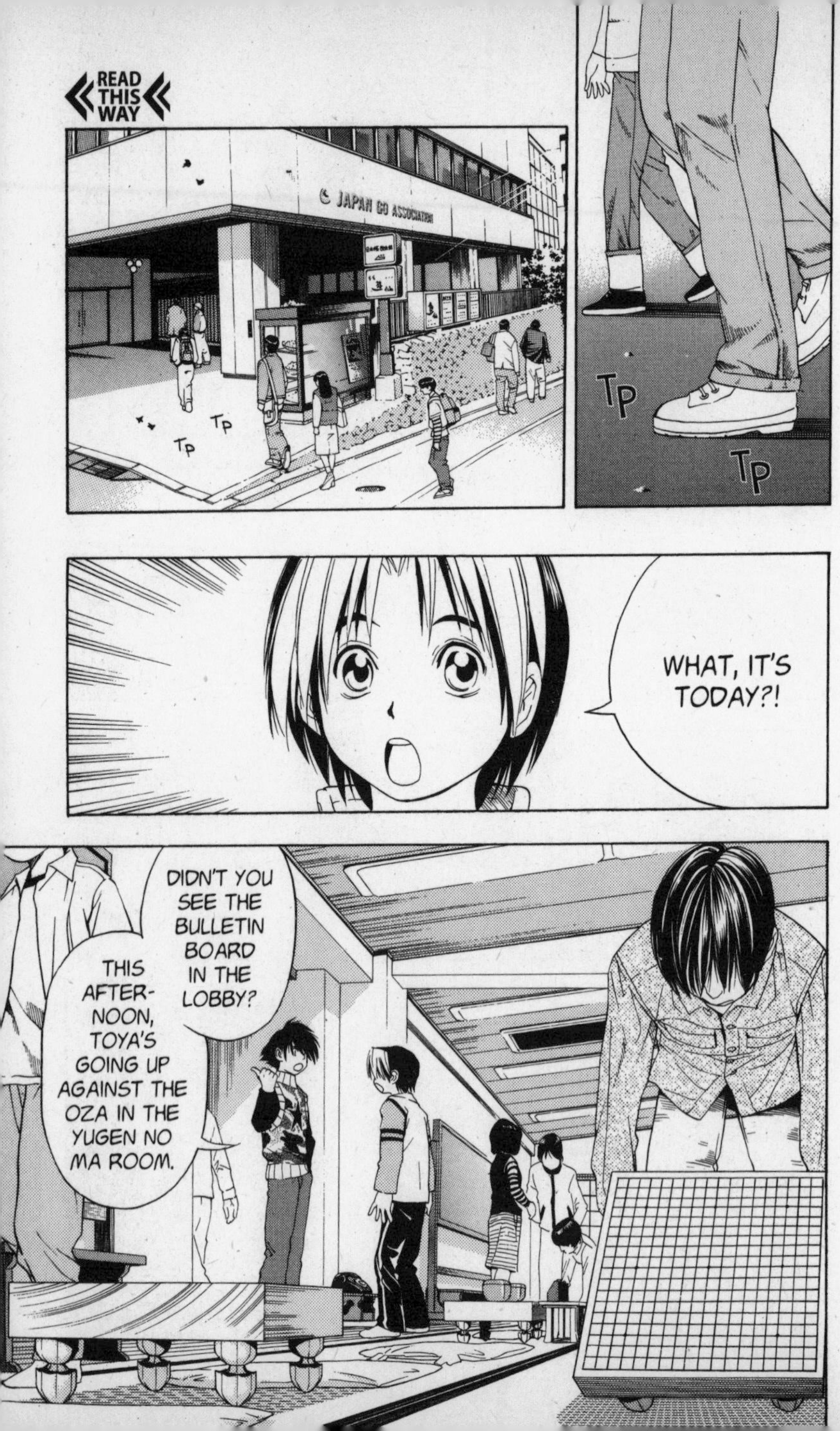
READ THIS WAY
TP
TP
JAPAN GO ASSOCIATION
TP
TP
WHAT, IT'S TODAY?!
DIDN'T YOU SEE THE BULLETIN BOARD IN THE LOBBY?
THIS AFTER-NOON, TOYA'S GOING UP AGAINST THE OZA IN THE YUGEN NO MA ROOM.

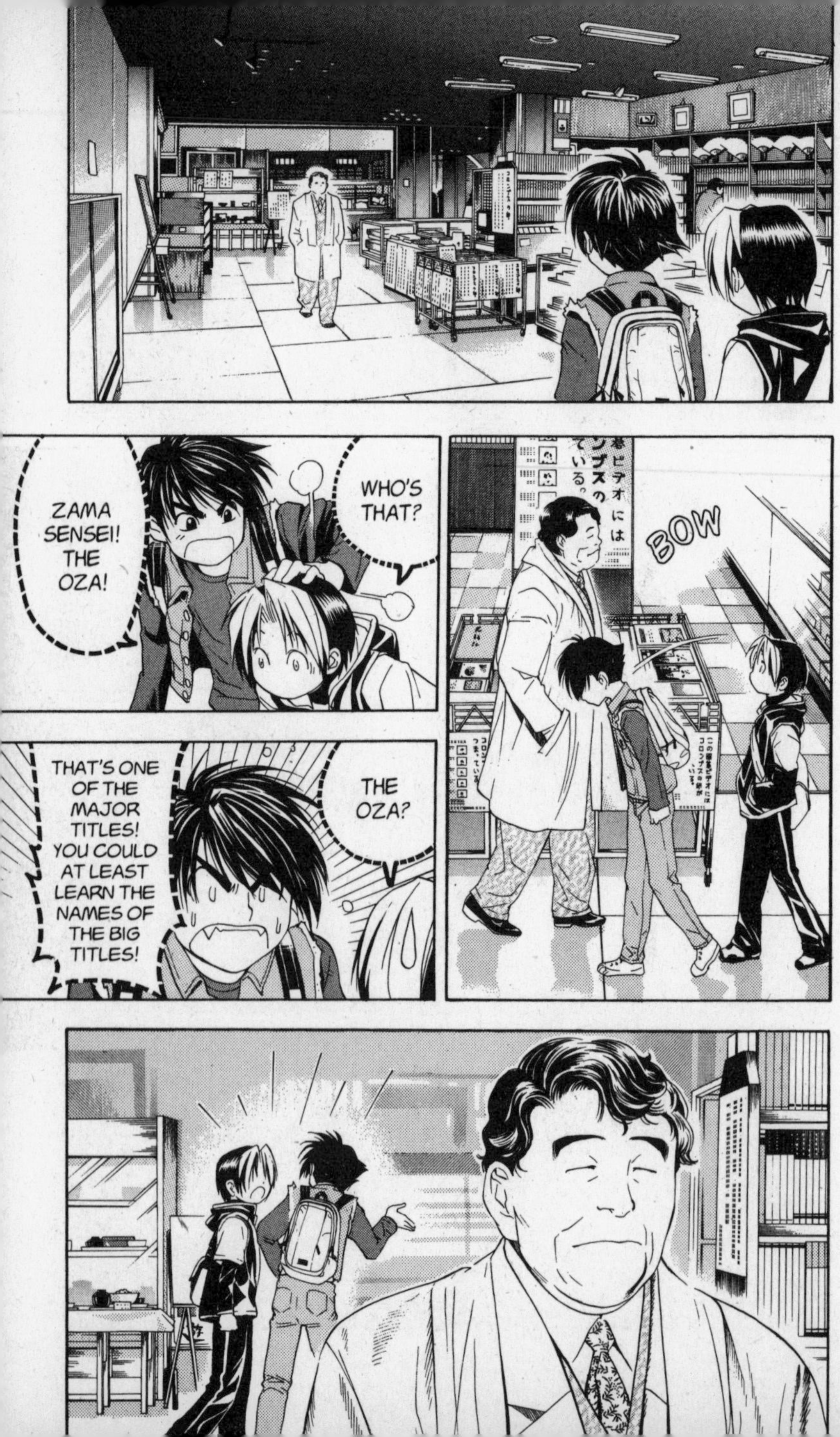
BOW
WHO'S THAT?
ZAMA SENSEI! THE OZA!
THE OZA?
THAT'S ONE OF THE MAJOR TITLES! YOU COULD AT LEAST LEARN THE NAMES OF THE BIG TITLES!

READ THIS WAY

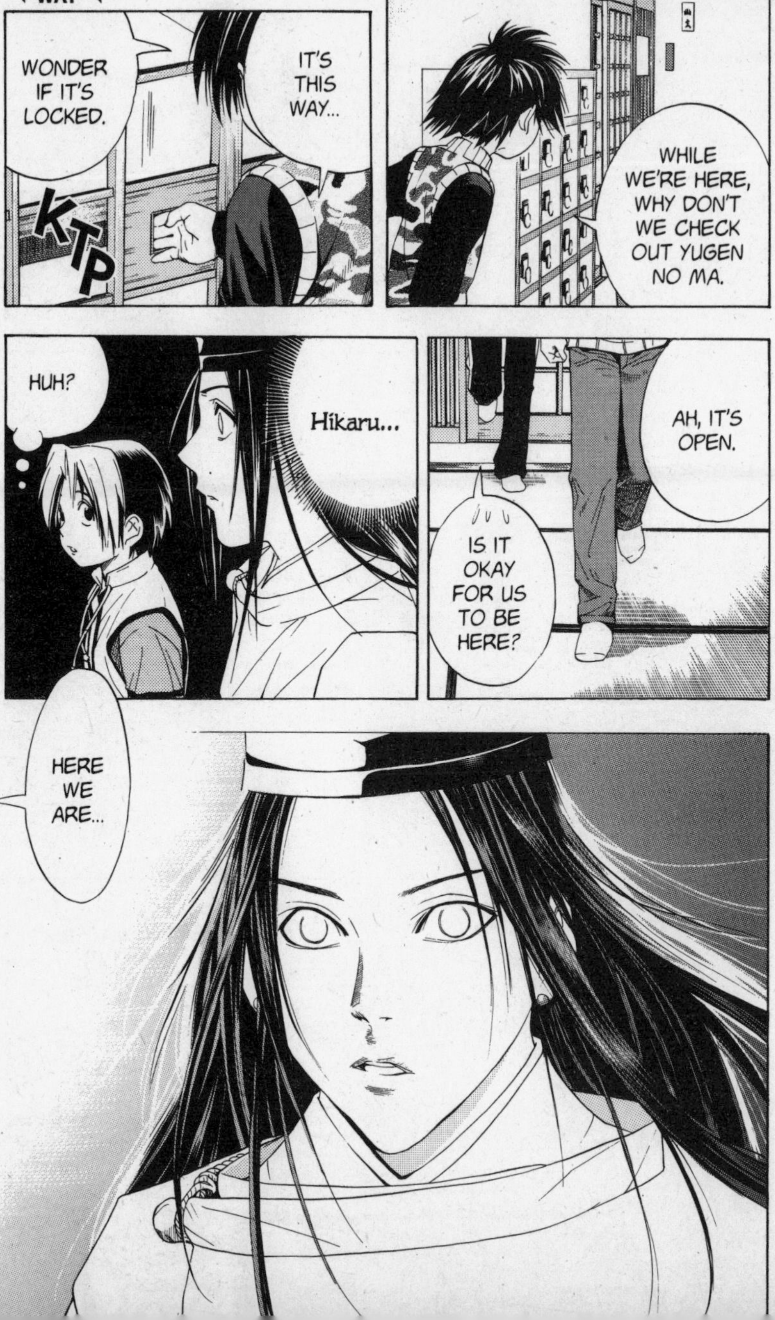

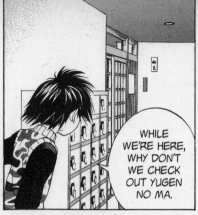

WHILE WE'RE HERE, WHY DON'T WE CHECK OUT YUGEN NO MA.
IT'S THIS WAY...
WONDER IF IT'S LOCKED.
KTP
AH, IT'S OPEN.
IS IT OKAY FOR US TO BE HERE?
Hikaru...
HUH?
HERE WE ARE...

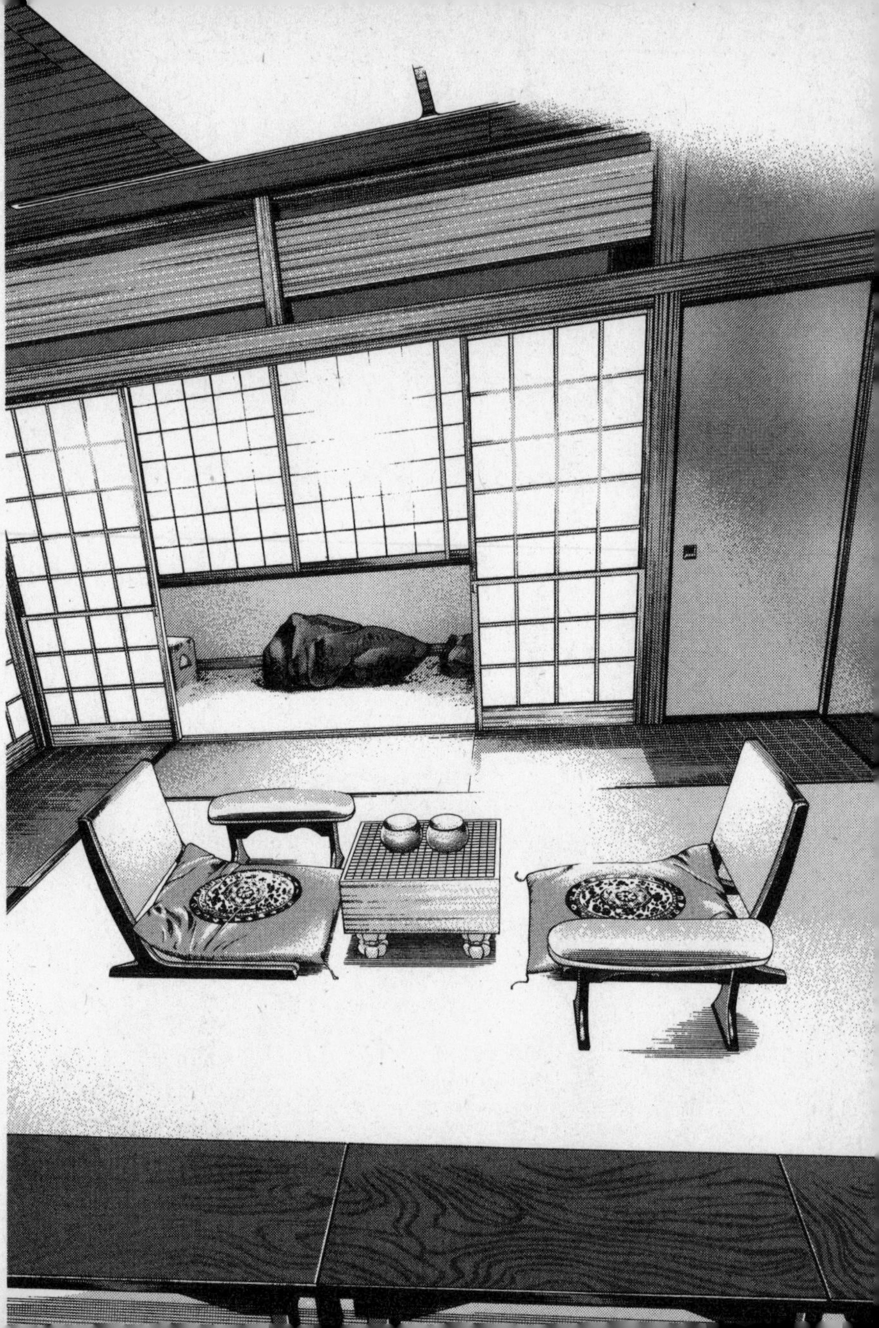

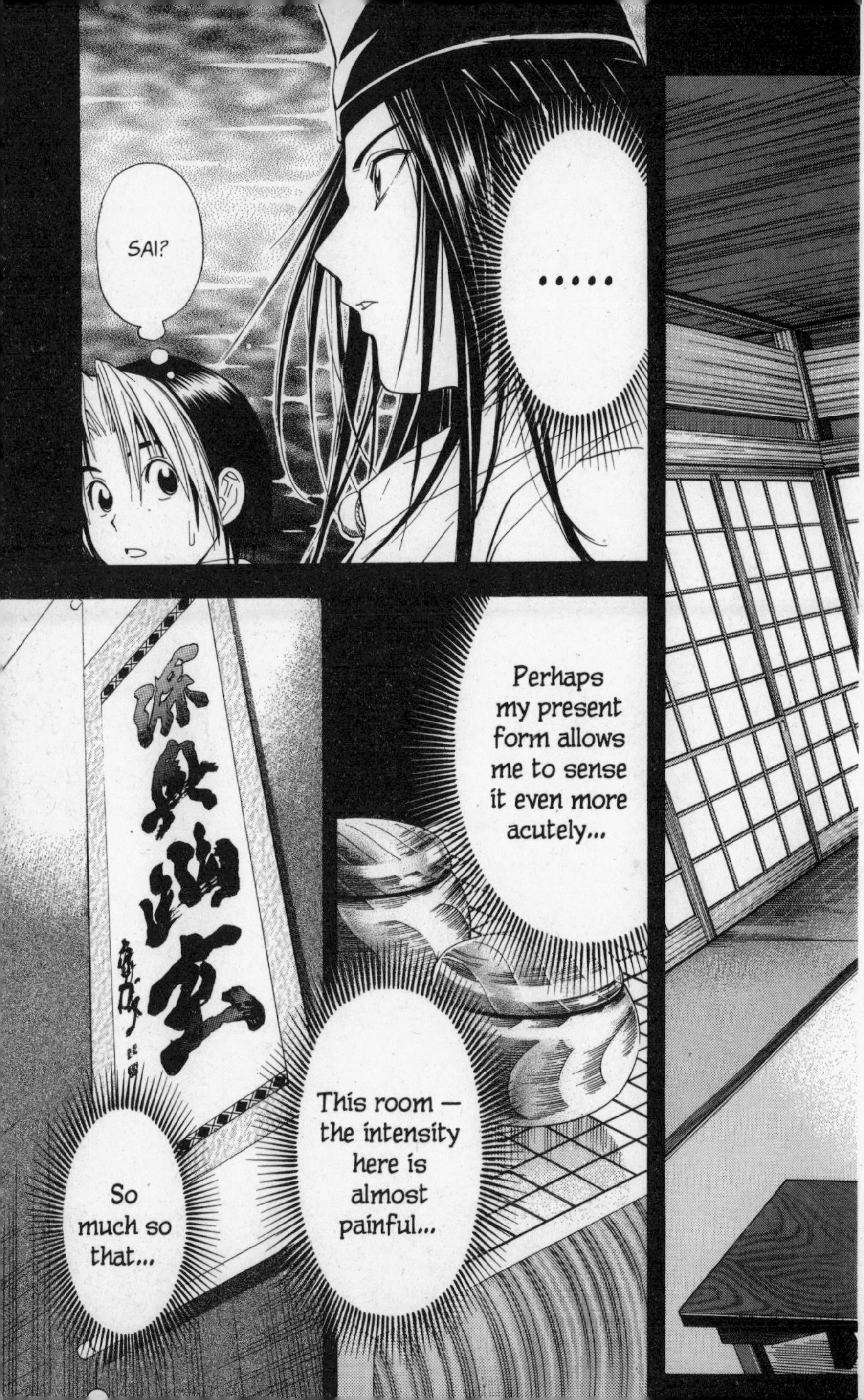
SAI?
.....
Perhaps my present form allows me to sense it even more acutely...
This room — the intensity here is almost painful...
So much so that...

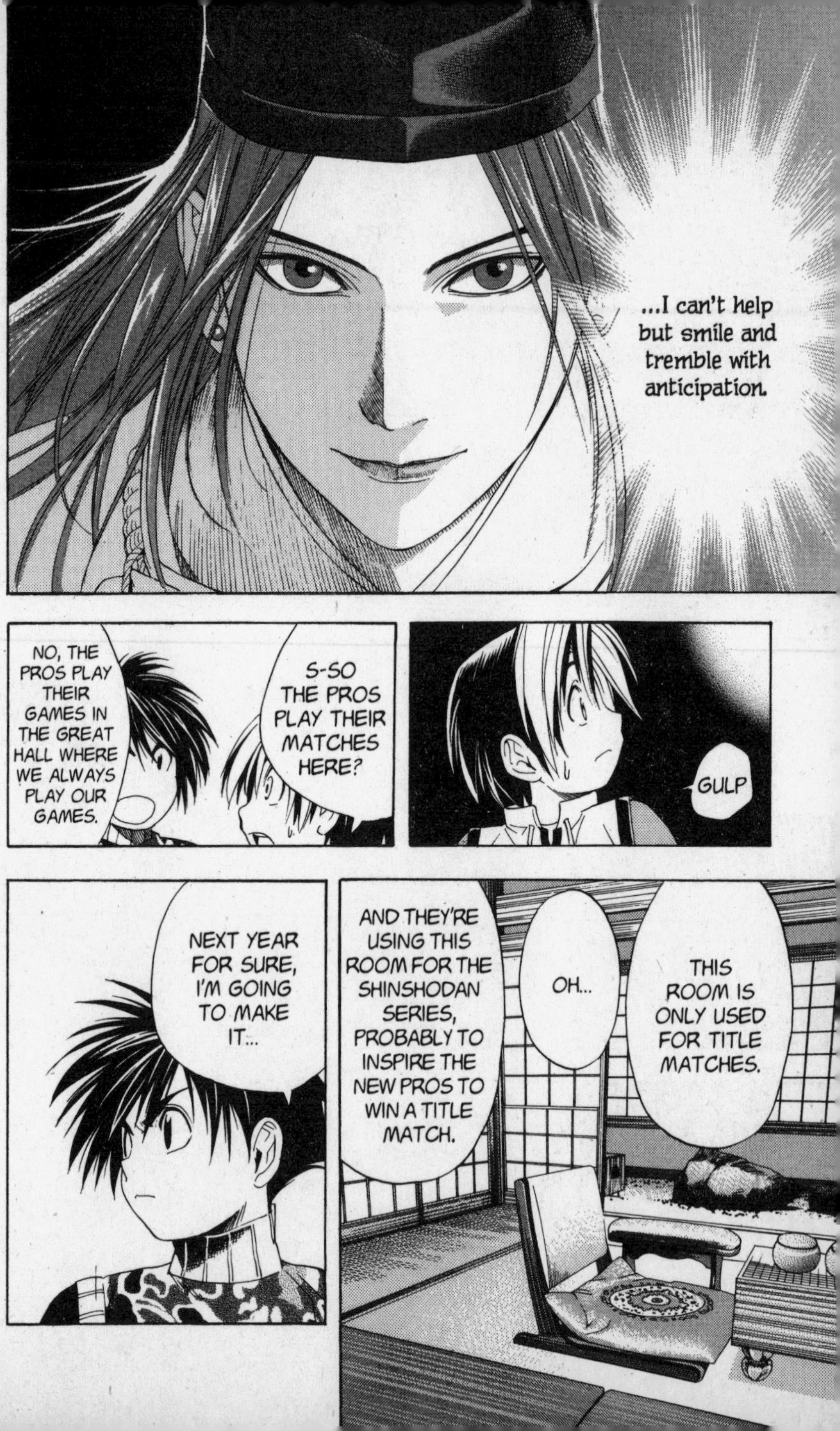
...I can't help but smile and tremble with anticipation.
GULP
S-SO THE PROS PLAY THEIR MATCHES HERE?
NO, THE PROS PLAY THEIR GAMES IN THE GREAT HALL WHERE WE ALWAYS PLAY OUR GAMES.
THIS ROOM IS ONLY USED FOR TITLE MATCHES.
OH...
AND THEY'RE USING THIS ROOM FOR THE SHINSHODAN SERIES, PROBABLY TO INSPIRE THE NEW PROS TO WIN A TITLE MATCH.
NEXT YEAR FOR SURE, I'M GOING TO MAKE IT...

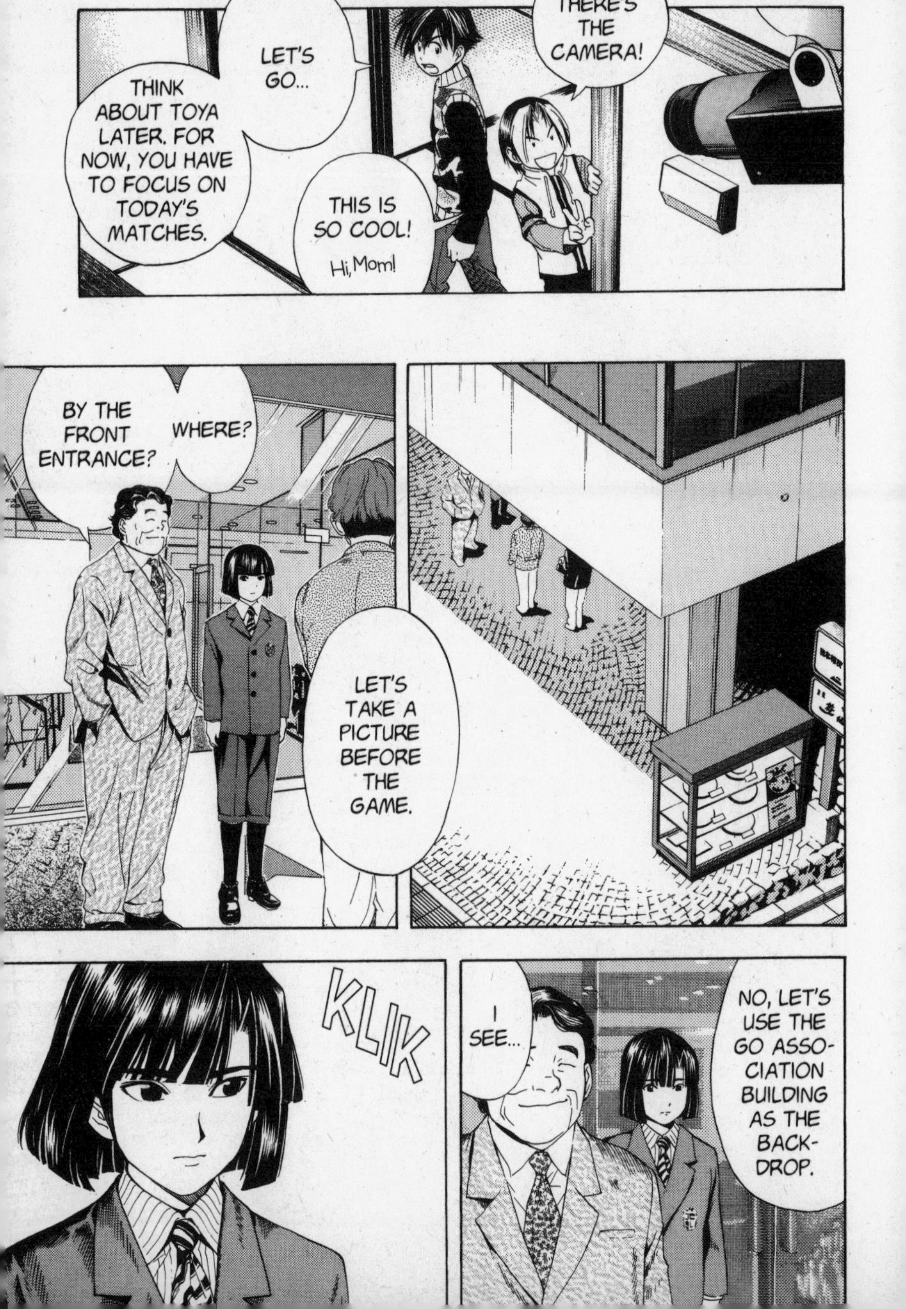
HEY, THERE'S THE CAMERA!
LET'S GO...
THINK ABOUT TOYA LATER. FOR NOW, YOU HAVE TO FOCUS ON TODAY'S MATCHES.
THIS IS SO COOL!
Hi, Mom!
WHERE?
BY THE FRONT ENTRANCE?
LET'S TAKE A PICTURE BEFORE THE GAME.
NO, LET'S USE THE GO ASSOCIATION BUILDING AS THE BACKDROP.
I SEE...
KLIK

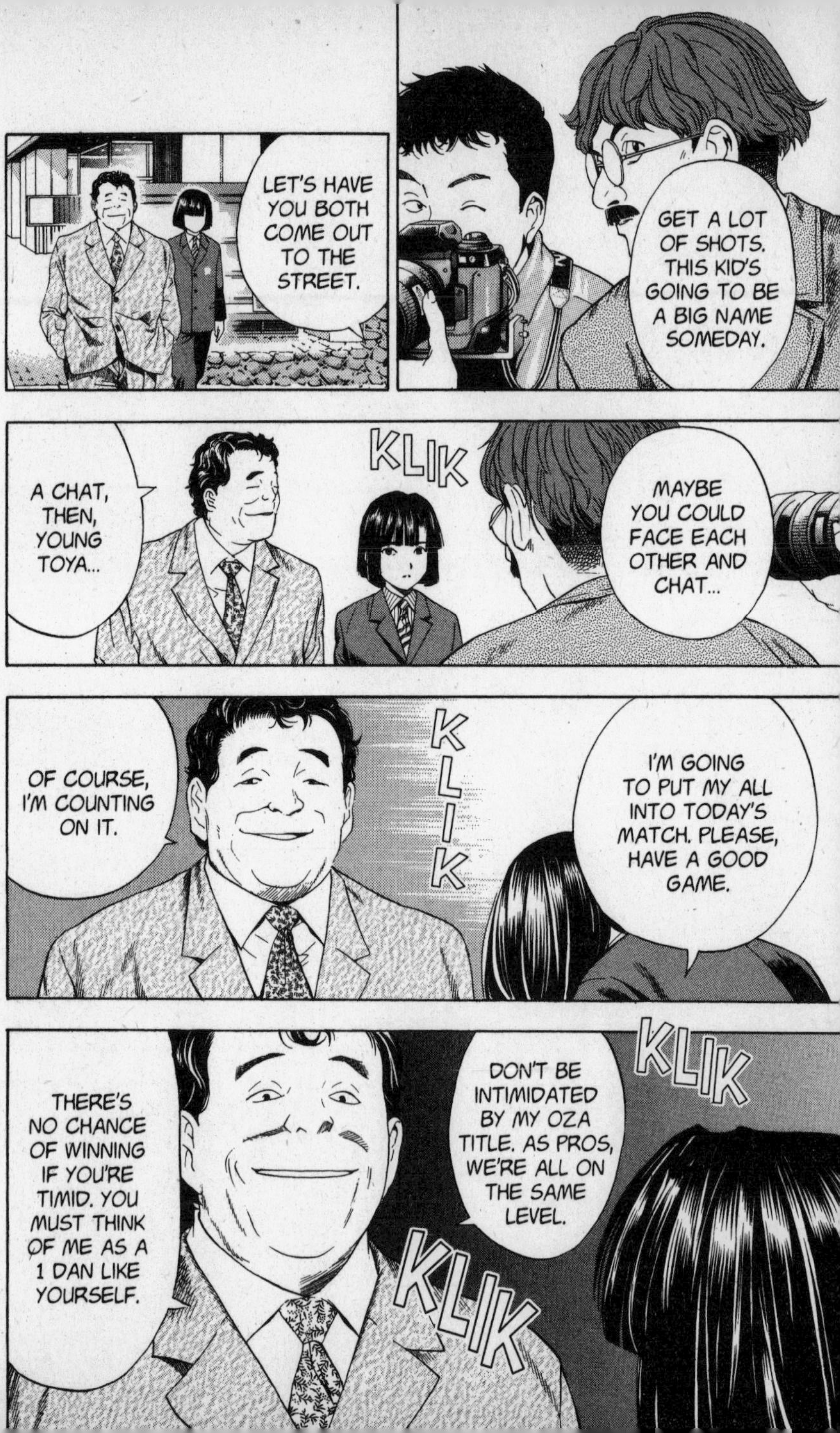
GET A LOT OF SHOTS. THIS KID'S GOING TO BE A BIG NAME SOMEDAY.
LET'S HAVE YOU BOTH COME OUT TO THE STREET.
MAYBE YOU COULD FACE EACH OTHER AND CHAT...
KLIK
A CHAT, THEN, YOUNG TOYA...
I'M GOING TO PUT MY ALL INTO TODAY'S MATCH. PLEASE, HAVE A GOOD GAME.
KLIK
OF COURSE, I'M COUNTING ON IT.
KLIK
DON'T BE INTIMIDATED BY MY OZA TITLE. AS PROS, WE'RE ALL ON THE SAME LEVEL.
KLIK
THERE'S NO CHANCE OF WINNING IF YOU'RE TIMID. YOU MUST THINK OF ME AS A 1 DAN LIKE YOURSELF.

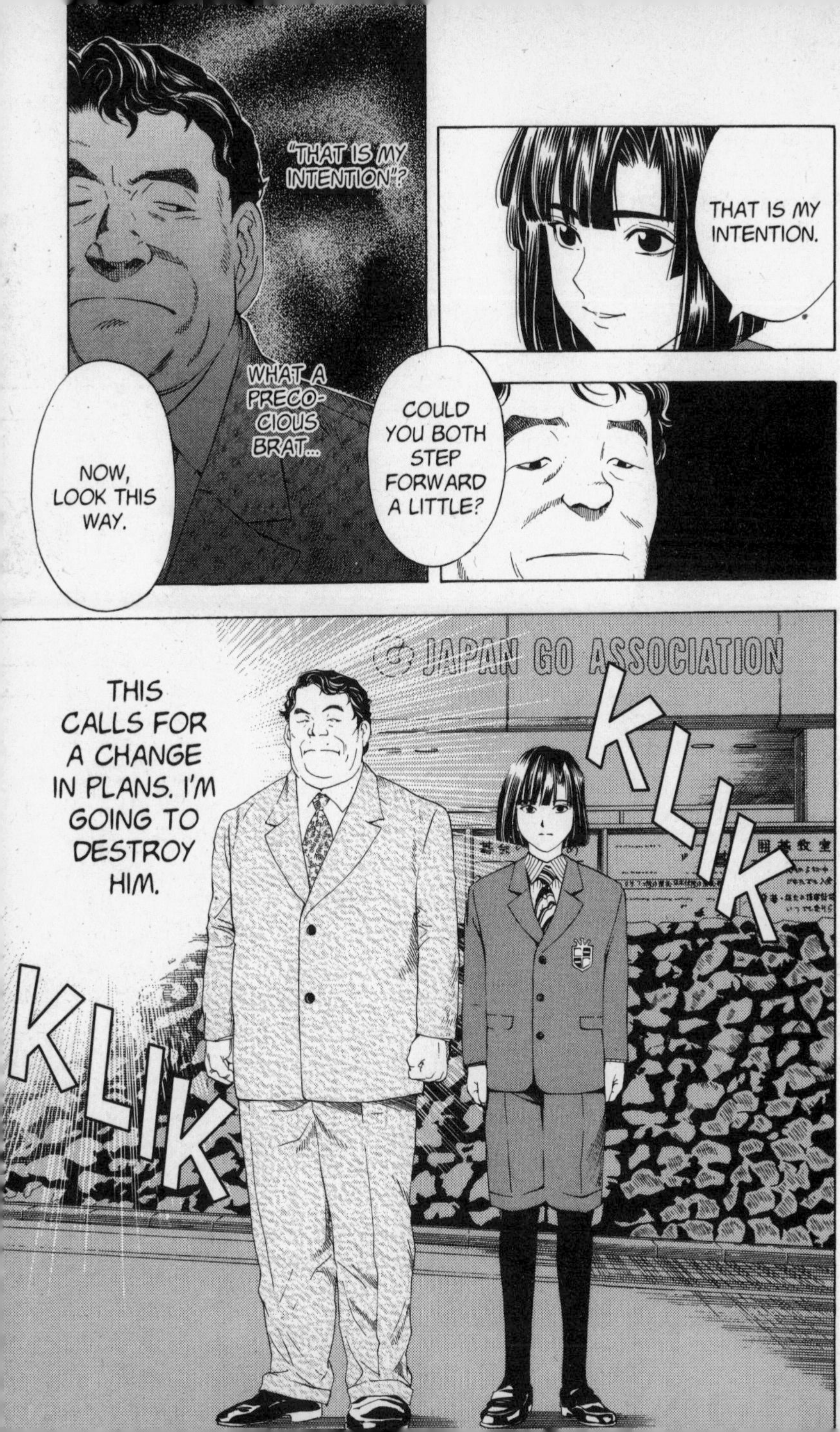
THAT IS MY INTENTION.
COULD YOU BOTH STEP FORWARD A LITTLE?
"THAT IS MY INTENTION"?
WHAT A PRECOCIOUS BRAT...
NOW, LOOK THIS WAY.
JAPAN GO ASSOCIATION
KLIK
THIS CALLS FOR A CHANGE IN PLANS. I'M GOING TO DESTROY HIM.
KLIK

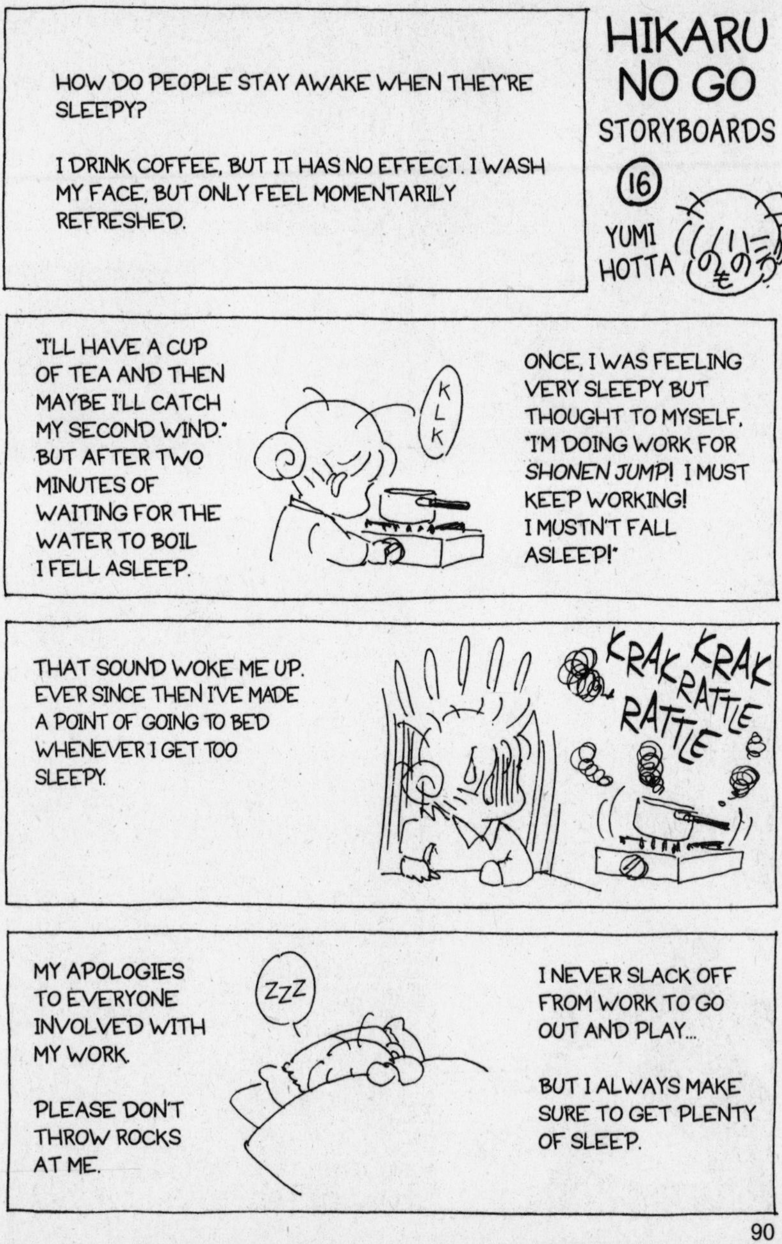
HIKARU NO GO
STORYBOARDS
16
YUMI HOTTA
HOW DO PEOPLE STAY AWAKE WHEN THEY'RE SLEEPY?
I DRINK COFFEE, BUT IT HAS NO EFFECT. I WASH MY FACE, BUT ONLY FEEL MOMENTARILY REFRESHED.
ONCE, I WAS FEELING VERY SLEEPY BUT THOUGHT TO MYSELF, "I'M DOING WORK FOR *SHONEN JUMP*! I MUST KEEP WORKING! I MUSTN'T FALL ASLEEP!"
KLK
"I'LL HAVE A CUP OF TEA AND THEN MAYBE I'LL CATCH MY SECOND WIND." BUT AFTER TWO MINUTES OF WAITING FOR THE WATER TO BOIL I FELL ASLEEP.
KRAK KRAK
RATTLE RATTLE
THAT SOUND WOKE ME UP. EVER SINCE THEN I'VE MADE A POINT OF GOING TO BED WHENEVER I GET TOO SLEEPY.
I NEVER SLACK OFF FROM WORK TO GO OUT AND PLAY...
BUT I ALWAYS MAKE SURE TO GET PLENTY OF SLEEP.
ZZZ
MY APOLOGIES TO EVERYONE INVOLVED WITH MY WORK.
PLEASE DON'T THROW ROCKS AT ME.

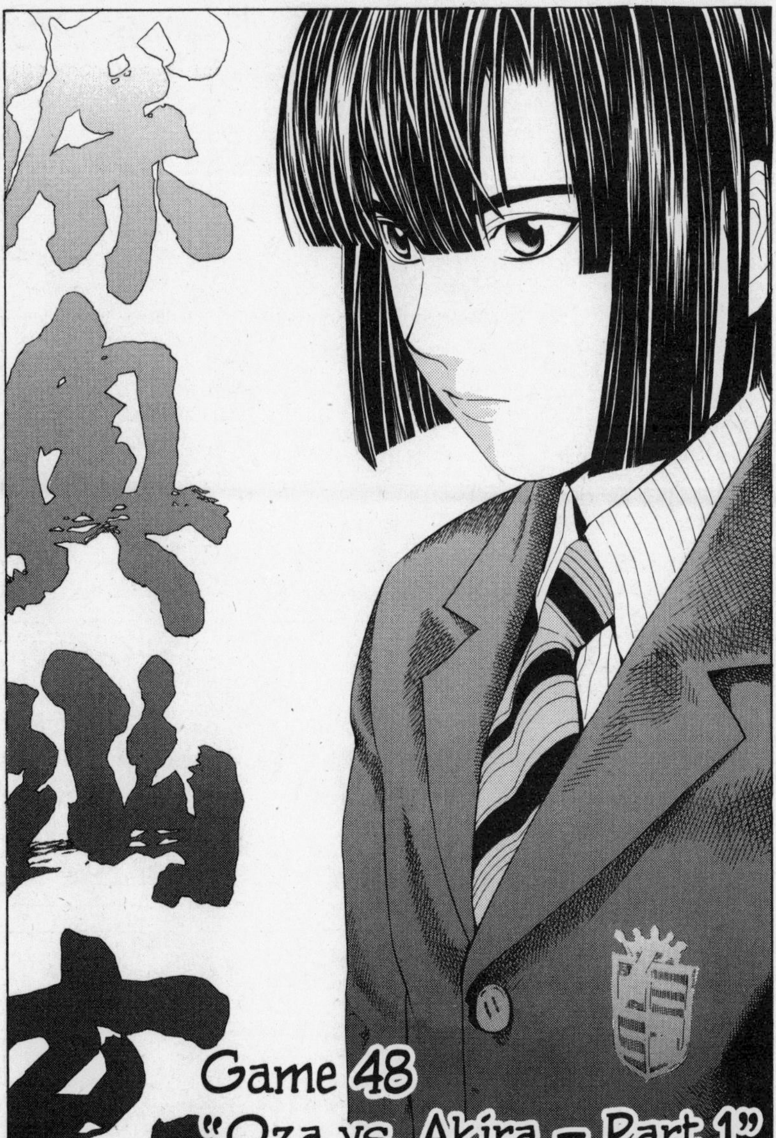
Game 48
"Oza vs. Akira – Part 1"

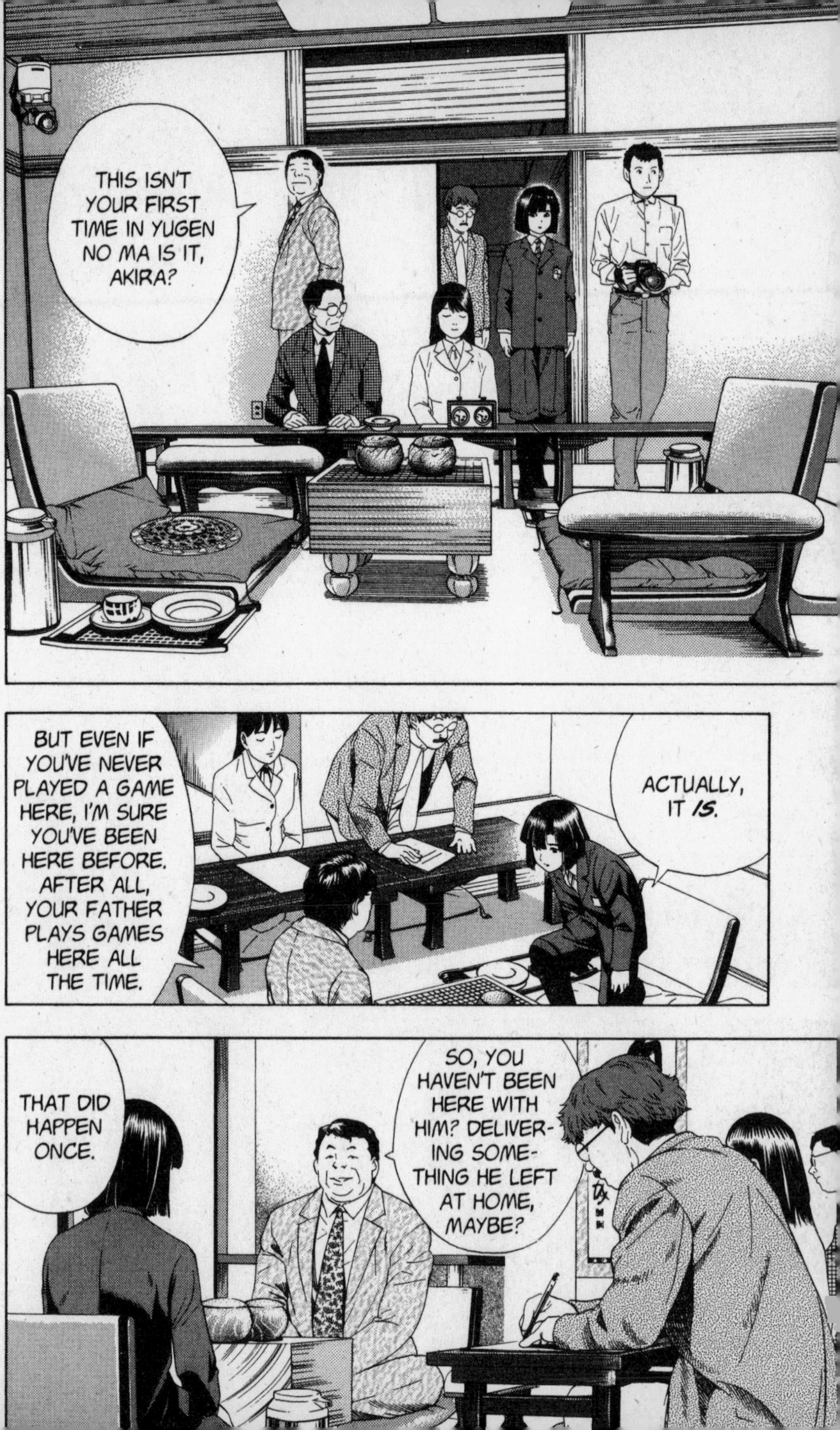
THIS ISN'T YOUR FIRST TIME IN YUGEN NO MA IS IT, AKIRA?
ACTUALLY, IT *IS*.
BUT EVEN IF YOU'VE NEVER PLAYED A GAME HERE, I'M SURE YOU'VE BEEN HERE BEFORE. AFTER ALL, YOUR FATHER PLAYS GAMES HERE ALL THE TIME.
SO, YOU HAVEN'T BEEN HERE WITH HIM? DELIVERING SOMETHING HE LEFT AT HOME, MAYBE?
THAT DID HAPPEN ONCE.

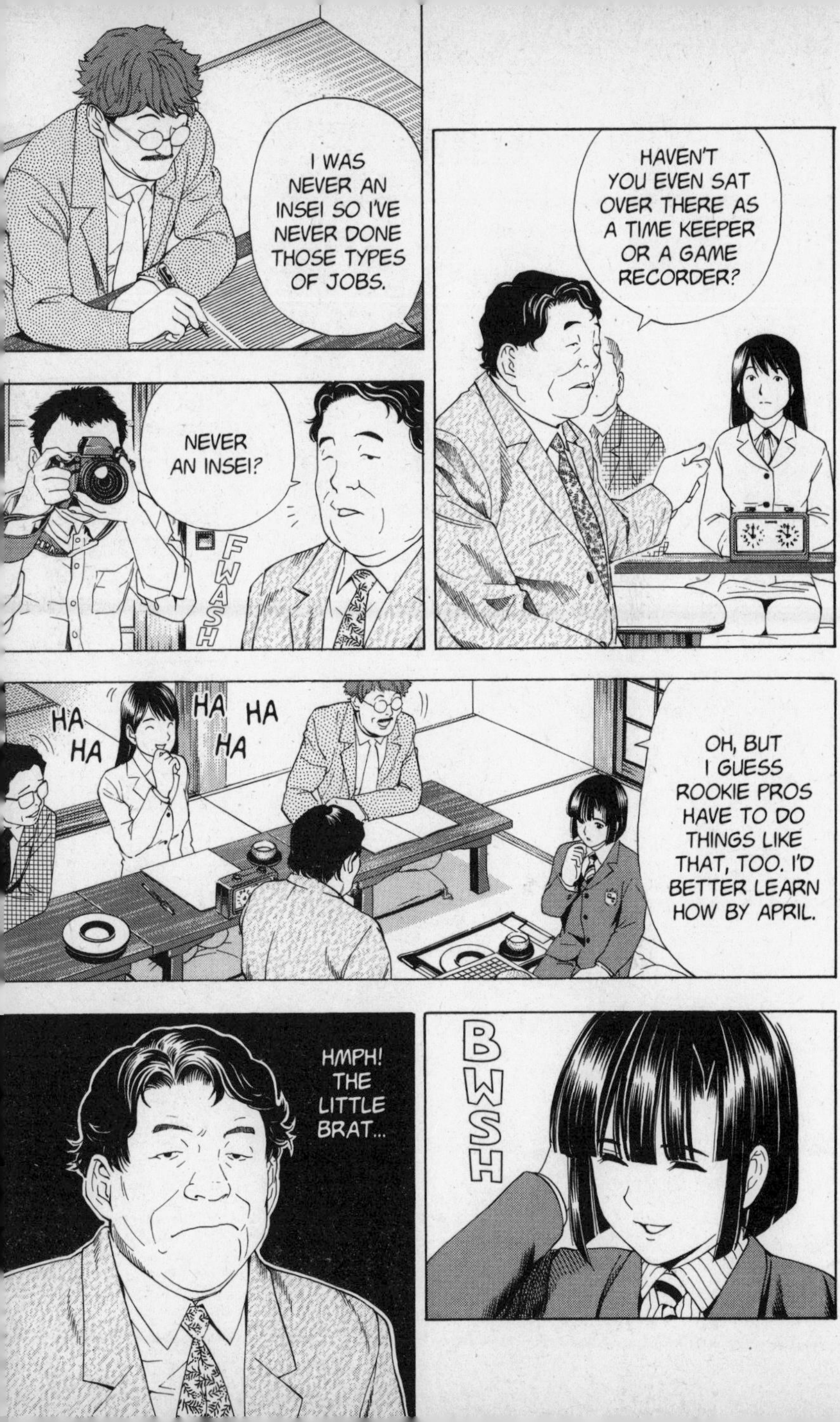
I WAS NEVER AN INSEI SO I'VE NEVER DONE THOSE TYPES OF JOBS.
NEVER AN INSEI?
FWASH
HAVEN'T YOU EVEN SAT OVER THERE AS A TIME KEEPER OR A GAME RECORDER?
OH, BUT I GUESS ROOKIE PROS HAVE TO DO THINGS LIKE THAT, TOO. I'D BETTER LEARN HOW BY APRIL.
HA HA
HA HA
HA
HA
BWSH
HMPH! THE LITTLE BRAT...

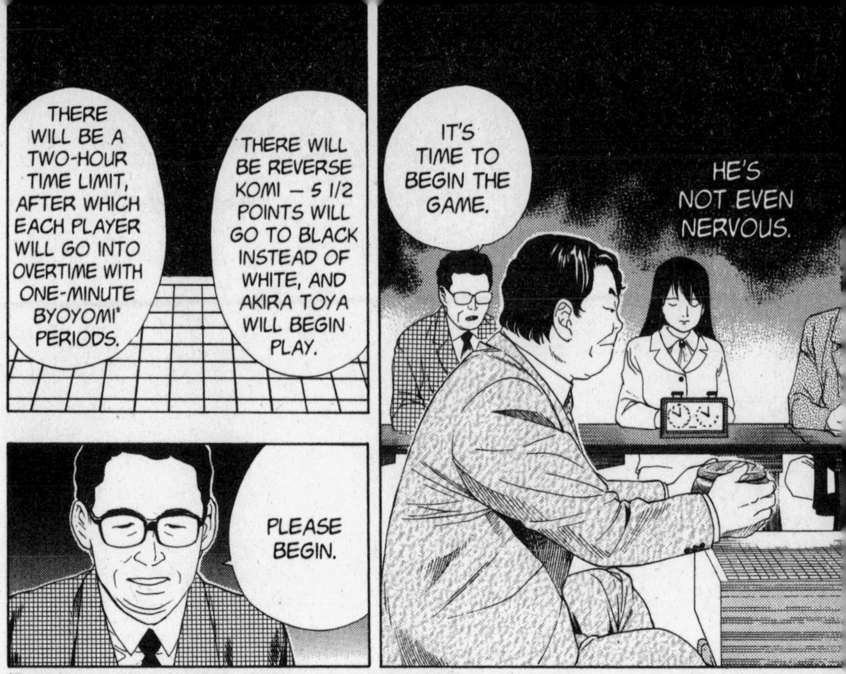
HE'S NOT EVEN NERVOUS.
IT'S TIME TO BEGIN THE GAME.
THERE WILL BE REVERSE KOMI — 5 1/2 POINTS WILL GO TO BLACK INSTEAD OF WHITE, AND AKIRA TOYA WILL BEGIN PLAY.
THERE WILL BE A TWO-HOUR TIME LIMIT, AFTER WHICH EACH PLAYER WILL GO INTO OVERTIME WITH ONE-MINUTE BYOYOMI* PERIODS.
PLEASE BEGIN.

*Byoyomi: overtime periods in which a set time limit is allotted and seconds are counted off.

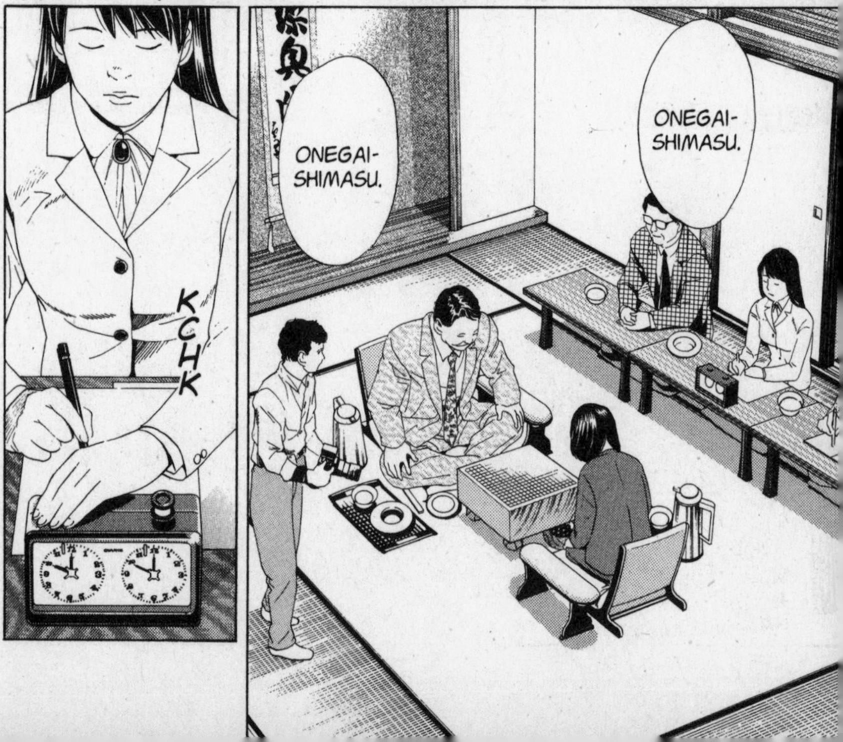
ONEGAI-SHIMASU.
ONEGAI-SHIMASU.
KCHK

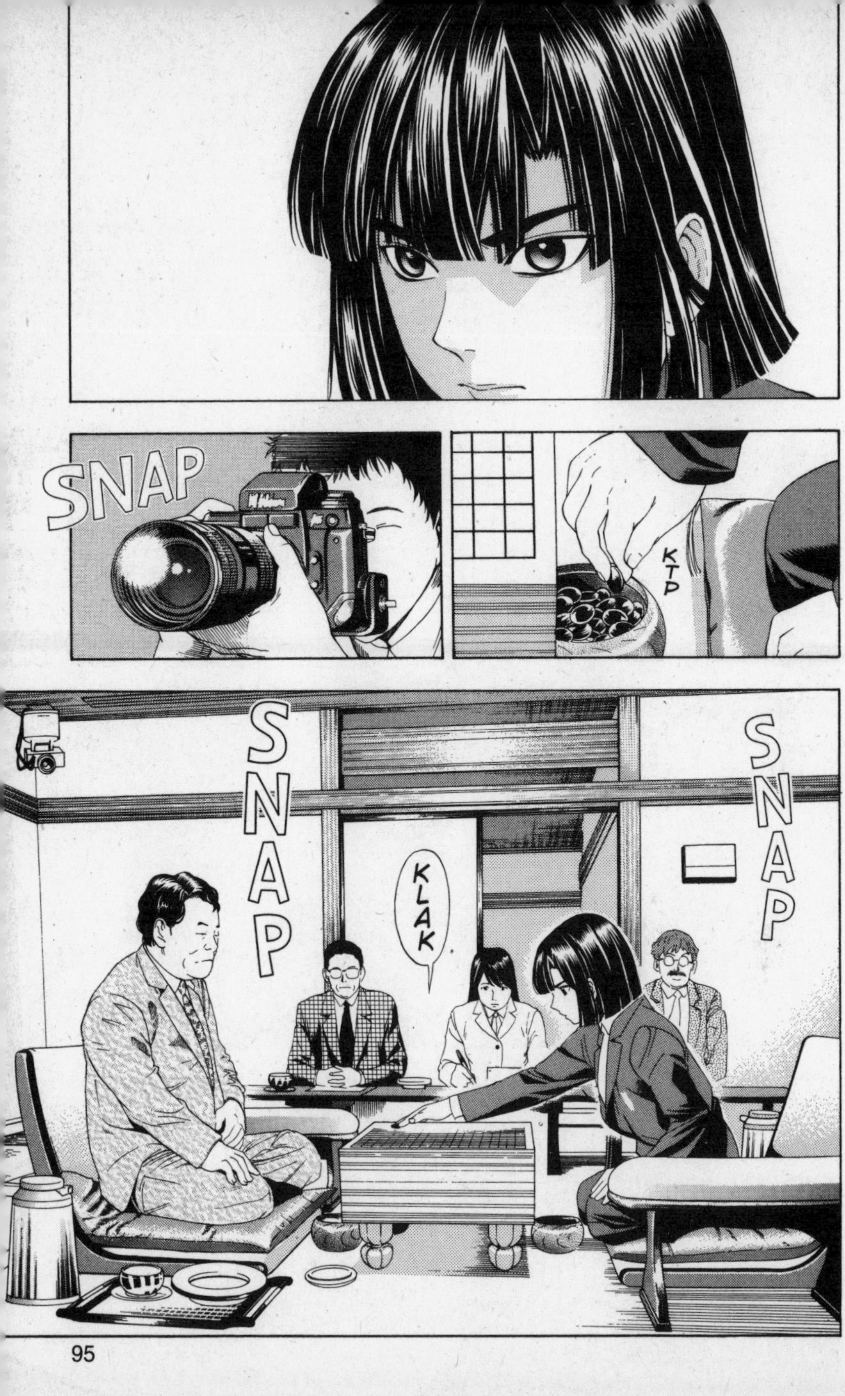
SNAP
KTP
SNAP
KLAK
SNAP

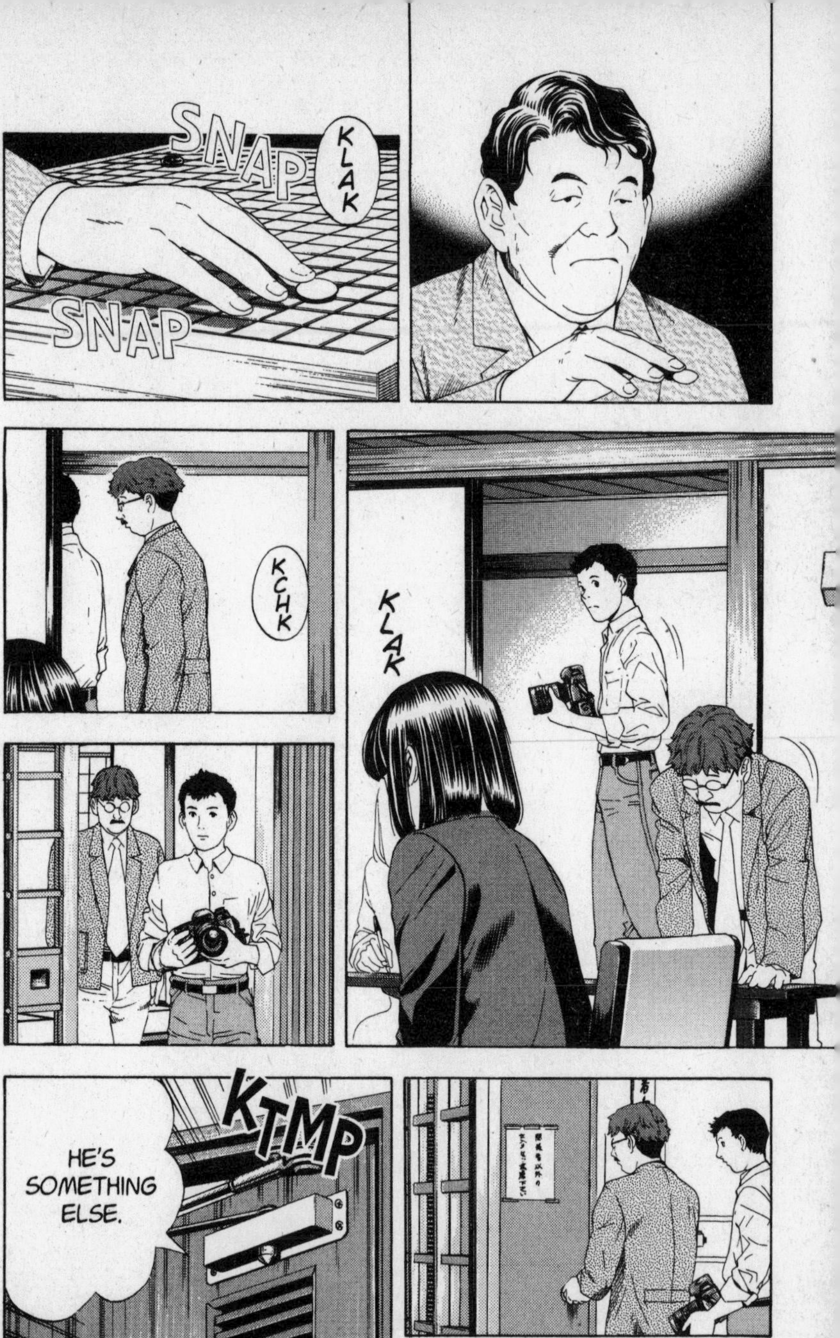
KLAK
SNAP
SNAP
KLAK
KCHK
KTMP
HE'S SOMETHING ELSE.

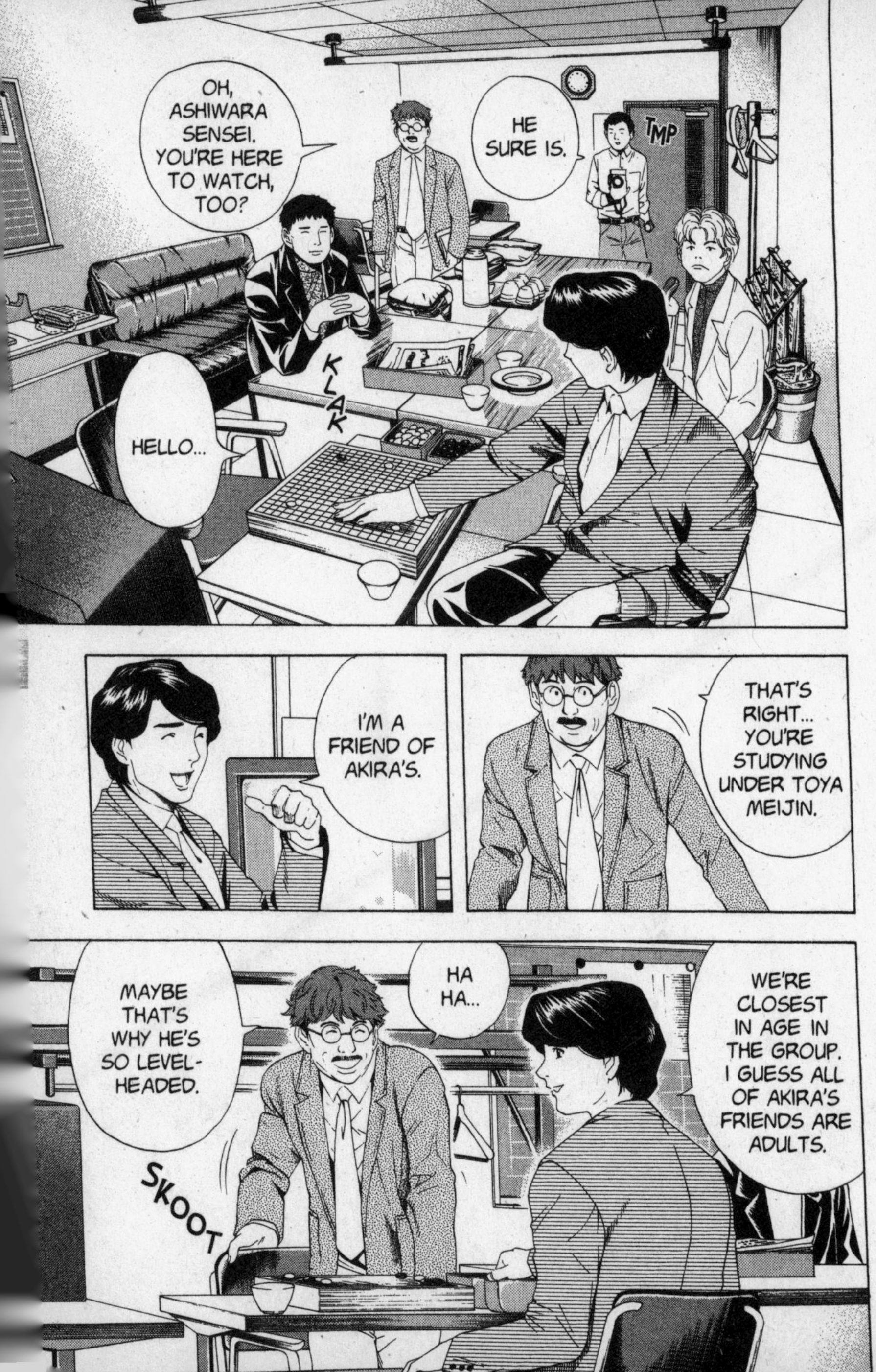
TMP
HE SURE IS.
OH, ASHIWARA SENSEI. YOU'RE HERE TO WATCH, TOO?
KLAK
HELLO...
THAT'S RIGHT... YOU'RE STUDYING UNDER TOYA MEIJIN.
I'M A FRIEND OF AKIRA'S.
WE'RE CLOSEST IN AGE IN THE GROUP. I GUESS ALL OF AKIRA'S FRIENDS ARE ADULTS.
HA HA...
MAYBE THAT'S WHY HE'S SO LEVEL-HEADED.
SKOOT

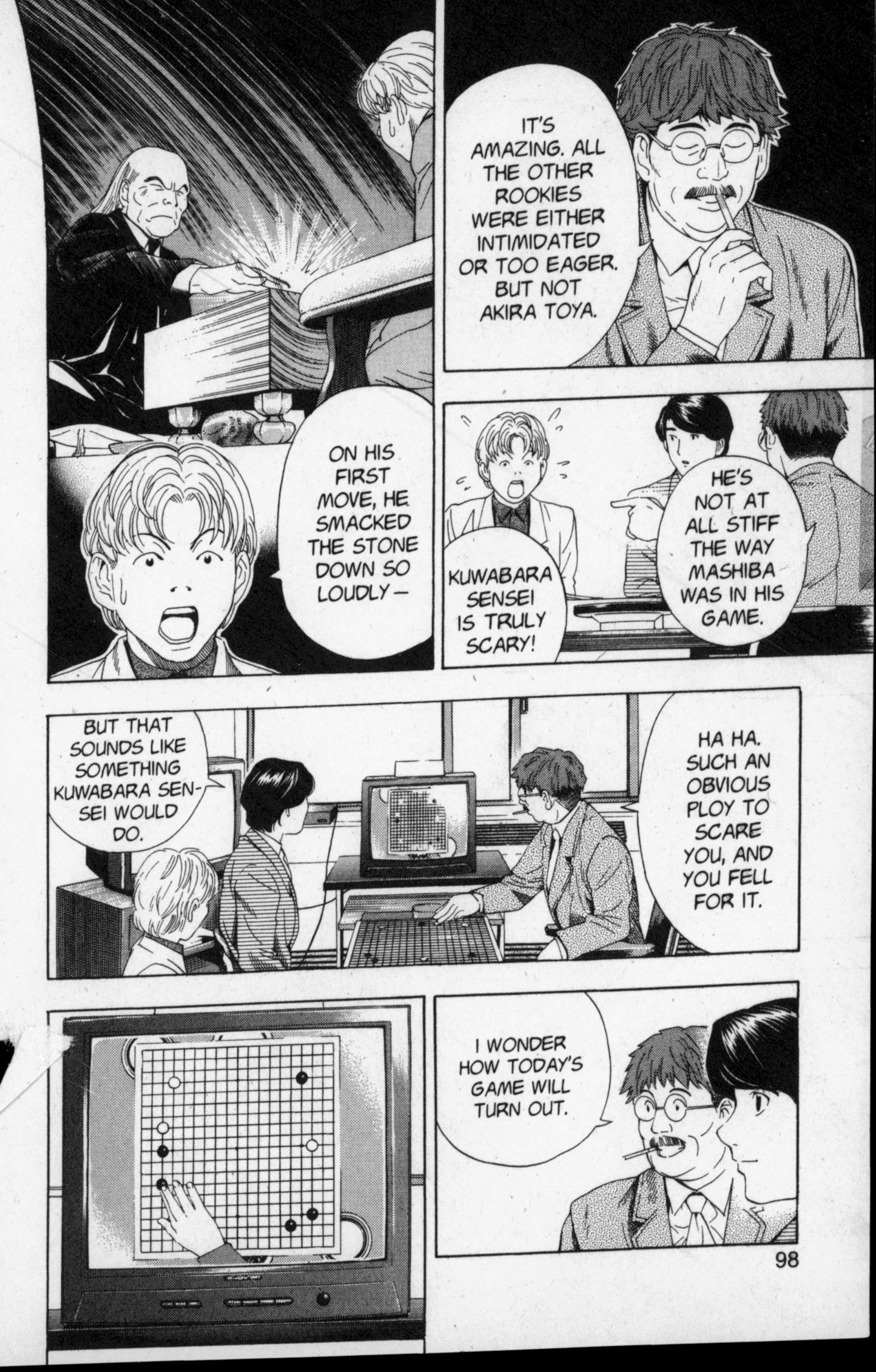
IT'S AMAZING. ALL THE OTHER ROOKIES WERE EITHER INTIMIDATED OR TOO EAGER. BUT NOT AKIRA TOYA.
HE'S NOT AT ALL STIFF THE WAY MASHIBA WAS IN HIS GAME.
KUWABARA SENSEI IS TRULY SCARY!
ON HIS FIRST MOVE, HE SMACKED THE STONE DOWN SO LOUDLY—
HA HA. SUCH AN OBVIOUS PLOY TO SCARE YOU, AND YOU FELL FOR IT.
BUT THAT SOUNDS LIKE SOMETHING KUWABARA SEN-SEI WOULD DO.
I WONDER HOW TODAY'S GAME WILL TURN OUT.

READ THIS WAY

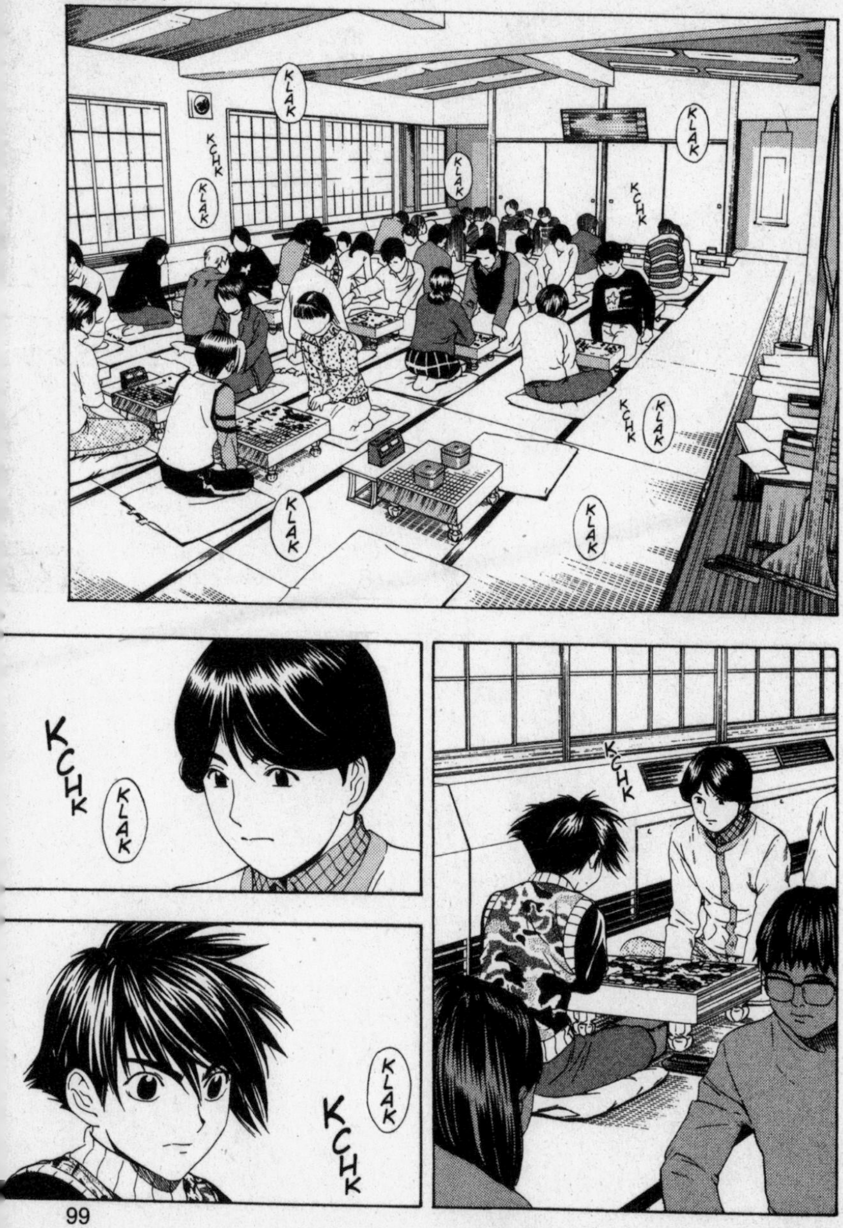

KLAK
KLAK
KCHK
KLAK
KLAK
KCHK
KLAK
KLAK
KLAK
KCHK
KLAK
KCHK
KLAK
KLAK
KCHK

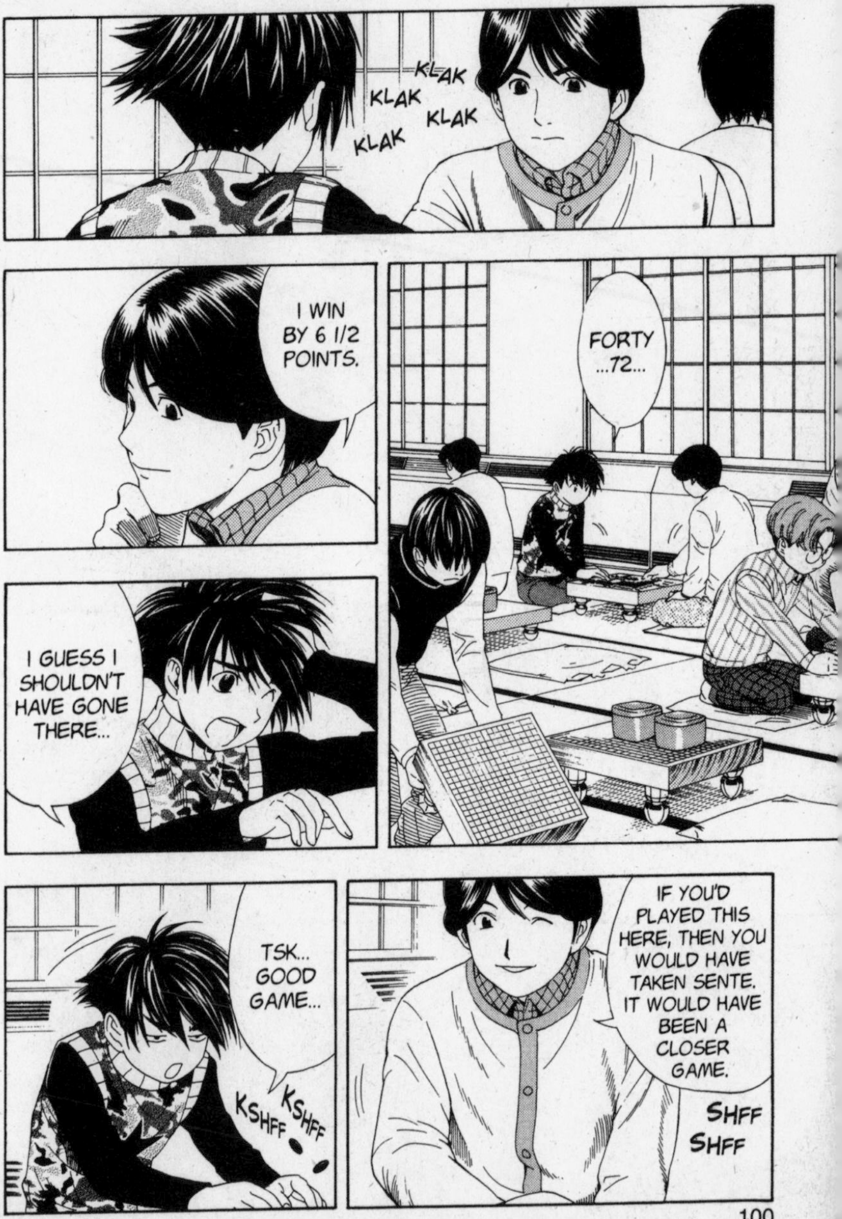
KLAK
KLAK
KLAK
KLAK
FORTY ...72...
I WIN BY 6 1/2 POINTS.
I GUESS I SHOULDN'T HAVE GONE THERE...
IF YOU'D PLAYED THIS HERE, THEN YOU WOULD HAVE TAKEN SENTE. IT WOULD HAVE BEEN A CLOSER GAME.
SHFF
SHFF
TSK... GOOD GAME...
KSHFF
KSHFF

READ THIS WAY

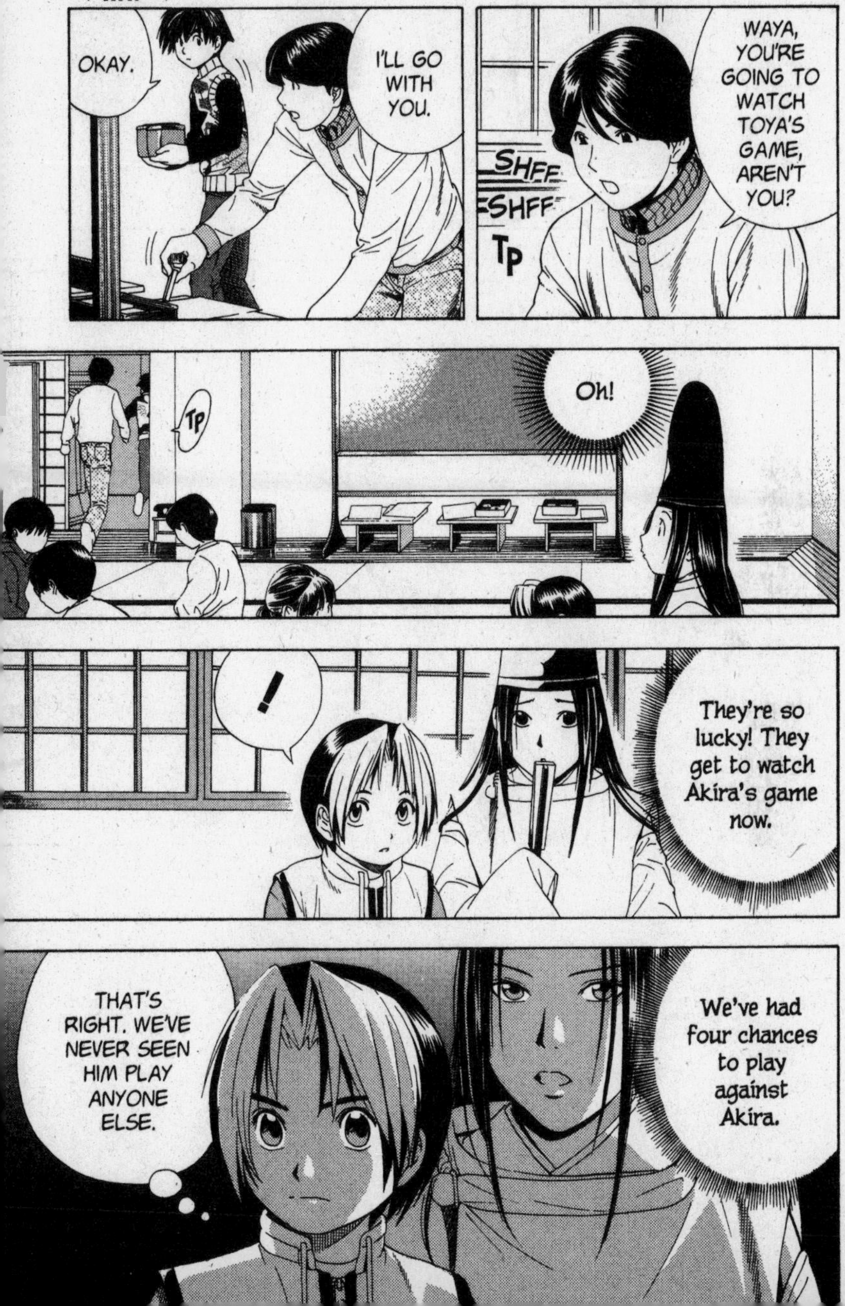
WAYA, YOU'RE GOING TO WATCH TOYA'S GAME, AREN'T YOU?
SHFF
SHFF
TP
I'LL GO WITH YOU.
OKAY.
Oh!
TP
They're so lucky! They get to watch Akira's game now.
!
We've had four chances to play against Akira.
THAT'S RIGHT. WE'VE NEVER SEEN HIM PLAY ANYONE ELSE.

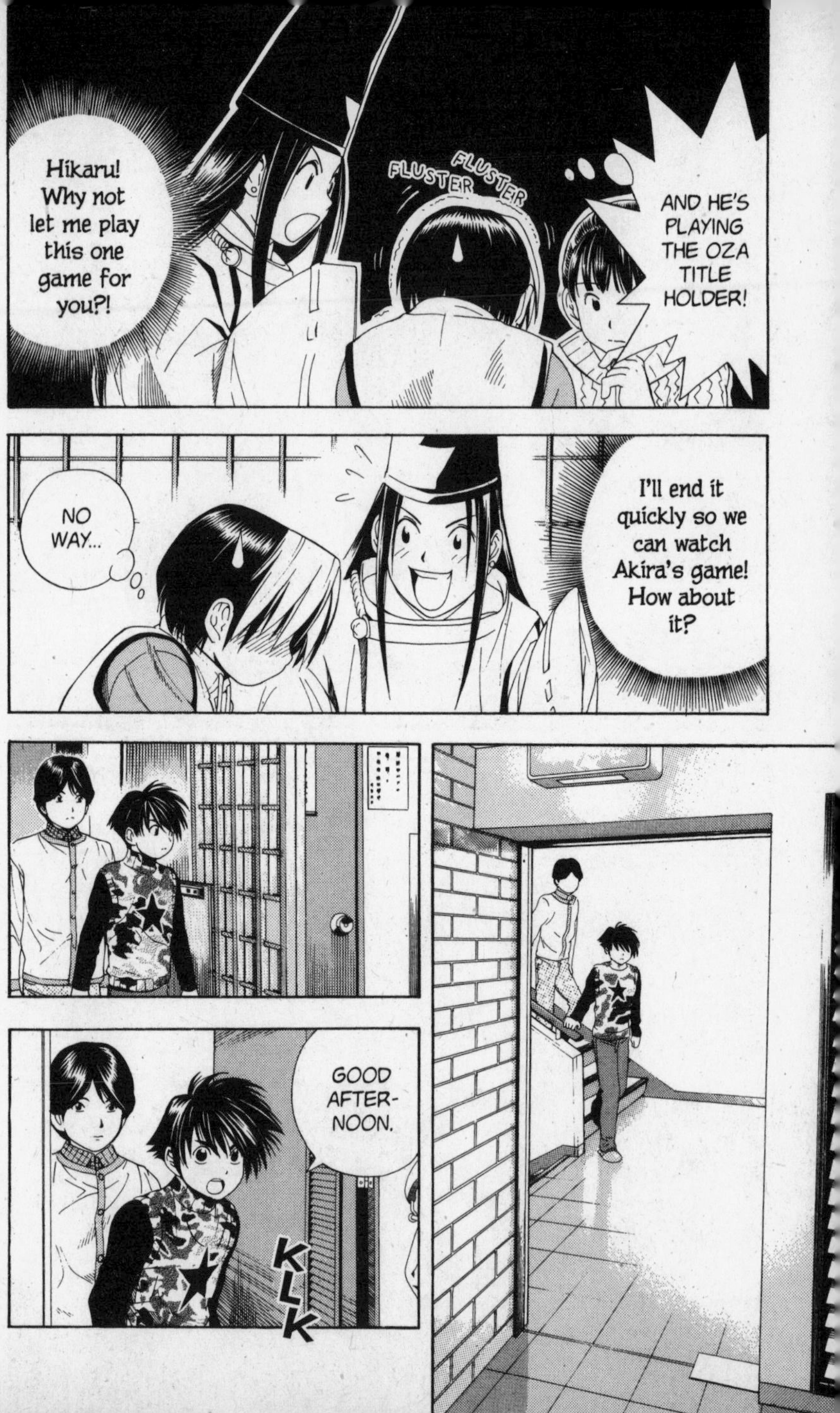
AND HE'S PLAYING THE OZA TITLE HOLDER!
FLUSTER FLUSTER
Hikaru! Why not let me play this one game for you?!
I'll end it quickly so we can watch Akira's game! How about it?
NO WAY...
GOOD AFTER-NOON.
KLK

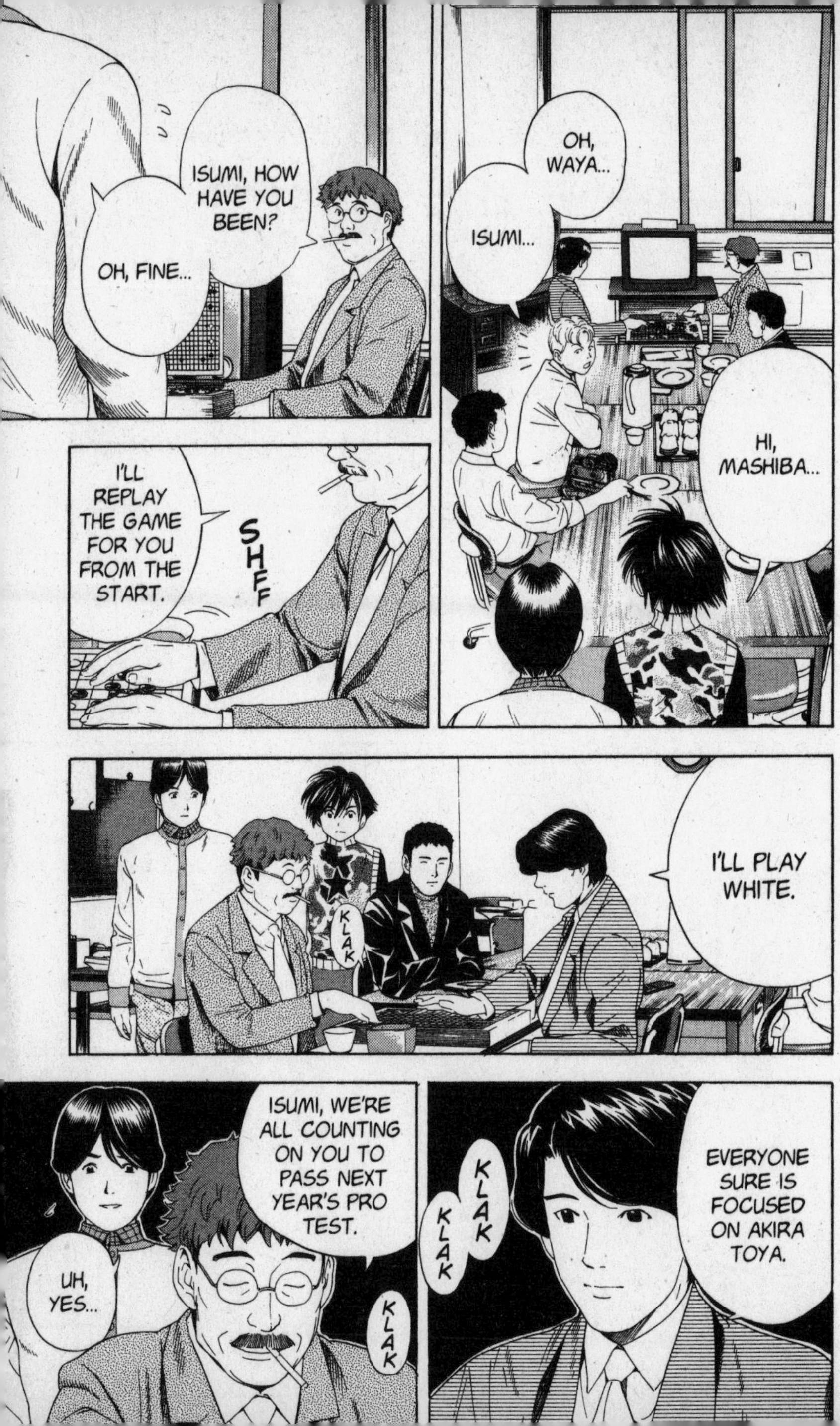
OH, WAYA...
ISUMI...
HI, MASHIBA...
ISUMI, HOW HAVE YOU BEEN?
OH, FINE...
I'LL REPLAY THE GAME FOR YOU FROM THE START.
SHFF
I'LL PLAY WHITE.
KLAK
EVERYONE SURE IS FOCUSED ON AKIRA TOYA.
KLAK
KLAK
ISUMI, WE'RE ALL COUNTING ON YOU TO PASS NEXT YEAR'S PRO TEST.
KLAK
UH, YES...

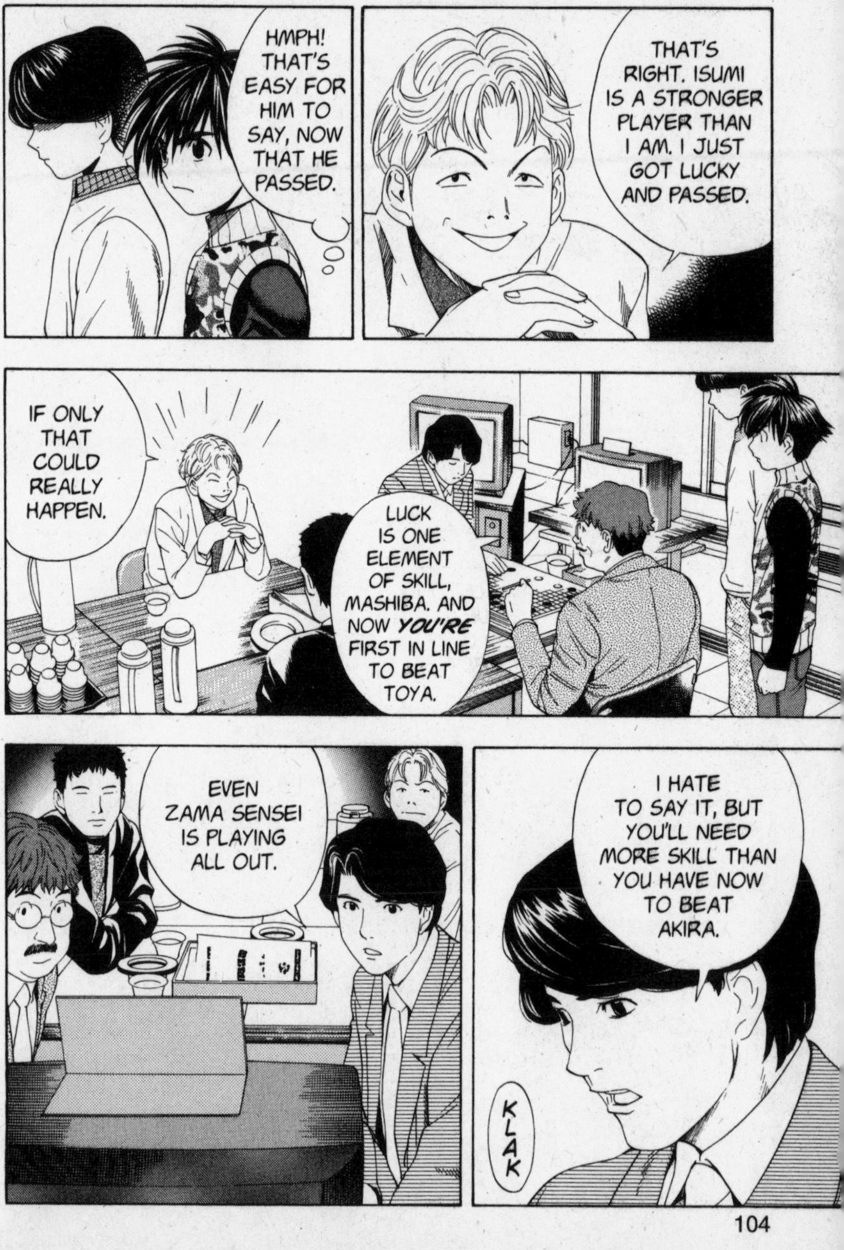
THAT'S RIGHT. ISUMI IS A STRONGER PLAYER THAN I AM. I JUST GOT LUCKY AND PASSED.
HMPH! THAT'S EASY FOR HIM TO SAY, NOW THAT HE PASSED.
LUCK IS ONE ELEMENT OF SKILL, MASHIBA. AND NOW *YOU'RE* FIRST IN LINE TO BEAT TOYA.
IF ONLY THAT COULD REALLY HAPPEN.
I HATE TO SAY IT, BUT YOU'LL NEED MORE SKILL THAN YOU HAVE NOW TO BEAT AKIRA.
KLAK
EVEN ZAMA SENSEI IS PLAYING ALL OUT.

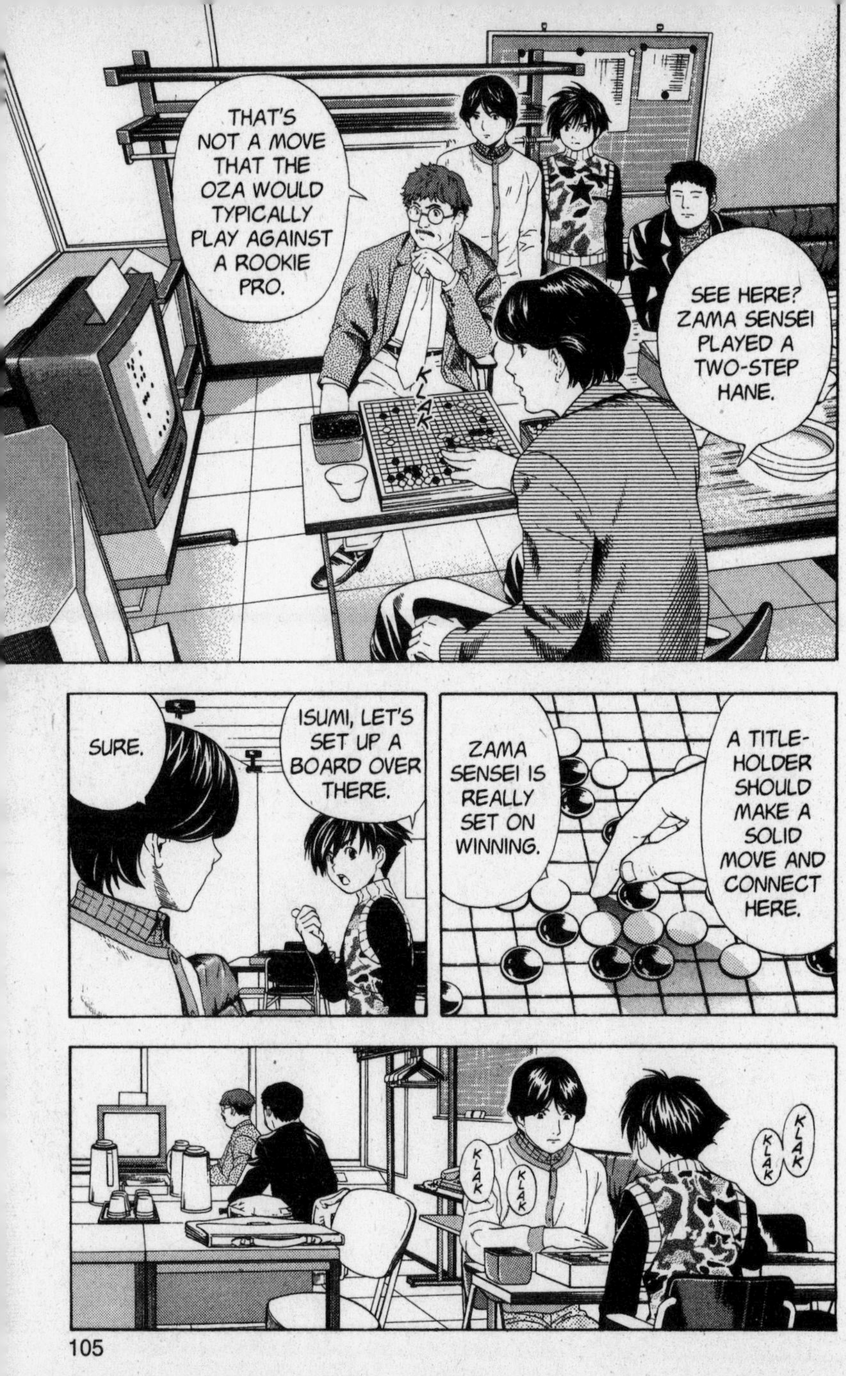
SEE HERE? ZAMA SENSEI PLAYED A TWO-STEP HANE.
KLAK
THAT'S NOT A MOVE THAT THE OZA WOULD TYPICALLY PLAY AGAINST A ROOKIE PRO.
A TITLE-HOLDER SHOULD MAKE A SOLID MOVE AND CONNECT HERE.
ZAMA SENSEI IS REALLY SET ON WINNING.
ISUMI, LET'S SET UP A BOARD OVER THERE.
SURE.
KLAK KLAK
KLAK KLAK

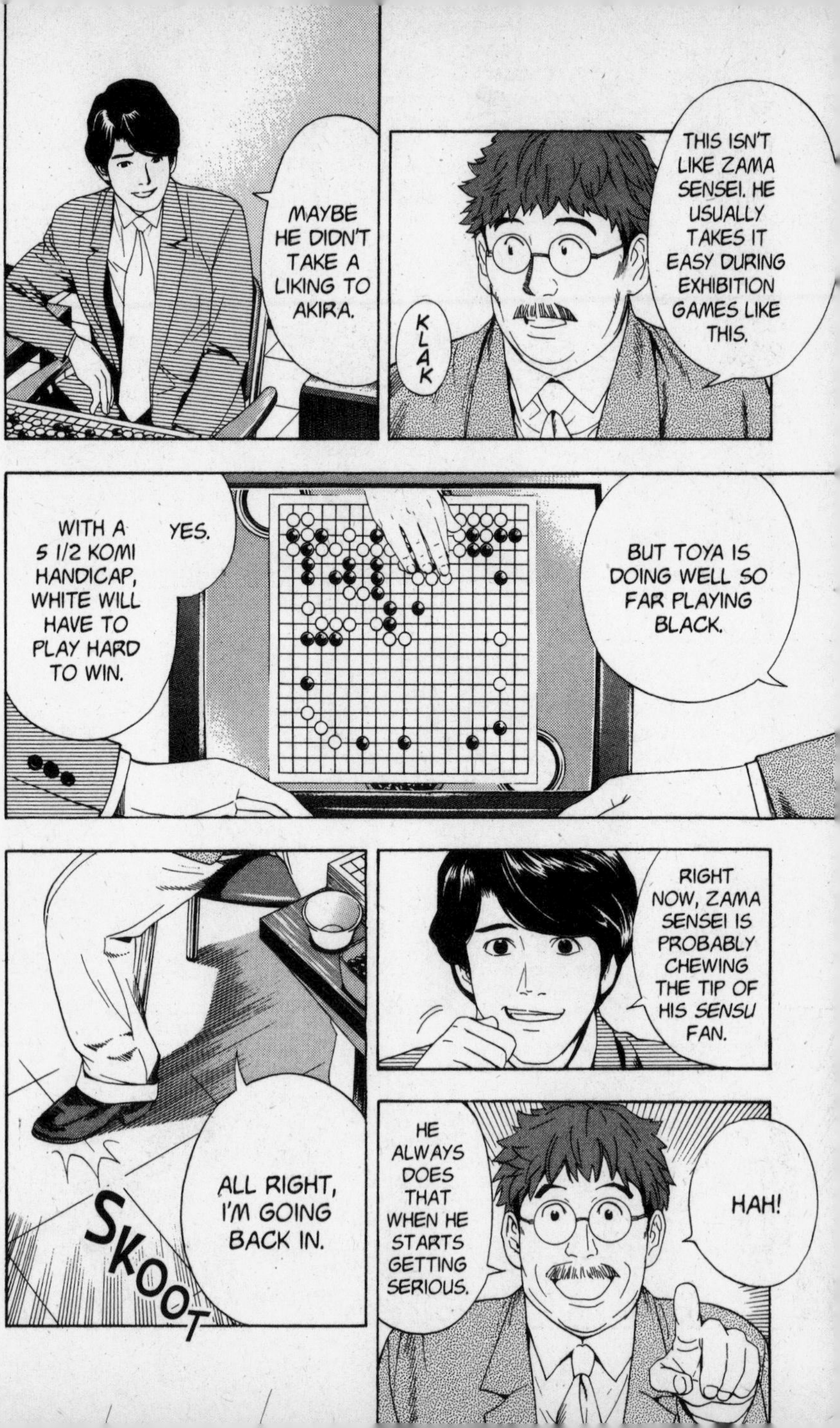
THIS ISN'T LIKE ZAMA SENSEI. HE USUALLY TAKES IT EASY DURING EXHIBITION GAMES LIKE THIS.
KLAK
MAYBE HE DIDN'T TAKE A LIKING TO AKIRA.
BUT TOYA IS DOING WELL SO FAR PLAYING BLACK.
YES.
WITH A 5 1/2 KOMI HANDICAP, WHITE WILL HAVE TO PLAY HARD TO WIN.
RIGHT NOW, ZAMA SENSEI IS PROBABLY CHEWING THE TIP OF HIS SENSU FAN.
HAH!
HE ALWAYS DOES THAT WHEN HE STARTS GETTING SERIOUS.
ALL RIGHT, I'M GOING BACK IN.
SKOOT

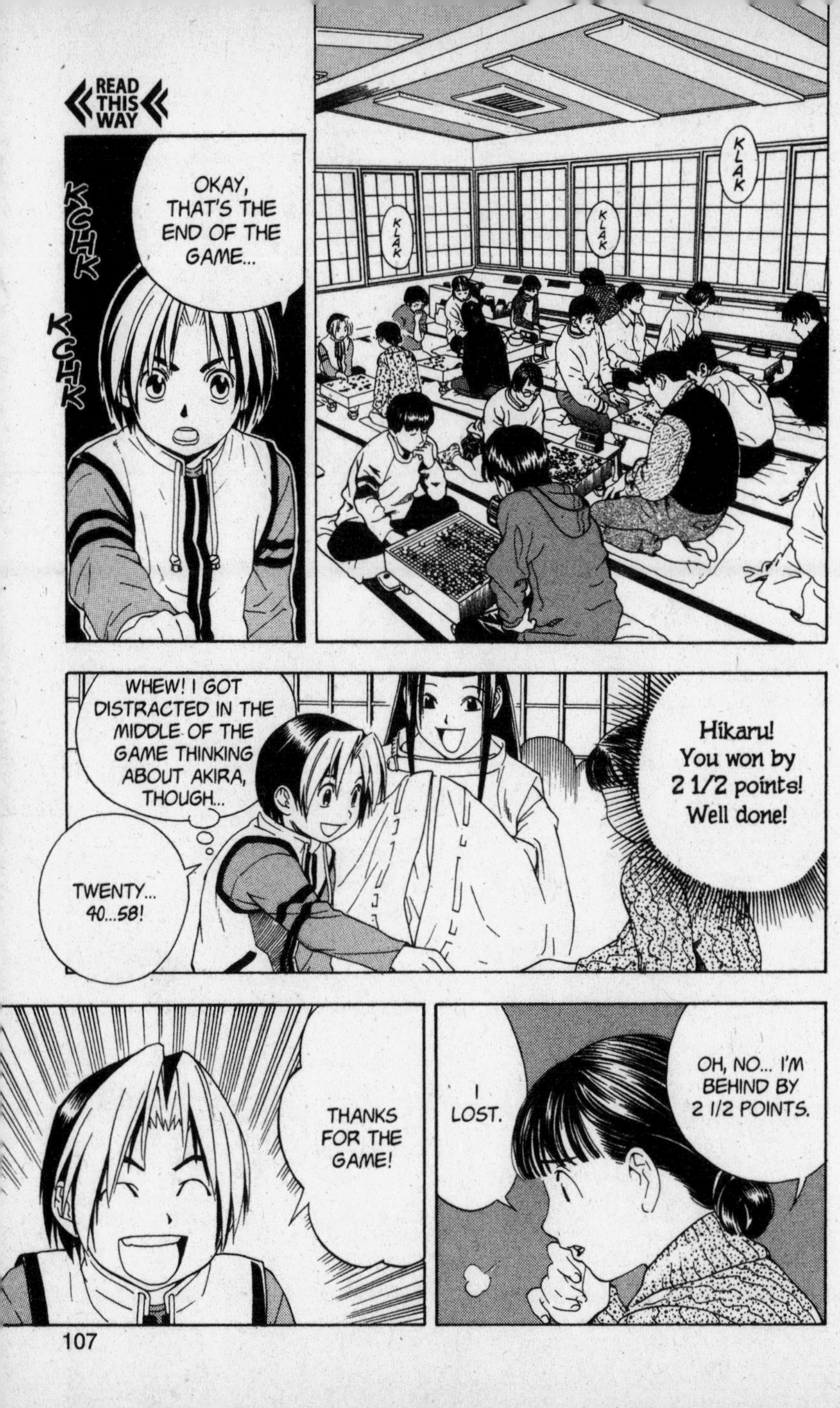
READ THIS WAY
KLAK
KLAK
KLAK
OKAY, THAT'S THE END OF THE GAME...
KCHK KCHK
Hikaru! You won by 2 1/2 points! Well done!
WHEW! I GOT DISTRACTED IN THE MIDDLE OF THE GAME THINKING ABOUT AKIRA, THOUGH...
TWENTY... 40...58!
OH, NO... I'M BEHIND BY 2 1/2 POINTS.
I LOST.
THANKS FOR THE GAME!

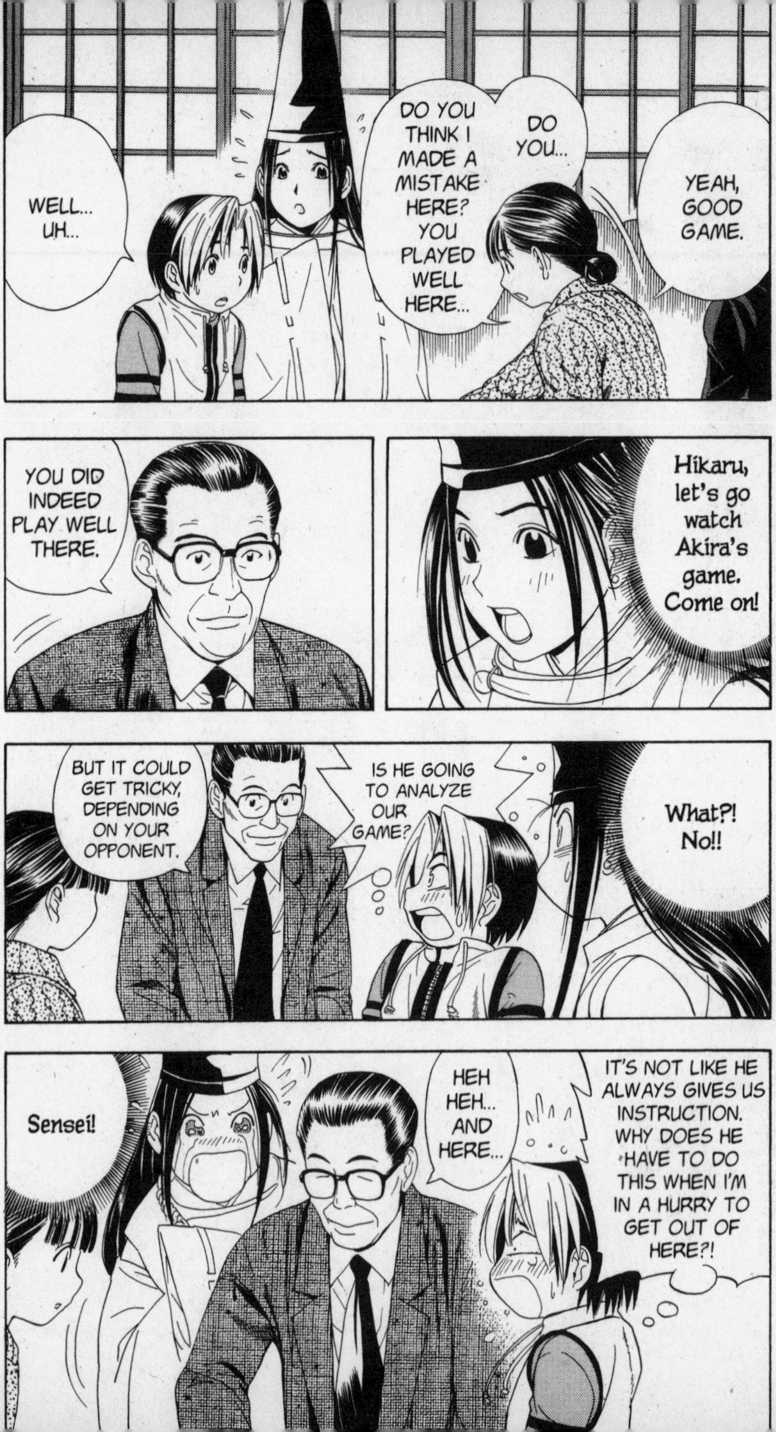
YEAH, GOOD GAME.
DO YOU...
DO YOU THINK I MADE A MISTAKE HERE? YOU PLAYED WELL HERE...
WELL... UH...
Hikaru, let's go watch Akira's game. Come on!
YOU DID INDEED PLAY WELL THERE.
What?! No!!
IS HE GOING TO ANALYZE OUR GAME?
BUT IT COULD GET TRICKY, DEPENDING ON YOUR OPPONENT.
IT'S NOT LIKE HE ALWAYS GIVES US INSTRUCTION. WHY DOES HE HAVE TO DO THIS WHEN I'M IN A HURRY TO GET OUT OF HERE?!
HEH HEH... AND HERE...
Sensei!

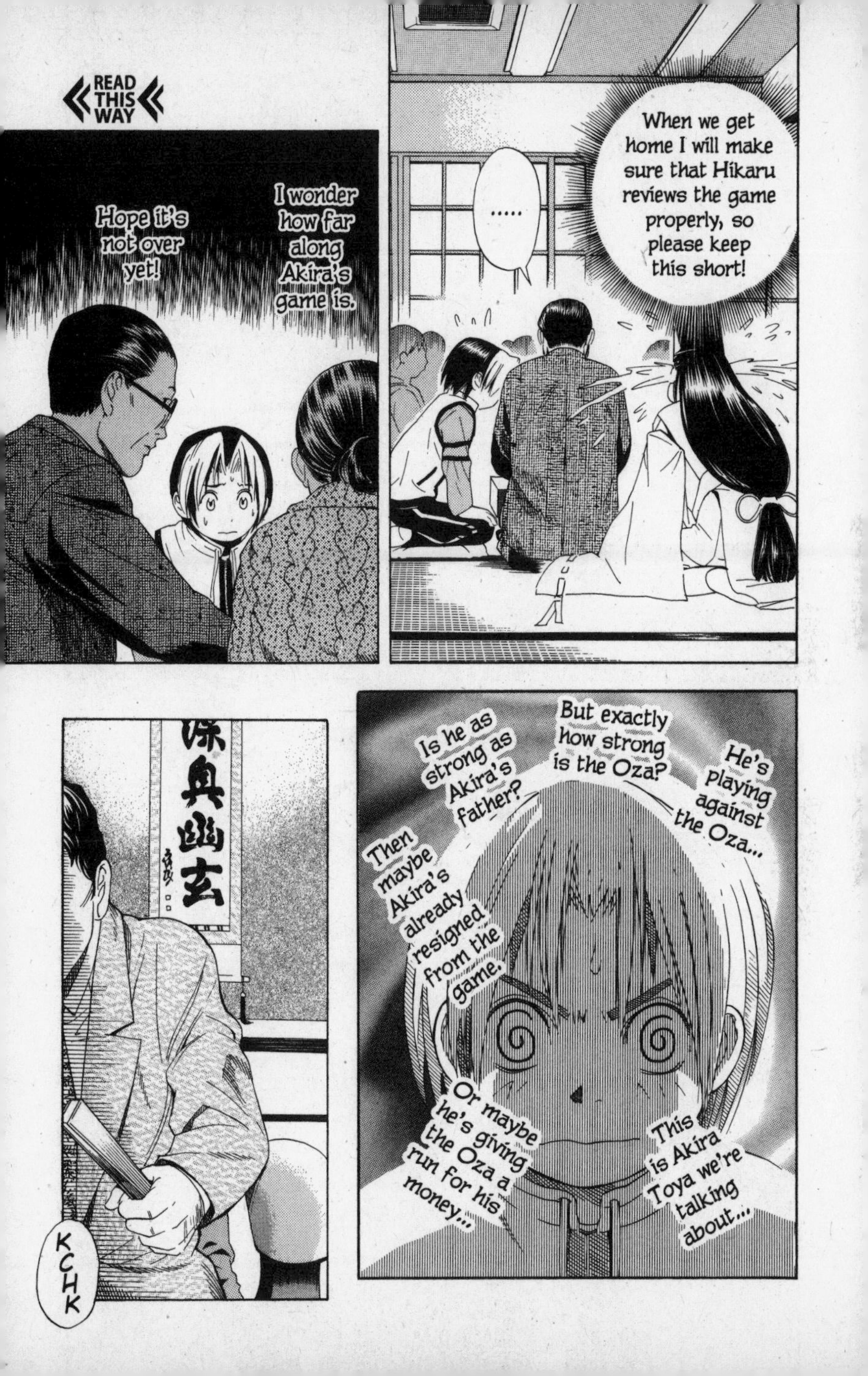
READ THIS WAY
When we get home I will make sure that Hikaru reviews the game properly, so please keep this short!
.....
I wonder how far along Akira's game is.
Hope it's not over yet!
He's playing against the Oza...
But exactly how strong is the Oza?
Is he as strong as Akira's father?
Then maybe Akira's already resigned from the game.
This is Akira Toya we're talking about...
Or maybe he's giving the Oza a run for his money...
深奥幽玄
KCHK

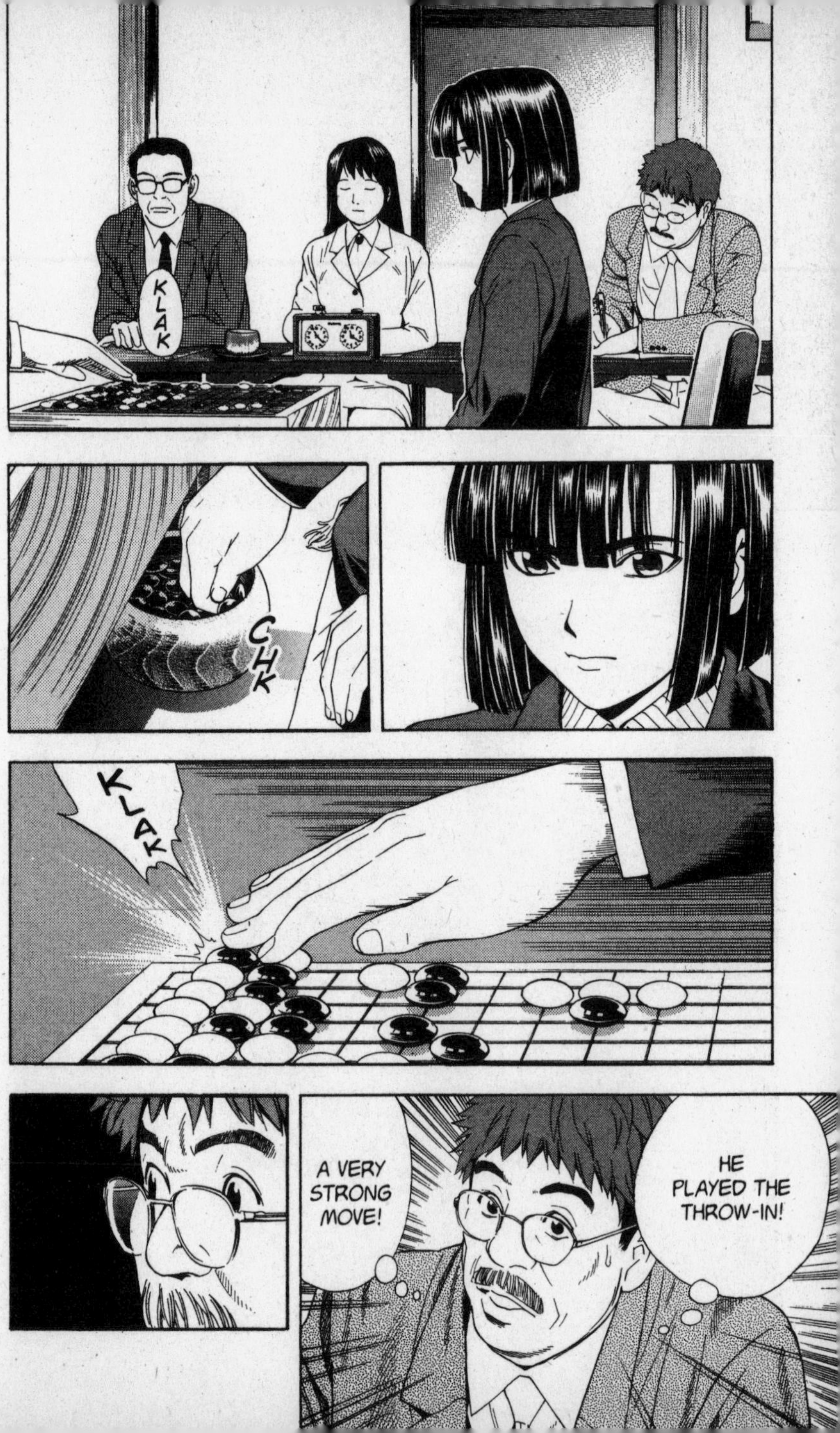
KLAK
CHK
KLAK
HE PLAYED THE THROW-IN!
A VERY STRONG MOVE!

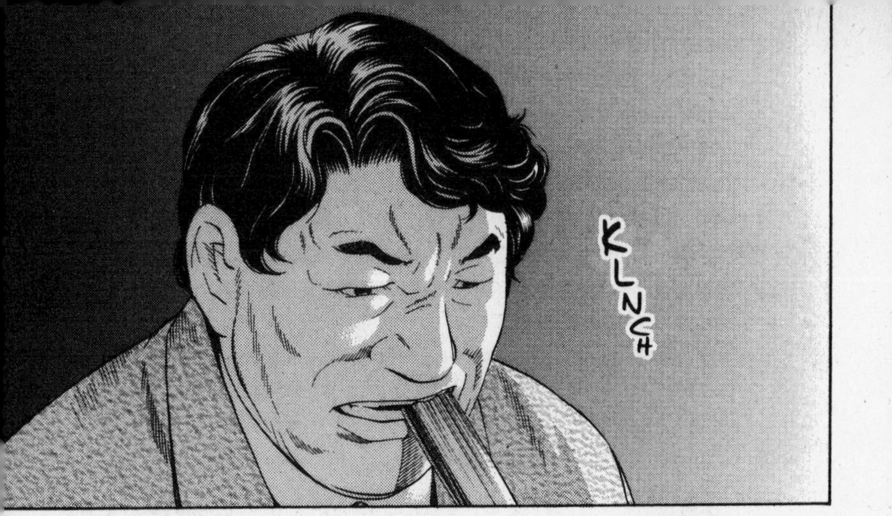
KLNCH
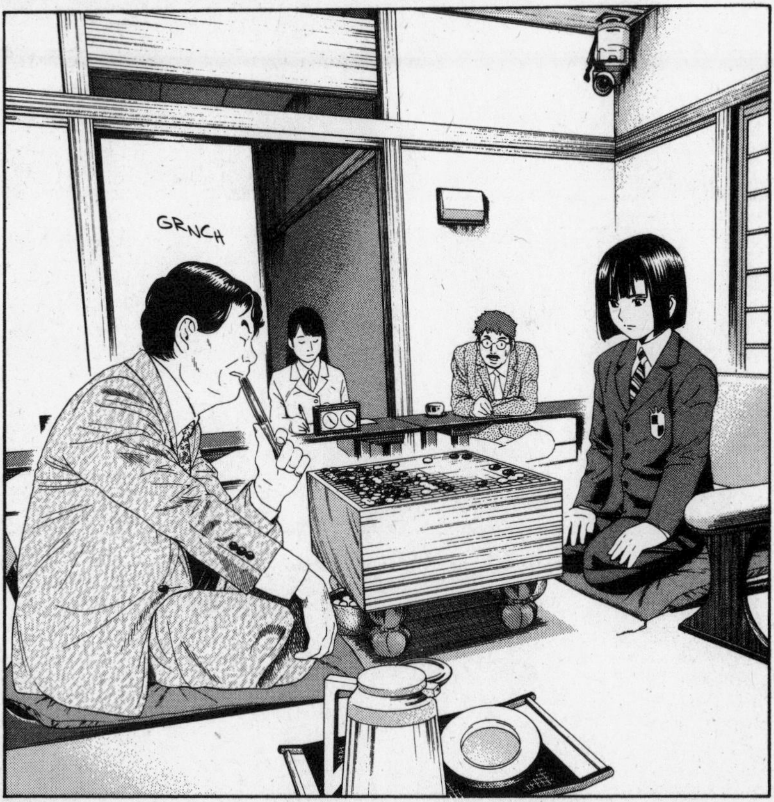
GRNCH

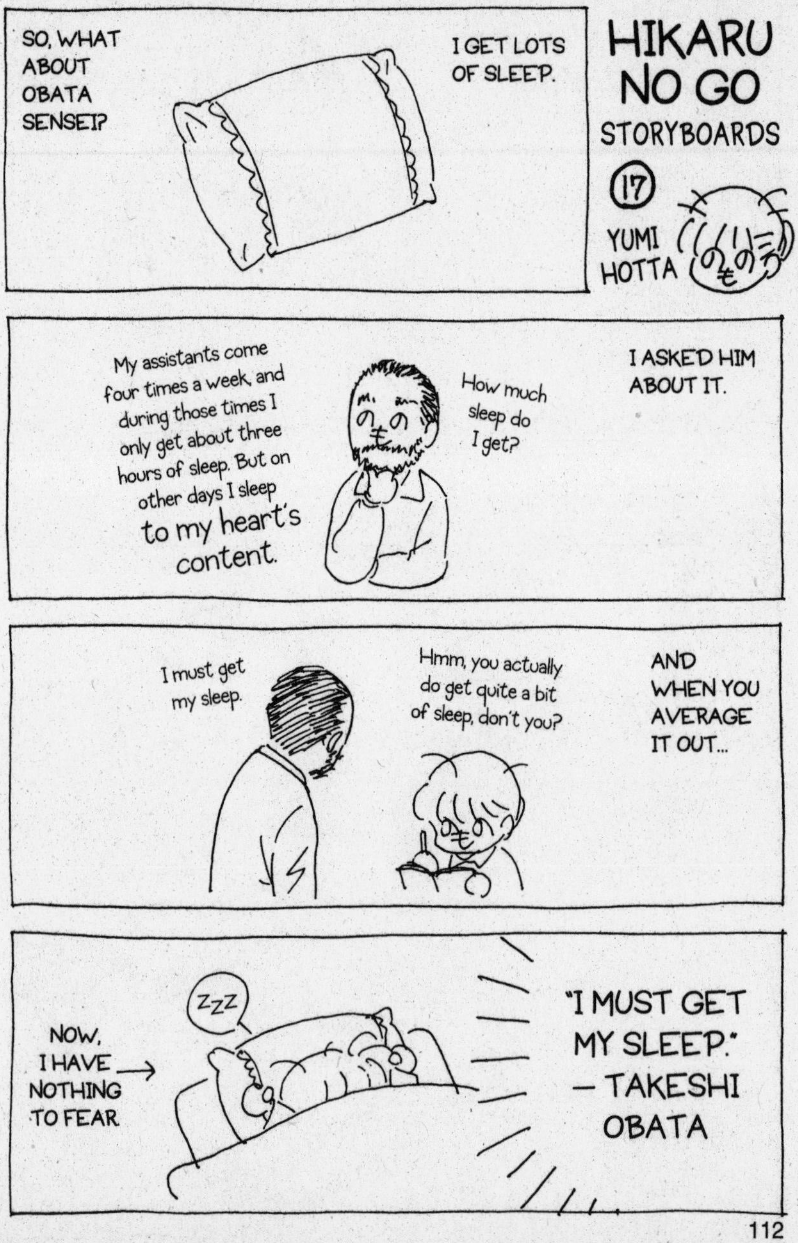
HIKARU NO GO STORYBOARDS
17
YUMI HOTTA
I GET LOTS OF SLEEP.
SO, WHAT ABOUT OBATA SENSEI?
I ASKED HIM ABOUT IT.
How much sleep do I get?
My assistants come four times a week, and during those times I only get about three hours of sleep. But on other days I sleep to my heart's content.
AND WHEN YOU AVERAGE IT OUT...
Hmm, you actually do get quite a bit of sleep, don't you?
I must get my sleep.
"I MUST GET MY SLEEP." — TAKESHI OBATA
ZZZ
NOW, I HAVE NOTHING TO FEAR

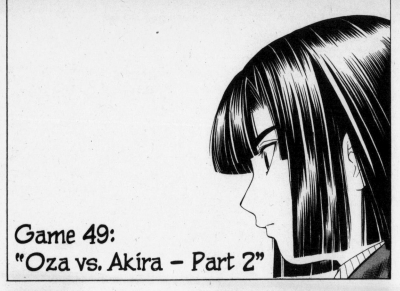

Game 49:
"Oza vs. Akira – Part 2"

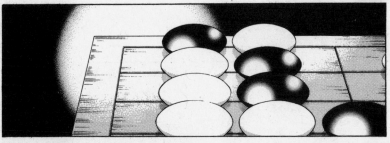

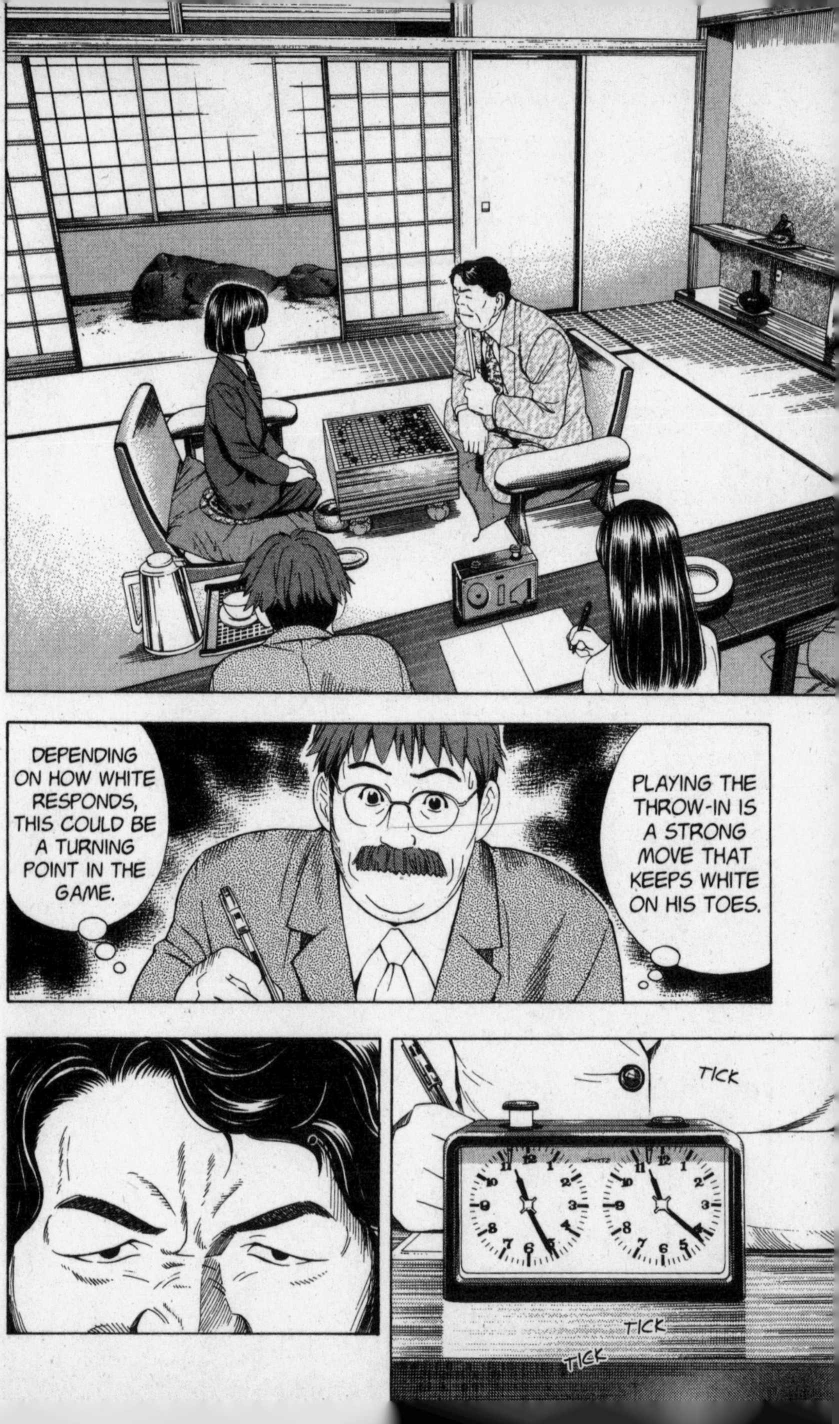
PLAYING THE THROW-IN IS A STRONG MOVE THAT KEEPS WHITE ON HIS TOES.
DEPENDING ON HOW WHITE RESPONDS, THIS COULD BE A TURNING POINT IN THE GAME.
TICK
TICK
TICK

READ THIS WAY

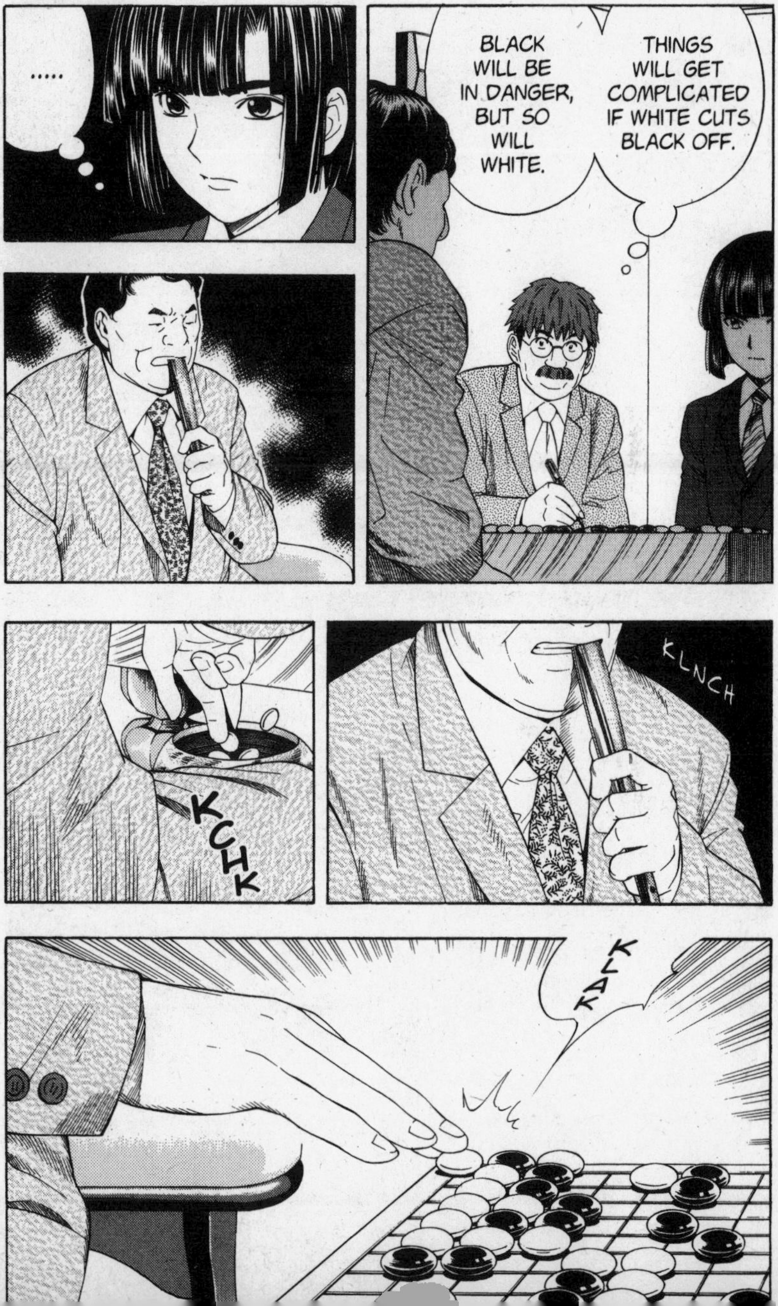
THINGS WILL GET COMPLICATED IF WHITE CUTS BLACK OFF.
BLACK WILL BE IN DANGER, BUT SO WILL WHITE.
.....
KLNCH
KCHK
KLAK

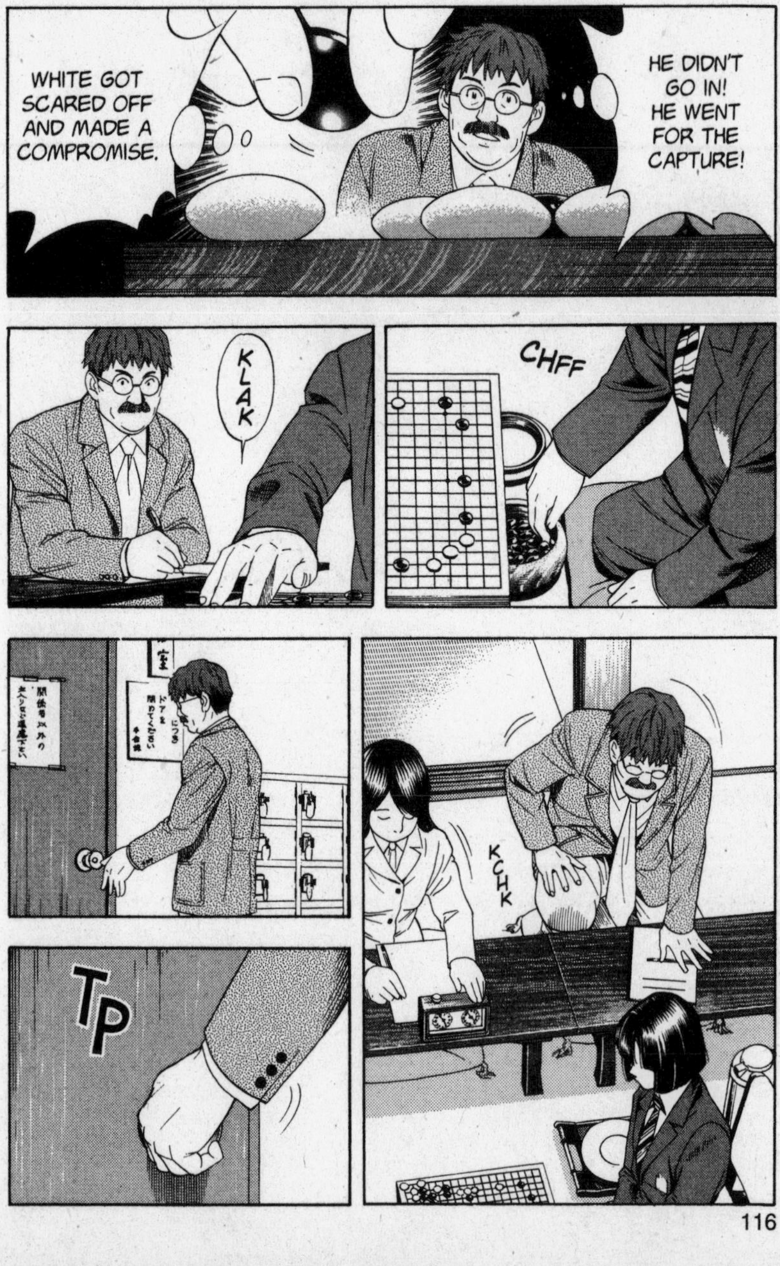
HE DIDN'T GO IN! HE WENT FOR THE CAPTURE!
WHITE GOT SCARED OFF AND MADE A COMPROMISE.
CHFF
KLAK
KCHK
TP

READ THIS WAY

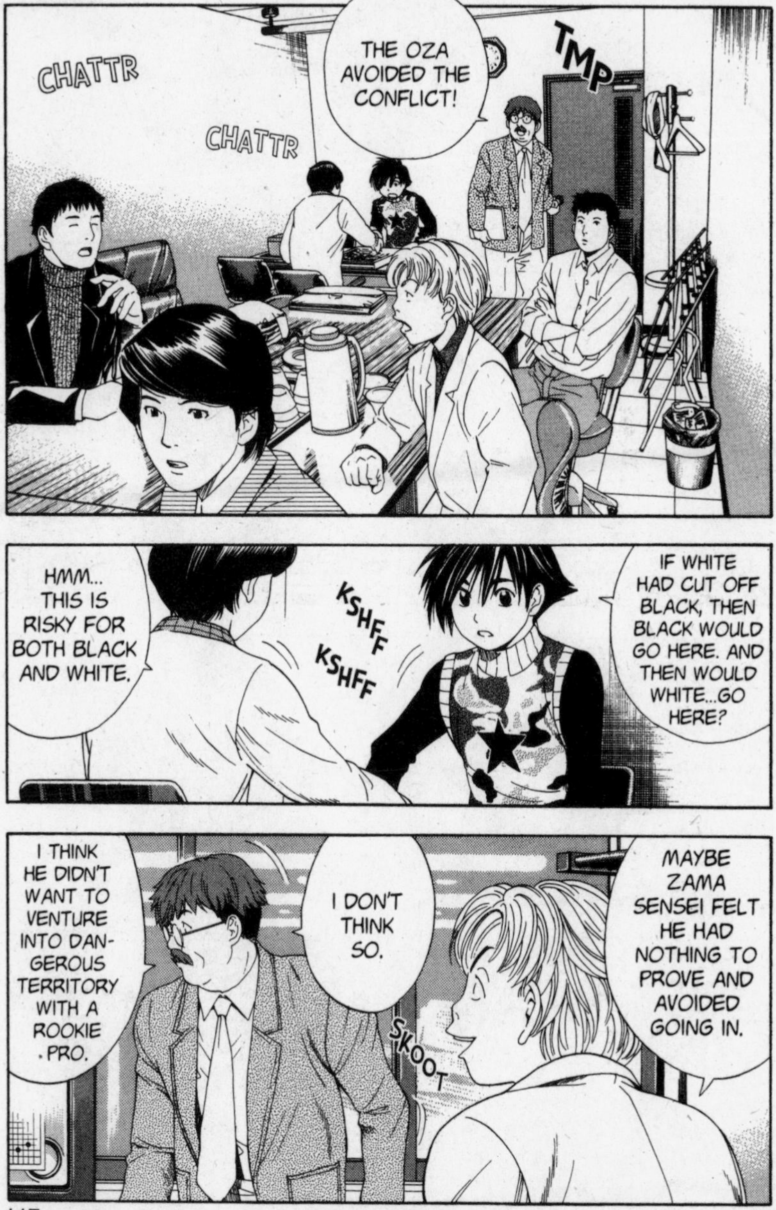
TMP
THE OZA AVOIDED THE CONFLICT!
CHATTR
CHATTR
IF WHITE HAD CUT OFF BLACK, THEN BLACK WOULD GO HERE. AND THEN WOULD WHITE...GO HERE?
KSHFF
KSHFF
HMM... THIS IS RISKY FOR BOTH BLACK AND WHITE.
MAYBE ZAMA SENSEI FELT HE HAD NOTHING TO PROVE AND AVOIDED GOING IN.
SKOOT
I DON'T THINK SO.
I THINK HE DIDN'T WANT TO VENTURE INTO DANGEROUS TERRITORY WITH A ROOKIE PRO.

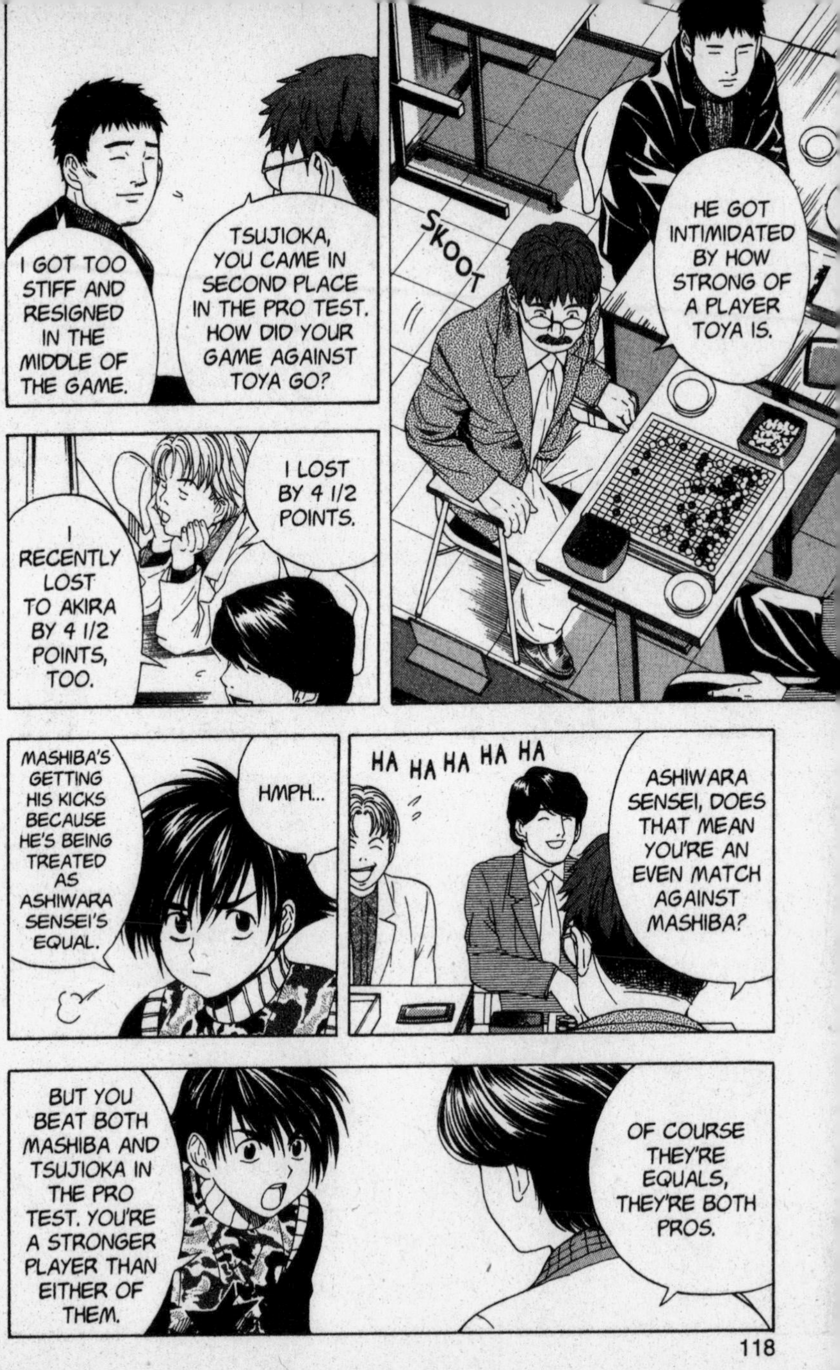
SKOOT
HE GOT INTIMIDATED BY HOW STRONG OF A PLAYER TOYA IS.
TSUJIOKA, YOU CAME IN SECOND PLACE IN THE PRO TEST. HOW DID YOUR GAME AGAINST TOYA GO?
I GOT TOO STIFF AND RESIGNED IN THE MIDDLE OF THE GAME.
I LOST BY 4 1/2 POINTS.
I RECENTLY LOST TO AKIRA BY 4 1/2 POINTS, TOO.
ASHIWARA SENSEI, DOES THAT MEAN YOU'RE AN EVEN MATCH AGAINST MASHIBA?
HA HA HA HA HA
HMPH...
MASHIBA'S GETTING HIS KICKS BECAUSE HE'S BEING TREATED AS ASHIWARA SENSEI'S EQUAL.
OF COURSE THEY'RE EQUALS, THEY'RE BOTH PROS.
BUT YOU BEAT BOTH MASHIBA AND TSUJIOKA IN THE PRO TEST. YOU'RE A STRONGER PLAYER THAN EITHER OF THEM.

READ THIS WAY

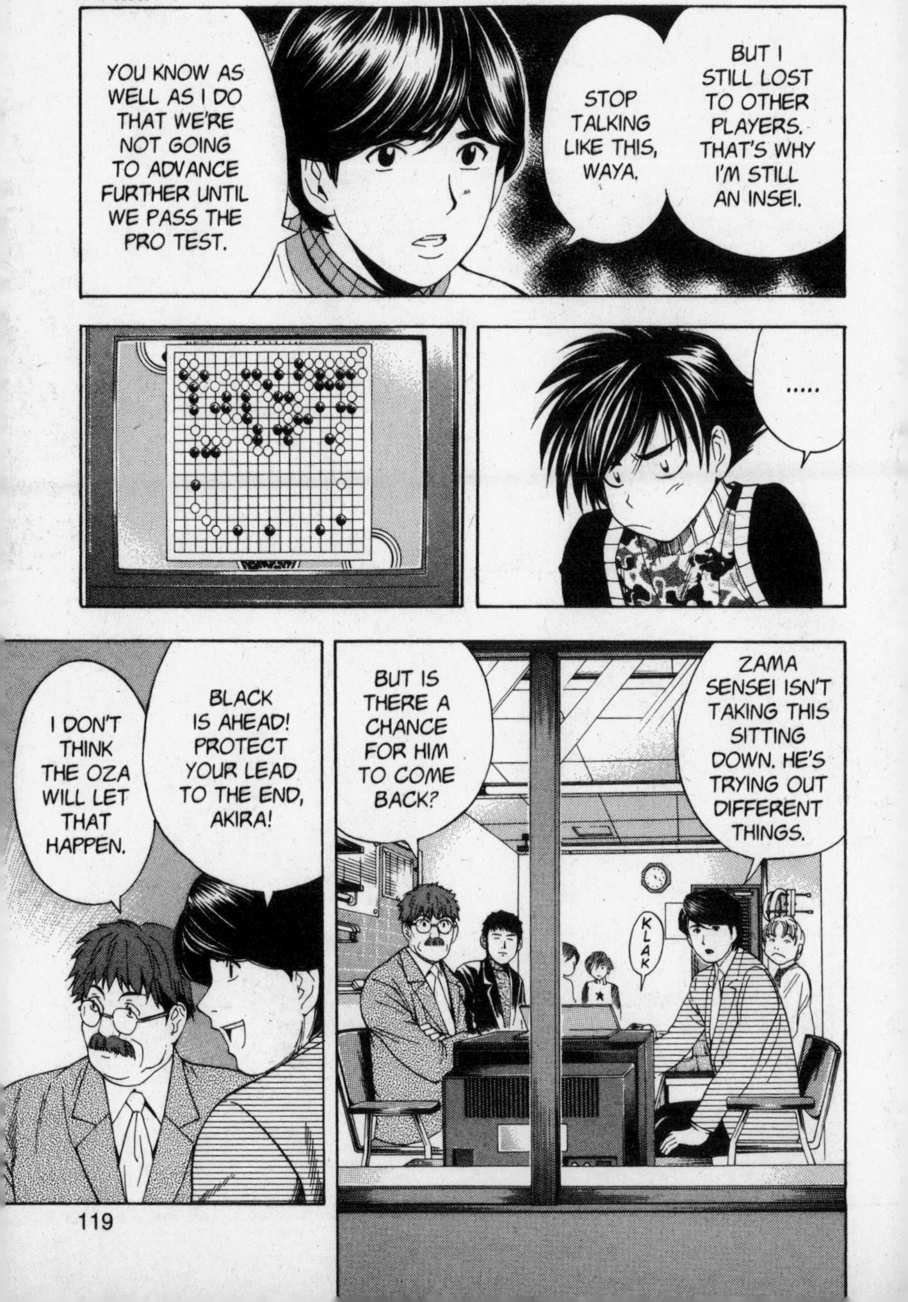
BUT I STILL LOST TO OTHER PLAYERS. THAT'S WHY I'M STILL AN INSEI.
STOP TALKING LIKE THIS, WAYA.
YOU KNOW AS WELL AS I DO THAT WE'RE NOT GOING TO ADVANCE FURTHER UNTIL WE PASS THE PRO TEST.
.....
ZAMA SENSEI ISN'T TAKING THIS SITTING DOWN. HE'S TRYING OUT DIFFERENT THINGS.
KLAK
BUT IS THERE A CHANCE FOR HIM TO COME BACK?
BLACK IS AHEAD! PROTECT YOUR LEAD TO THE END, AKIRA!
I DON'T THINK THE OZA WILL LET THAT HAPPEN.

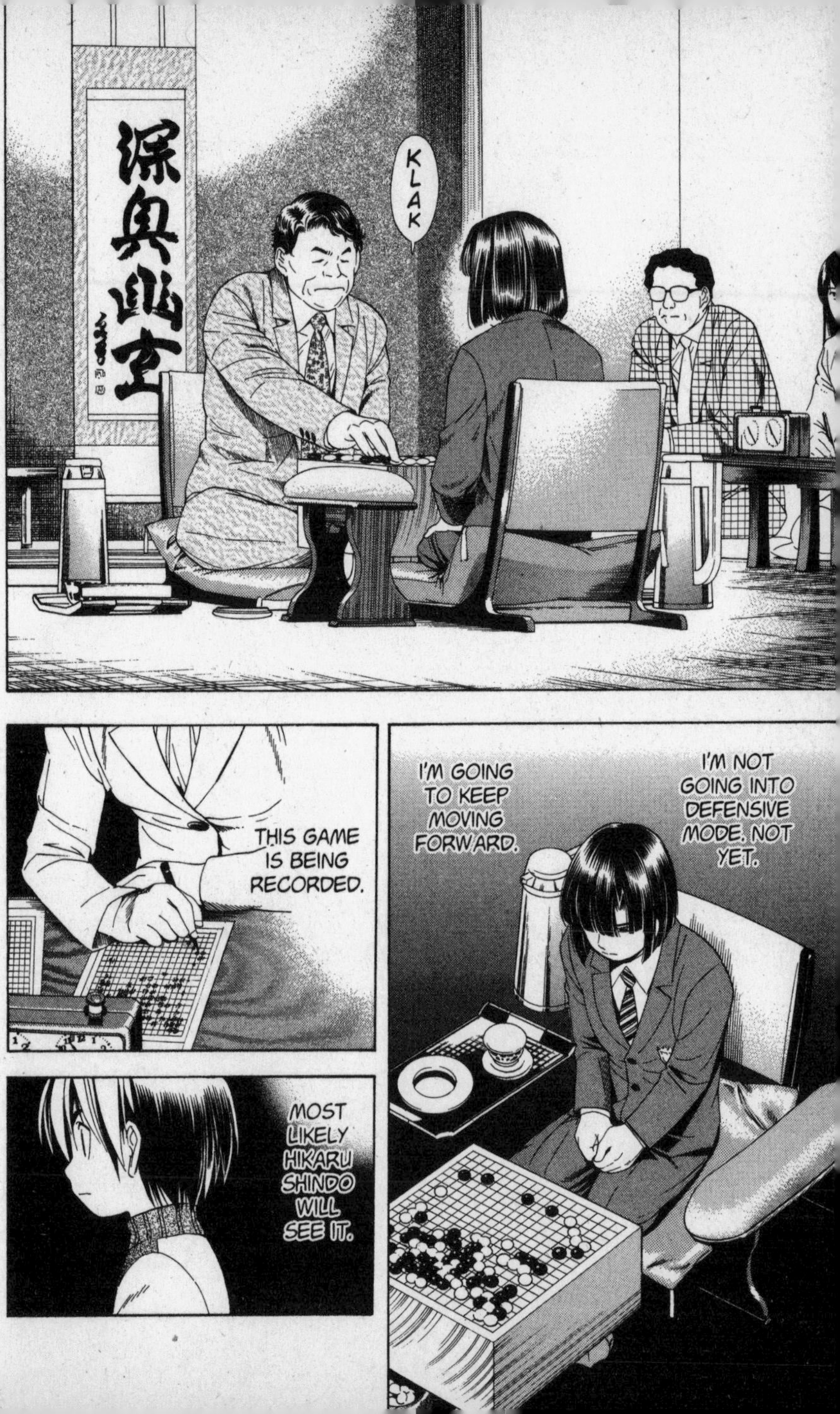
深奥幽玄
KLAK
I'M NOT GOING INTO DEFENSIVE MODE. NOT YET.
I'M GOING TO KEEP MOVING FORWARD.
THIS GAME IS BEING RECORDED.
MOST LIKELY HIKARU SHINDO WILL SEE IT.

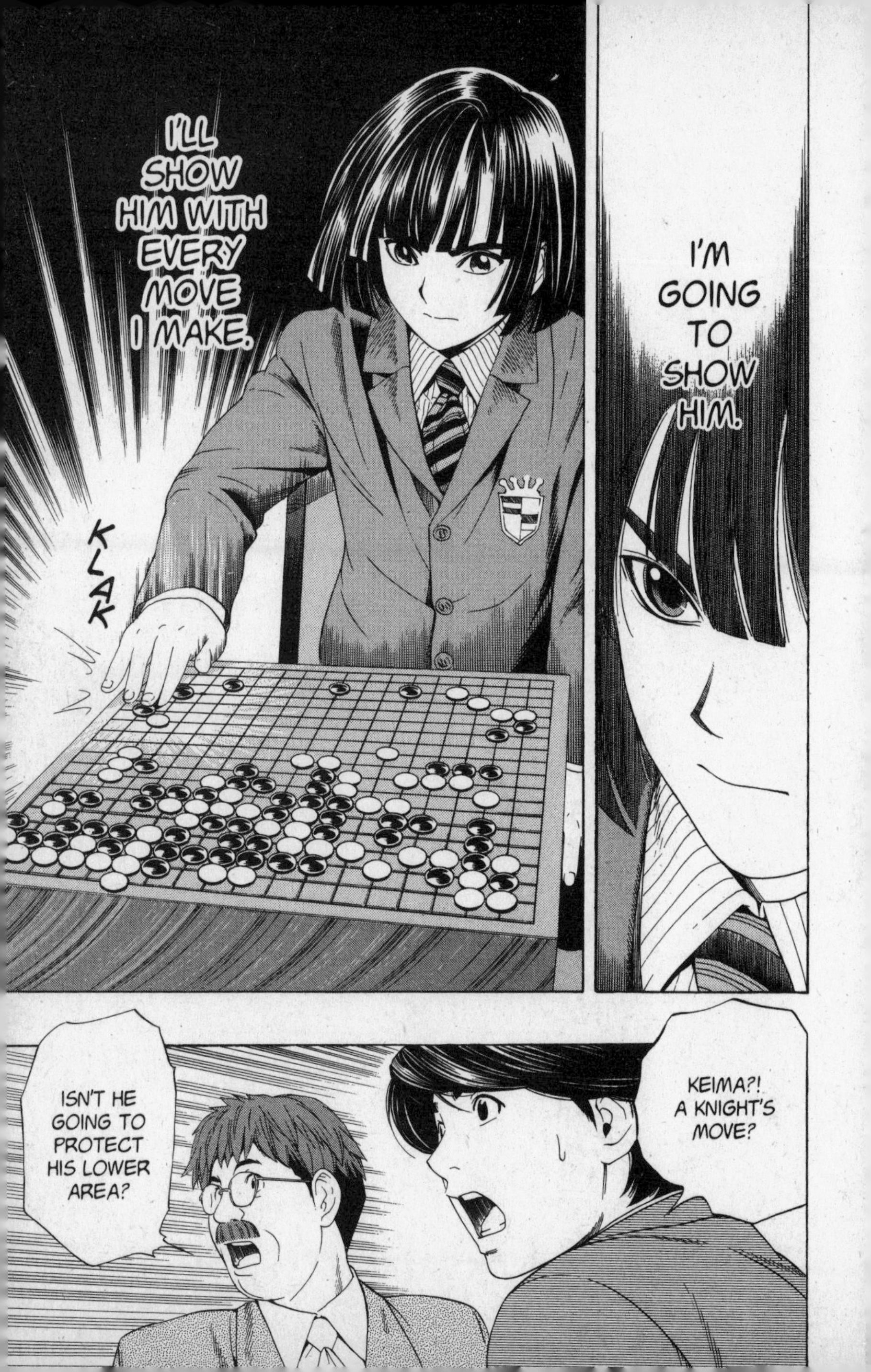
I'M GOING TO SHOW HIM.
I'LL SHOW HIM WITH EVERY MOVE I MAKE.
KLAK
KEIMA?! A KNIGHT'S MOVE?
ISN'T HE GOING TO PROTECT HIS LOWER AREA?

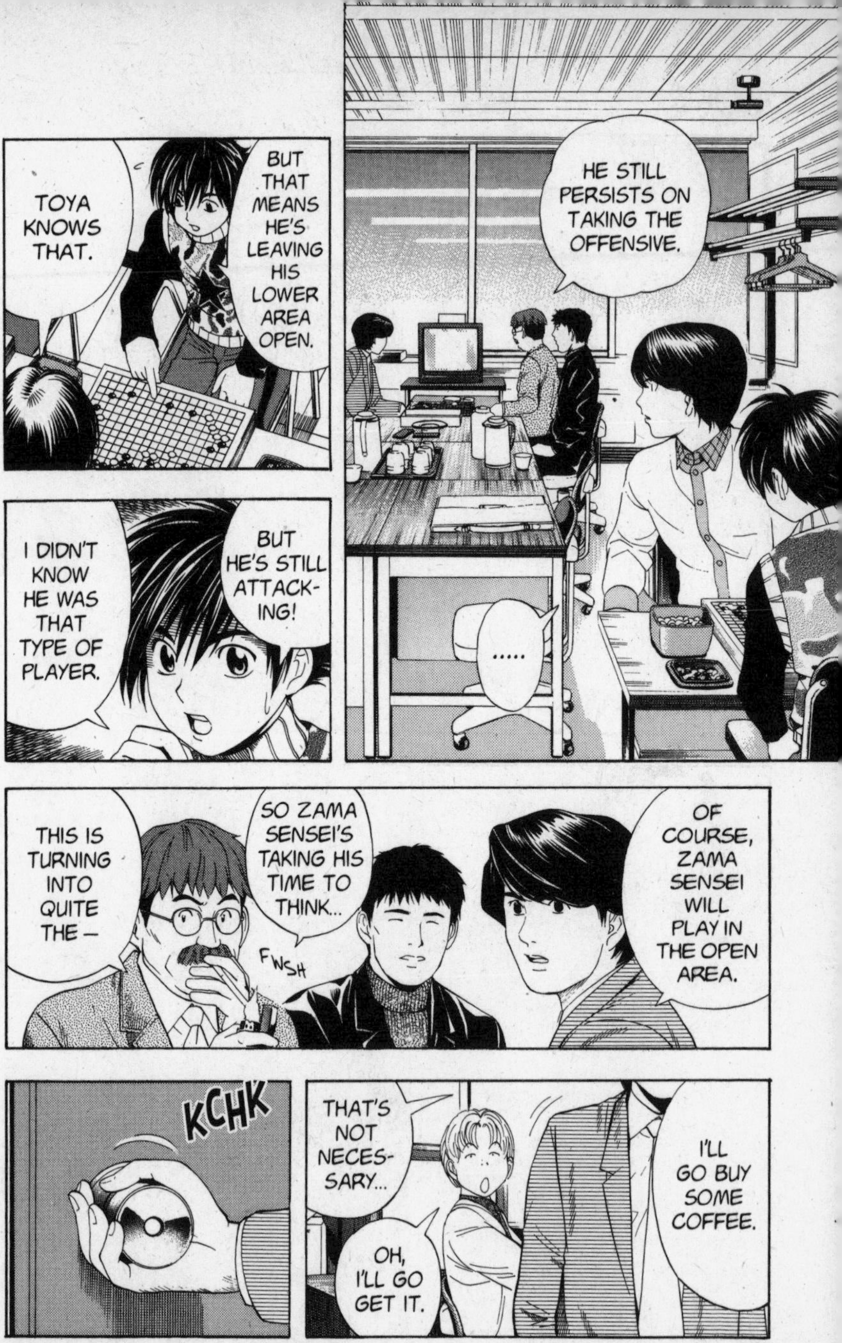
HE STILL PERSISTS ON TAKING THE OFFENSIVE.
.....
BUT THAT MEANS HE'S LEAVING HIS LOWER AREA OPEN.
TOYA KNOWS THAT.
BUT HE'S STILL ATTACK-ING!
I DIDN'T KNOW HE WAS THAT TYPE OF PLAYER.
OF COURSE, ZAMA SENSEI WILL PLAY IN THE OPEN AREA.
SO ZAMA SENSEI'S TAKING HIS TIME TO THINK...
FWSH
THIS IS TURNING INTO QUITE THE —
I'LL GO BUY SOME COFFEE.
THAT'S NOT NECES-SARY...
OH, I'LL GO GET IT.
KCHK

READ THIS WAY

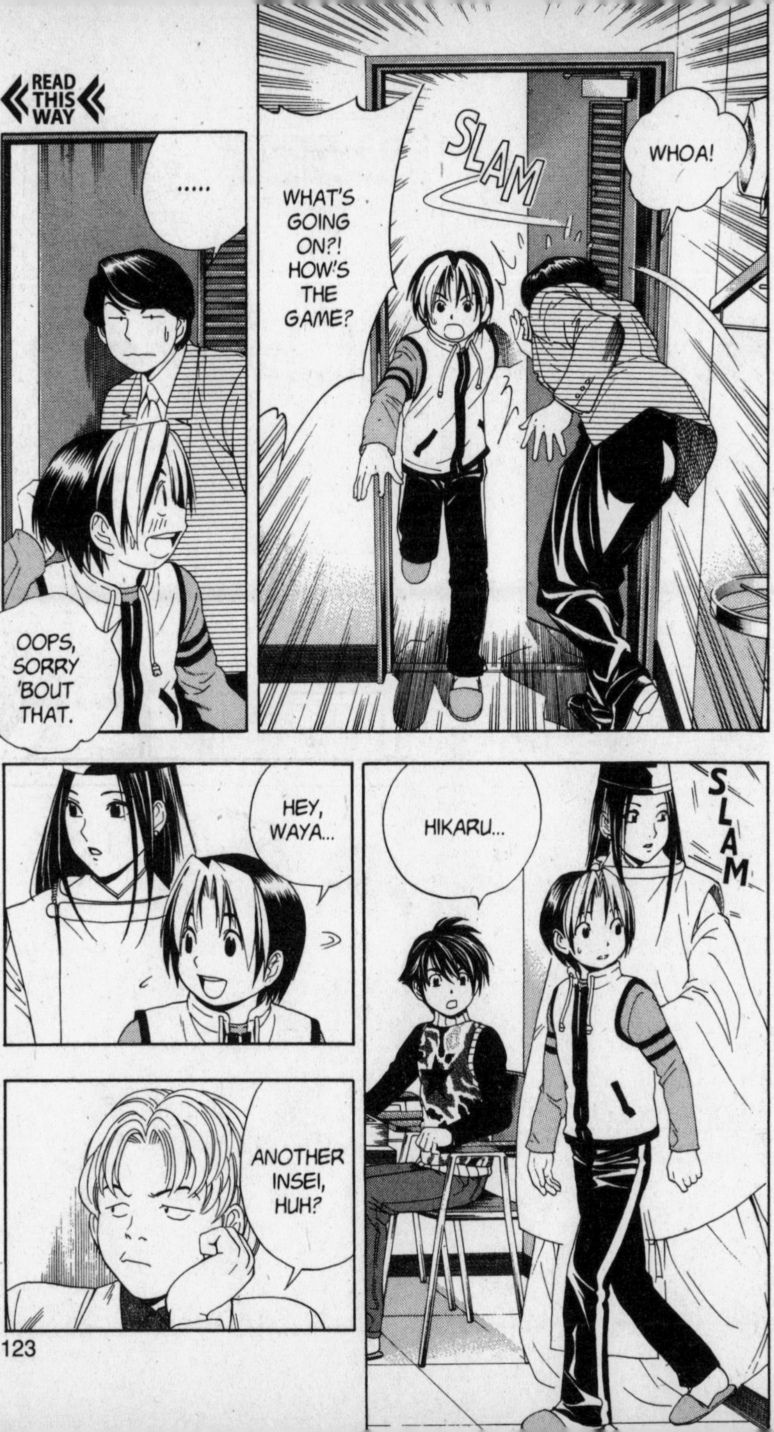
WHOA!
SLAM
WHAT'S GOING ON?! HOW'S THE GAME?
.....
OOPS, SORRY 'BOUT THAT.
SLAM
HIKARU...
HEY, WAYA...
ANOTHER INSEI, HUH?

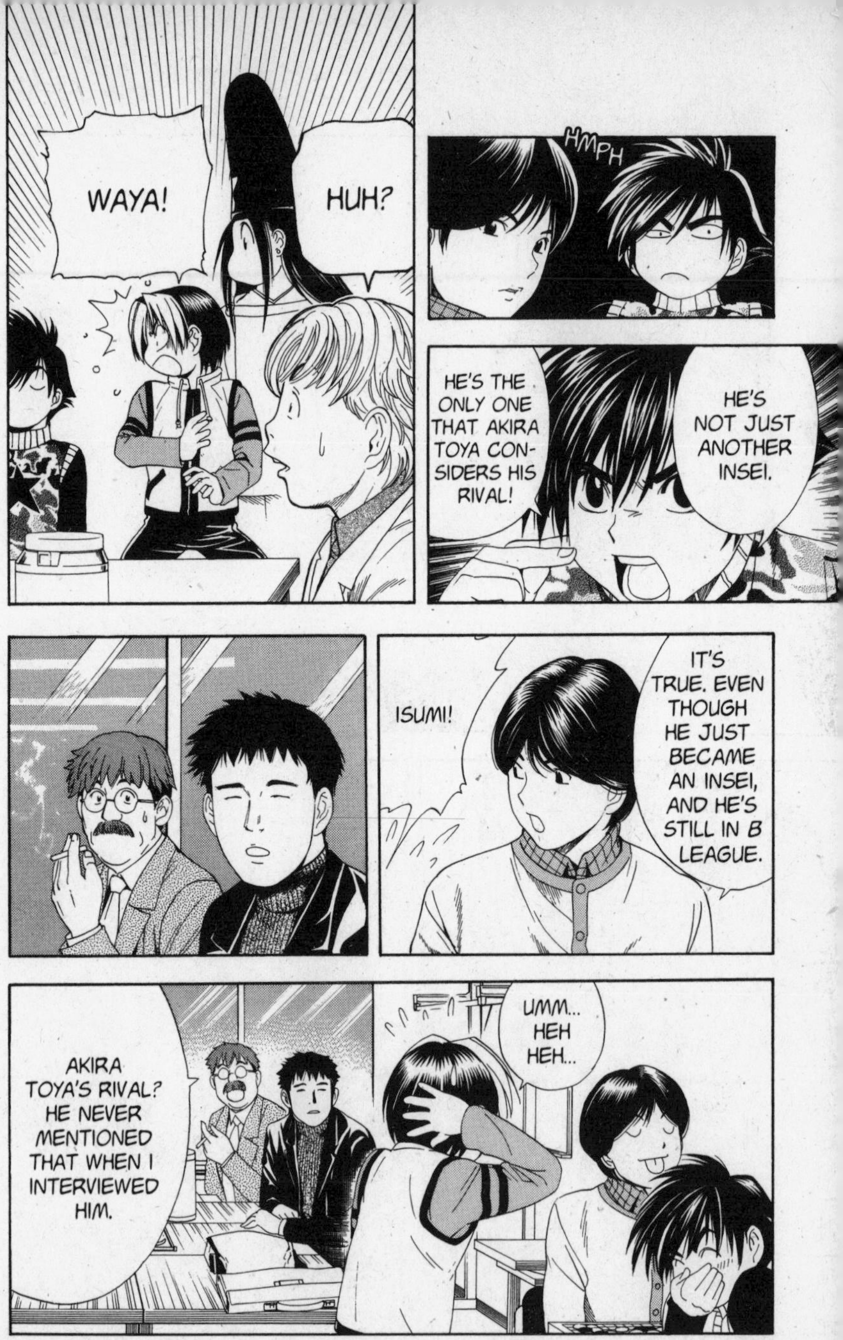
HMPH
HE'S NOT JUST ANOTHER INSEI.
HE'S THE ONLY ONE THAT AKIRA TOYA CONSIDERS HIS RIVAL!
HUH?
WAYA!
IT'S TRUE. EVEN THOUGH HE JUST BECAME AN INSEI, AND HE'S STILL IN B LEAGUE.
ISUMI!
UMM... HEH HEH...
AKIRA TOYA'S RIVAL? HE NEVER MENTIONED THAT WHEN I INTERVIEWED HIM.

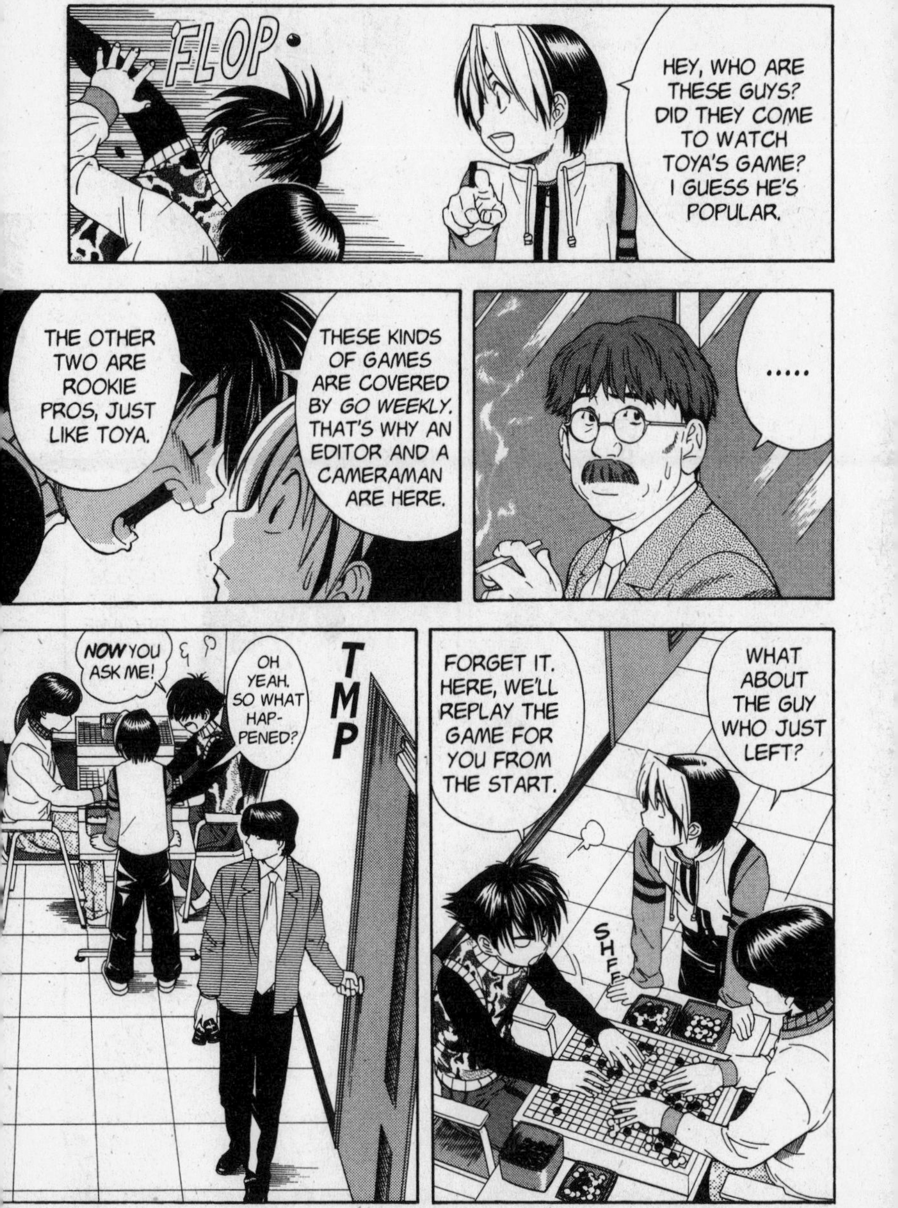
HEY, WHO ARE THESE GUYS? DID THEY COME TO WATCH TOYA'S GAME? I GUESS HE'S POPULAR.
FLOP
.....
THESE KINDS OF GAMES ARE COVERED BY GO WEEKLY. THAT'S WHY AN EDITOR AND A CAMERAMAN ARE HERE.
THE OTHER TWO ARE ROOKIE PROS, JUST LIKE TOYA.
WHAT ABOUT THE GUY WHO JUST LEFT?
FORGET IT. HERE, WE'LL REPLAY THE GAME FOR YOU FROM THE START.
SHFF
TMP
OH YEAH. SO WHAT HAP-PENED?
NOW YOU ASK ME!

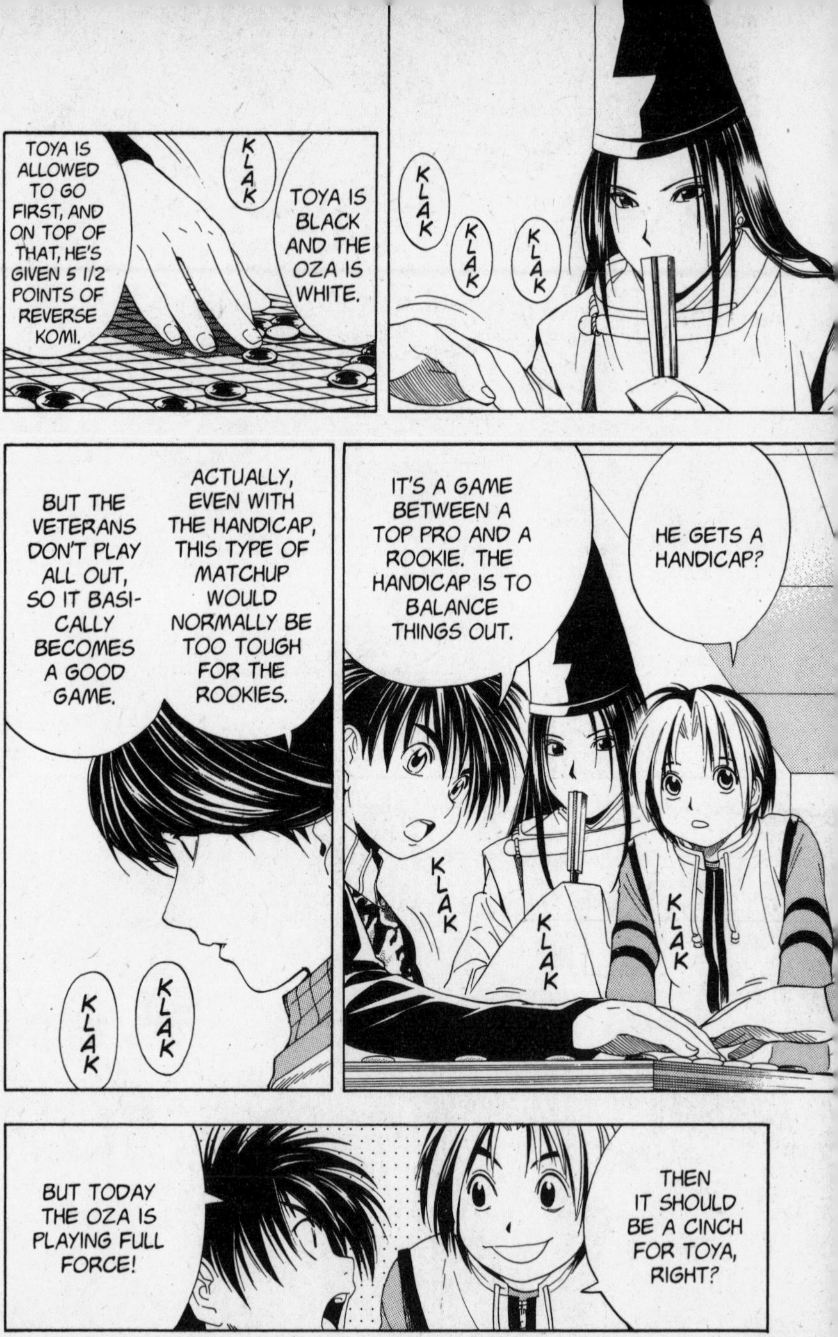
KLAK
KLAK
KLAK
KLAK
TOYA IS BLACK AND THE OZA IS WHITE.
TOYA IS ALLOWED TO GO FIRST, AND ON TOP OF THAT, HE'S GIVEN 5 1/2 POINTS OF REVERSE KOMI.
HE GETS A HANDICAP?
IT'S A GAME BETWEEN A TOP PRO AND A ROOKIE. THE HANDICAP IS TO BALANCE THINGS OUT.
KLAK
KLAK
KLAK
ACTUALLY, EVEN WITH THE HANDICAP, THIS TYPE OF MATCHUP WOULD NORMALLY BE TOO TOUGH FOR THE ROOKIES.
BUT THE VETERANS DON'T PLAY ALL OUT, SO IT BASICALLY BECOMES A GOOD GAME.
KLAK
KLAK
THEN IT SHOULD BE A CINCH FOR TOYA, RIGHT?
BUT TODAY THE OZA IS PLAYING FULL FORCE!

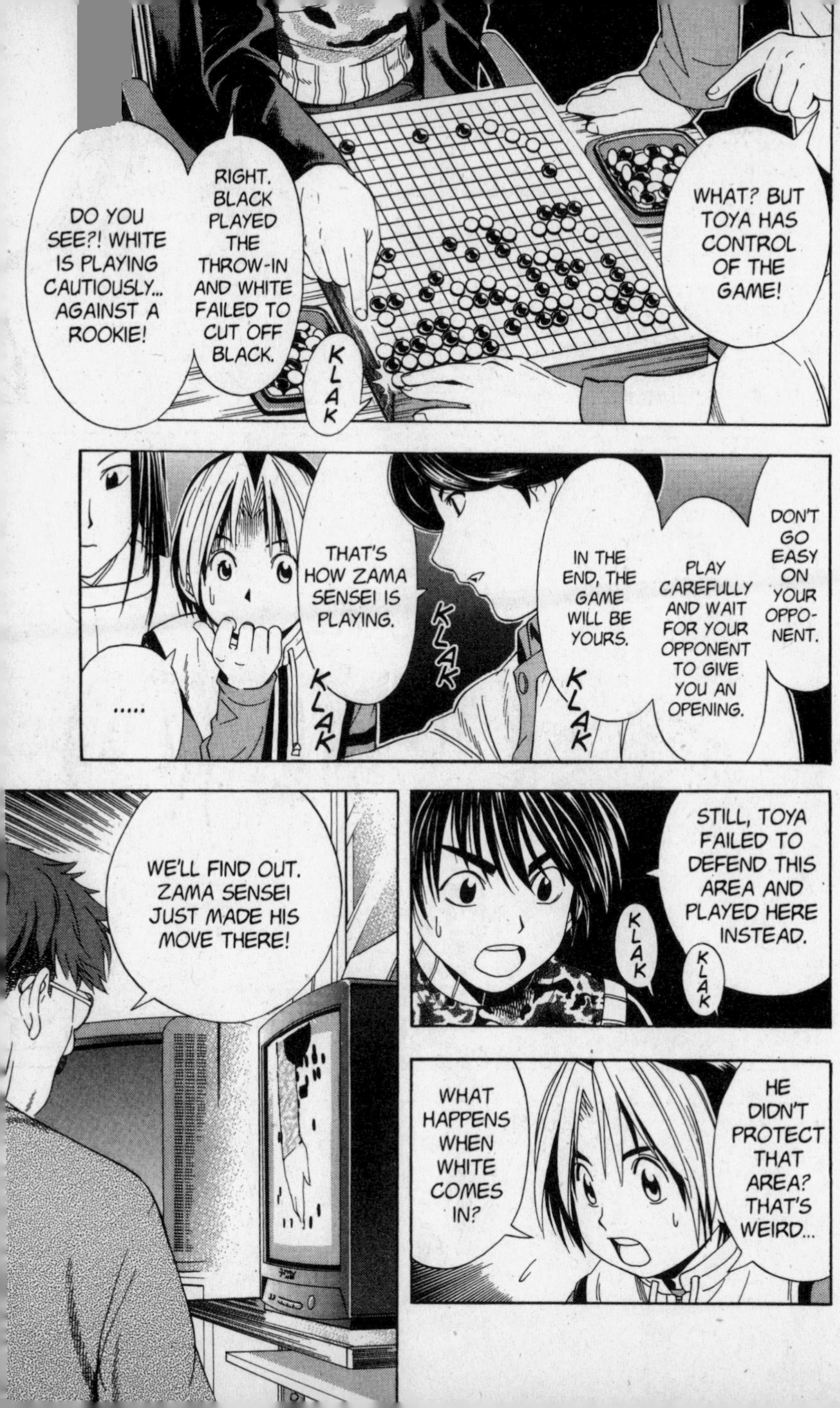
WHAT? BUT TOYA HAS CONTROL OF THE GAME!
RIGHT. BLACK PLAYED THE THROW-IN AND WHITE FAILED TO CUT OFF BLACK.
KLAK
DO YOU SEE?! WHITE IS PLAYING CAUTIOUSLY... AGAINST A ROOKIE!
DON'T GO EASY ON YOUR OPPONENT.
PLAY CAREFULLY AND WAIT FOR YOUR OPPONENT TO GIVE YOU AN OPENING.
IN THE END, THE GAME WILL BE YOURS.
KLAK
KLAK
THAT'S HOW ZAMA SENSEI IS PLAYING.
KLAK
.....
STILL, TOYA FAILED TO DEFEND THIS AREA AND PLAYED HERE INSTEAD.
KLAK
KLAK
HE DIDN'T PROTECT THAT AREA? THAT'S WEIRD...
WHAT HAPPENS WHEN WHITE COMES IN?
WE'LL FIND OUT. ZAMA SENSEI JUST MADE HIS MOVE THERE!

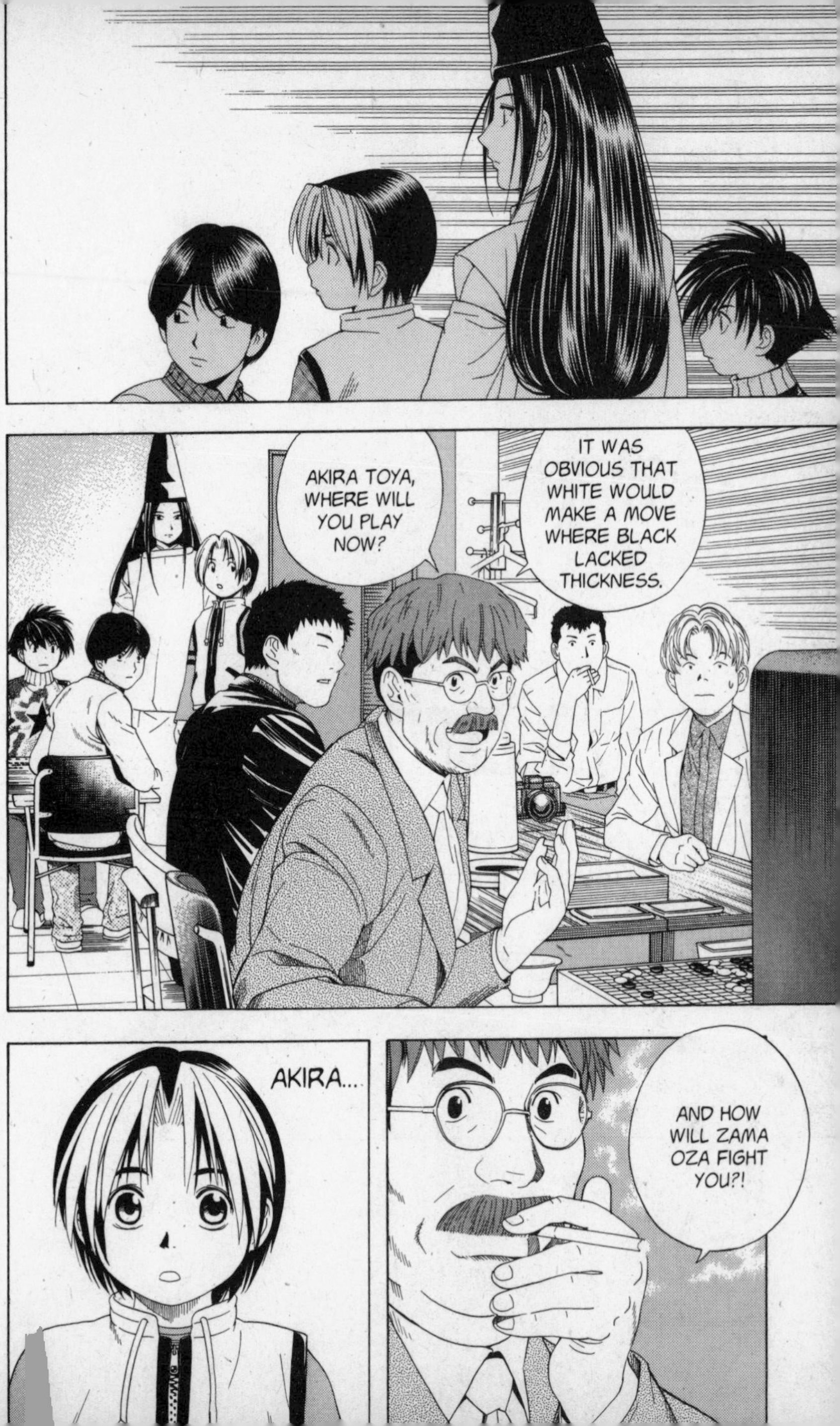
IT WAS OBVIOUS THAT WHITE WOULD MAKE A MOVE WHERE BLACK LACKED THICKNESS.
AKIRA TOYA, WHERE WILL YOU PLAY NOW?
AND HOW WILL ZAMA OZA FIGHT YOU?!
AKIRA...

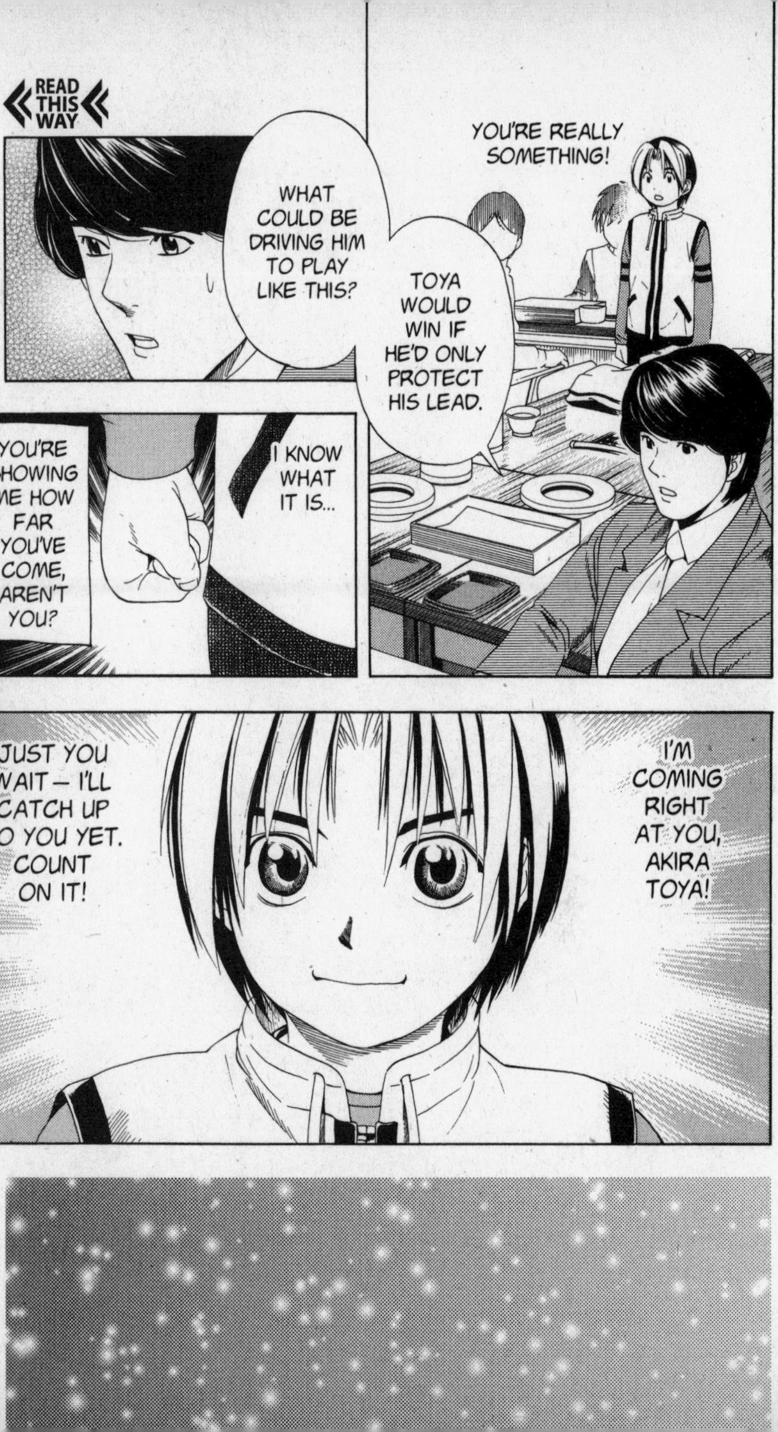
READ THIS WAY
YOU'RE REALLY SOMETHING!
TOYA WOULD WIN IF HE'D ONLY PROTECT HIS LEAD.
WHAT COULD BE DRIVING HIM TO PLAY LIKE THIS?
I KNOW WHAT IT IS...
YOU'RE SHOWING ME HOW FAR YOU'VE COME, AREN'T YOU?
I'M COMING RIGHT AT YOU, AKIRA TOYA!
JUST YOU WAIT— I'LL CATCH UP TO YOU YET. COUNT ON IT!

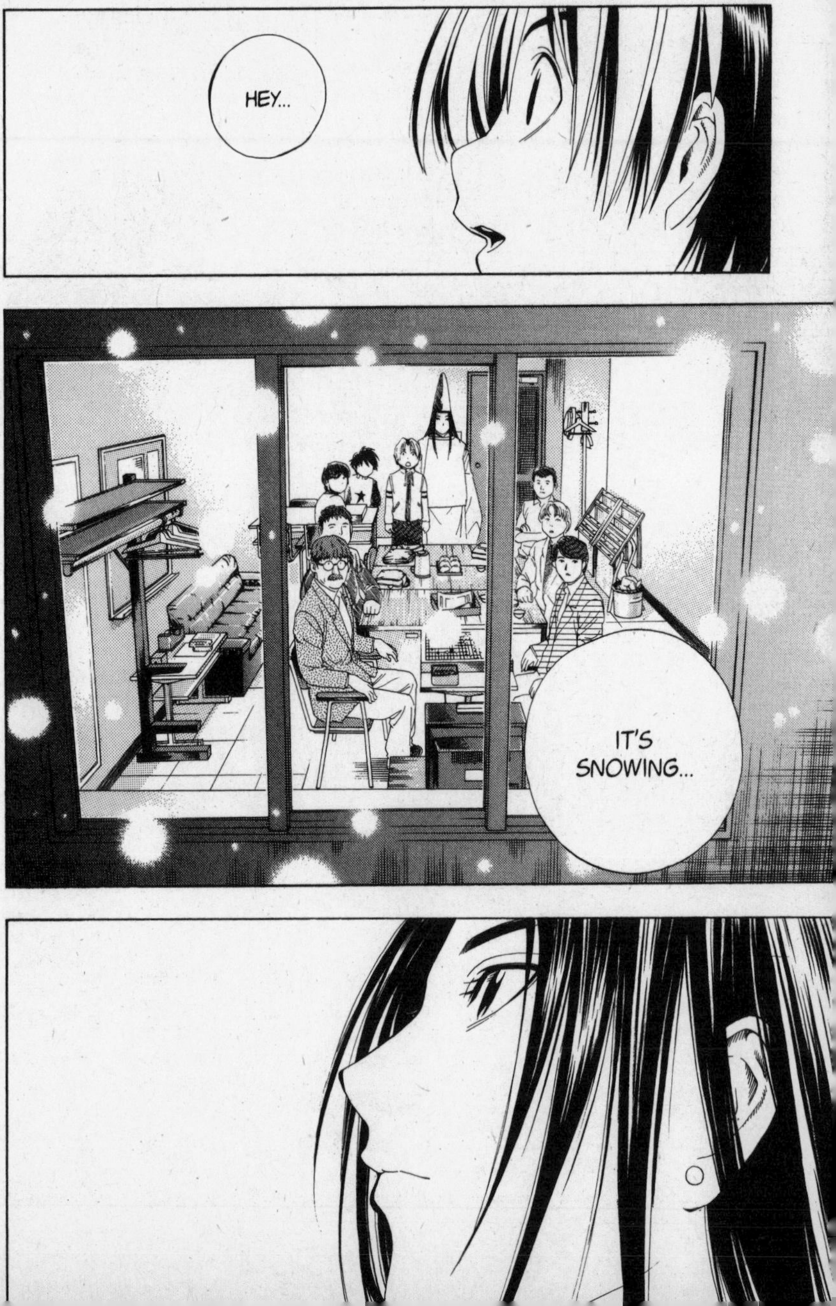
HEY...
IT'S SNOWING...

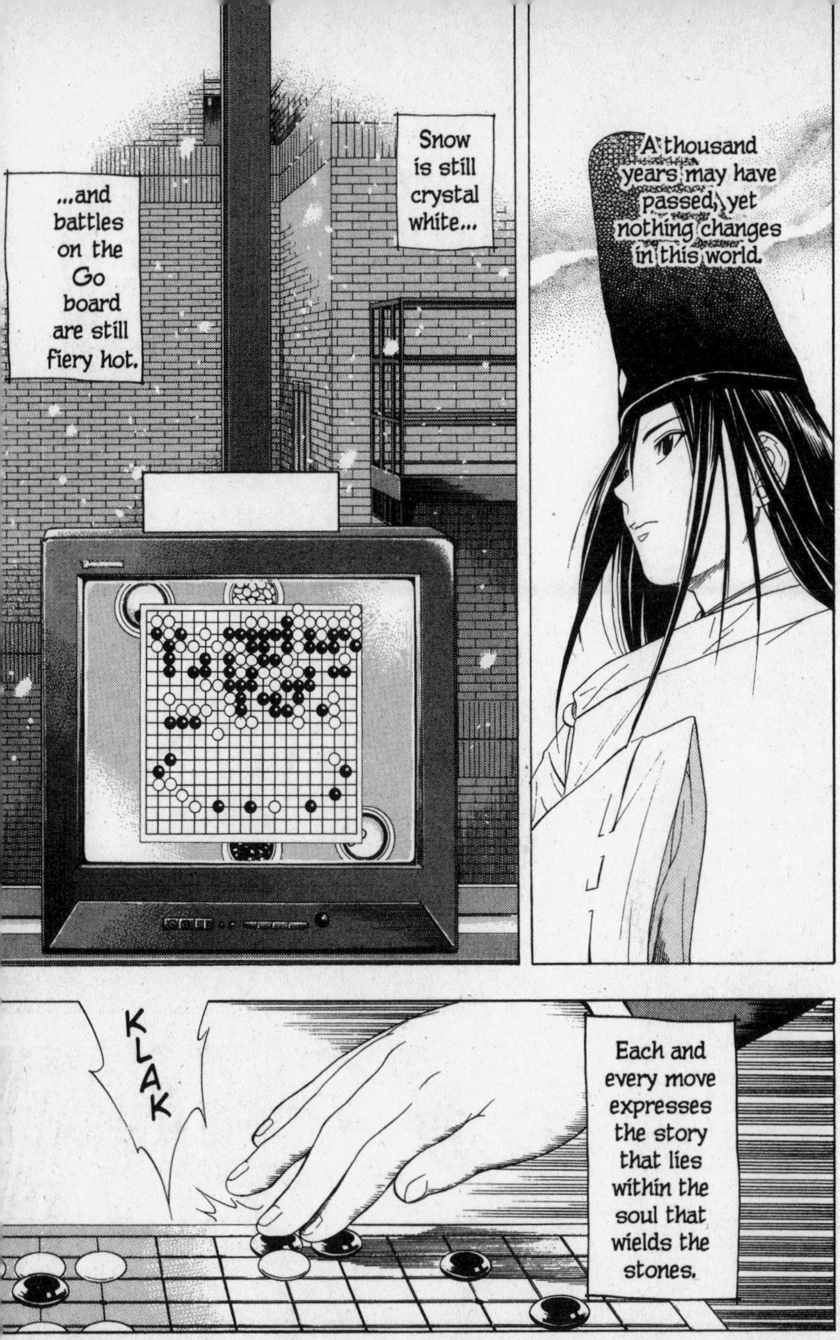
A thousand years may have passed, yet nothing changes in this world.
Snow is still crystal white...
...and battles on the Go board are still fiery hot.
Each and every move expresses the story that lies within the soul that wields the stones.
KLAK

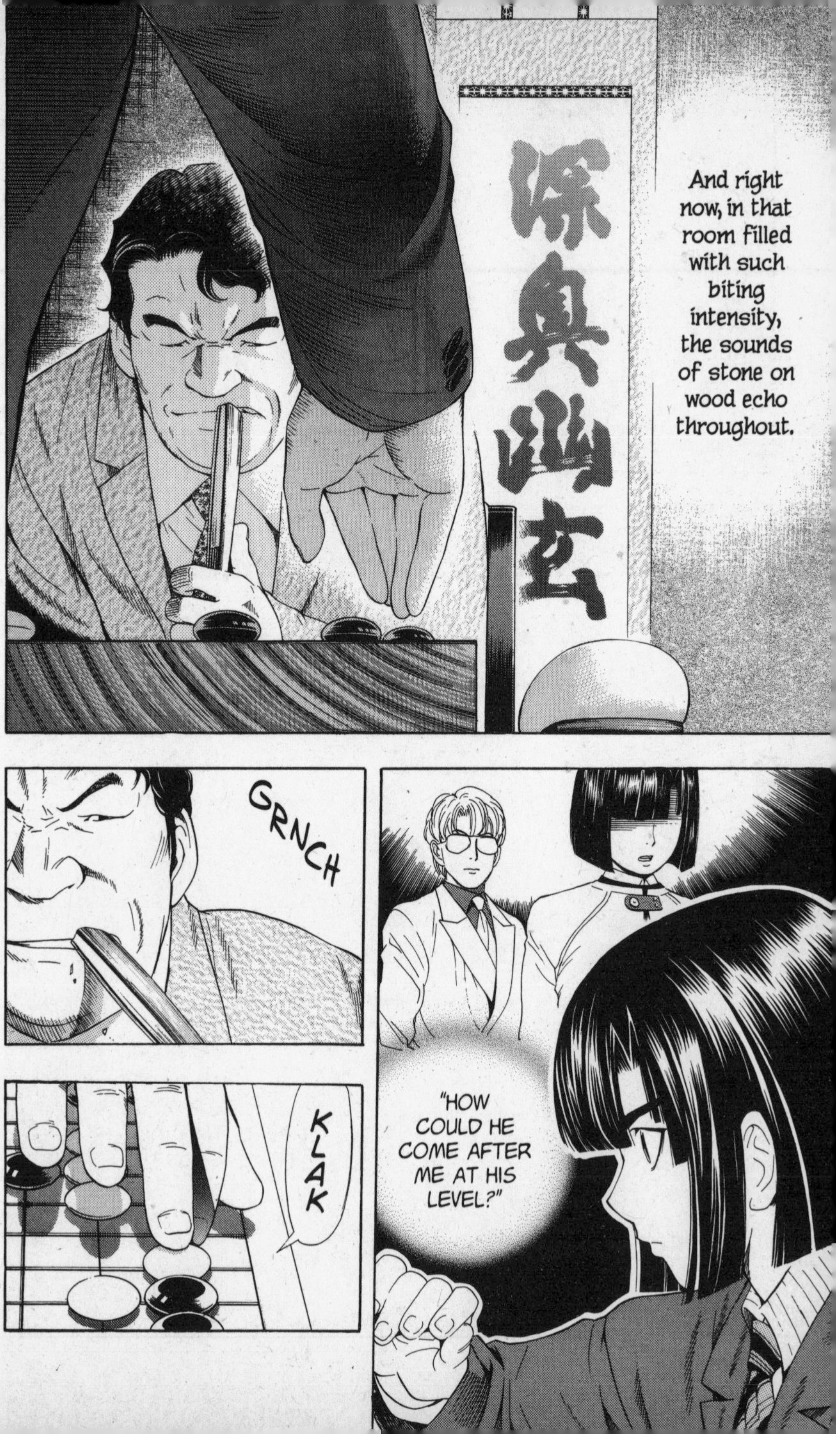
深奥幽玄
And right now, in that room filled with such biting intensity, the sounds of stone on wood echo throughout.
"HOW COULD HE COME AFTER ME AT HIS LEVEL?"
GRNCH
KLAK

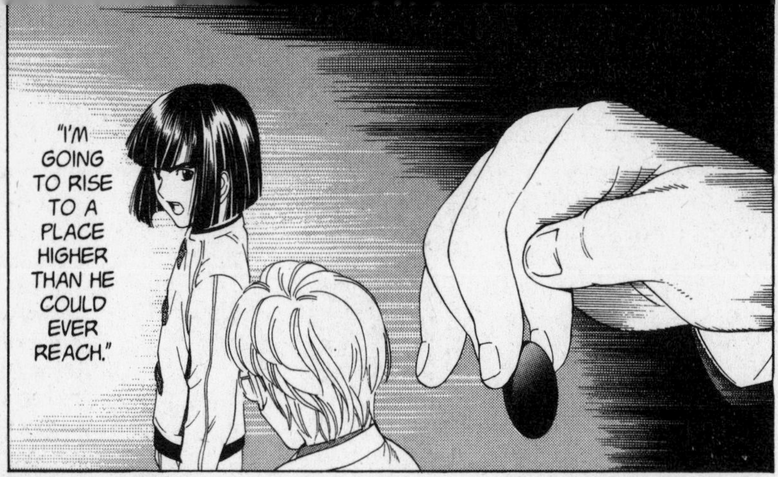
"I'M GOING TO RISE TO A PLACE HIGHER THAN HE COULD EVER REACH."
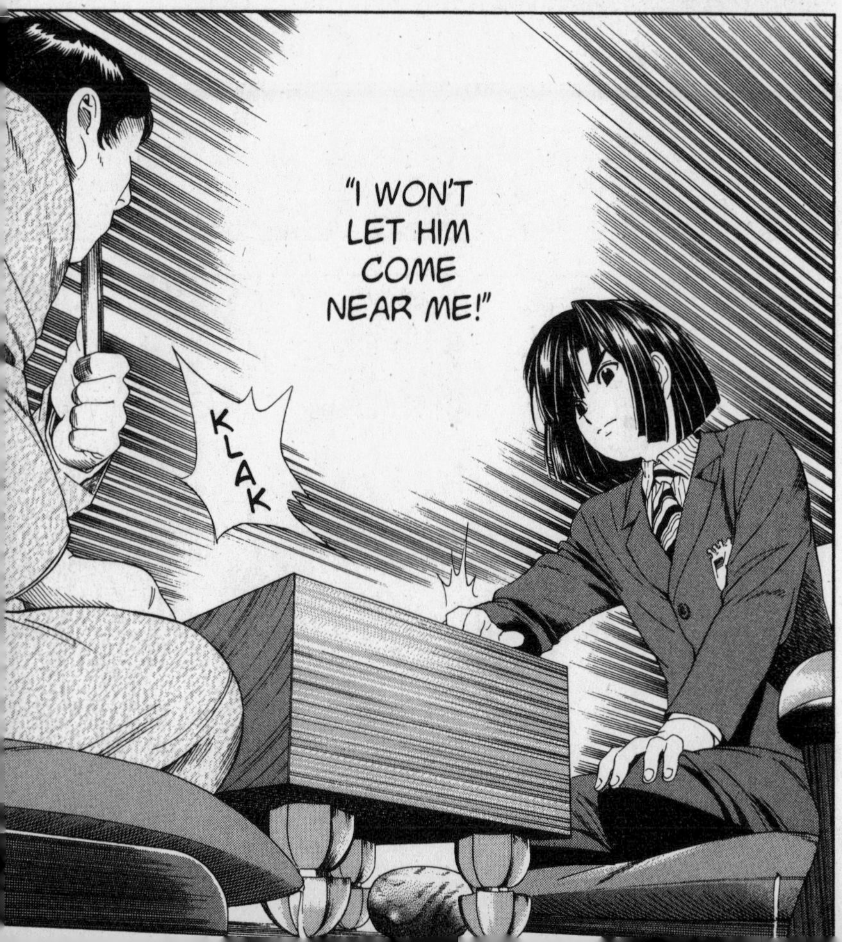
"I WON'T LET HIM COME NEAR ME!"
KLAK

YOU'RE STILL GREEN.

KLAK

CHFF

DID YOU THINK I'D BE DRAWN IN TO RESPOND HERE?

GASP!

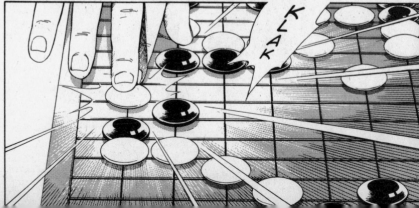

KLAK

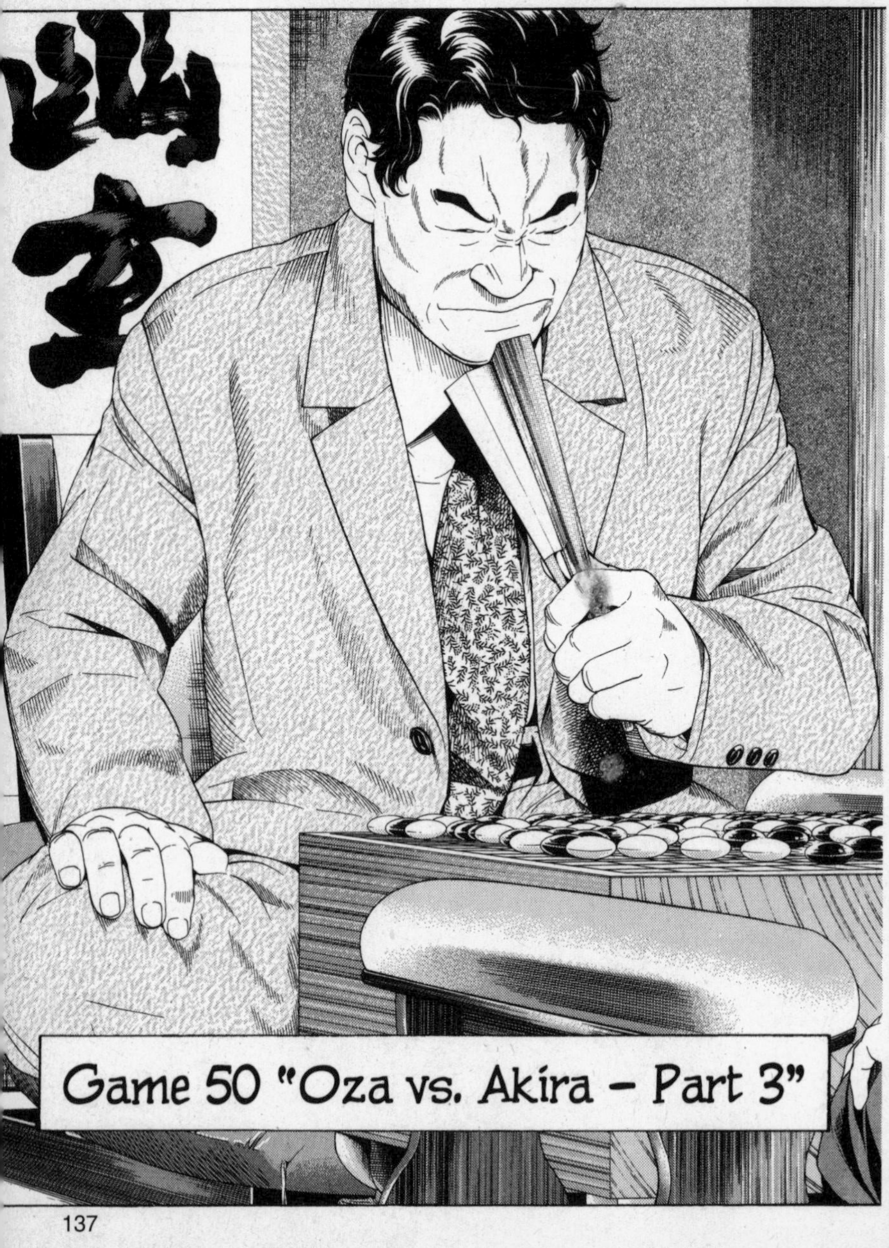
Game 50 "Oza vs. Akira – Part 3"

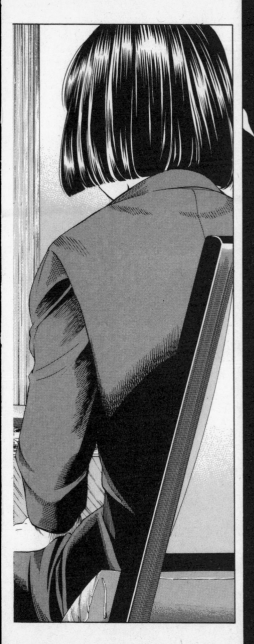

I WILL NOT BE DISTRACTED...

...BY THE LIKES OF YOU.

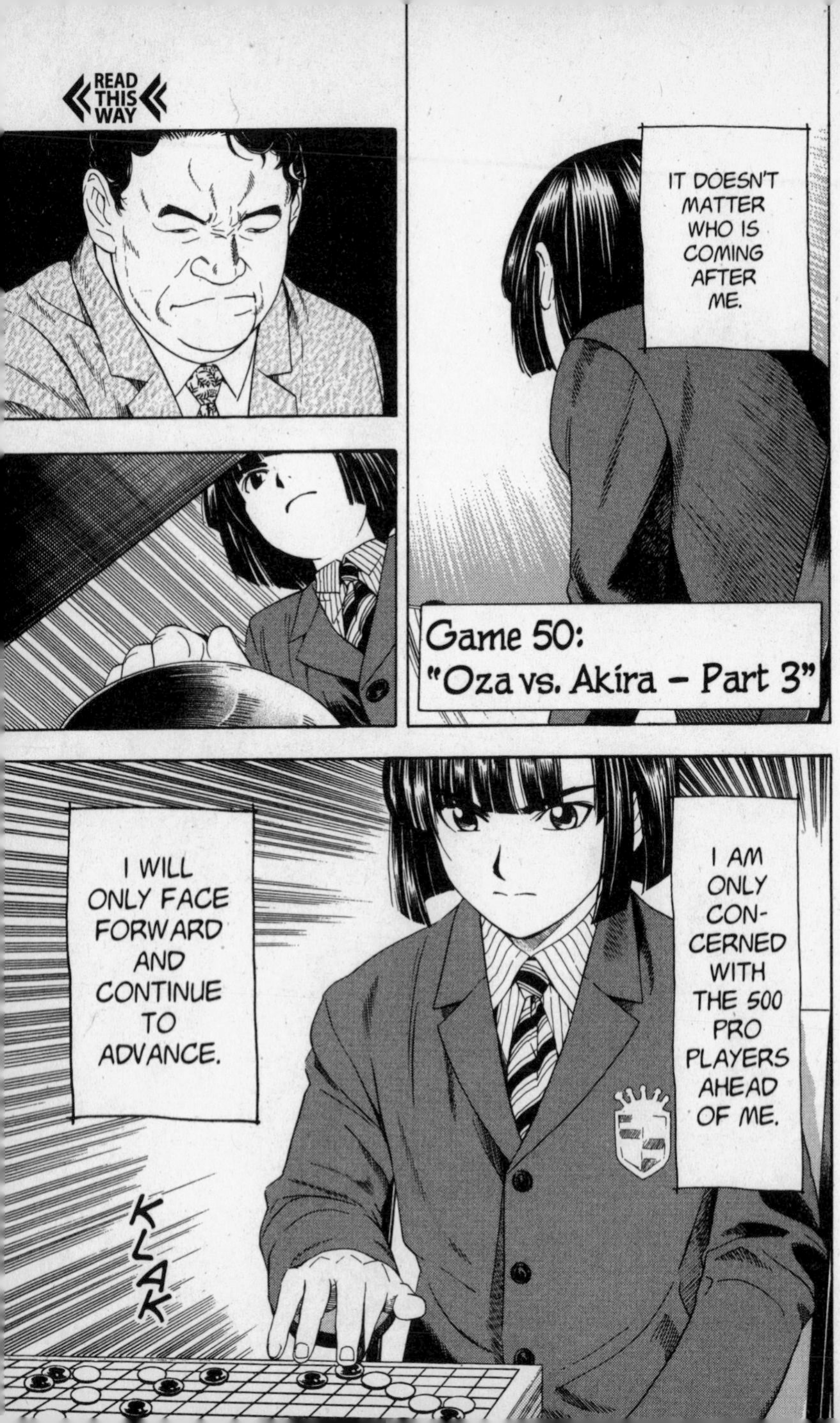
READ THIS WAY
IT DOESN'T MATTER WHO IS COMING AFTER ME.
Game 50: "Oza vs. Akira – Part 3"
I AM ONLY CON-CERNED WITH THE 500 PRO PLAYERS AHEAD OF ME.
I WILL ONLY FACE FORWARD AND CONTINUE TO ADVANCE.
KLAK

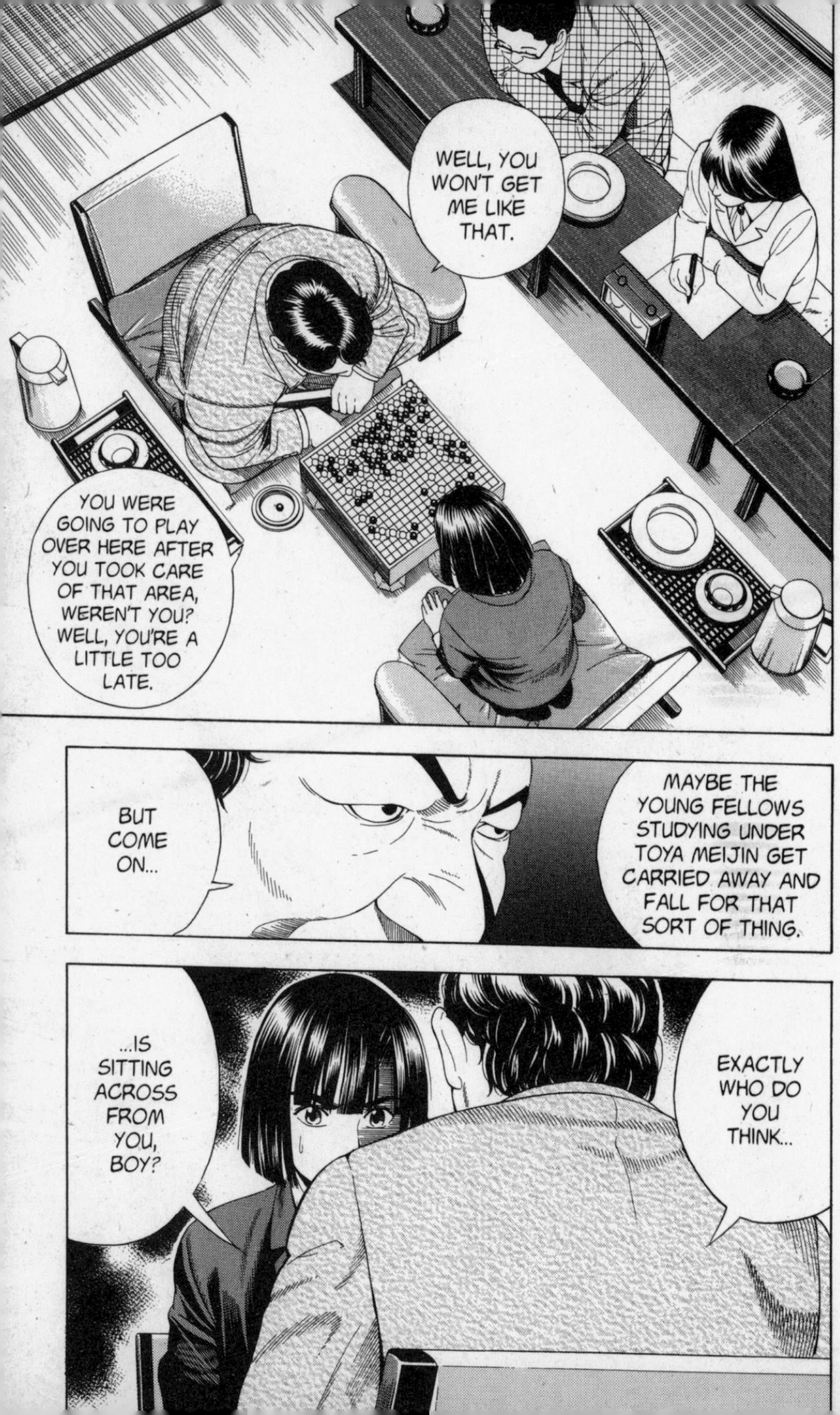
WELL, YOU WON'T GET ME LIKE THAT.
YOU WERE GOING TO PLAY OVER HERE AFTER YOU TOOK CARE OF THAT AREA, WEREN'T YOU? WELL, YOU'RE A LITTLE TOO LATE.
MAYBE THE YOUNG FELLOWS STUDYING UNDER TOYA MEIJIN GET CARRIED AWAY AND FALL FOR THAT SORT OF THING.
BUT COME ON...
EXACTLY WHO DO YOU THINK...
...IS SITTING ACROSS FROM YOU, BOY?

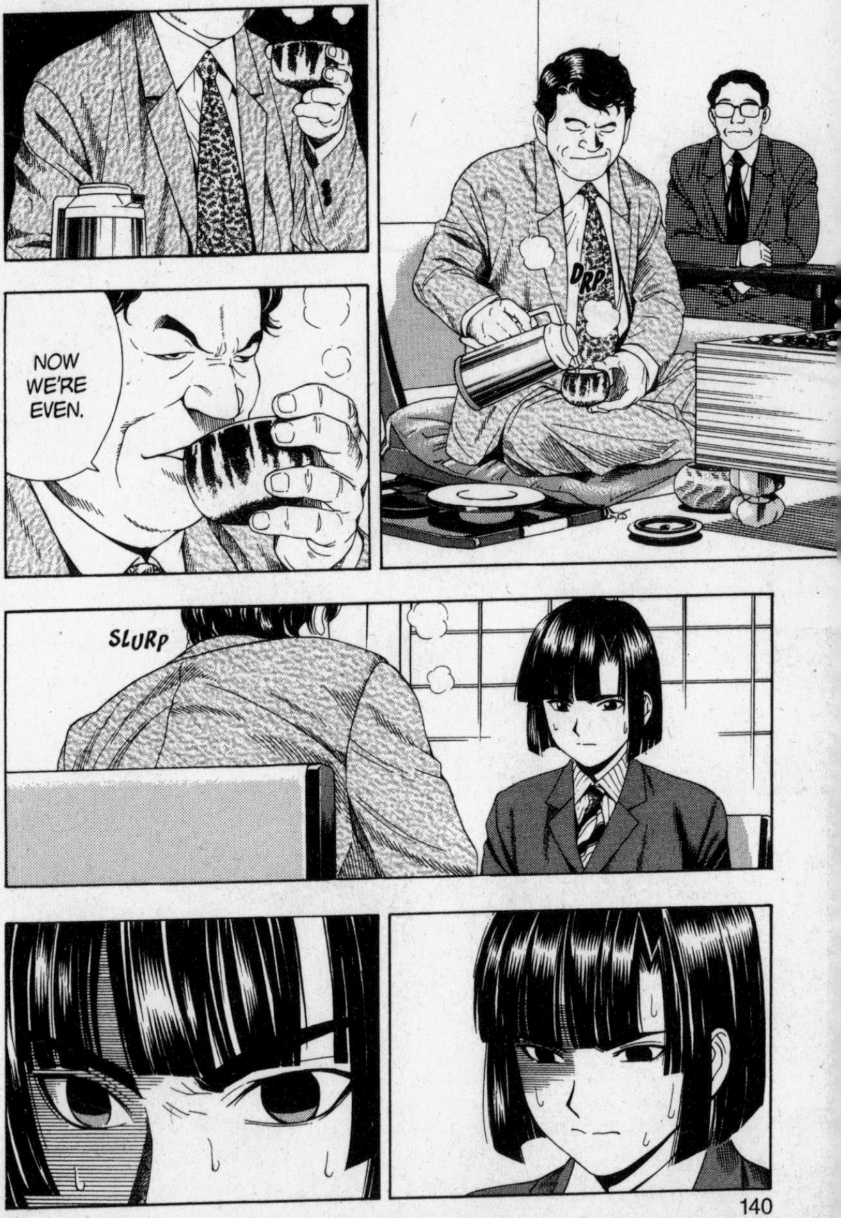
DRP
NOW WE'RE EVEN.
SLURP

CHFF

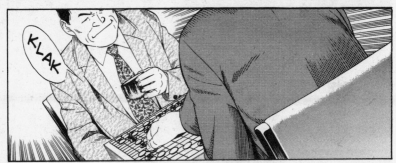

KLAK

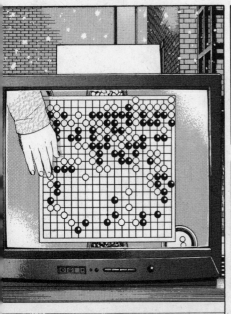

KLNK

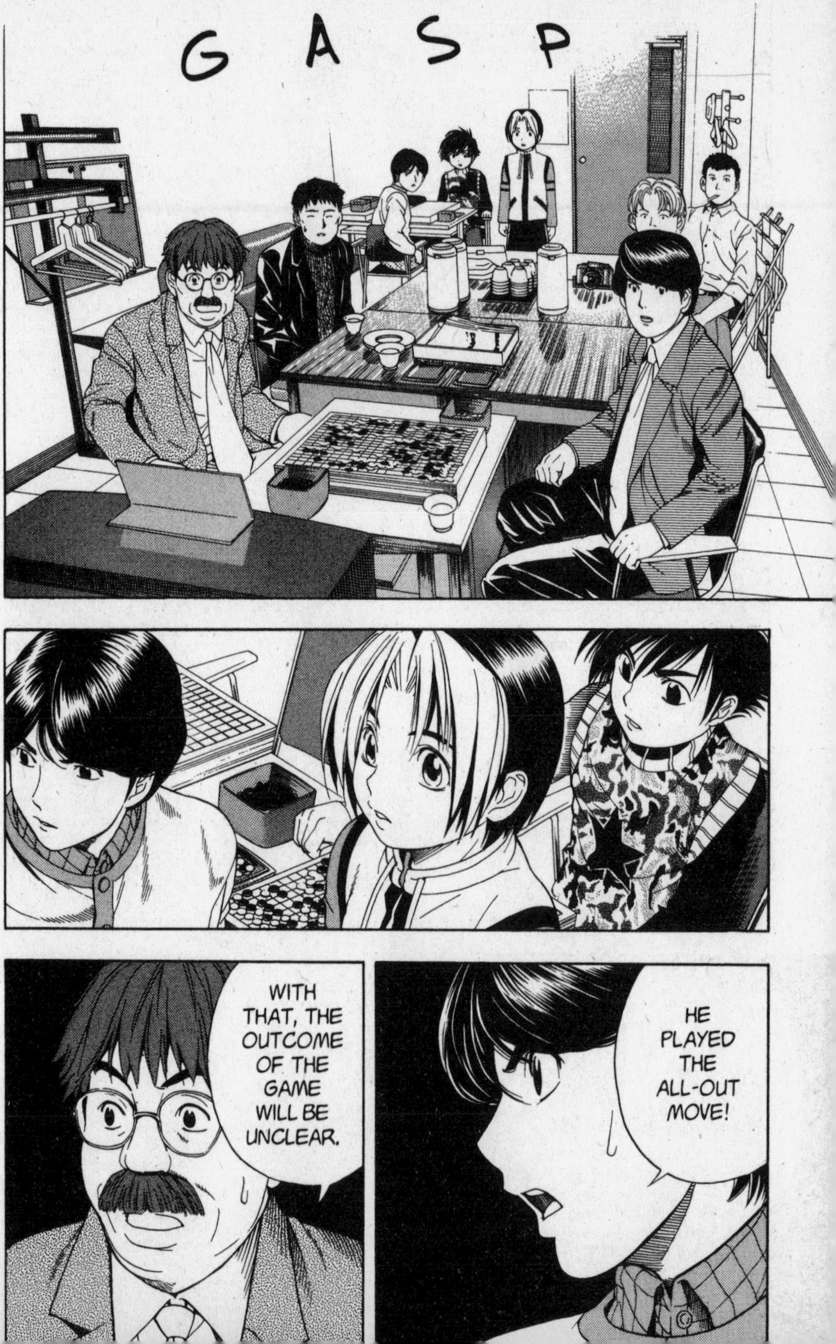
GASP
HE PLAYED THE ALL-OUT MOVE!
WITH THAT, THE OUTCOME OF THE GAME WILL BE UNCLEAR.

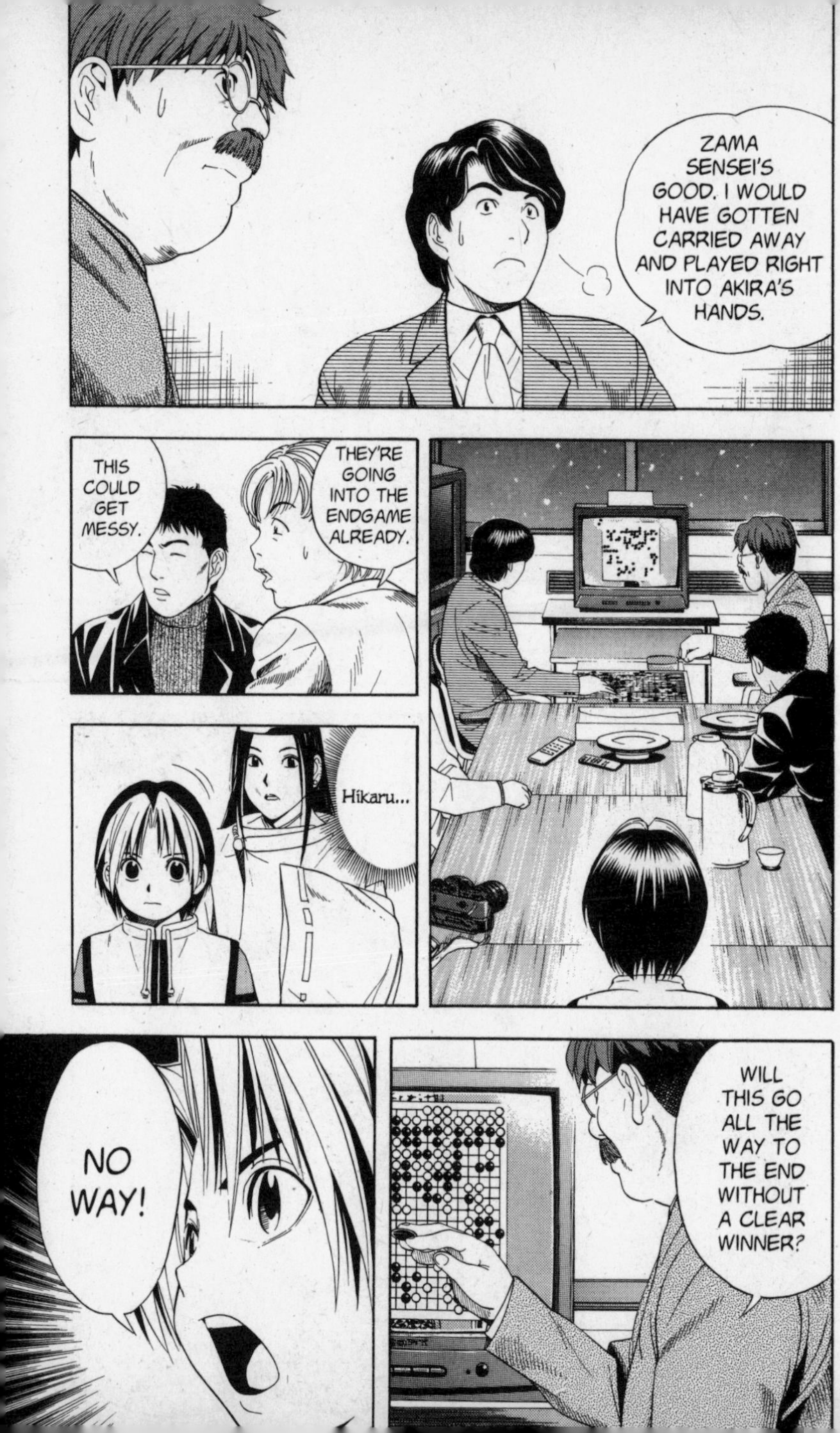
ZAMA SENSEI'S GOOD. I WOULD HAVE GOTTEN CARRIED AWAY AND PLAYED RIGHT INTO AKIRA'S HANDS.
THEY'RE GOING INTO THE ENDGAME ALREADY.
THIS COULD GET MESSY.
Hikaru...
WILL THIS GO ALL THE WAY TO THE END WITHOUT A CLEAR WINNER?
NO WAY!

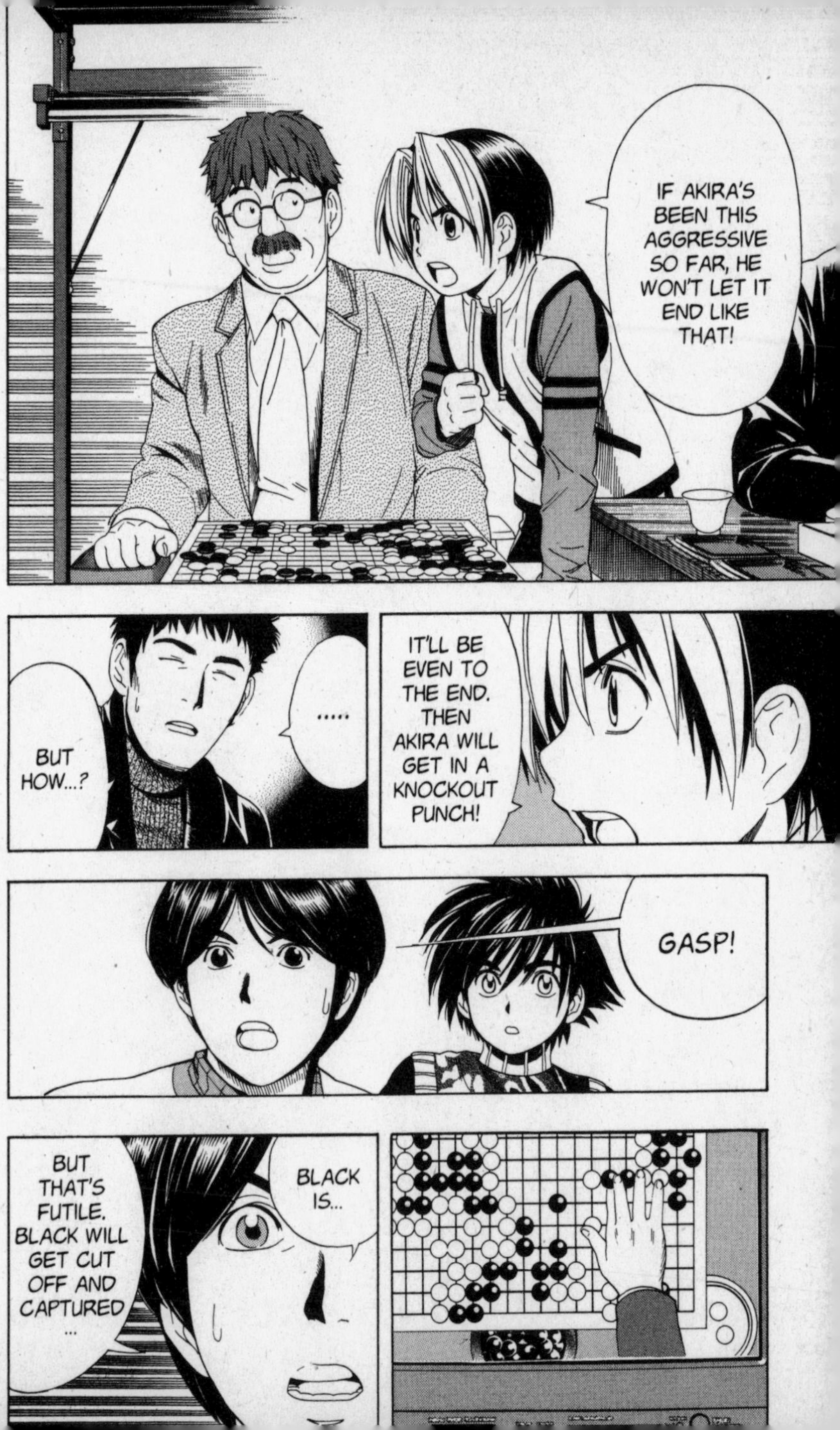
IF AKIRA'S BEEN THIS AGGRESSIVE SO FAR, HE WON'T LET IT END LIKE THAT!
IT'LL BE EVEN TO THE END. THEN AKIRA WILL GET IN A KNOCKOUT PUNCH!
.....
BUT HOW...?
GASP!
BLACK IS...
BUT THAT'S FUTILE. BLACK WILL GET CUT OFF AND CAPTURED ...

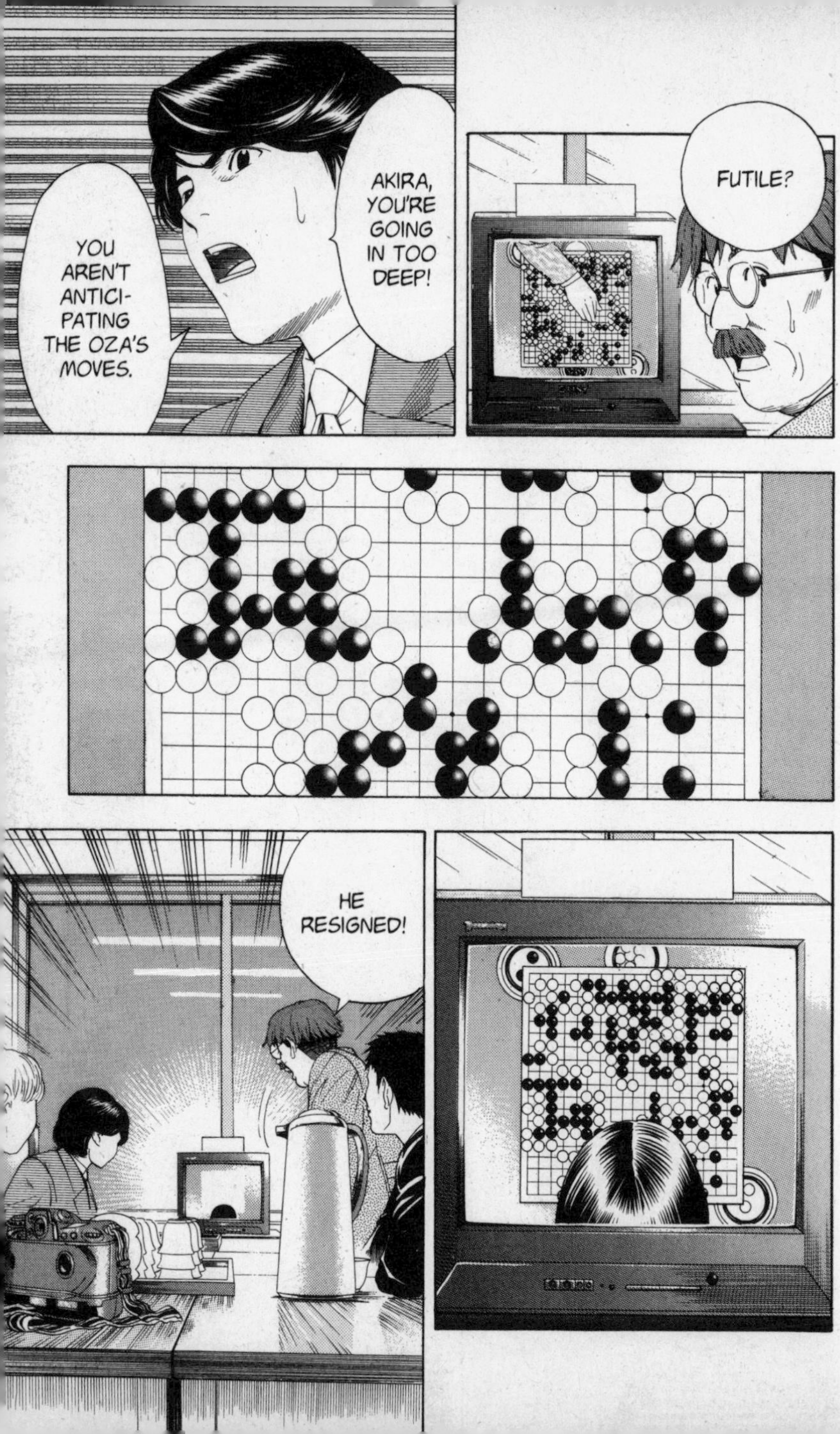
FUTILE?
AKIRA, YOU'RE GOING IN TOO DEEP!
YOU AREN'T ANTICI-PATING THE OZA'S MOVES.
HE RESIGNED!

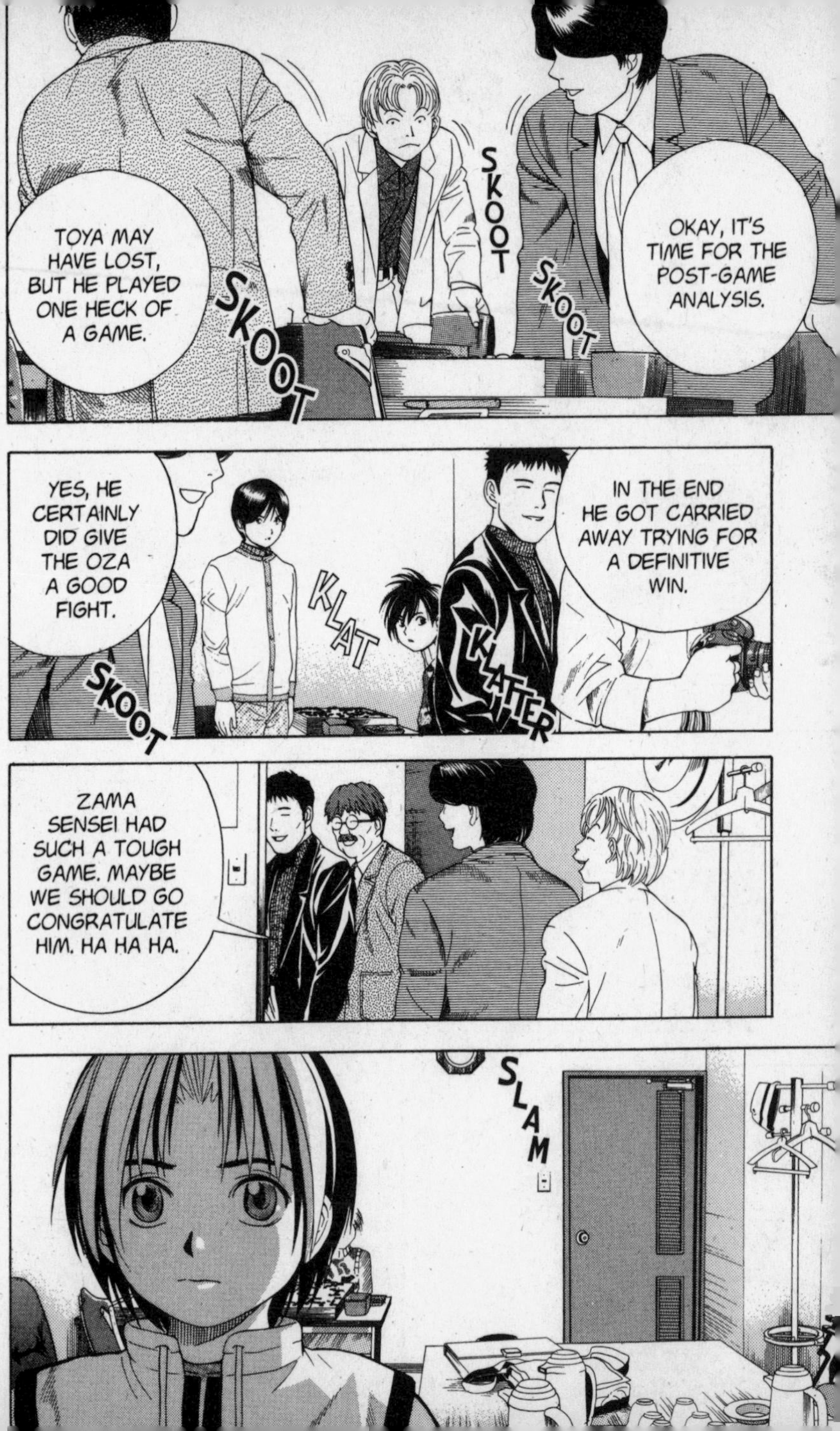
OKAY, IT'S TIME FOR THE POST-GAME ANALYSIS.
SKOOT
SKOOT
TOYA MAY HAVE LOST, BUT HE PLAYED ONE HECK OF A GAME.
SKOOT
IN THE END HE GOT CARRIED AWAY TRYING FOR A DEFINITIVE WIN.
KLATTER
KLAT
YES, HE CERTAINLY DID GIVE THE OZA A GOOD FIGHT.
SKOOT
ZAMA SENSEI HAD SUCH A TOUGH GAME. MAYBE WE SHOULD GO CONGRATULATE HIM. HA HA HA.
SLAM

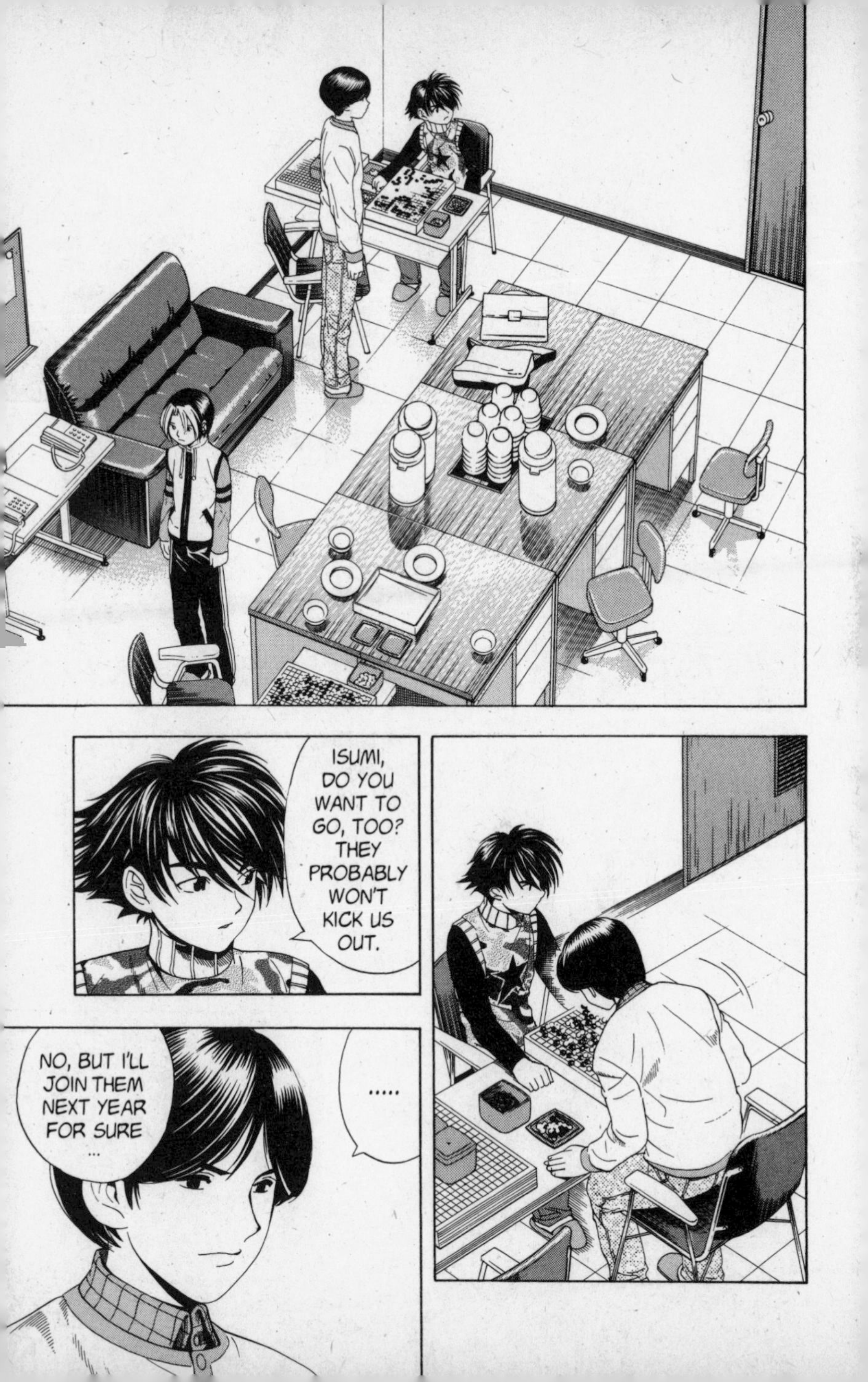
ISUMI, DO YOU WANT TO GO, TOO? THEY PROBABLY WON'T KICK US OUT.
.....
NO, BUT I'LL JOIN THEM NEXT YEAR FOR SURE ...

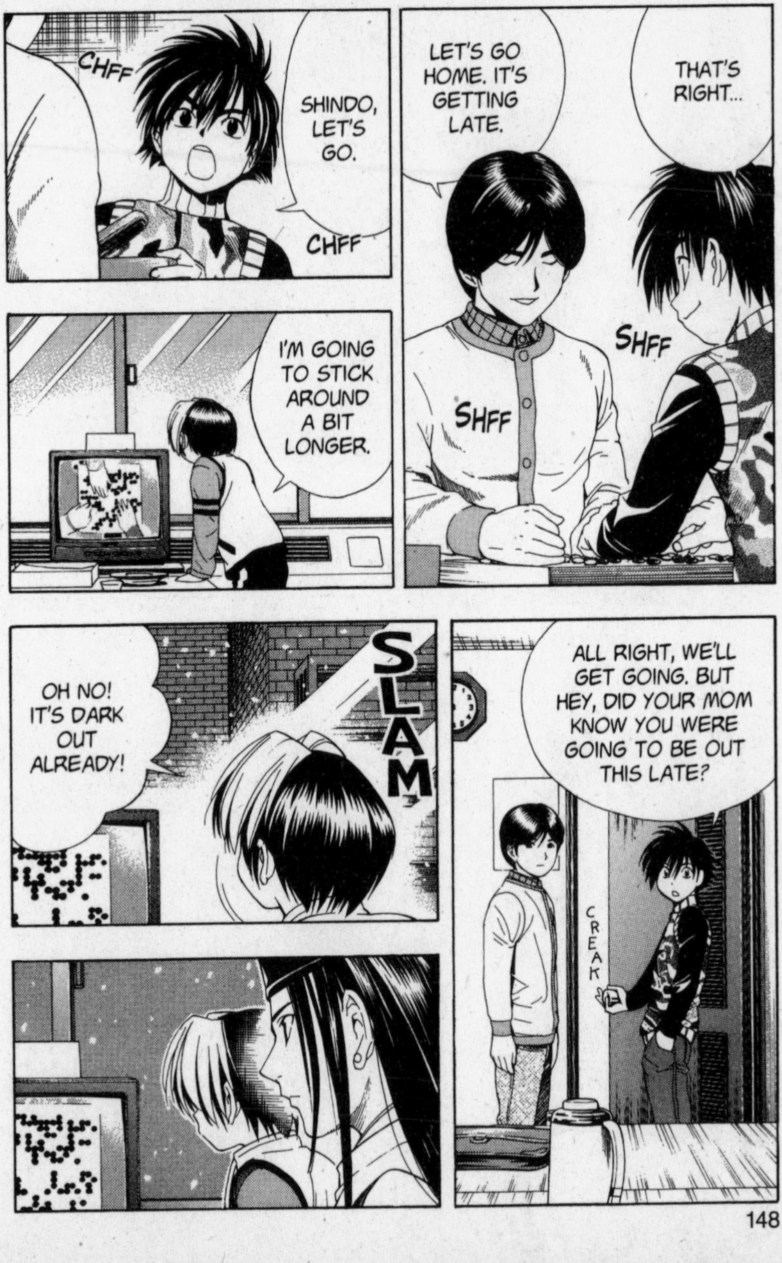
THAT'S RIGHT...
LET'S GO HOME. IT'S GETTING LATE.
SHFF
SHFF
CHFF
SHINDO, LET'S GO.
CHFF
I'M GOING TO STICK AROUND A BIT LONGER.
ALL RIGHT, WE'LL GET GOING. BUT HEY, DID YOUR MOM KNOW YOU WERE GOING TO BE OUT THIS LATE?
CREAK
SLAM
OH NO! IT'S DARK OUT ALREADY!

READ THIS WAY

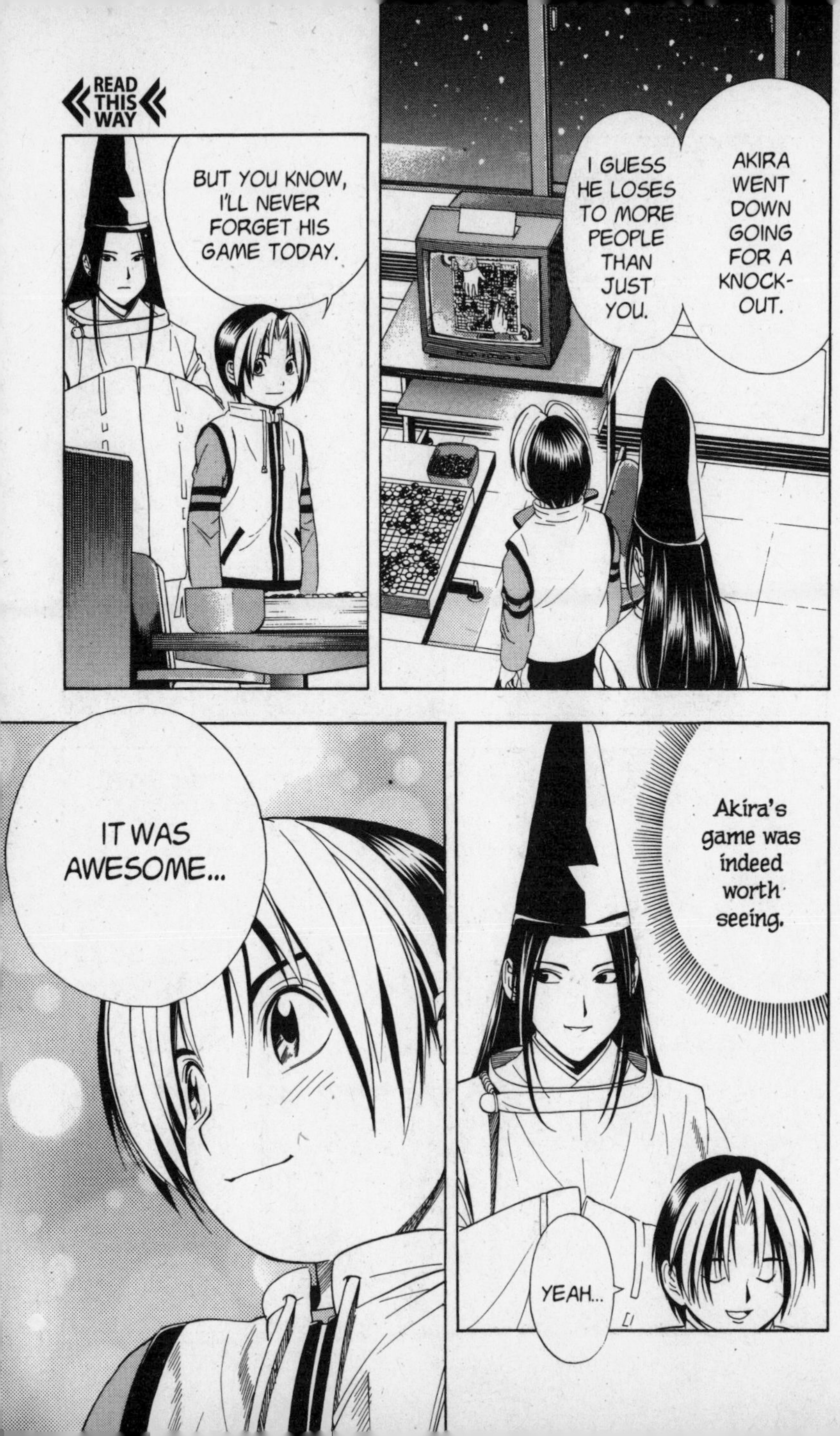
AKIRA WENT DOWN GOING FOR A KNOCK-OUT.
I GUESS HE LOSES TO MORE PEOPLE THAN JUST YOU.
BUT YOU KNOW, I'LL NEVER FORGET HIS GAME TODAY.
Akira's game was indeed worth seeing.
YEAH...
IT WAS AWESOME...

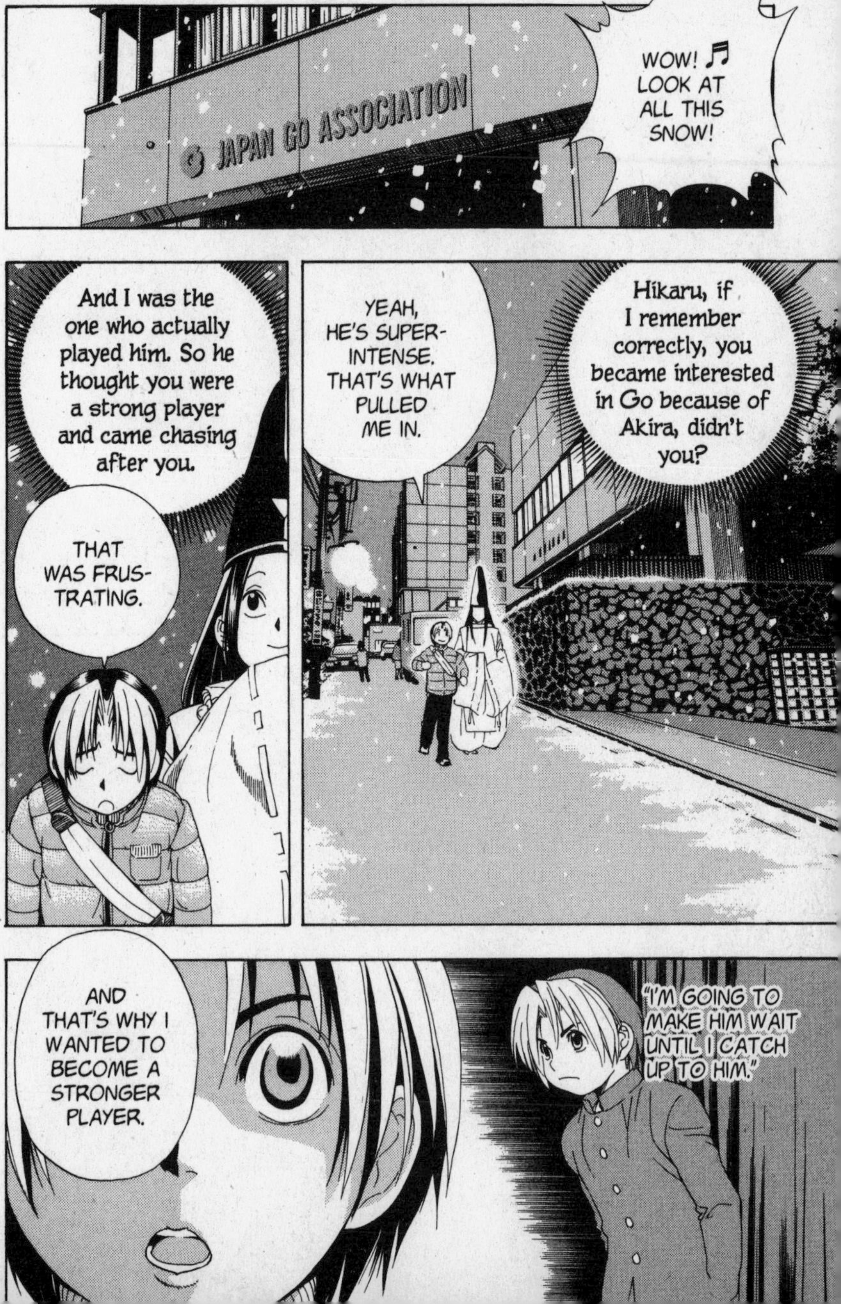
JAPAN GO ASSOCIATION
WOW! ♬ LOOK AT ALL THIS SNOW!
Hikaru, if I remember correctly, you became interested in Go because of Akira, didn't you?
YEAH, HE'S SUPER-INTENSE. THAT'S WHAT PULLED ME IN.
And I was the one who actually played him. So he thought you were a strong player and came chasing after you.
THAT WAS FRUS-TRATING.
"I'M GOING TO MAKE HIM WAIT UNTIL I CATCH UP TO HIM."
AND THAT'S WHY I WANTED TO BECOME A STRONGER PLAYER.

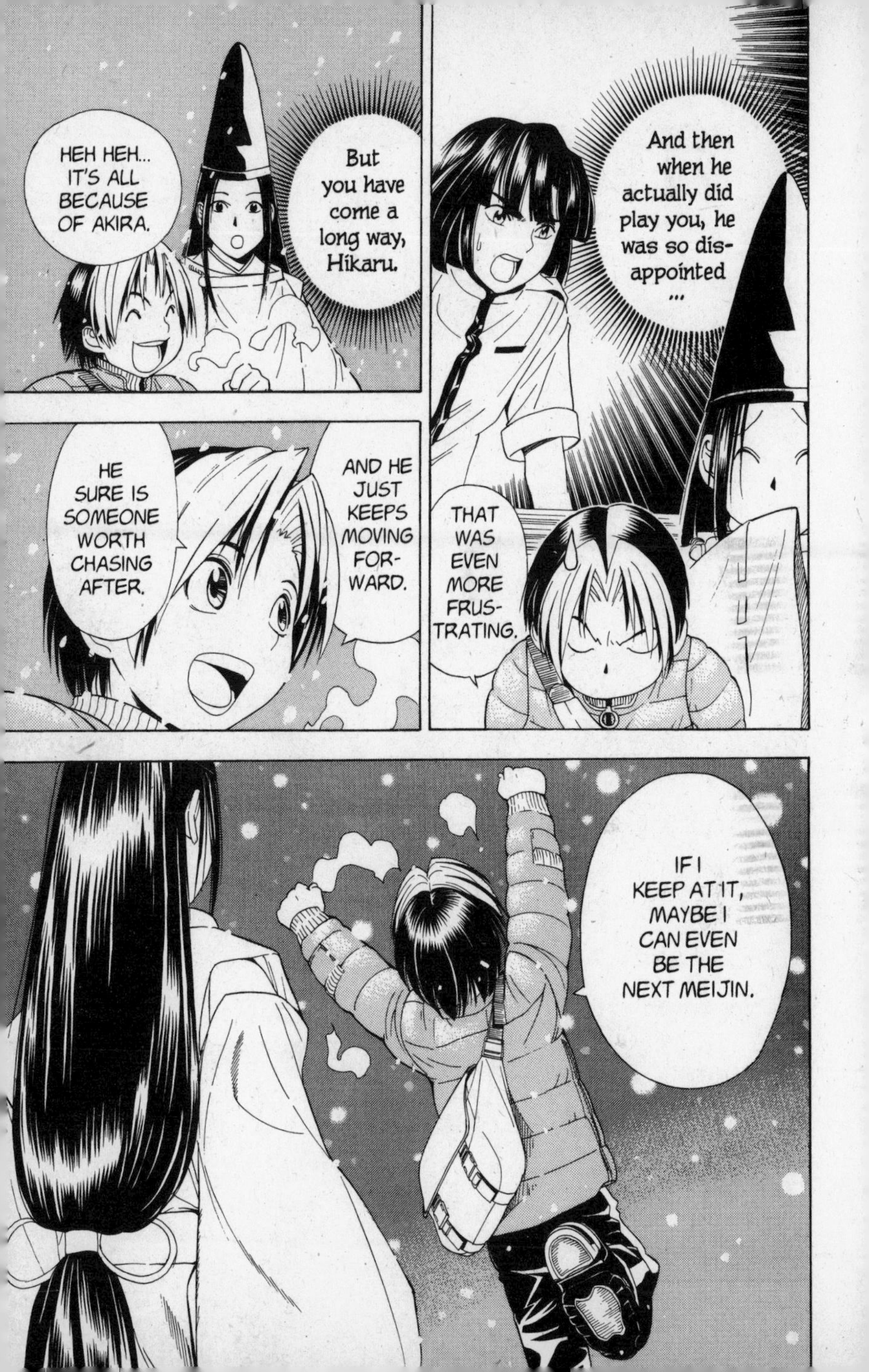

And then when he actually did play you, he was so disappointed ...
THAT WAS EVEN MORE FRUSTRATING.
But you have come a long way, Hikaru.
HEH HEH... IT'S ALL BECAUSE OF AKIRA.
AND HE JUST KEEPS MOVING FORWARD.
HE SURE IS SOMEONE WORTH CHASING AFTER.
IF I KEEP AT IT, MAYBE I CAN EVEN BE THE NEXT MEIJIN.

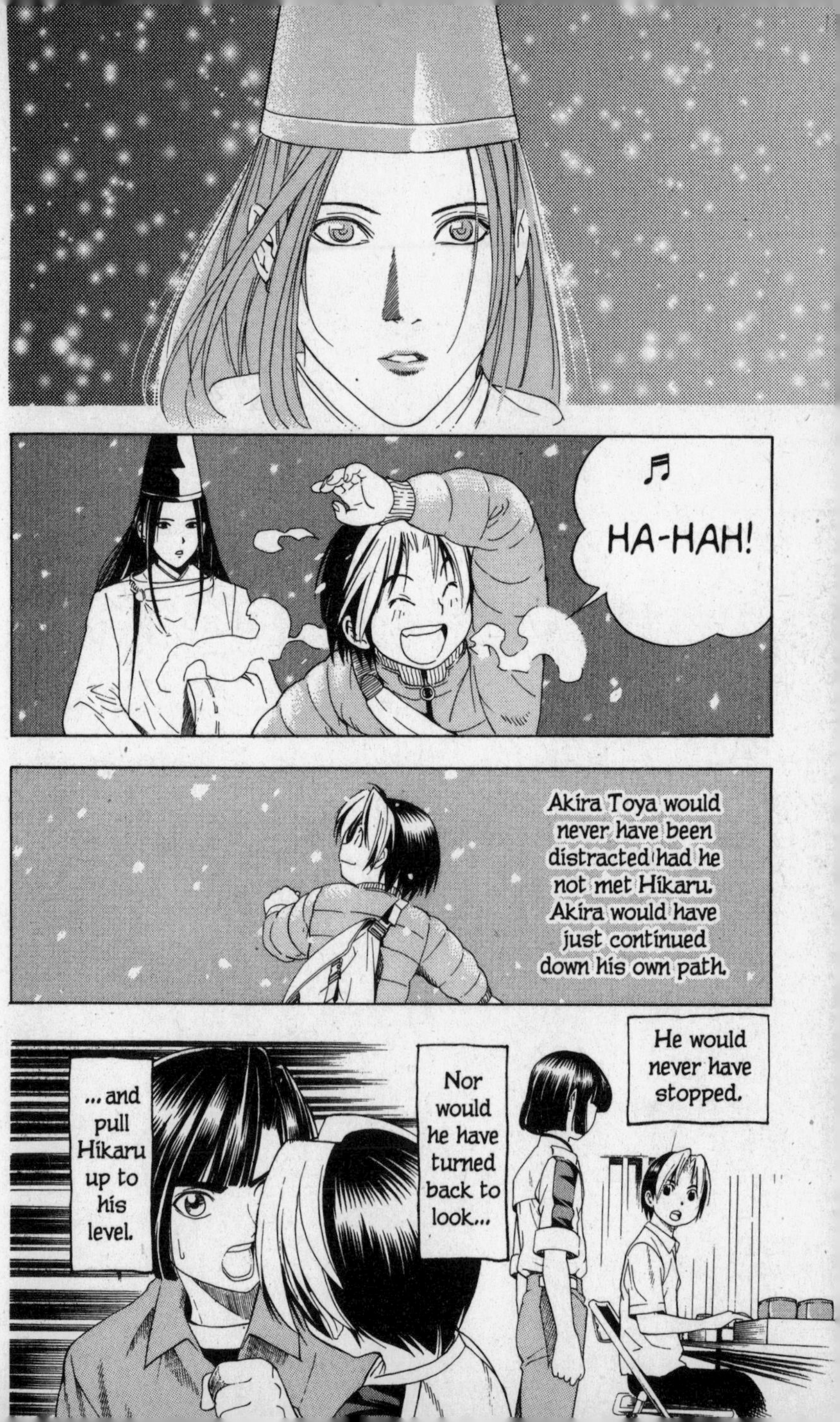
♬ HA-HAH!
Akira Toya would never have been distracted had he not met Hikaru. Akira would have just continued down his own path.
He would never have stopped.
Nor would he have turned back to look...
...and pull Hikaru up to his level.

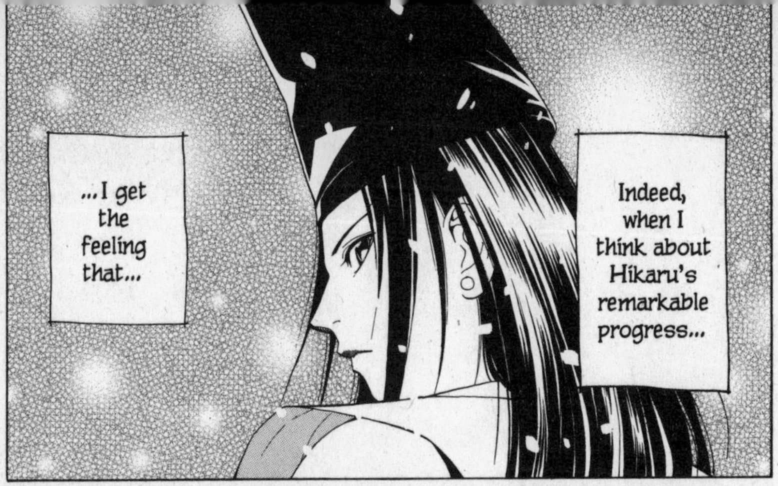
Indeed, when I think about Hikaru's remarkable progress...
...I get the feeling that...

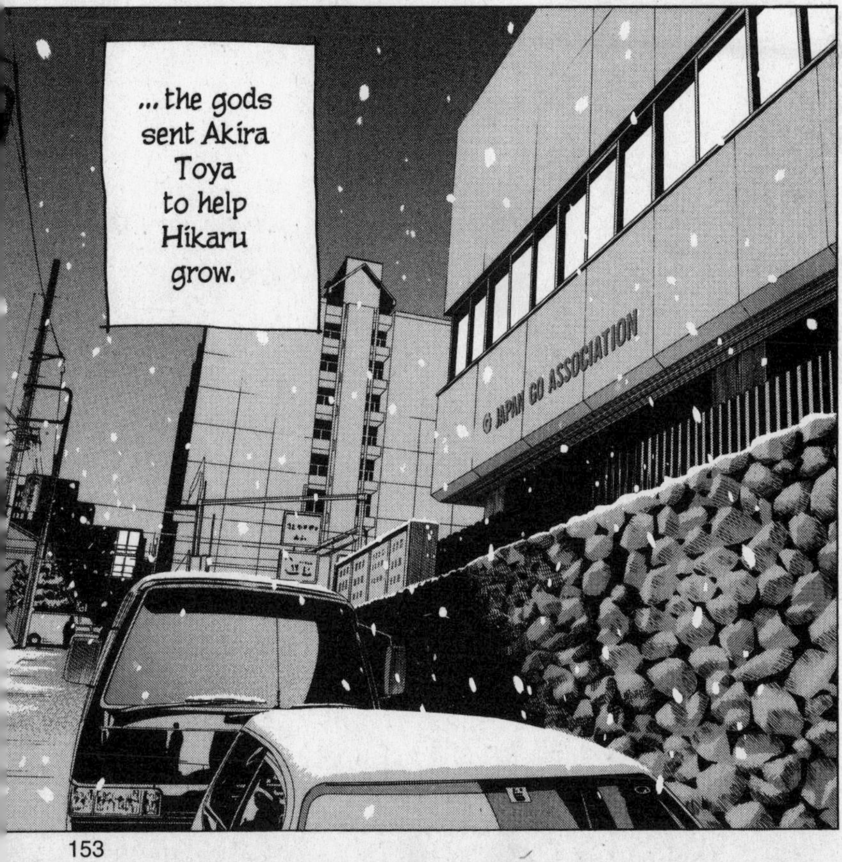
...the gods sent Akira Toya to help Hikaru grow.
JAPAN GO ASSOCIATION

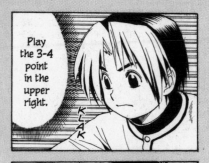

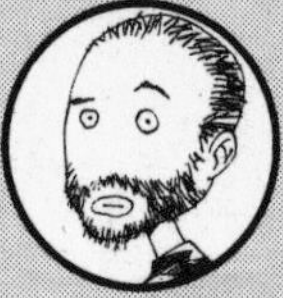

Play the 3-4 point in the upper right.
KLAK
Next play 4-15.
Now the 3-5 point in the lower left.
KLAK
Cut off White's head.
Now just hold out at the center and the left, and see what happens!
KLAK
Look, Hikaru!
2000
DA DUMM
WHAT THE —?!

HIKARU NO GO

NOSTRADAMUS PREDICTED THAT, IN 1999, A "GREAT AND TERRIFYING LEADER" WOULD APPEAR, BUT ONE NEVER SHOWED UP. STILL, THAT DOESN'T MEAN WE CAN RELAX. EVEN NOW I FEEL ANXIOUS ABOUT IT.
—TAKESHI OBATA

THIS FOUR-PANEL MANGA ABOUT THE COMING OF THE YEAR 2000 WAS PUBLISHED IN *E-JUMP*, A SPECIAL COLLABORATIVE EFFORT BETWEEN *WEEKLY SHONEN JUMP* AND *V JUMP* (PUBLISHED DECEMBER 10, 1999).

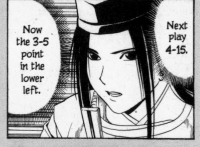

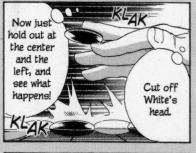

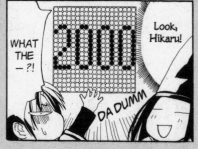

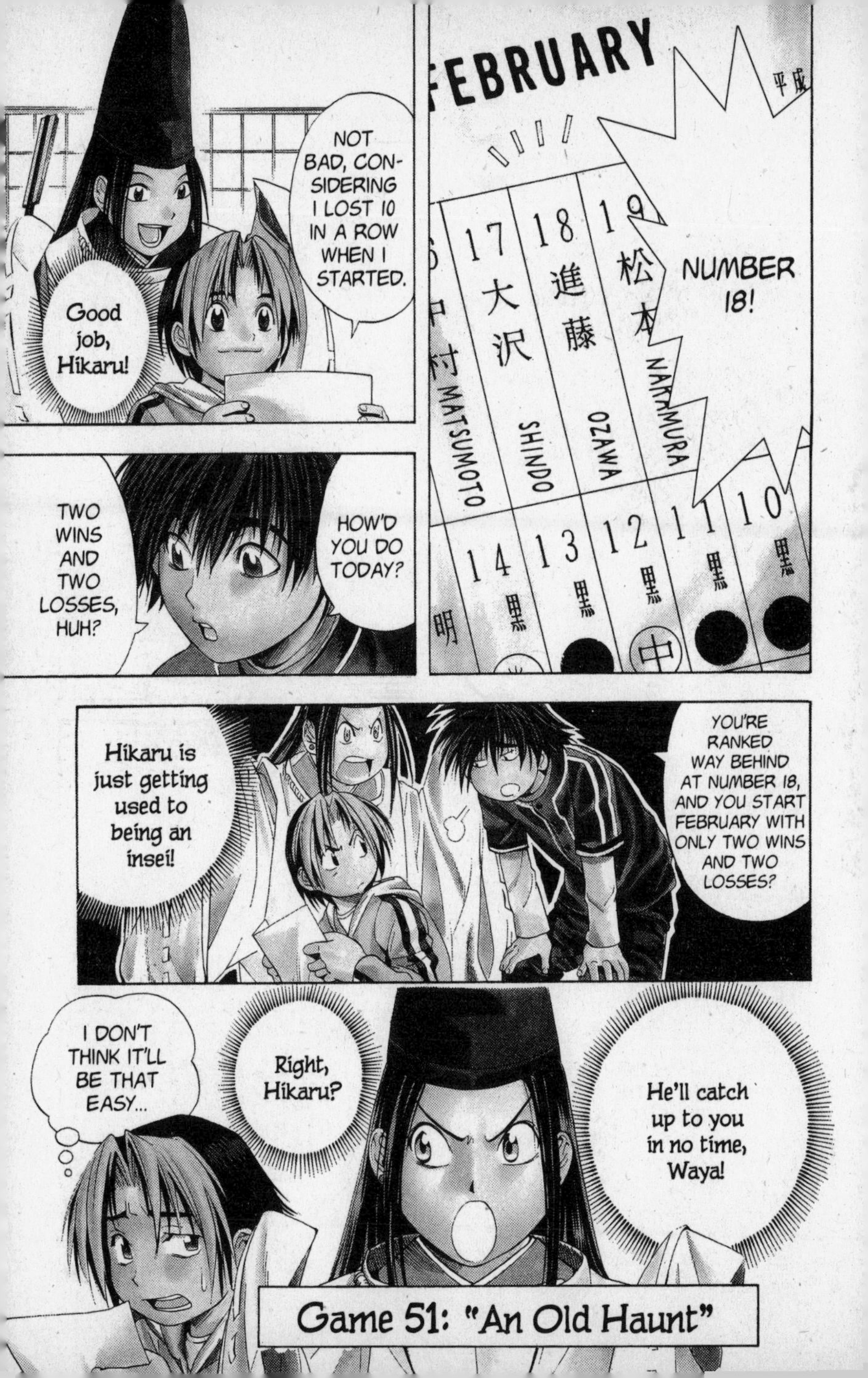
FEBRUARY
平成
NUMBER 18!
17 18 19
大沢 進藤 松本
中村
MATSUMOTO
SHINDO
OZAWA
NAKAMURA
14 13 12 11 10
NOT BAD, CONSIDERING I LOST 10 IN A ROW WHEN I STARTED.
Good job, Hikaru!
HOW'D YOU DO TODAY?
TWO WINS AND TWO LOSSES, HUH?
YOU'RE RANKED WAY BEHIND AT NUMBER 18, AND YOU START FEBRUARY WITH ONLY TWO WINS AND TWO LOSSES?
Hikaru is just getting used to being an insei!
He'll catch up to you in no time, Waya!
Right, Hikaru?
I DON'T THINK IT'LL BE THAT EASY...
Game 51: "An Old Haunt"

Game 51
"An Old Haunt"

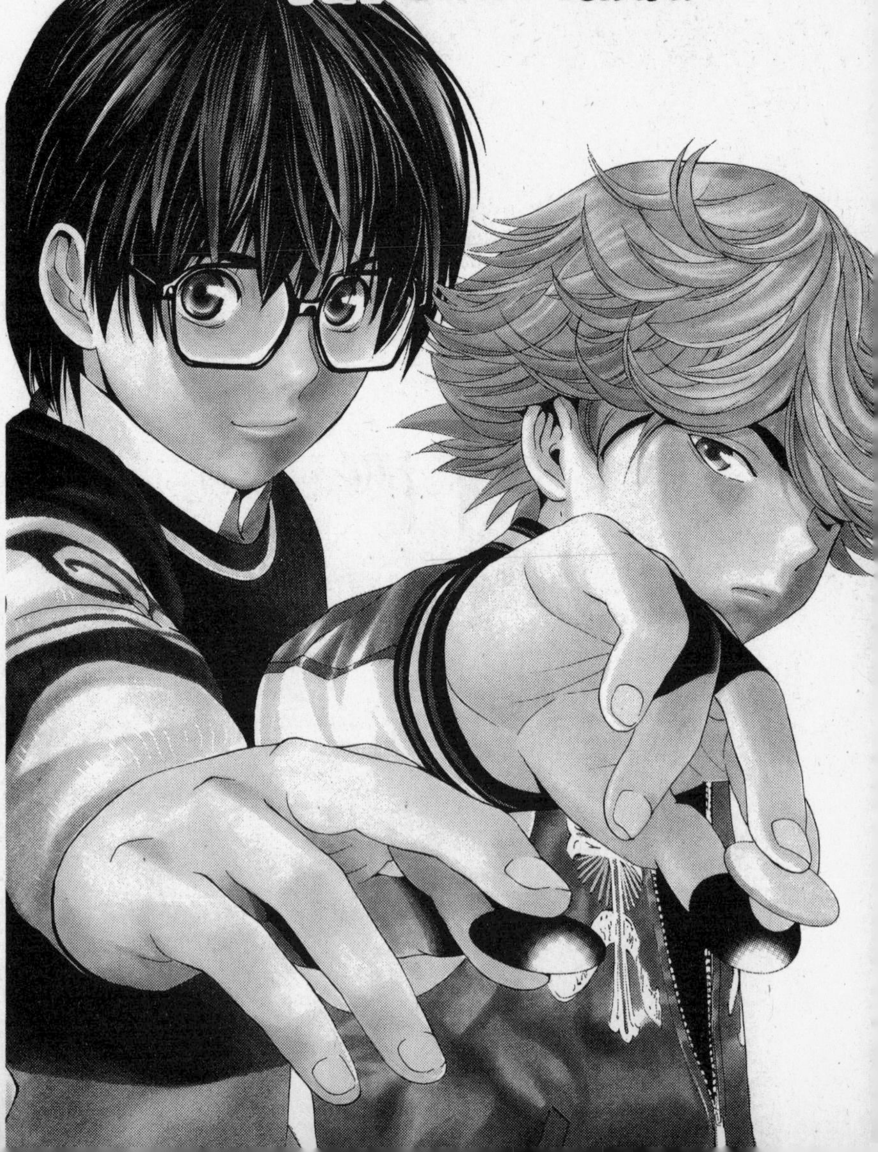

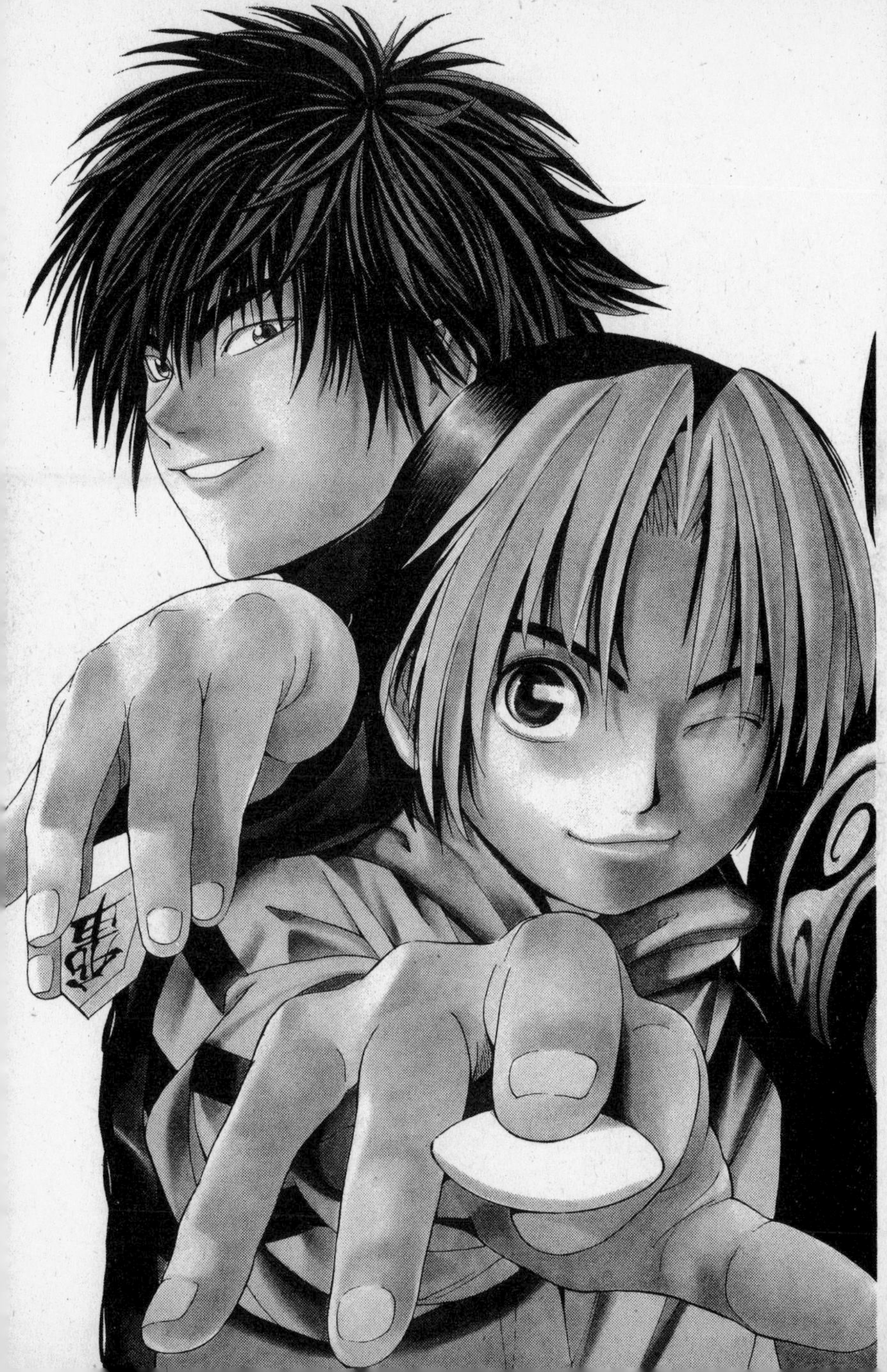

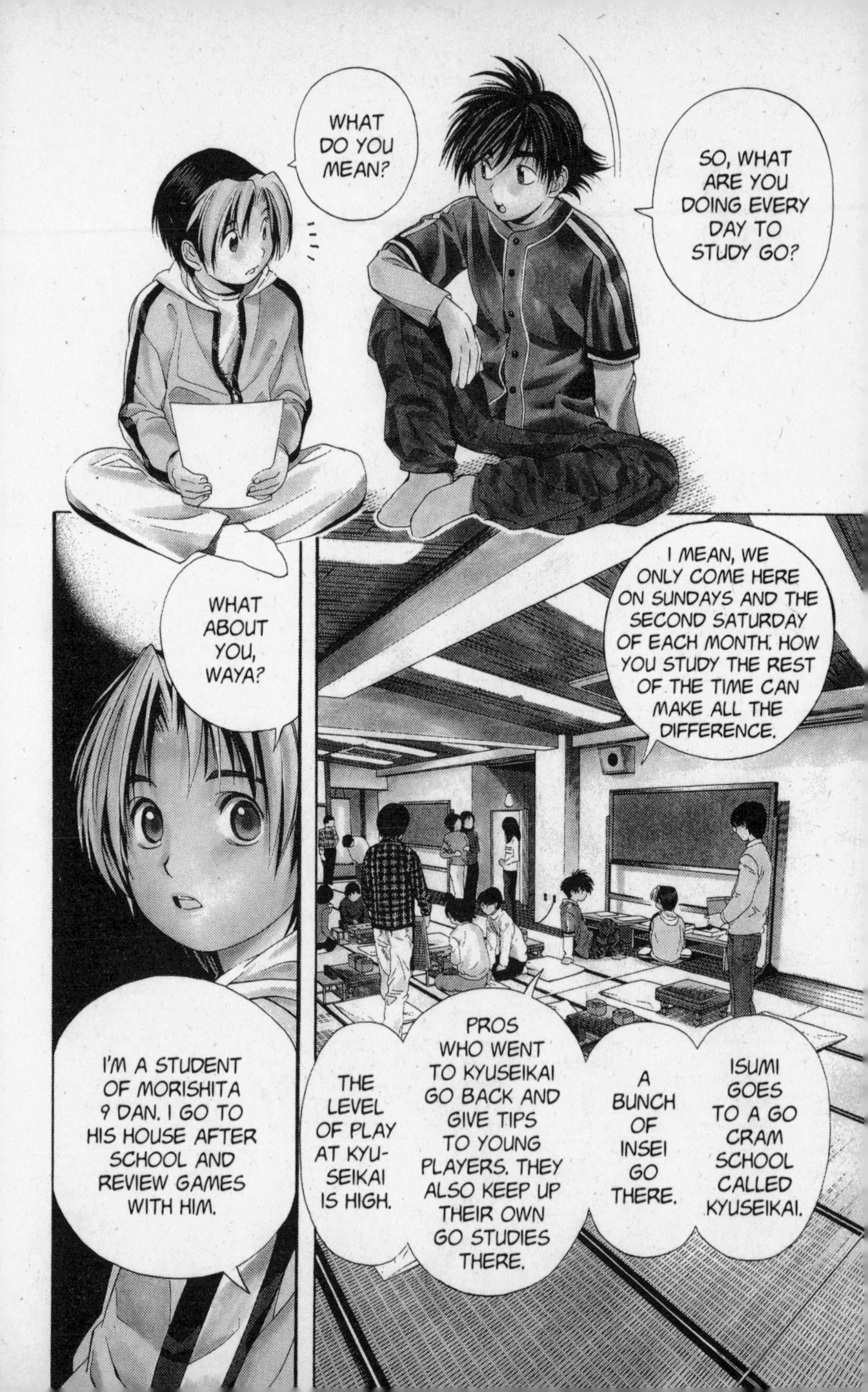
SO, WHAT ARE YOU DOING EVERY DAY TO STUDY GO?
WHAT DO YOU MEAN?
I MEAN, WE ONLY COME HERE ON SUNDAYS AND THE SECOND SATURDAY OF EACH MONTH. HOW YOU STUDY THE REST OF THE TIME CAN MAKE ALL THE DIFFERENCE.
ISUMI GOES TO A GO CRAM SCHOOL CALLED KYUSEIKAI.
A BUNCH OF INSEI GO THERE.
PROS WHO WENT TO KYUSEIKAI GO BACK AND GIVE TIPS TO YOUNG PLAYERS. THEY ALSO KEEP UP THEIR OWN GO STUDIES THERE.
THE LEVEL OF PLAY AT KYU-SEIKAI IS HIGH.
WHAT ABOUT YOU, WAYA?
I'M A STUDENT OF MORISHITA 9 DAN. I GO TO HIS HOUSE AFTER SCHOOL AND REVIEW GAMES WITH HIM.

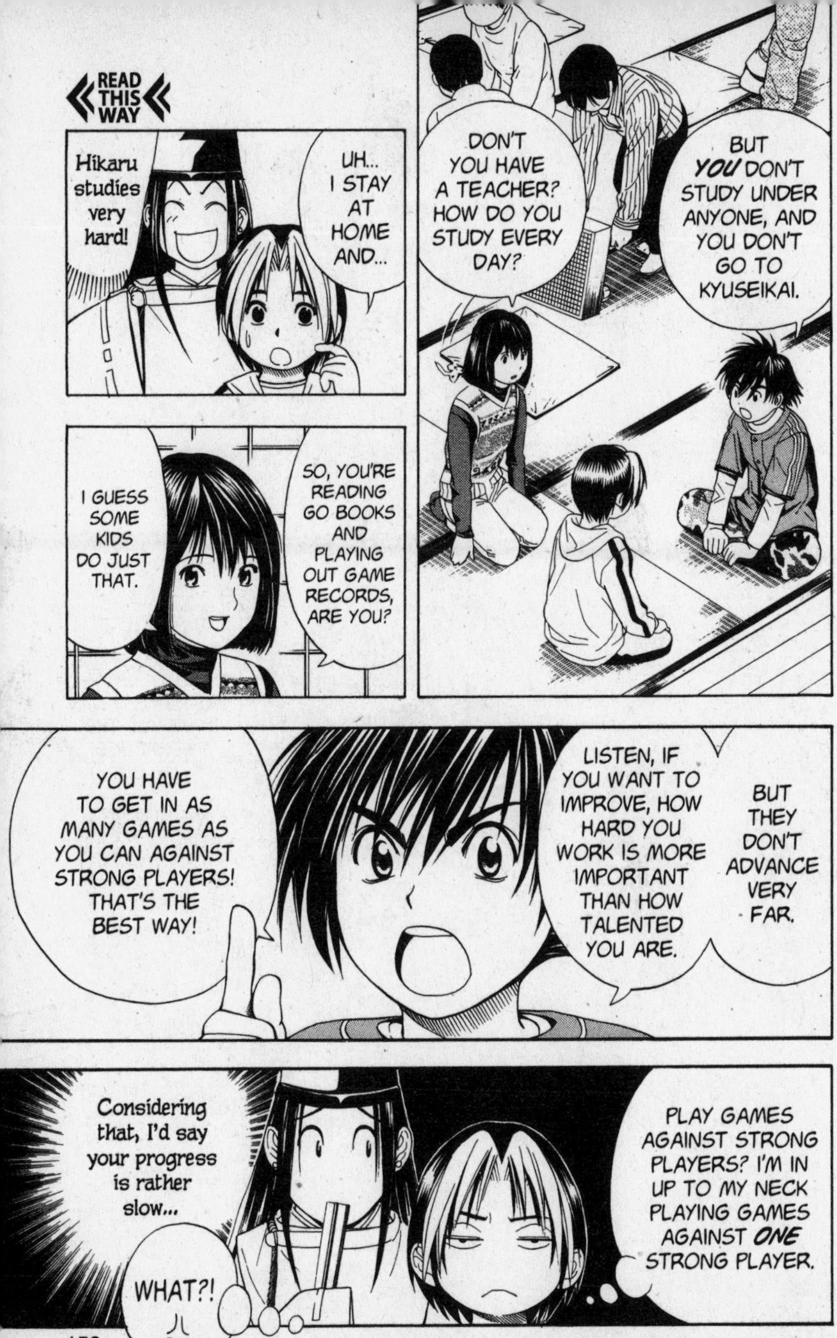
READ THIS WAY
BUT YOU DON'T STUDY UNDER ANYONE, AND YOU DON'T GO TO KYUSEIKAI.
DON'T YOU HAVE A TEACHER? HOW DO YOU STUDY EVERY DAY?
UH... I STAY AT HOME AND...
Hikaru studies very hard!
SO, YOU'RE READING GO BOOKS AND PLAYING OUT GAME RECORDS, ARE YOU?
I GUESS SOME KIDS DO JUST THAT.
BUT THEY DON'T ADVANCE VERY FAR.
LISTEN, IF YOU WANT TO IMPROVE, HOW HARD YOU WORK IS MORE IMPORTANT THAN HOW TALENTED YOU ARE.
YOU HAVE TO GET IN AS MANY GAMES AS YOU CAN AGAINST STRONG PLAYERS! THAT'S THE BEST WAY!
PLAY GAMES AGAINST STRONG PLAYERS? I'M IN UP TO MY NECK PLAYING GAMES AGAINST ONE STRONG PLAYER.
Considering that, I'd say your progress is rather slow...
WHAT?!

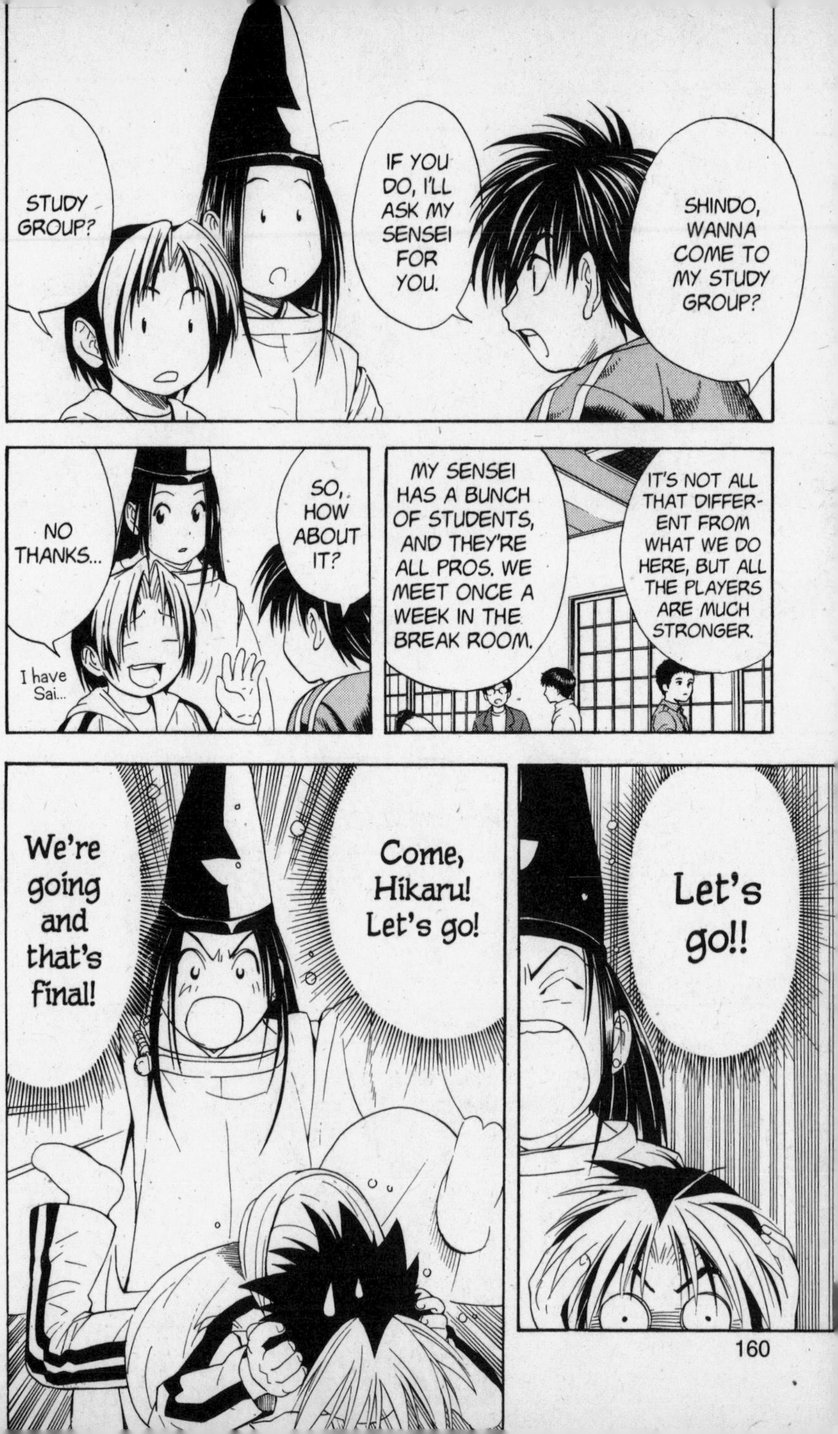
SHINDO, WANNA COME TO MY STUDY GROUP?
IF YOU DO, I'LL ASK MY SENSEI FOR YOU.
STUDY GROUP?
IT'S NOT ALL THAT DIFFER-ENT FROM WHAT WE DO HERE, BUT ALL THE PLAYERS ARE MUCH STRONGER.
MY SENSEI HAS A BUNCH OF STUDENTS, AND THEY'RE ALL PROS. WE MEET ONCE A WEEK IN THE BREAK ROOM.
SO, HOW ABOUT IT?
NO THANKS...
I have Sai...
Let's go!!
Come, Hikaru! Let's go!
We're going and that's final!

READ THIS WAY

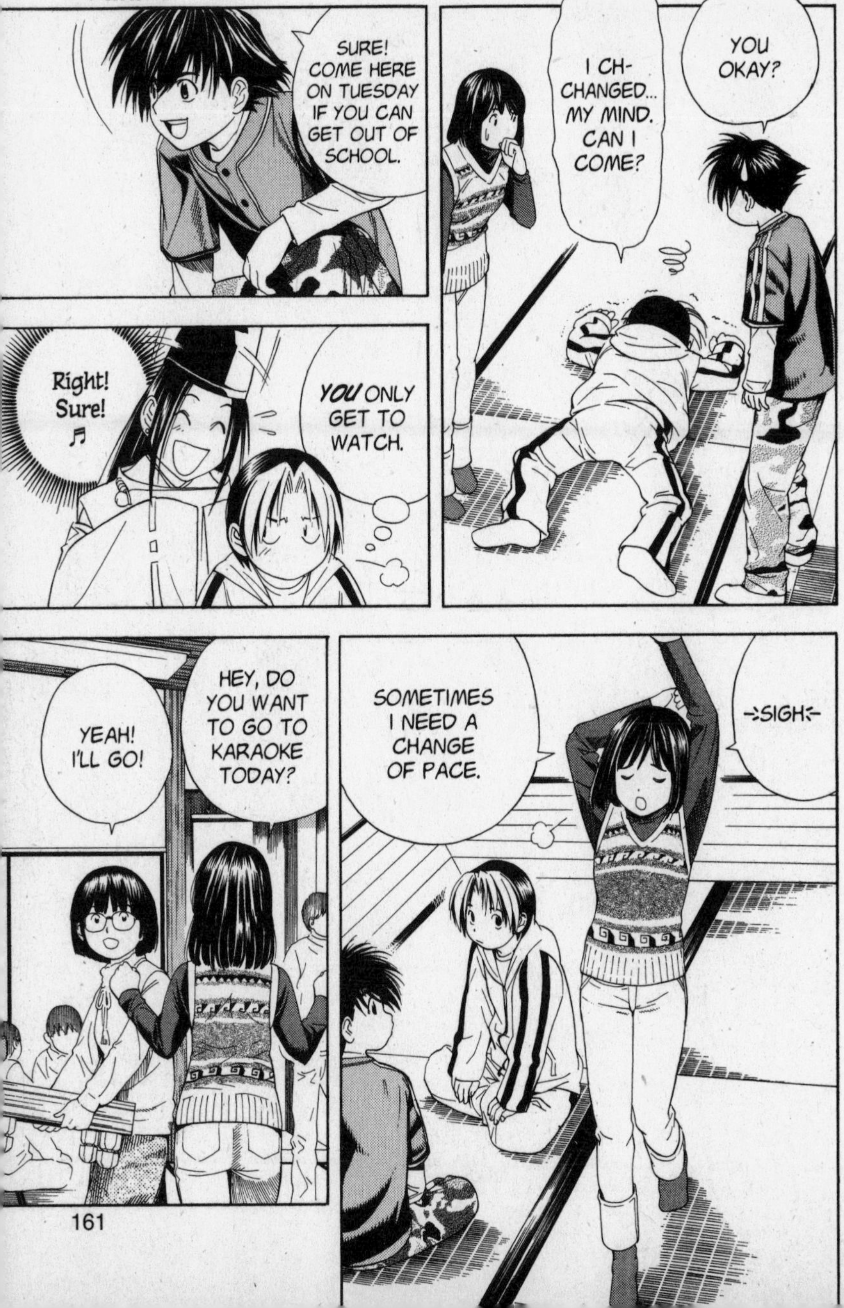
YOU OKAY?
I CH-CHANGED... MY MIND. CAN I COME?
SURE! COME HERE ON TUESDAY IF YOU CAN GET OUT OF SCHOOL.
YOU ONLY GET TO WATCH.
Right! Sure! ♬
~SIGH~
SOMETIMES I NEED A CHANGE OF PACE.
HEY, DO YOU WANT TO GO TO KARAOKE TODAY?
YEAH! I'LL GO!

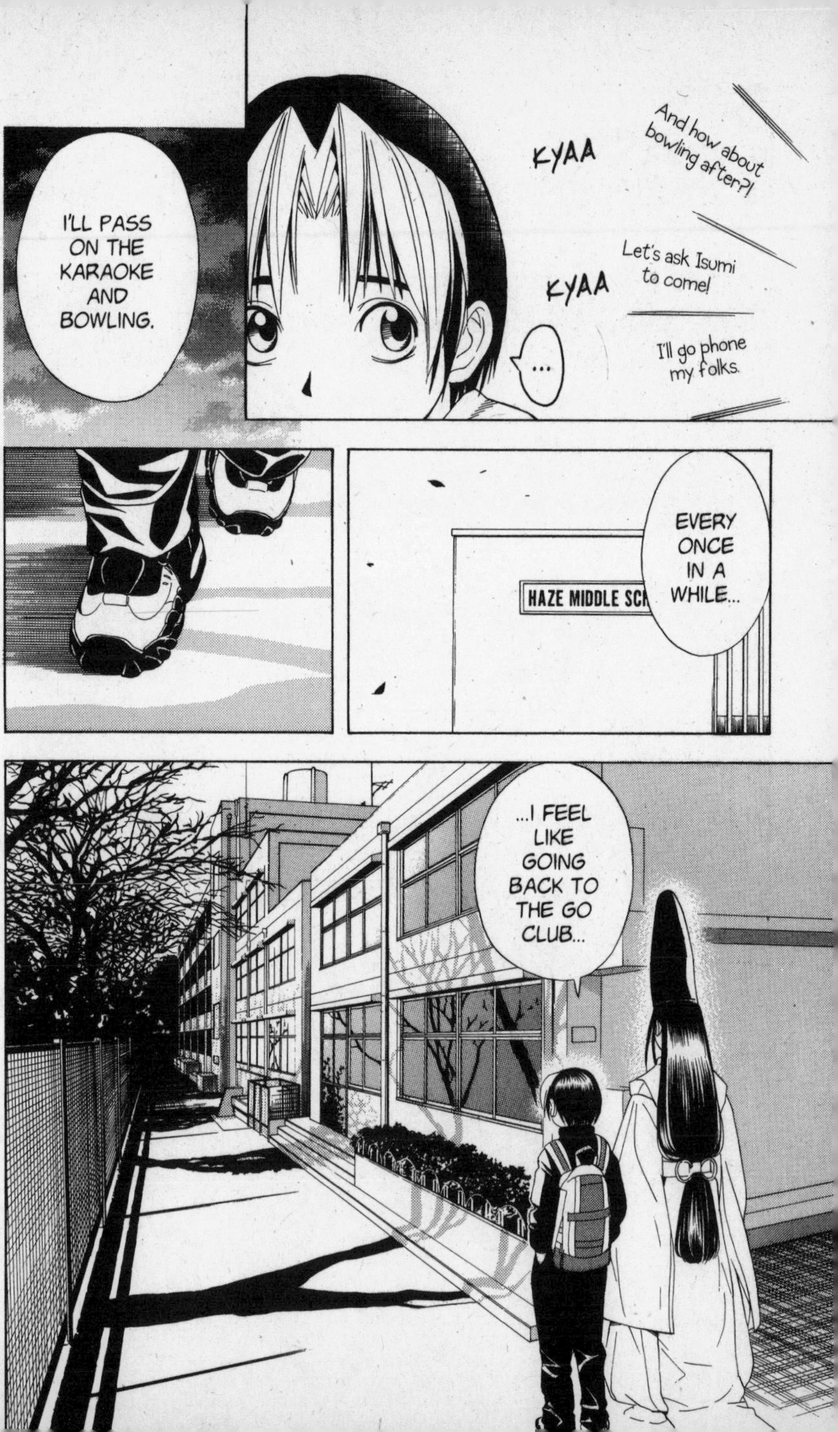
And how about bowling after?!
KYAA
Let's ask Isumi to come!
KYAA
I'll go phone my folks.
...
I'LL PASS ON THE KARAOKE AND BOWLING.
HAZE MIDDLE SC
EVERY ONCE IN A WHILE...
...I FEEL LIKE GOING BACK TO THE GO CLUB...

READ THIS WAY

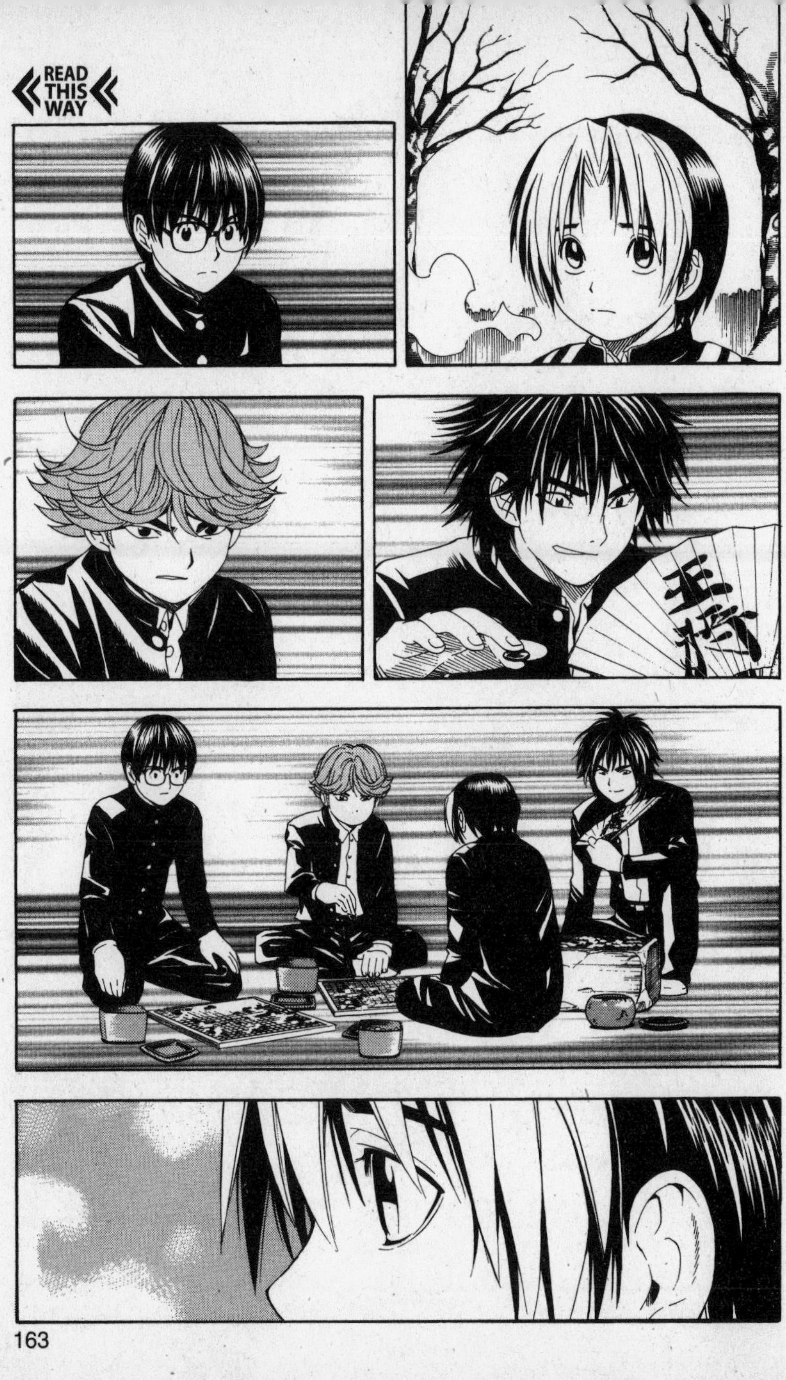

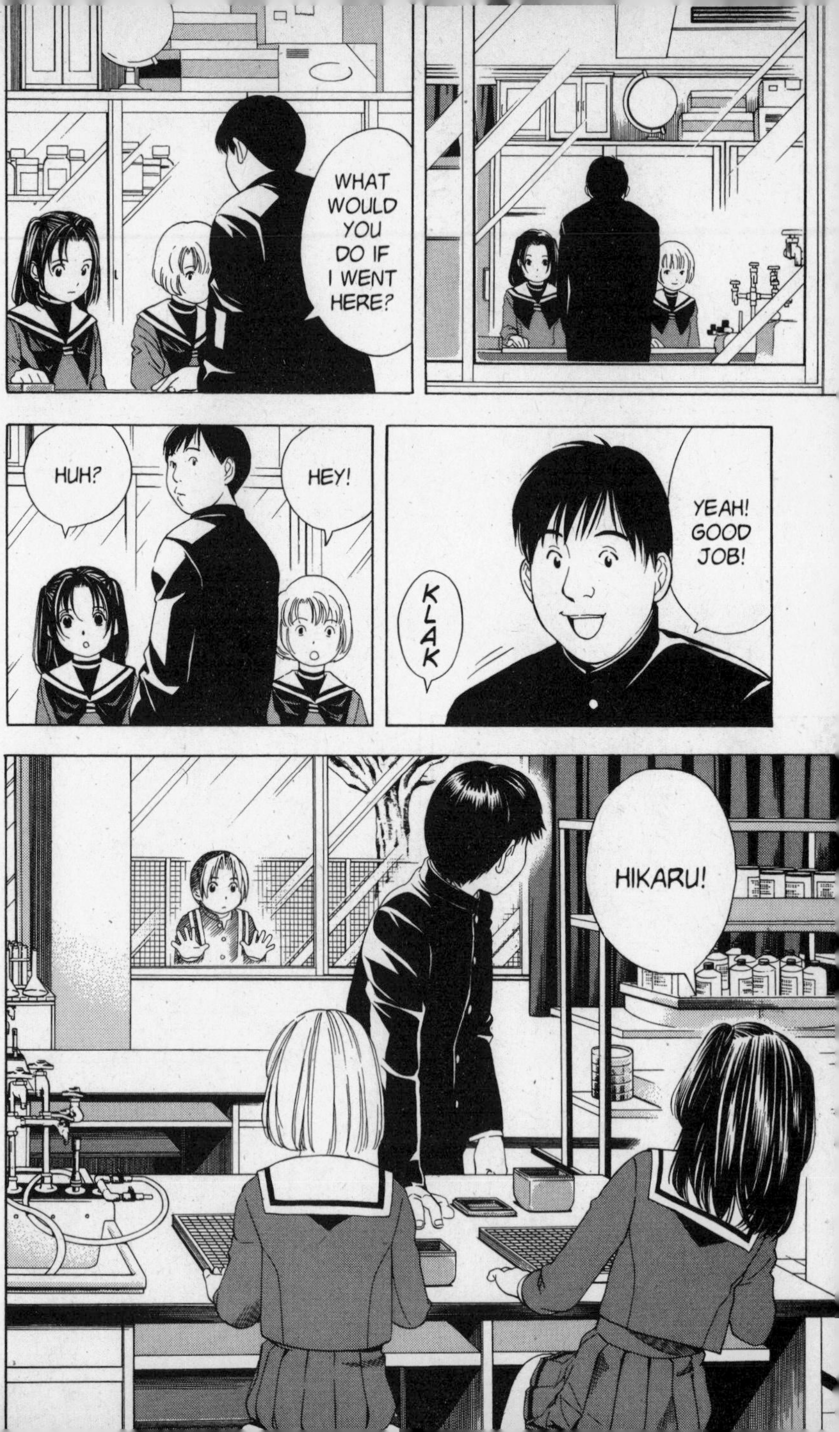
WHAT WOULD YOU DO IF I WENT HERE?
YEAH! GOOD JOB!
KLAK
HEY!
HUH?
HIKARU!

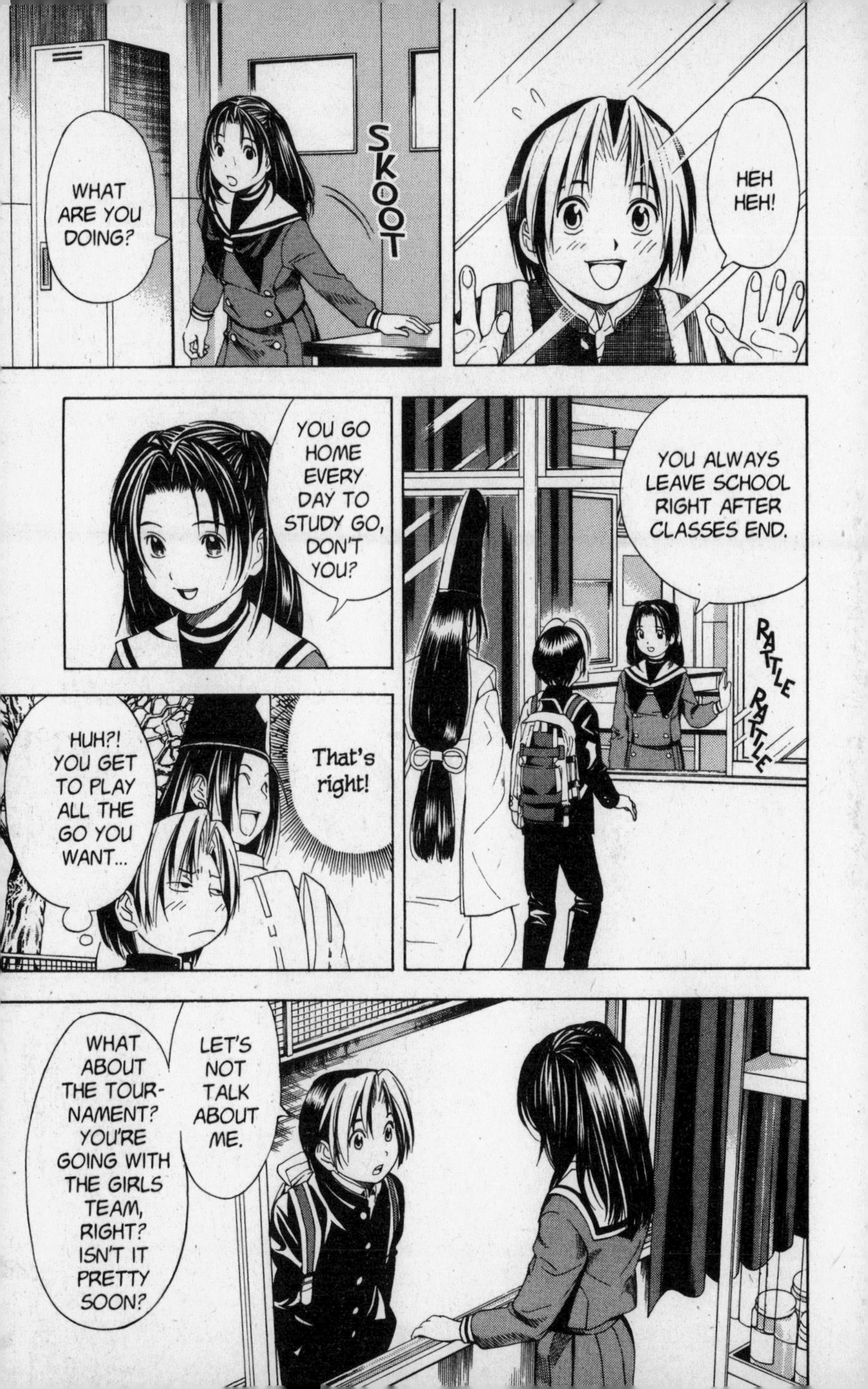
HEH HEH!
SKOOT
WHAT ARE YOU DOING?
YOU ALWAYS LEAVE SCHOOL RIGHT AFTER CLASSES END.
RATTLE RATTLE
YOU GO HOME EVERY DAY TO STUDY GO, DON'T YOU?
That's right!
HUH?! YOU GET TO PLAY ALL THE GO YOU WANT...
LET'S NOT TALK ABOUT ME.
WHAT ABOUT THE TOUR-NAMENT? YOU'RE GOING WITH THE GIRLS TEAM, RIGHT? ISN'T IT PRETTY SOON?

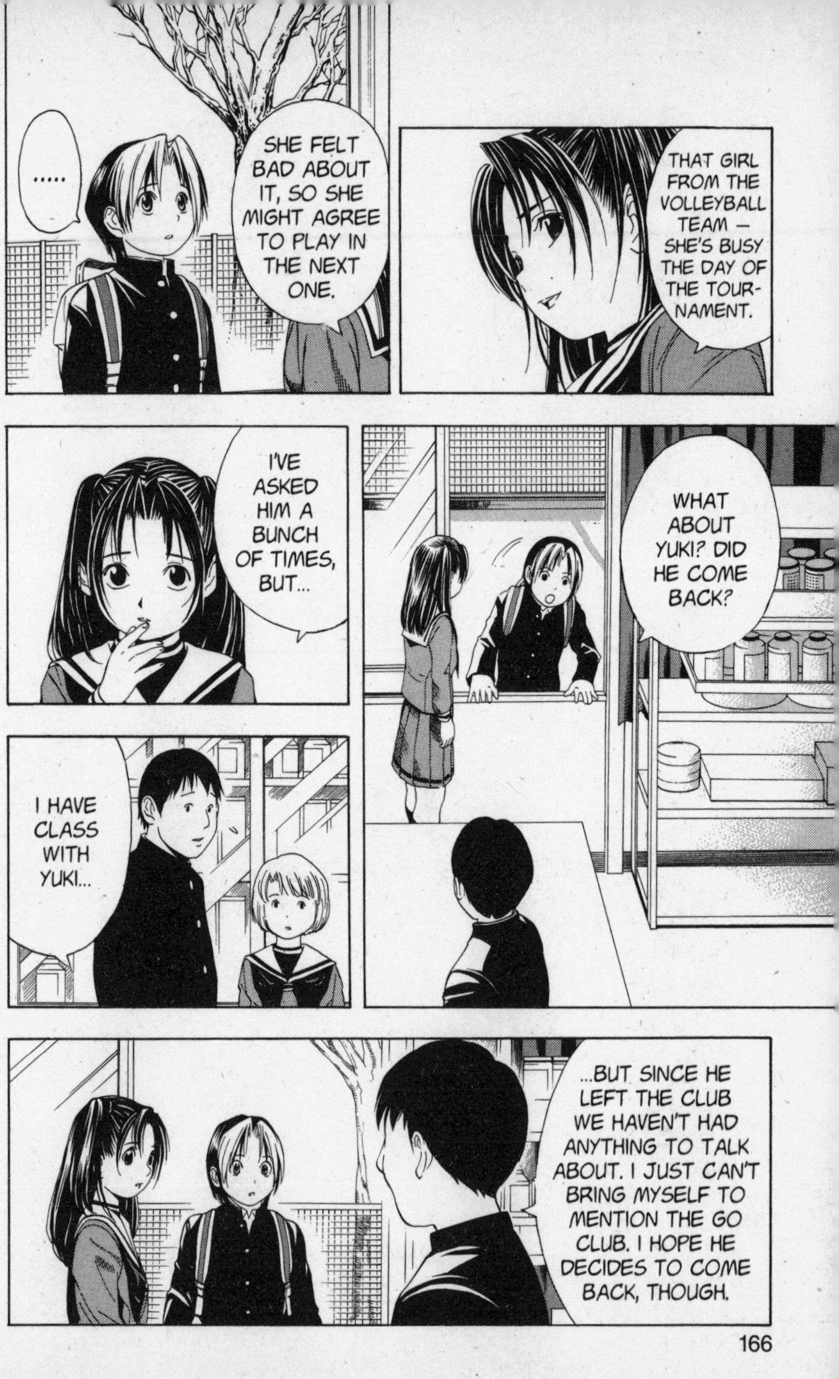
THAT GIRL FROM THE VOLLEYBALL TEAM — SHE'S BUSY THE DAY OF THE TOURNAMENT.
SHE FELT BAD ABOUT IT, SO SHE MIGHT AGREE TO PLAY IN THE NEXT ONE.
.....
WHAT ABOUT YUKI? DID HE COME BACK?
I'VE ASKED HIM A BUNCH OF TIMES, BUT...
I HAVE CLASS WITH YUKI...
...BUT SINCE HE LEFT THE CLUB WE HAVEN'T HAD ANYTHING TO TALK ABOUT. I JUST CAN'T BRING MYSELF TO MENTION THE GO CLUB. I HOPE HE DECIDES TO COME BACK, THOUGH.

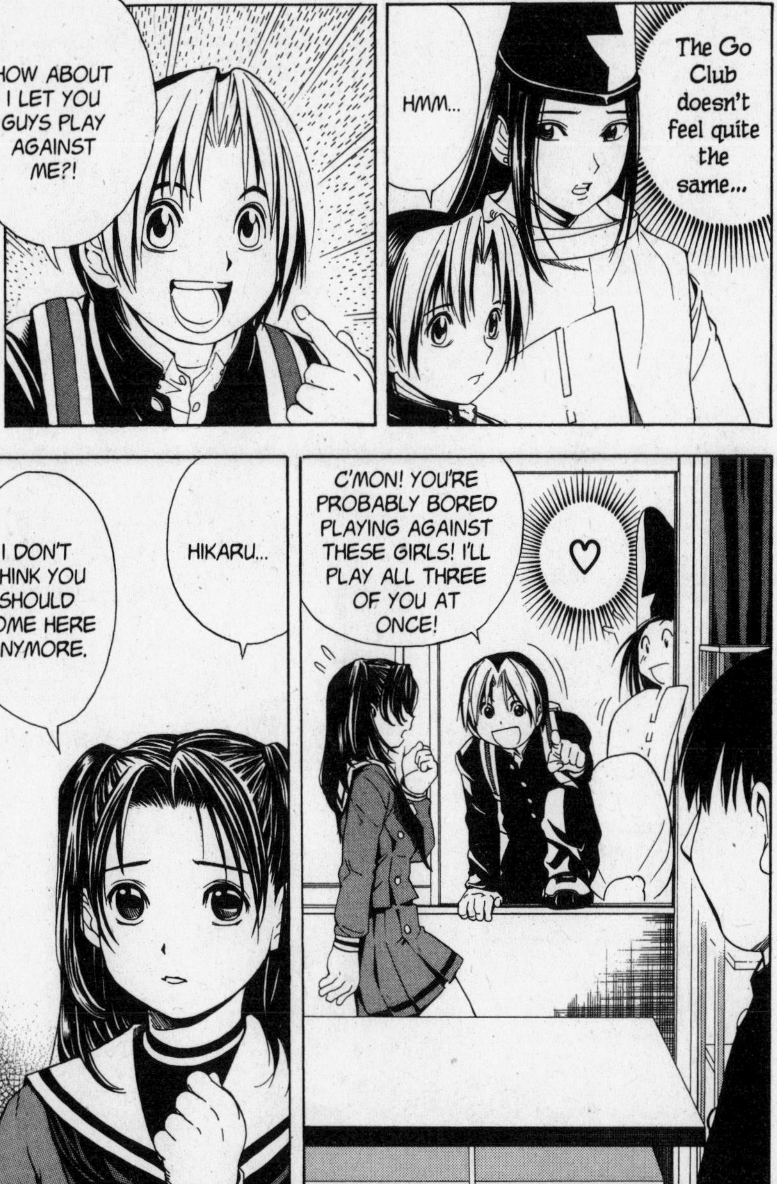
The Go Club doesn't feel quite the same...
HMM...
HOW ABOUT I LET YOU GUYS PLAY AGAINST ME?!
C'MON! YOU'RE PROBABLY BORED PLAYING AGAINST THESE GIRLS! I'LL PLAY ALL THREE OF YOU AT ONCE!
HIKARU...
I DON'T THINK YOU SHOULD COME HERE ANYMORE.

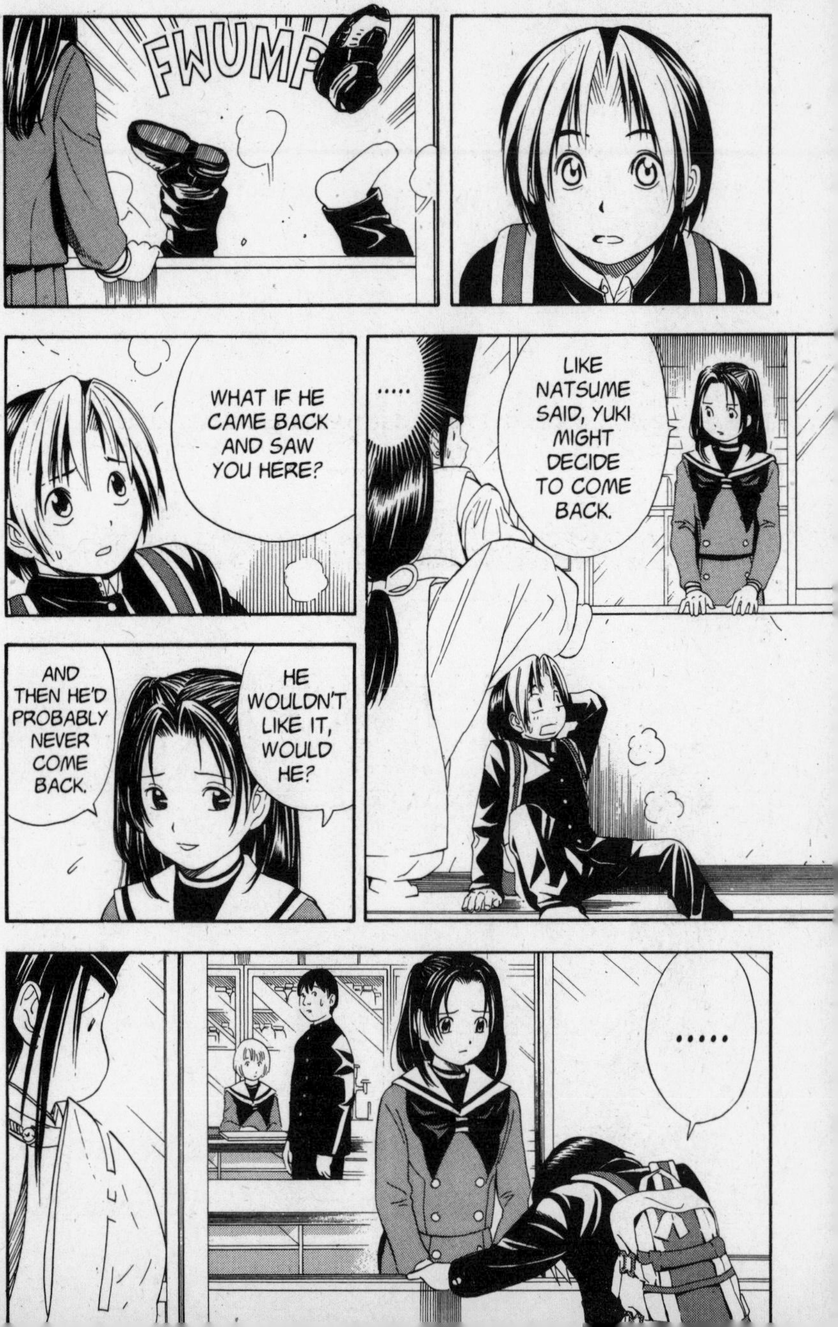
FWUMP
LIKE NATSUME SAID, YUKI MIGHT DECIDE TO COME BACK.
.....
WHAT IF HE CAME BACK AND SAW YOU HERE?
HE WOULDN'T LIKE IT, WOULD HE?
AND THEN HE'D PROBABLY NEVER COME BACK.
.....

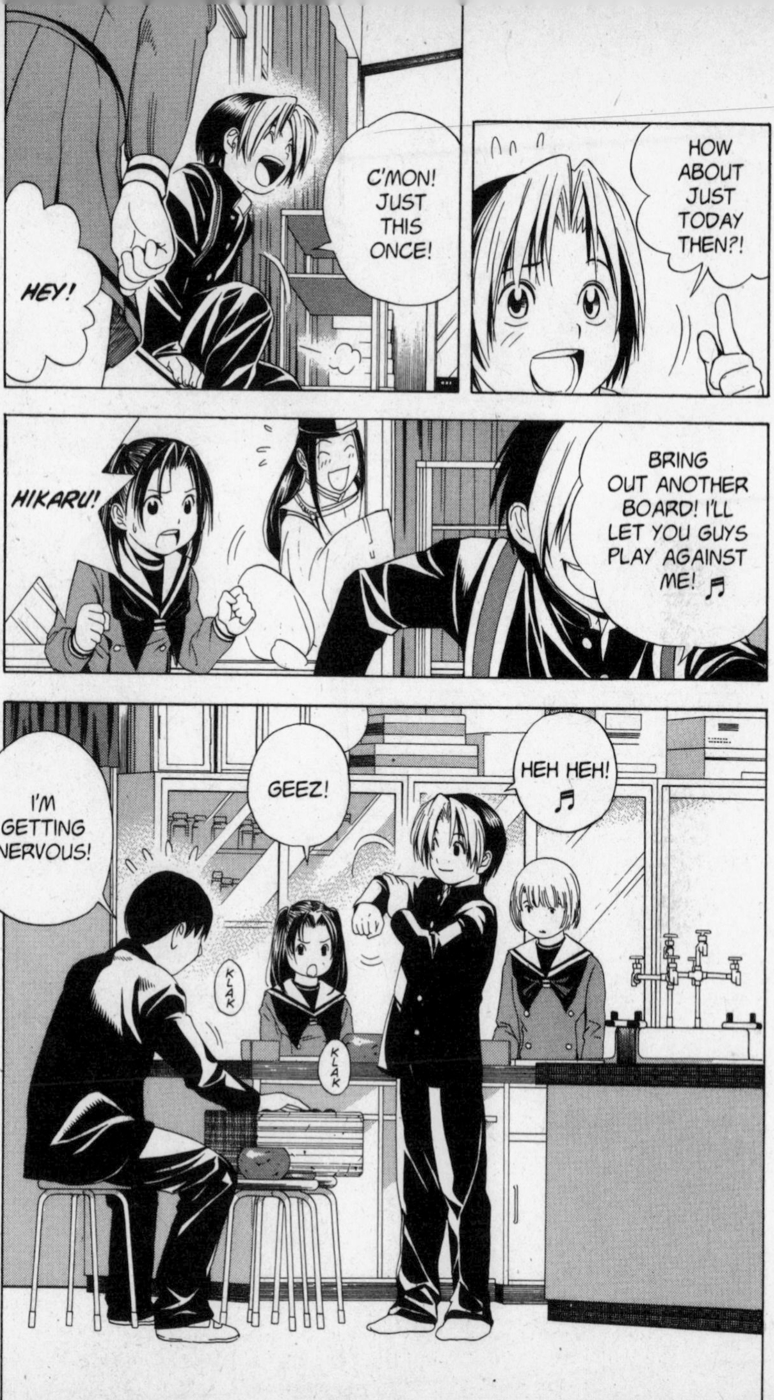
HOW ABOUT JUST TODAY THEN?!
C'MON! JUST THIS ONCE!
HEY!
BRING OUT ANOTHER BOARD! I'LL LET YOU GUYS PLAY AGAINST ME! ♬
HIKARU!
HEH HEH! ♫
GEEZ!
I'M GETTING NERVOUS!
KLAK
KLAK

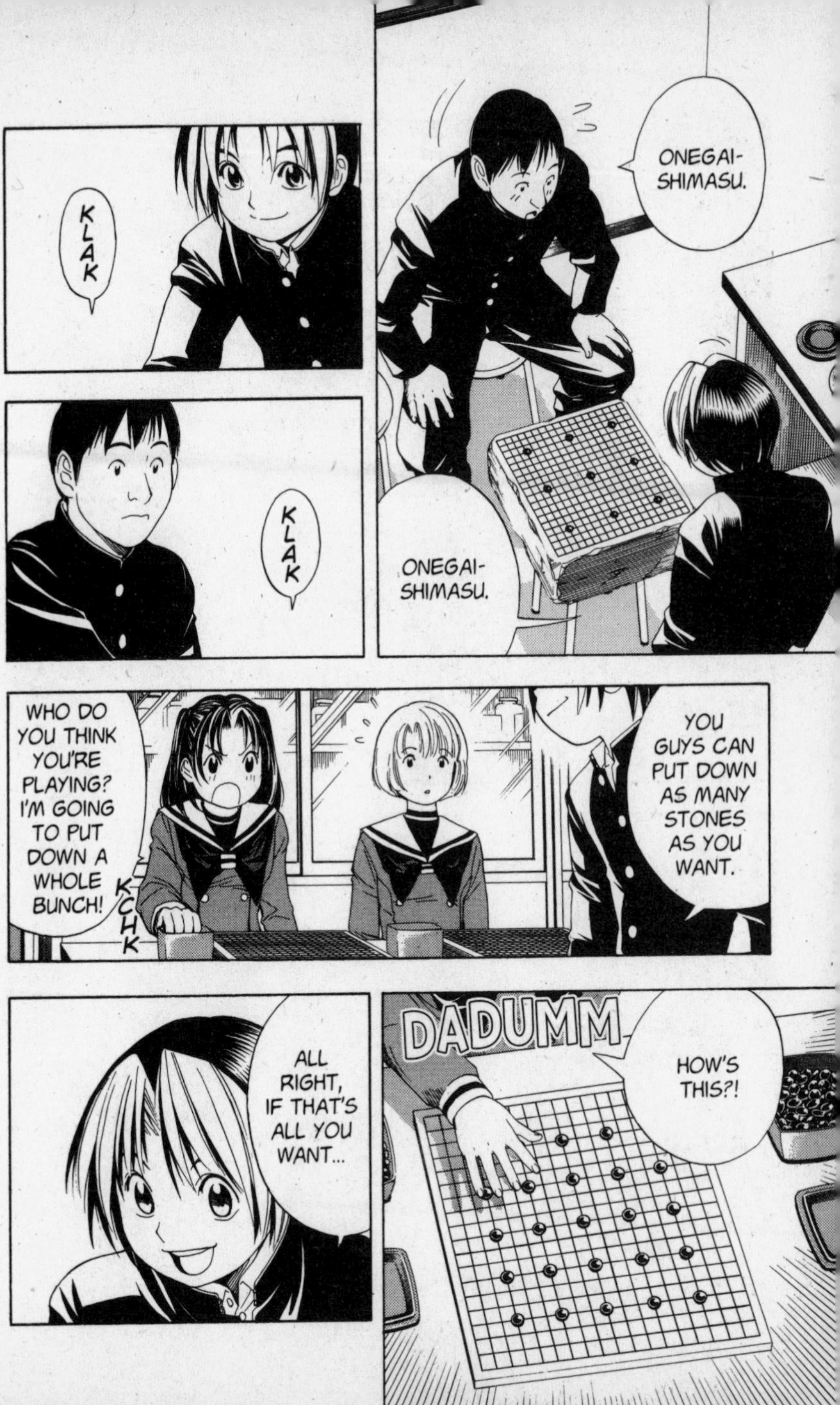
ONEGAI-SHIMASU.
ONEGAI-SHIMASU.
KLAK
KLAK
YOU GUYS CAN PUT DOWN AS MANY STONES AS YOU WANT.
WHO DO YOU THINK YOU'RE PLAYING? I'M GOING TO PUT DOWN A WHOLE BUNCH!
KCHK
HOW'S THIS?!
DADUMM
ALL RIGHT, IF THAT'S ALL YOU WANT...

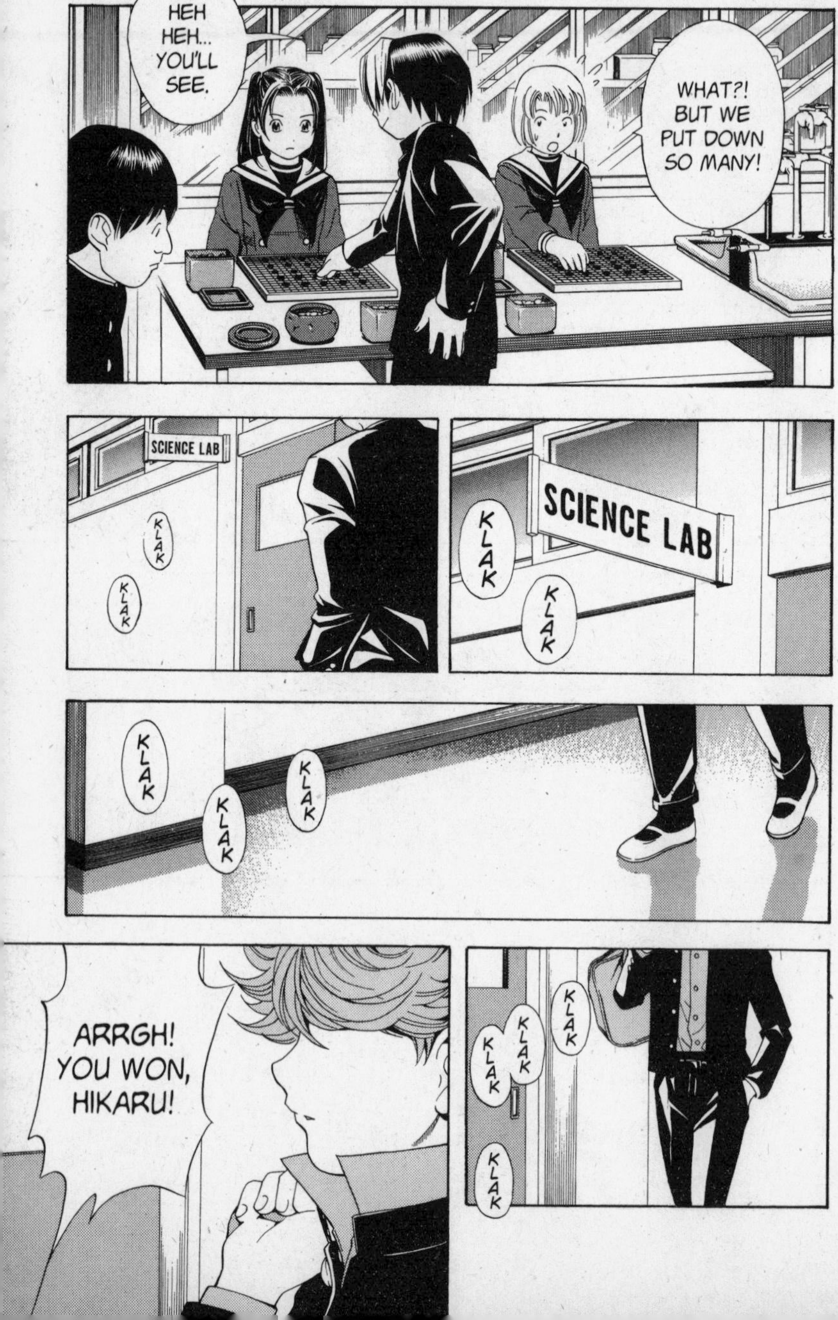
WHAT?! BUT WE PUT DOWN SO MANY!
HEH HEH... YOU'LL SEE.
SCIENCE LAB
KLAK
KLAK
SCIENCE LAB
KLAK
KLAK
KLAK
KLAK
KLAK
KLAK
KLAK
KLAK
KLAK
ARRGH! YOU WON, HIKARU!

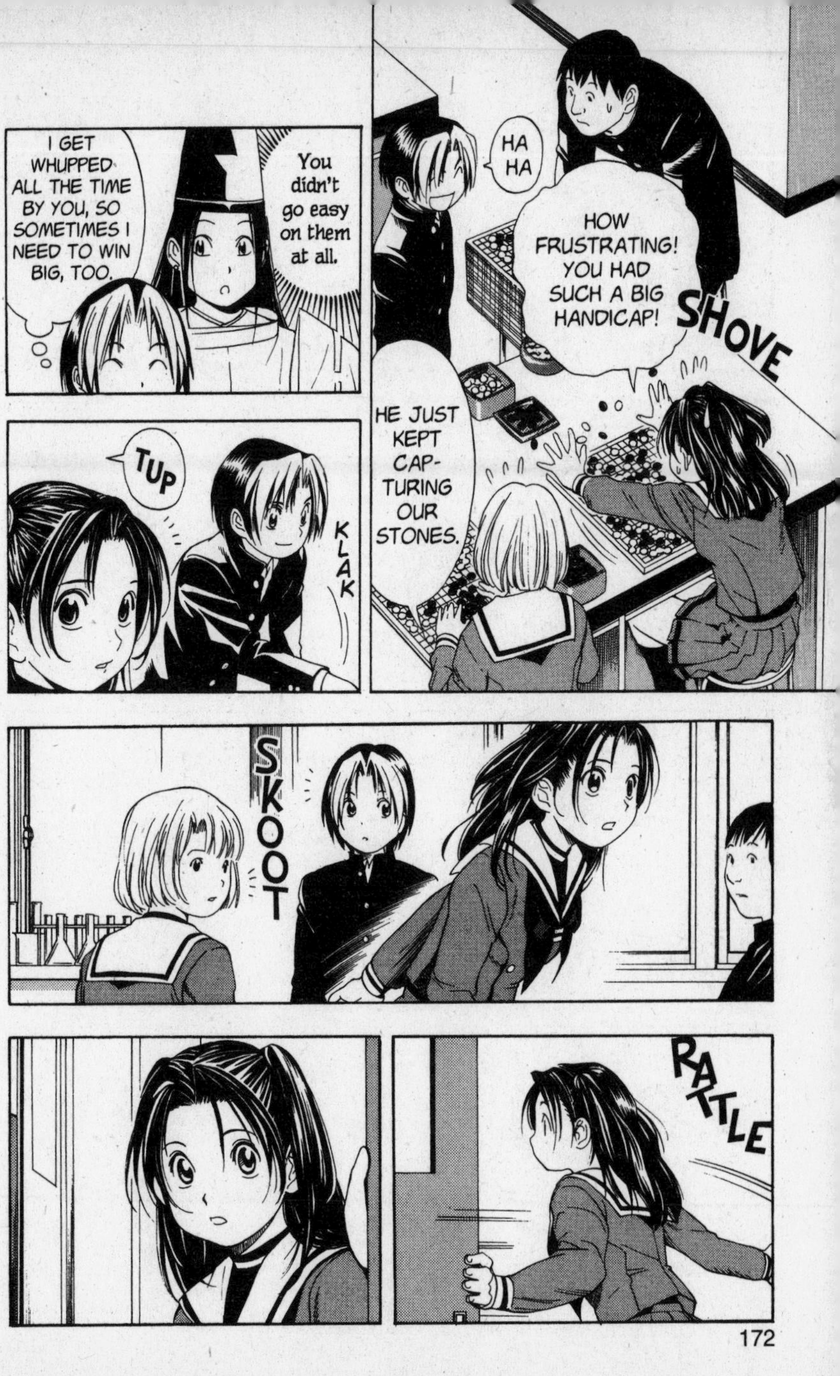
HA HA
HOW FRUSTRATING! YOU HAD SUCH A BIG HANDICAP!
SHOVE
HE JUST KEPT CAP-TURING OUR STONES.
You didn't go easy on them at all.
I GET WHUPPED ALL THE TIME BY YOU, SO SOMETIMES I NEED TO WIN BIG, TOO.
KLAK
TUP
SKOOT
RATTLE

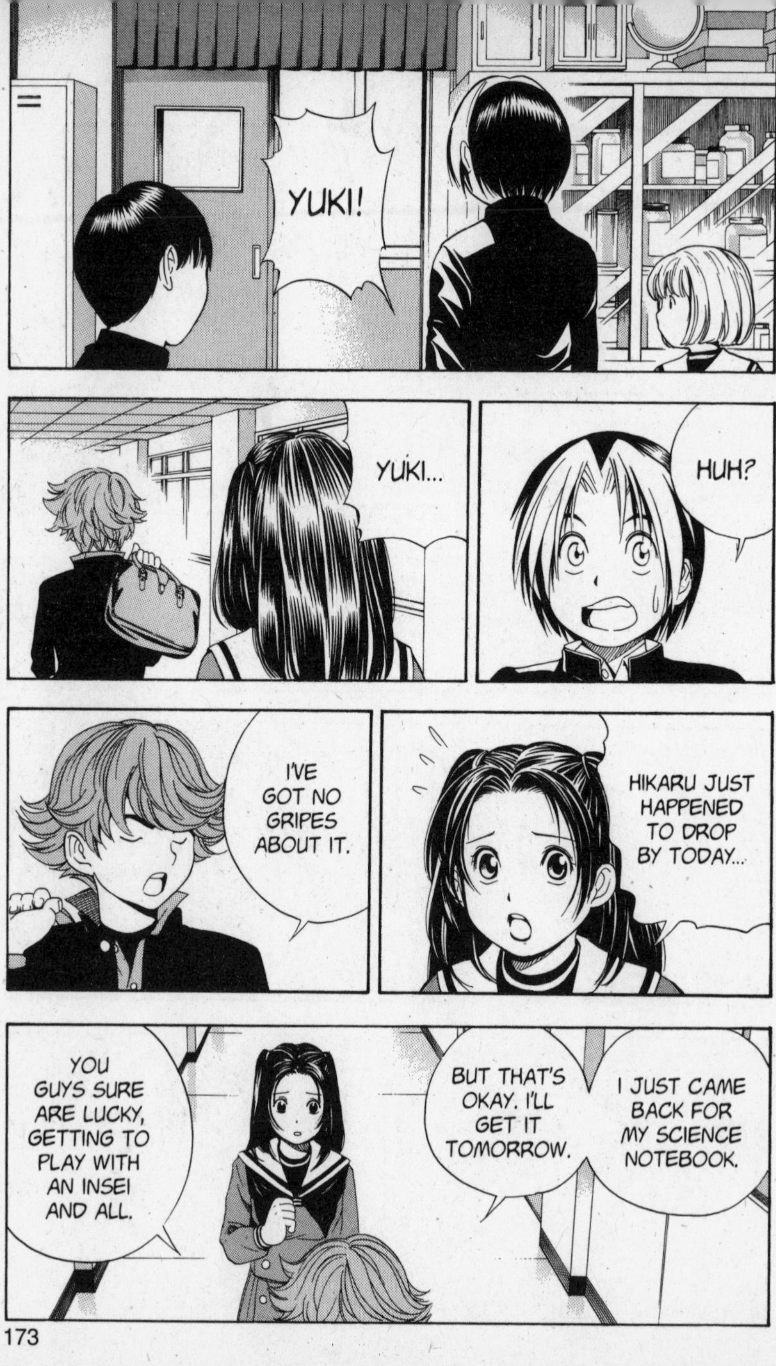
YUKI!
HUH?
YUKI...
HIKARU JUST HAPPENED TO DROP BY TODAY...
I'VE GOT NO GRIPES ABOUT IT.
I JUST CAME BACK FOR MY SCIENCE NOTEBOOK.
BUT THAT'S OKAY. I'LL GET IT TOMORROW.
YOU GUYS SURE ARE LUCKY, GETTING TO PLAY WITH AN INSEI AND ALL.

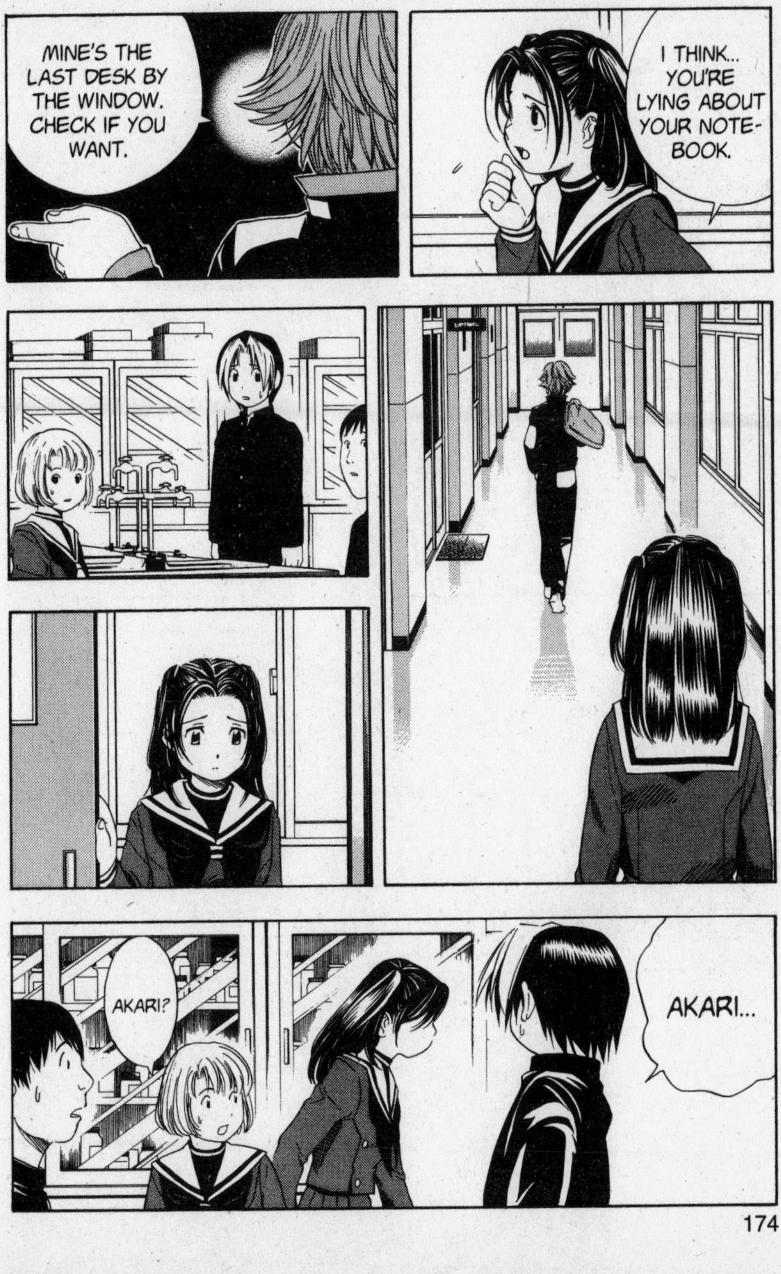
I THINK... YOU'RE LYING ABOUT YOUR NOTE-BOOK.
MINE'S THE LAST DESK BY THE WINDOW. CHECK IF YOU WANT.
AKARI...
AKARI?

READ THIS WAY

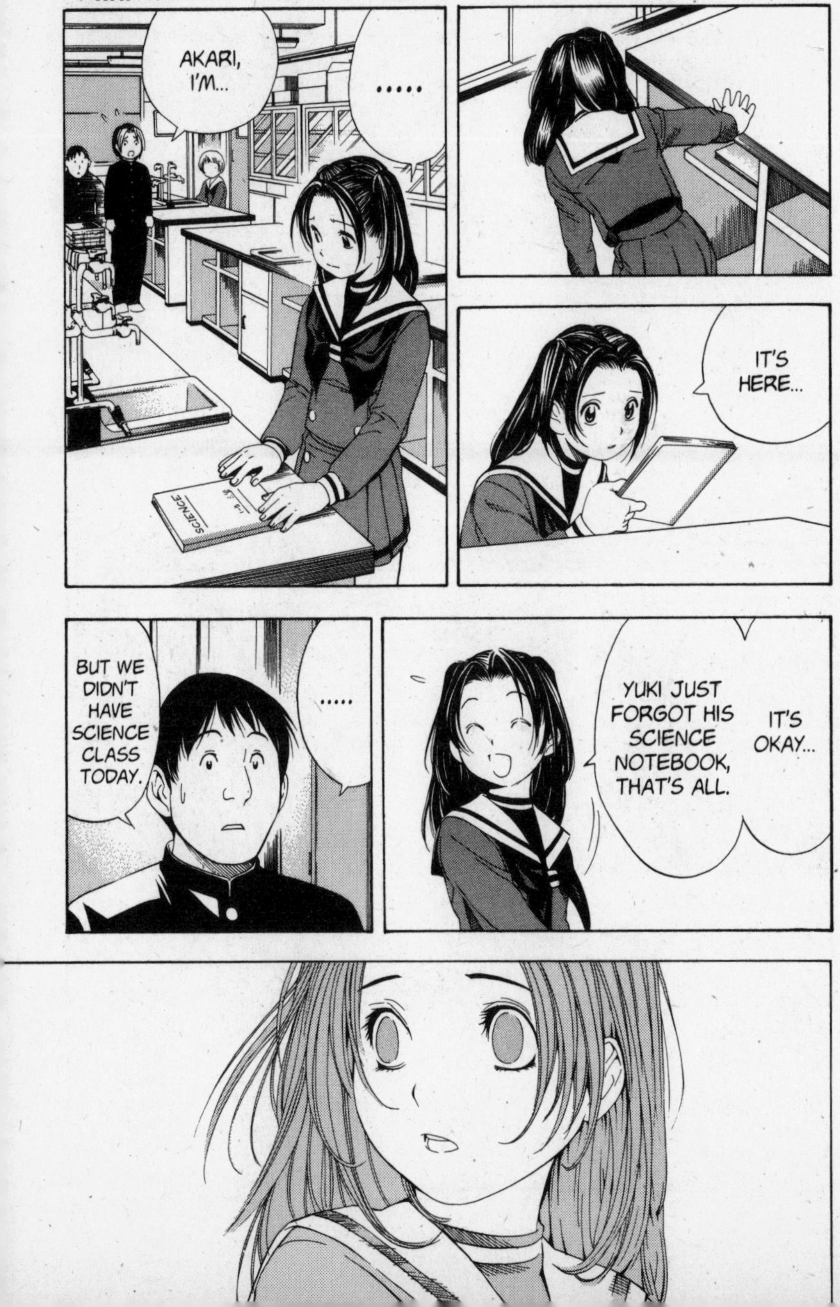
IT'S HERE...
.....
AKARI, I'M...
IT'S OKAY...
YUKI JUST FORGOT HIS SCIENCE NOTEBOOK, THAT'S ALL.
.....
BUT WE DIDN'T HAVE SCIENCE CLASS TODAY.
SCIENCE

HAZE MIDDLE S

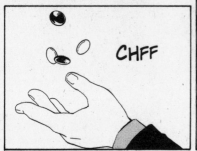

CHFF

NATSUME'S IN MY SCIENCE CLASS.

CHK

OOPS...

HMPH...

READ THIS WAY

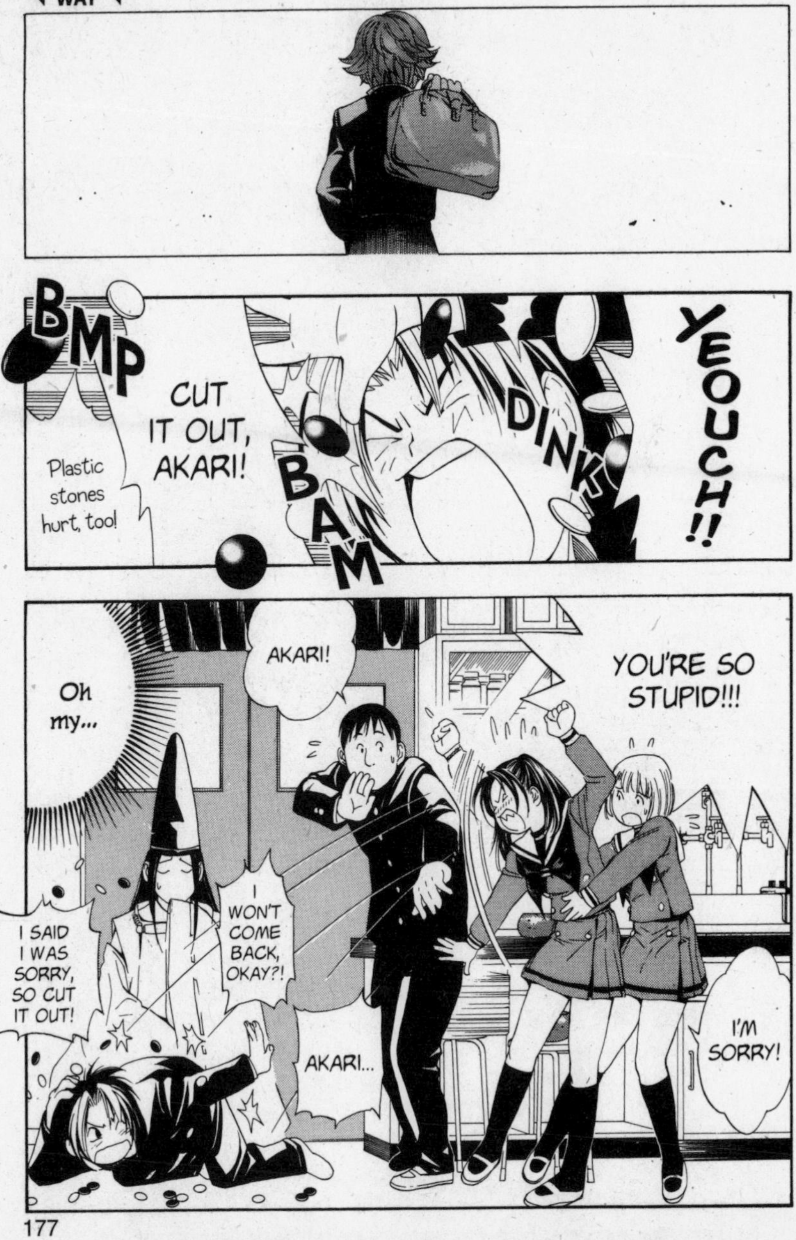

YEOUCH!!
DINK
BAM
CUT IT OUT, AKARI!
Plastic stones hurt, too!
BMP
YOU'RE SO STUPID!!!
AKARI!
Oh my...
I'M SORRY!
AKARI...
I WON'T COME BACK, OKAY?!
I SAID I WAS SORRY, SO CUT IT OUT!

A WORD ABOUT HIKARU NO GO

THE KANSAI GO ASSOCIATION

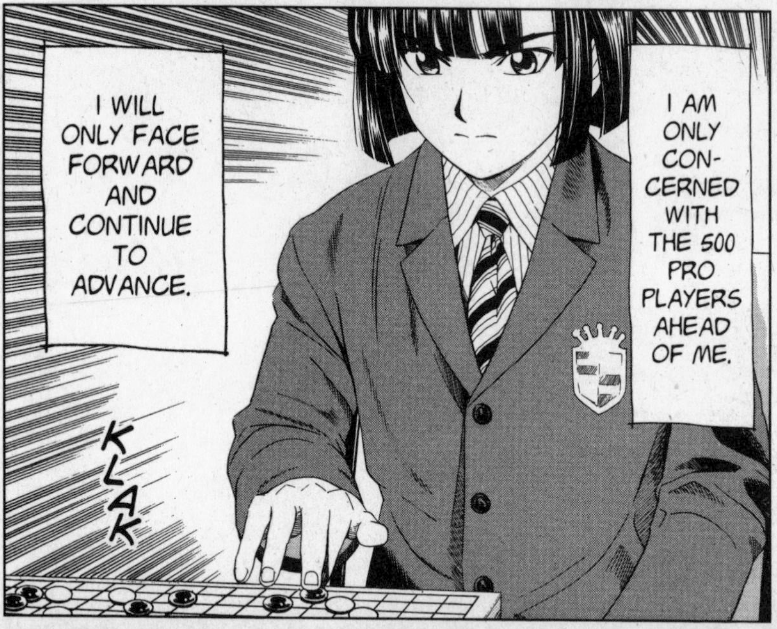
I AM ONLY CON-CERNED WITH THE 500 PRO PLAYERS AHEAD OF ME.
I WILL ONLY FACE FORWARD AND CONTINUE TO ADVANCE.
KLAK

IT HASN'T BEEN MENTIONED YET, BUT IN ADDITION TO THE JAPAN GO ASSOCIATION (NIHON KI-IN) THERE'S ALSO THE KANSAI GO ASSOCIATION (KANSAI KI-IN). THEY ARE RUN AS SEPARATE ORGANIZATIONS, BUT MEMBERS OF BOTH COMPETE IN TITLE MATCHES SUCH AS THE MEIJIN AND HON'INBO TITLES. SO THE 500 PEOPLE MENTIONED ABOVE COUNT ALL OF THE PROS IN JAPAN, NOT JUST THE PROS IN THE JAPAN GO ASSOCIATION.

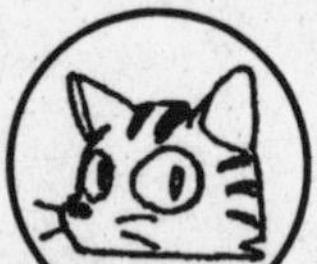

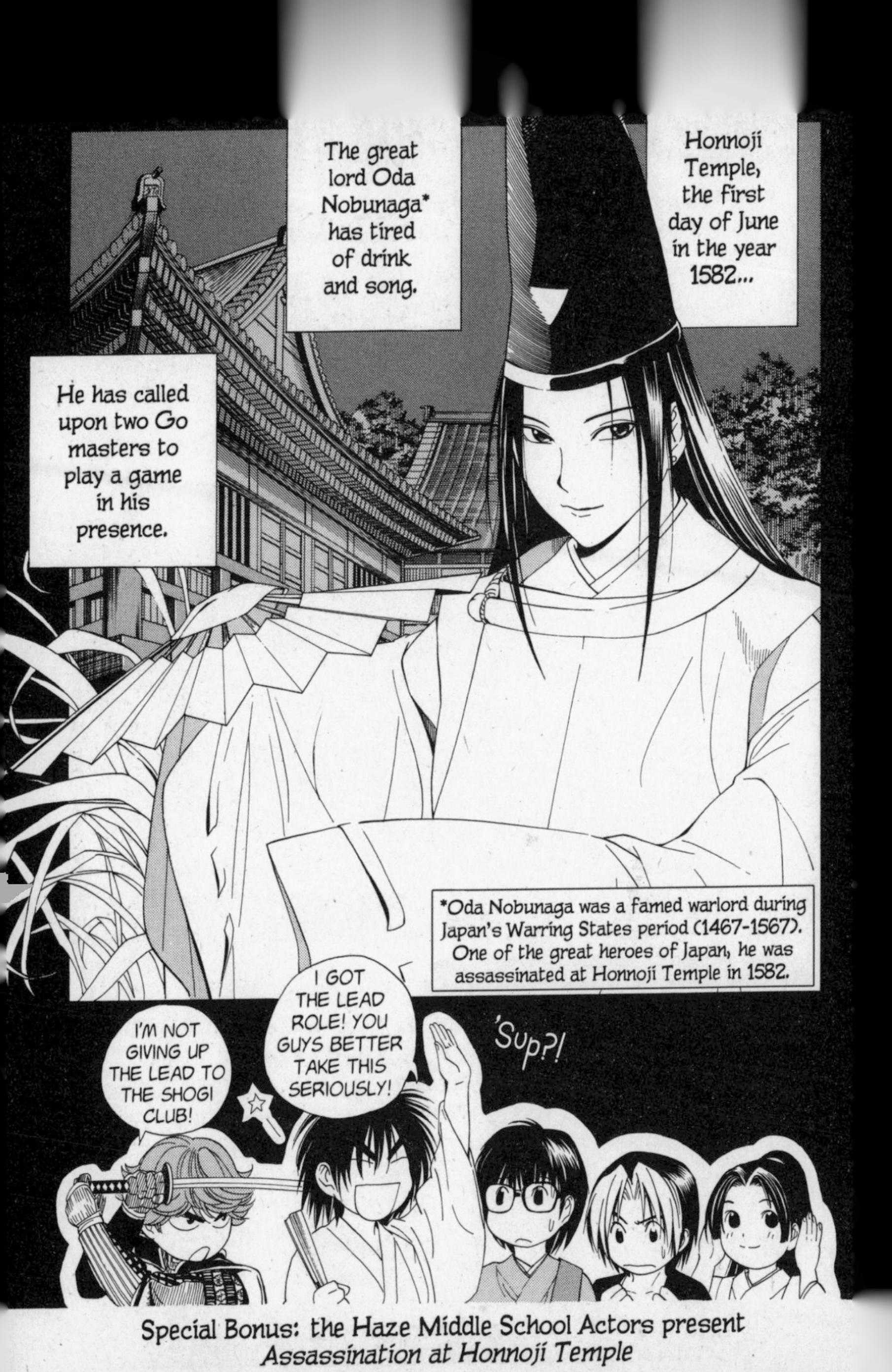
Honnoji Temple, the first day of June in the year 1582...
The great lord Oda Nobunaga* has tired of drink and song.
He has called upon two Go masters to play a game in his presence.
*Oda Nobunaga was a famed warlord during Japan's Warring States period (1467-1567). One of the great heroes of Japan, he was assassinated at Honnoji Temple in 1582.
'Sup?!
I GOT THE LEAD ROLE! YOU GUYS BETTER TAKE THIS SERIOUSLY!
I'M NOT GIVING UP THE LEAD TO THE SHOGI CLUB!

Special Bonus: the Haze Middle School Actors present *Assassination at Honnoji Temple*

SPECIAL BONUS

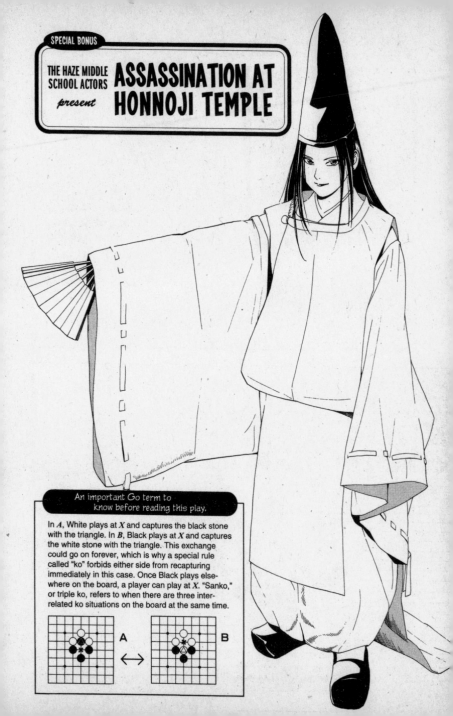

THE HAZE MIDDLE SCHOOL ACTORS *present*

ASSASSINATION AT HONNOJI TEMPLE

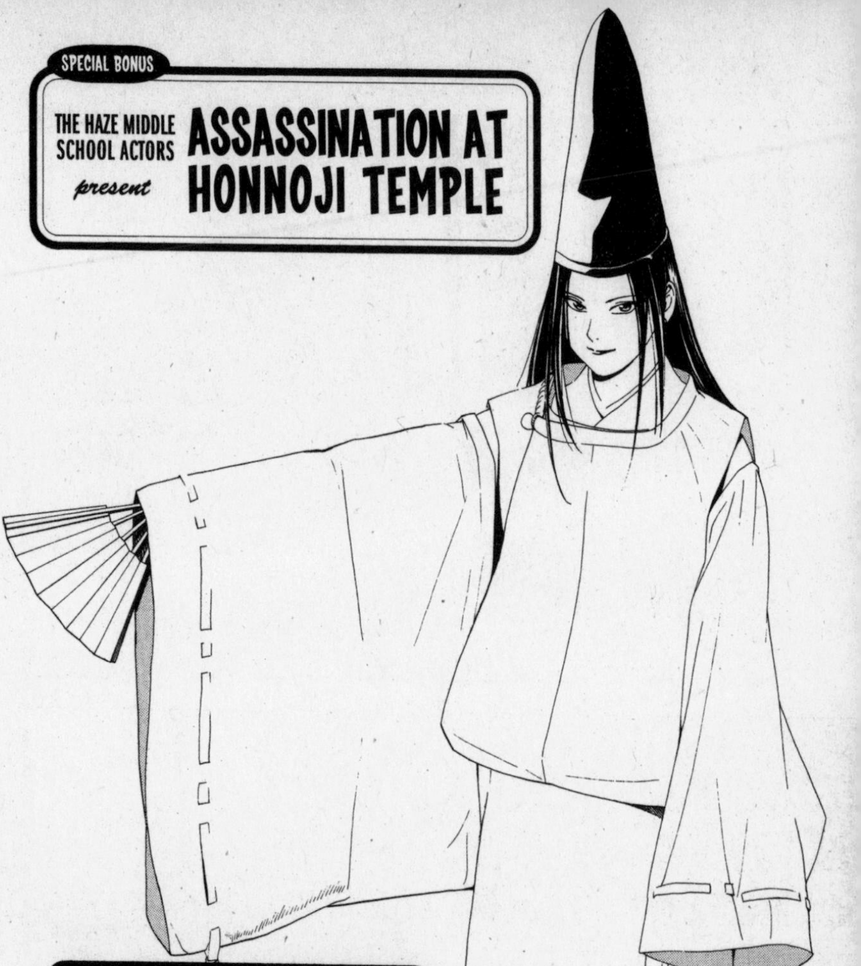

An important Go term to know before reading this play.

In *A*, White plays at *X* and captures the black stone with the triangle. In *B*, Black plays at *X* and captures the white stone with the triangle. This exchange could go on forever, which is why a special rule called "ko" forbids either side from recapturing immediately in this case. Once Black plays elsewhere on the board, a player can play at *X*. "Sanko," or triple ko, refers to when there are three interrelated ko situations on the board at the same time.

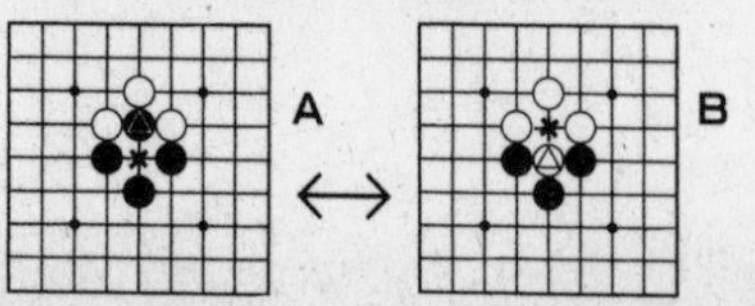
A
B

READ THIS WAY

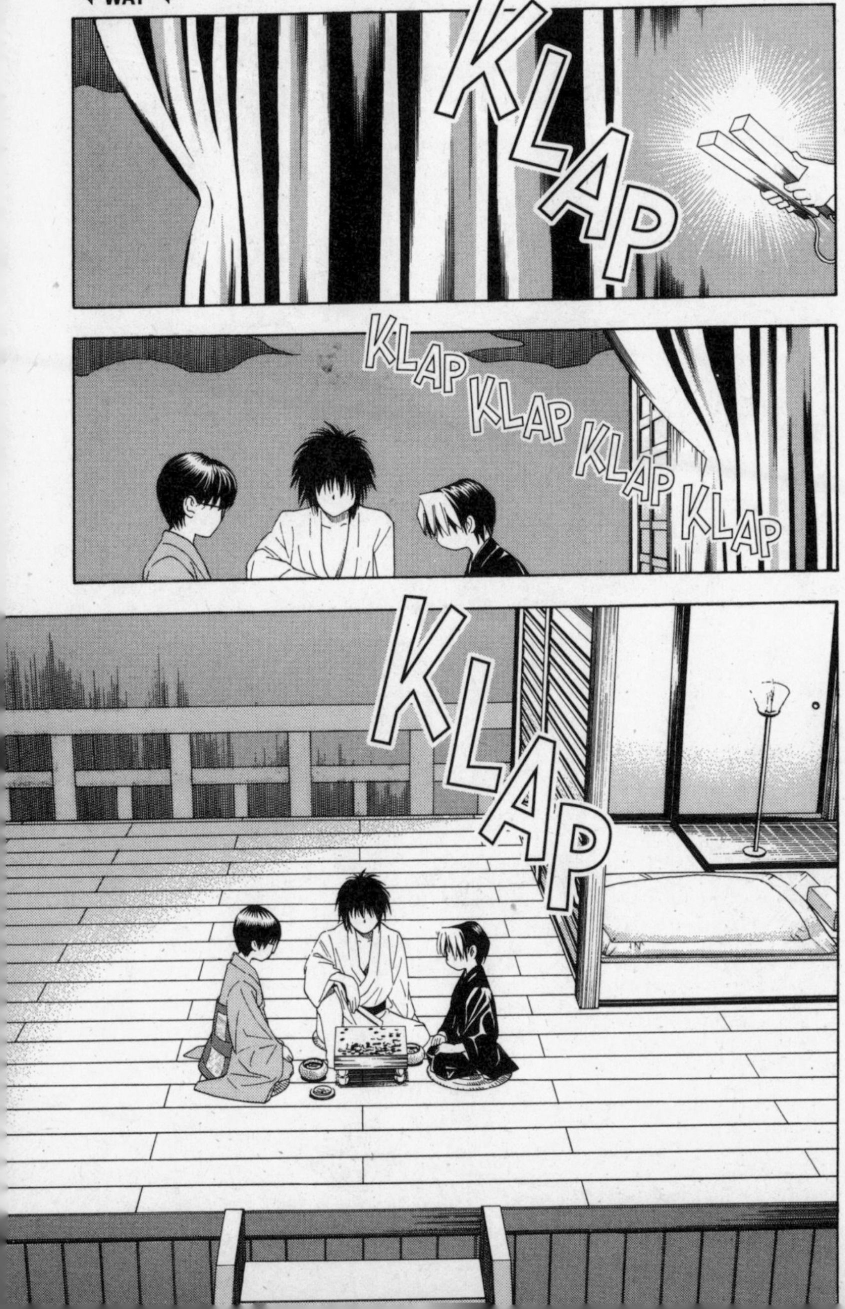
KLAP
KLAP
KLAP
KLAP
KLAP
KLAP

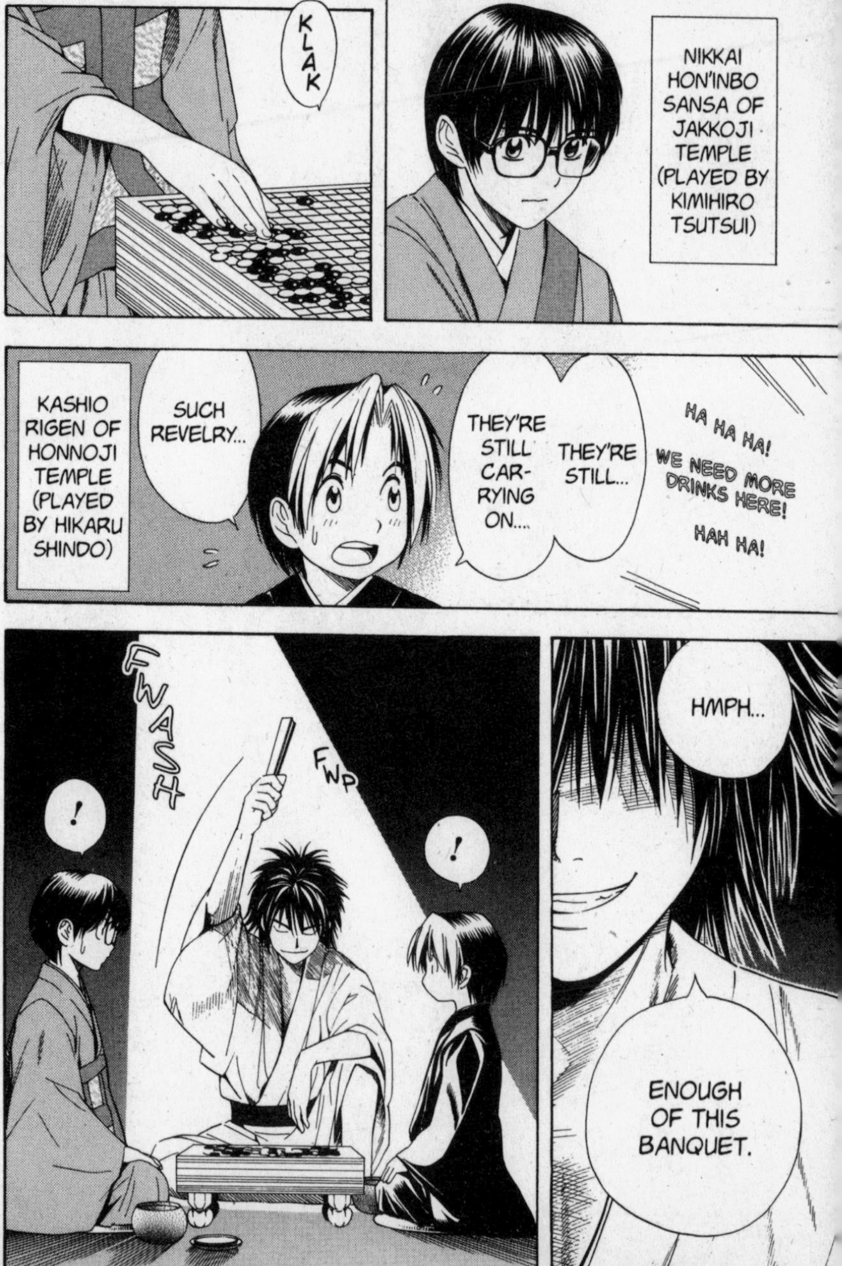
NIKKAI HON'INBO SANSA OF JAKKOJI TEMPLE (PLAYED BY KIMIHIRO TSUTSUI)
KLAK
HA HA HA!
WE NEED MORE DRINKS HERE!
HAH HA!
THEY'RE STILL...
THEY'RE STILL CAR-RYING ON....
SUCH REVELRY...
KASHIO RIGEN OF HONNOJI TEMPLE (PLAYED BY HIKARU SHINDO)
HMPH...
ENOUGH OF THIS BANQUET.
FWP
!
FWASH
!

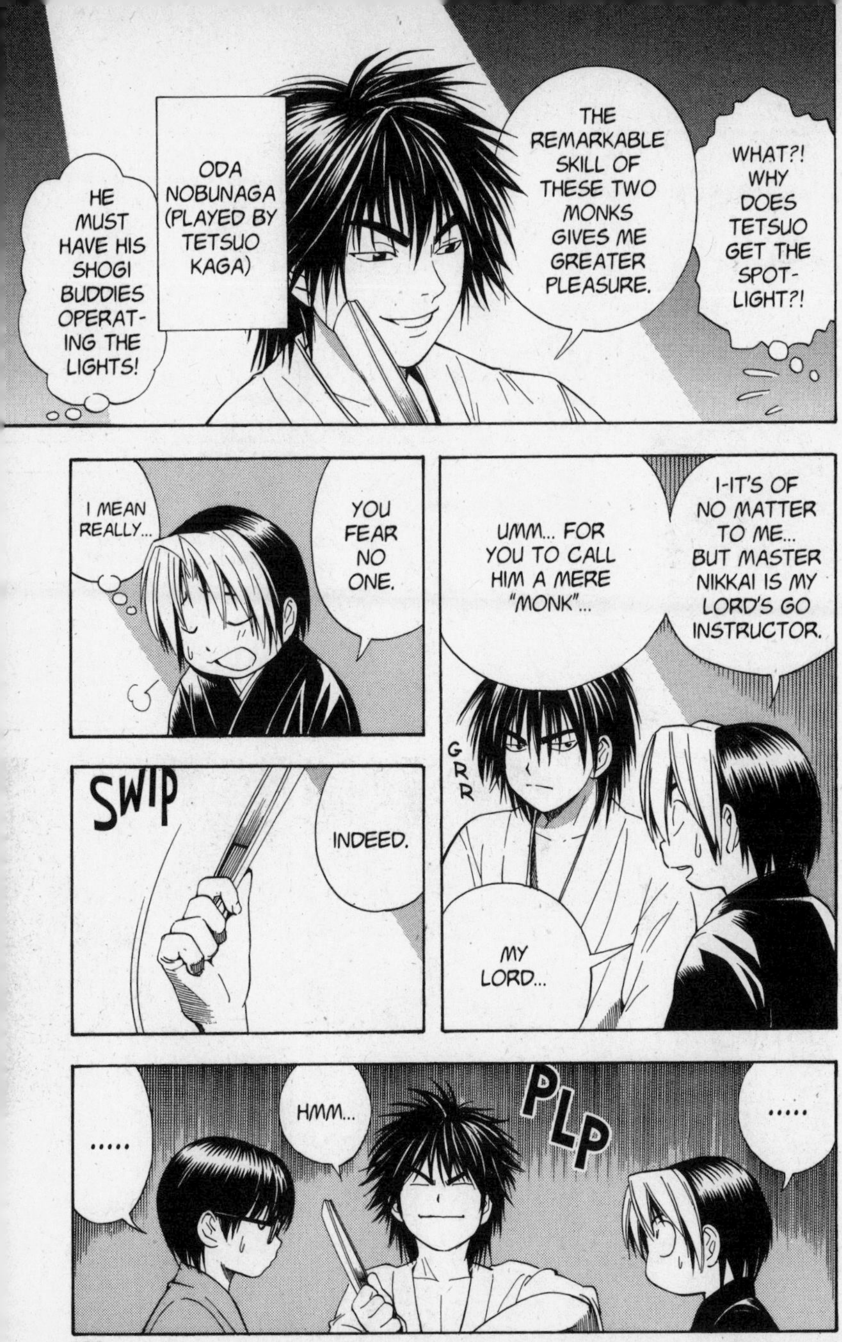
WHAT?! WHY DOES TETSUO GET THE SPOT-LIGHT?!
THE REMARKABLE SKILL OF THESE TWO MONKS GIVES ME GREATER PLEASURE.
ODA NOBUNAGA (PLAYED BY TETSUO KAGA)
HE MUST HAVE HIS SHOGI BUDDIES OPERAT-ING THE LIGHTS!
I-IT'S OF NO MATTER TO ME... BUT MASTER NIKKAI IS MY LORD'S GO INSTRUCTOR.
UMM... FOR YOU TO CALL HIM A MERE "MONK"...
GRR
MY LORD...
YOU FEAR NO ONE.
I MEAN REALLY...
INDEED.
SWIP
.....
PLP
HMM...
.....

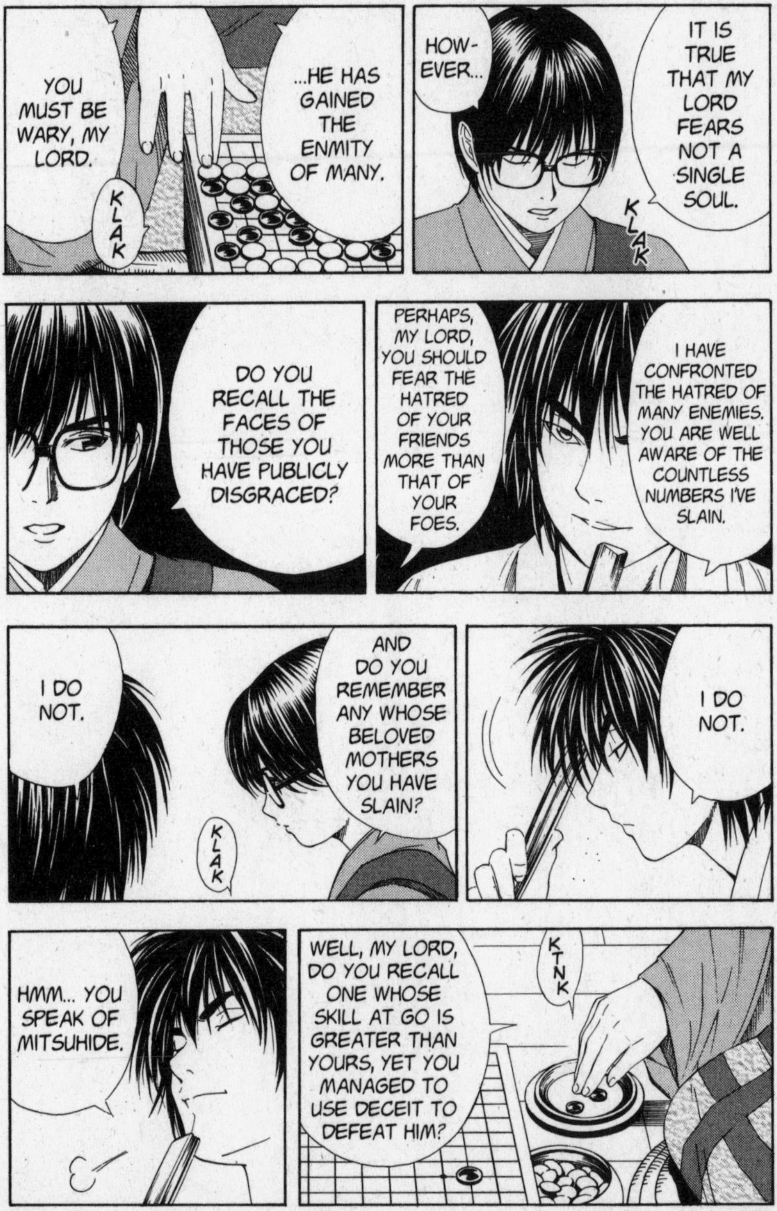
IT IS TRUE THAT MY LORD FEARS NOT A SINGLE SOUL.
KLAK
HOW-EVER...
...HE HAS GAINED THE ENMITY OF MANY.
YOU MUST BE WARY, MY LORD.
KLAK
I HAVE CONFRONTED THE HATRED OF MANY ENEMIES. YOU ARE WELL AWARE OF THE COUNTLESS NUMBERS I'VE SLAIN.
PERHAPS, MY LORD, YOU SHOULD FEAR THE HATRED OF YOUR FRIENDS MORE THAN THAT OF YOUR FOES.
DO YOU RECALL THE FACES OF THOSE YOU HAVE PUBLICLY DISGRACED?
I DO NOT.
AND DO YOU REMEMBER ANY WHOSE BELOVED MOTHERS YOU HAVE SLAIN?
KLAK
I DO NOT.
KTNK
WELL, MY LORD, DO YOU RECALL ONE WHOSE SKILL AT GO IS GREATER THAN YOURS, YET YOU MANAGED TO USE DECEIT TO DEFEAT HIM?
HMM... YOU SPEAK OF MITSUHIDE.

READ THIS WAY

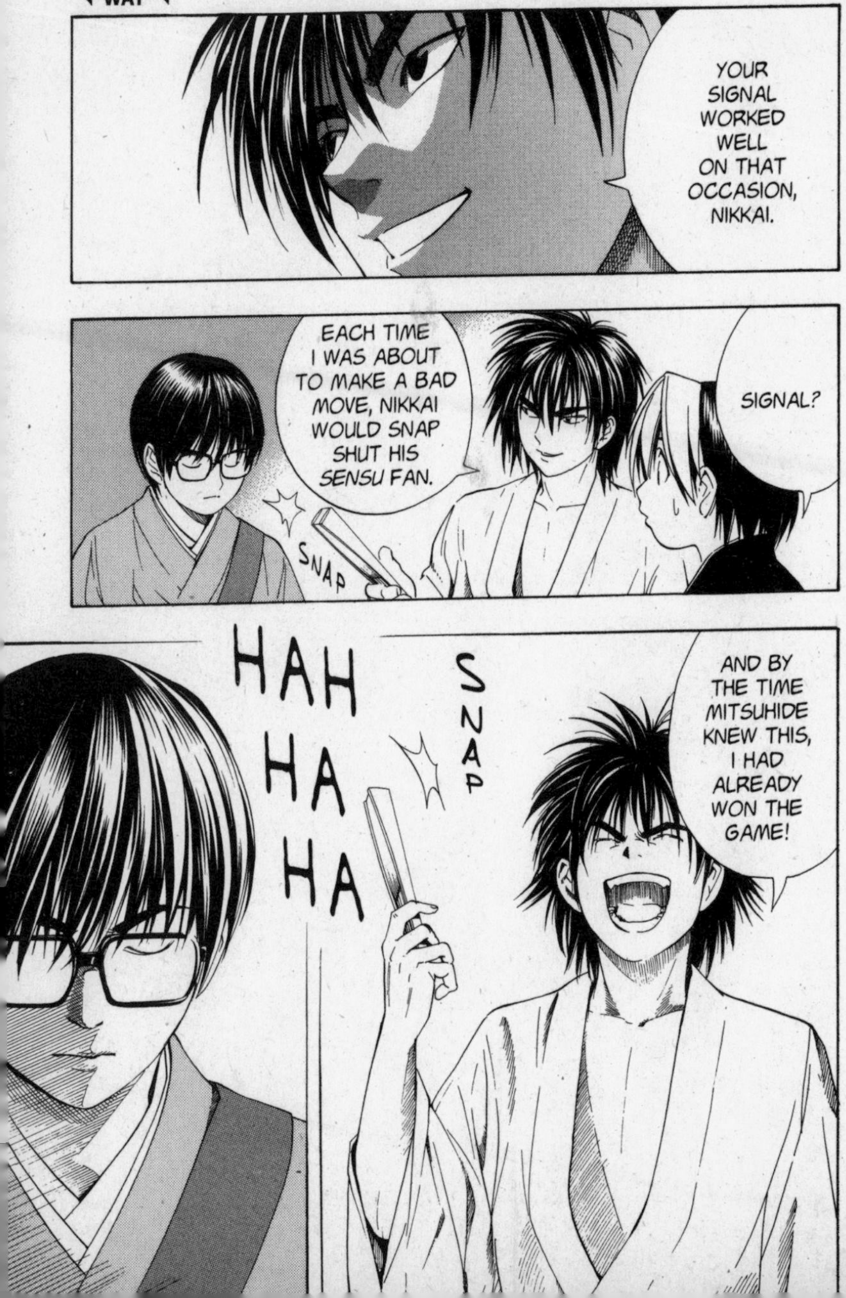
YOUR SIGNAL WORKED WELL ON THAT OCCASION, NIKKAI.
SIGNAL?
EACH TIME I WAS ABOUT TO MAKE A BAD MOVE, NIKKAI WOULD SNAP SHUT HIS SENSU FAN.
SNAP
AND BY THE TIME MITSUHIDE KNEW THIS, I HAD ALREADY WON THE GAME!
SNAP
HAH HA HA HA

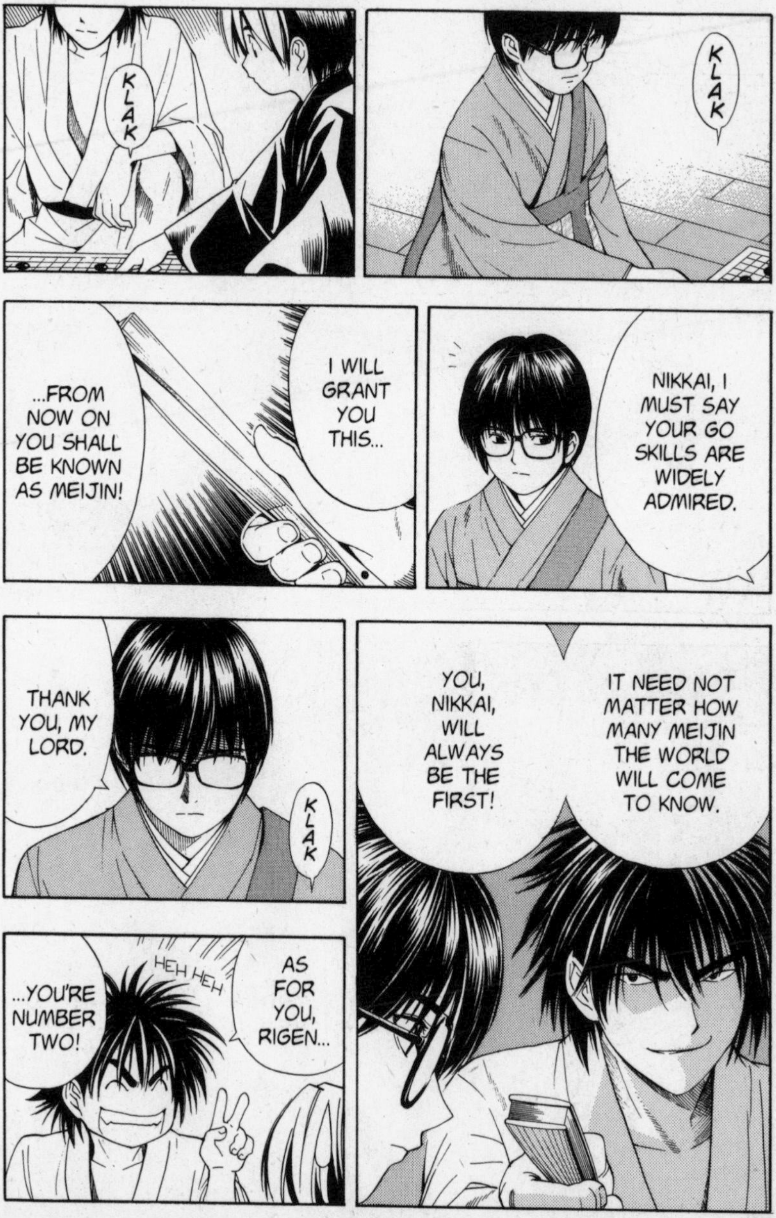
KLAK
KLAK
NIKKAI, I MUST SAY YOUR GO SKILLS ARE WIDELY ADMIRED.
I WILL GRANT YOU THIS...
...FROM NOW ON YOU SHALL BE KNOWN AS MEIJIN!
IT NEED NOT MATTER HOW MANY MEIJIN THE WORLD WILL COME TO KNOW.
YOU, NIKKAI, WILL ALWAYS BE THE FIRST!
THANK YOU, MY LORD.
KLAK
AS FOR YOU, RIGEN...
HEH HEH
...YOU'RE NUMBER TWO!

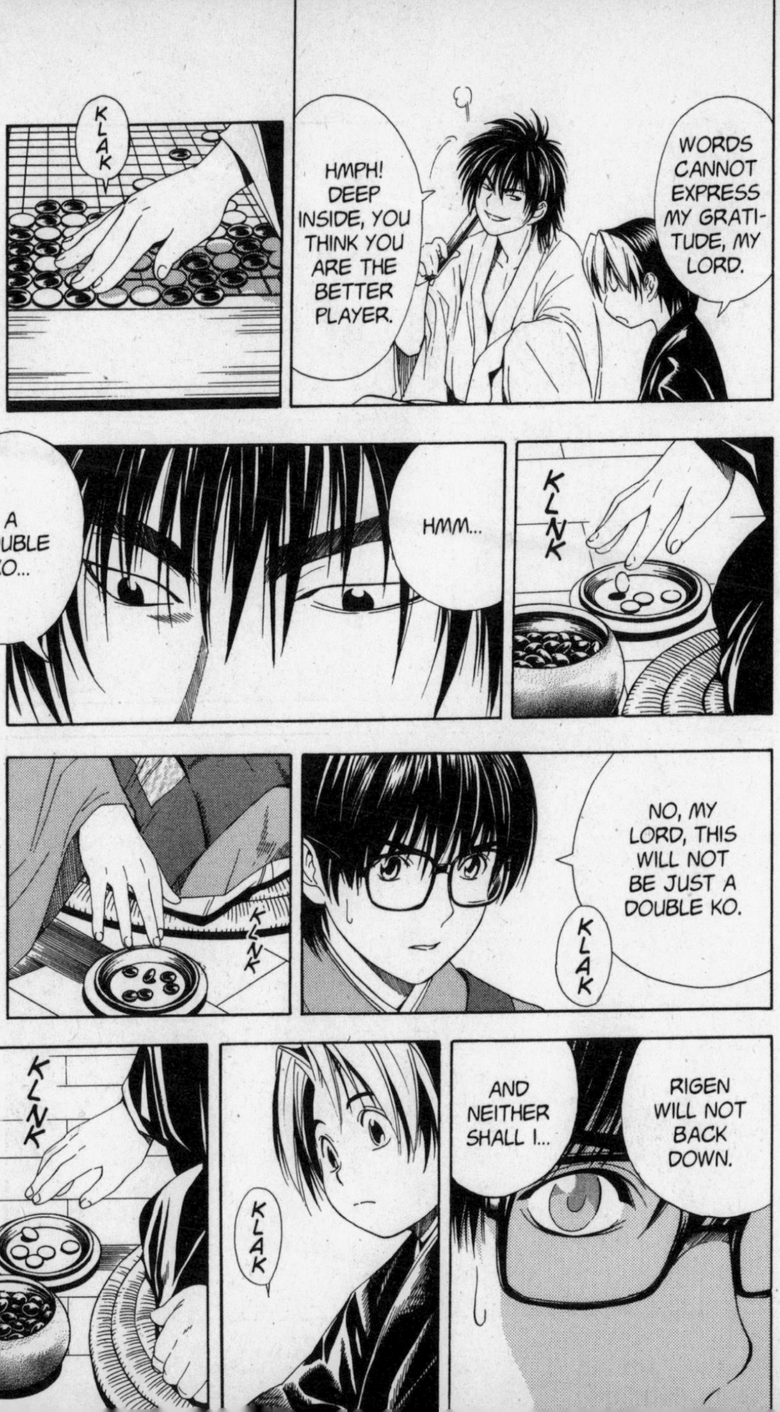
WORDS CANNOT EXPRESS MY GRATITUDE, MY LORD.
HMPH! DEEP INSIDE, YOU THINK YOU ARE THE BETTER PLAYER.
KLAK
KLNK
HMM...
A DOUBLE KO...
NO, MY LORD, THIS WILL NOT BE JUST A DOUBLE KO.
KLAK
KLNK
RIGEN WILL NOT BACK DOWN.
AND NEITHER SHALL I...
KLAK
KLNK

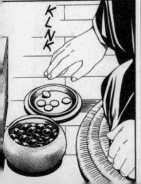

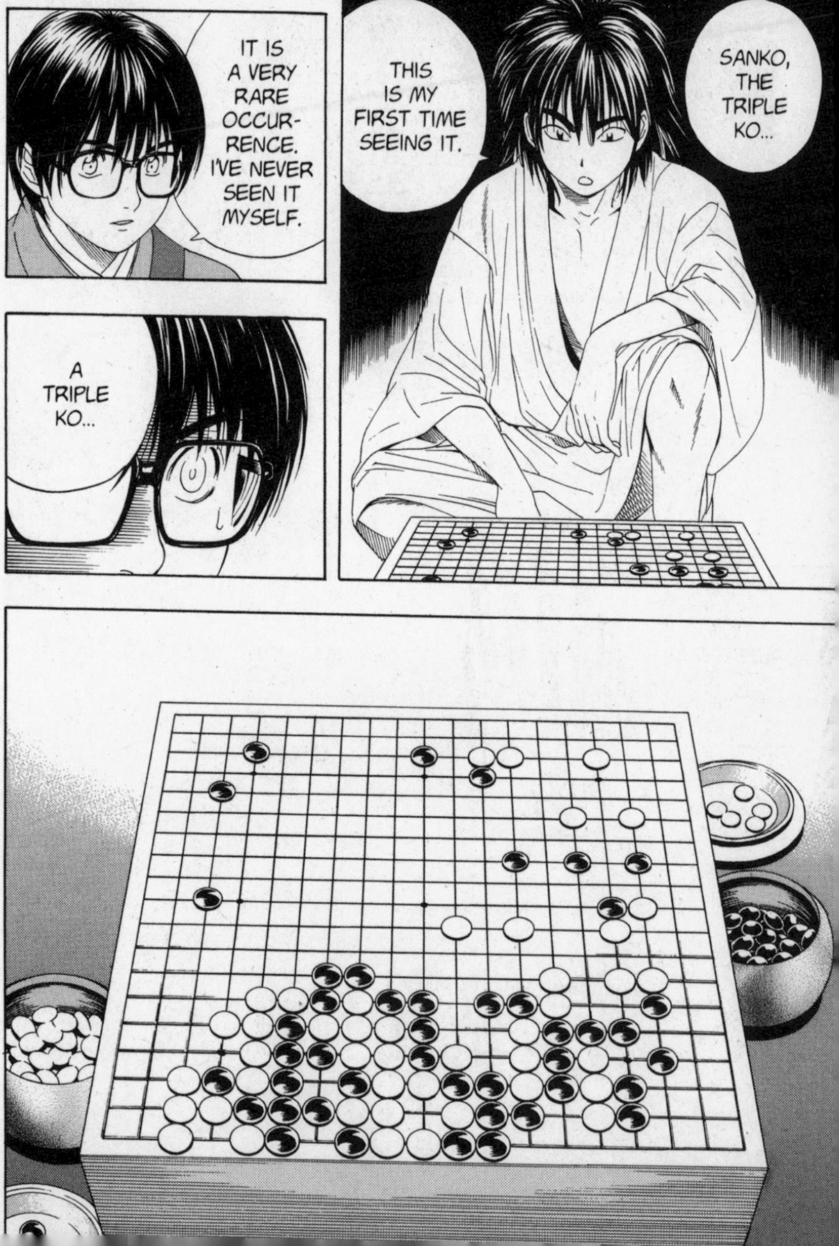
SANKO, THE TRIPLE KO...
THIS IS MY FIRST TIME SEEING IT.
IT IS A VERY RARE OCCURRENCE. I'VE NEVER SEEN IT MYSELF.
A TRIPLE KO...

READ THIS WAY

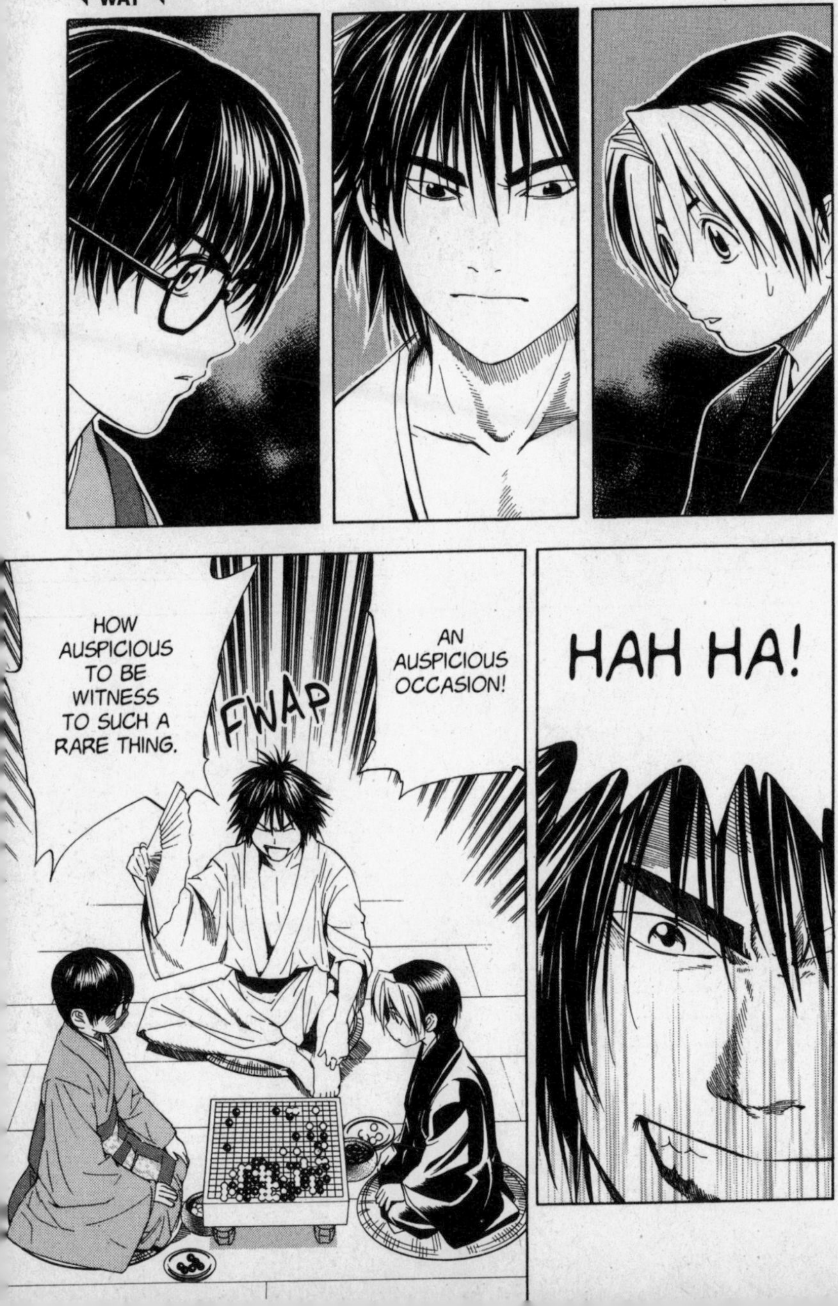
HAH HA!
AN AUSPICIOUS OCCASION!
FWAP
HOW AUSPICIOUS TO BE WITNESS TO SUCH A RARE THING.

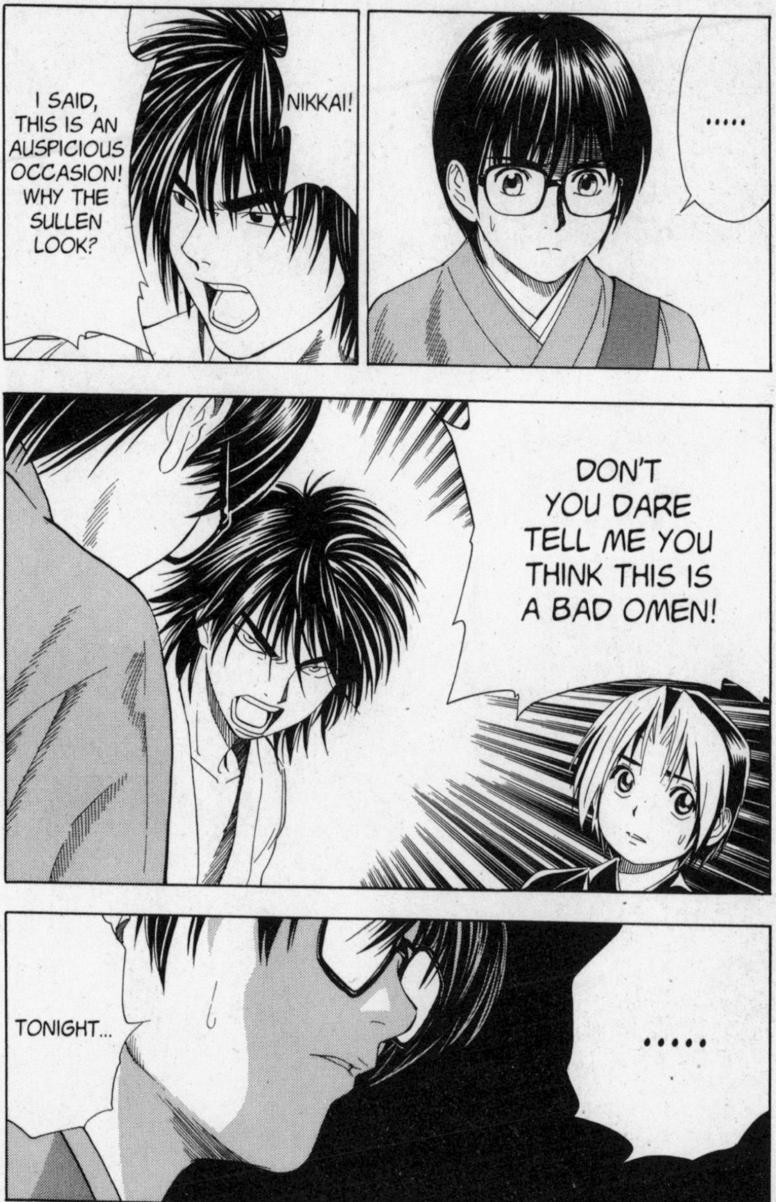
.....
NIKKAI!
I SAID, THIS IS AN AUSPICIOUS OCCASION! WHY THE SULLEN LOOK?
DON'T YOU DARE TELL ME YOU THINK THIS IS A BAD OMEN!
.....
TONIGHT...

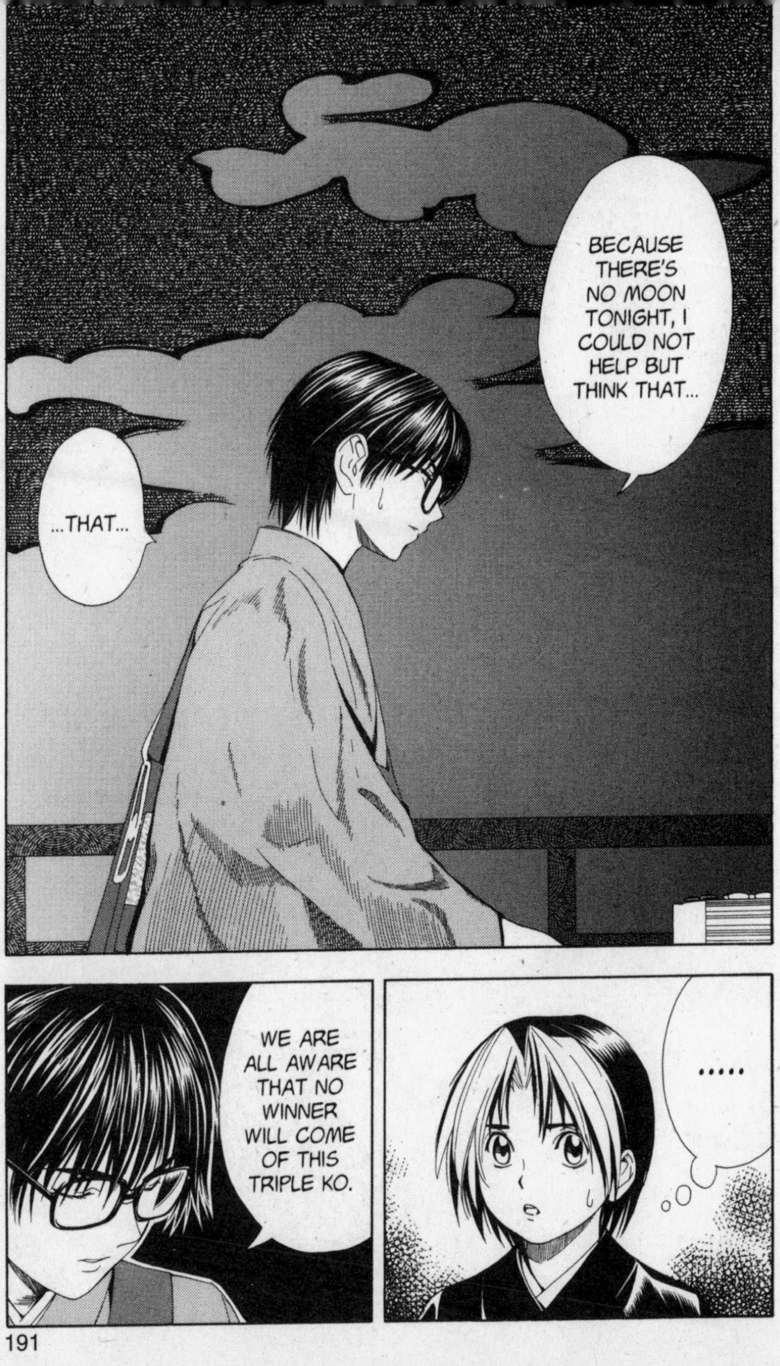
BECAUSE THERE'S NO MOON TONIGHT, I COULD NOT HELP BUT THINK THAT...
...THAT...
.....
WE ARE ALL AWARE THAT NO WINNER WILL COME OF THIS TRIPLE KO.

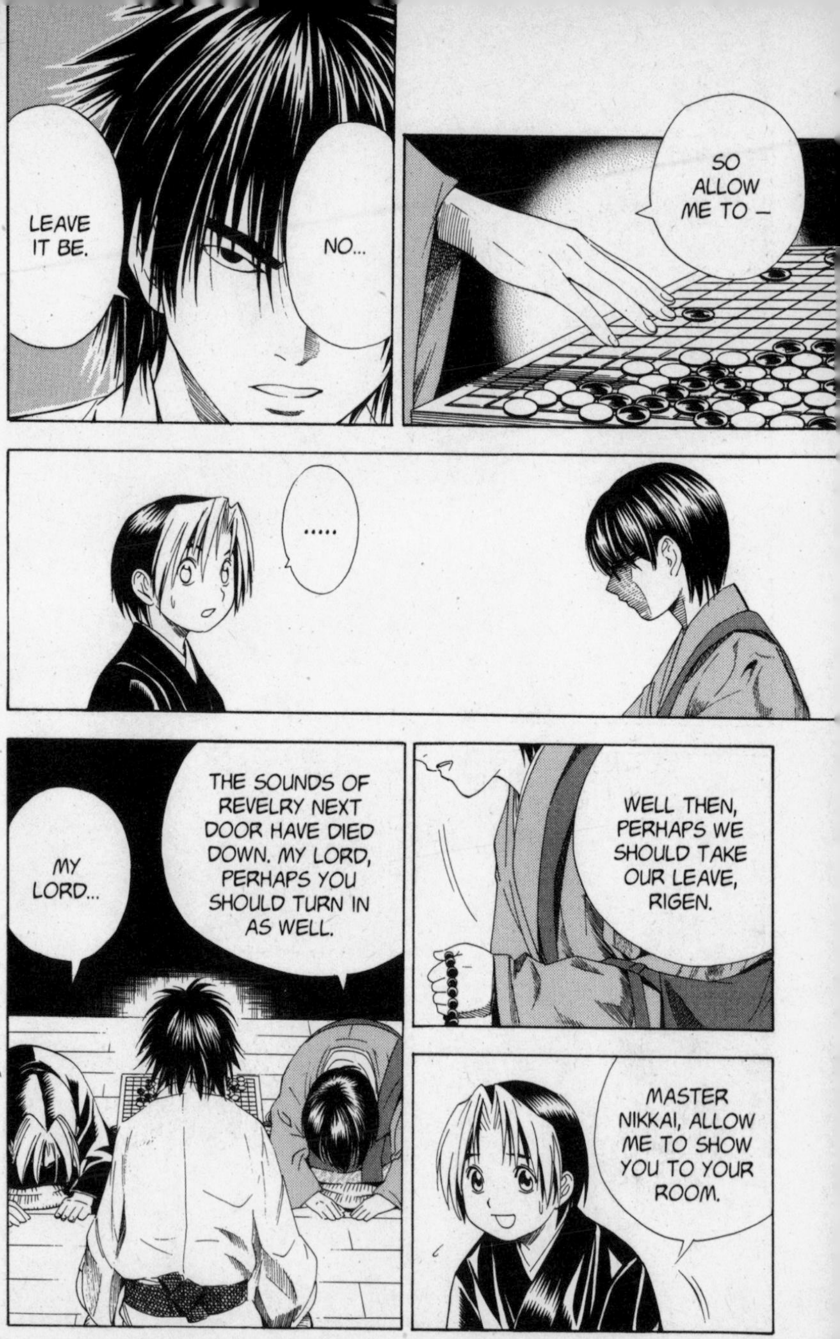
SO ALLOW ME TO –
NO...
LEAVE IT BE.
.....
WELL THEN, PERHAPS WE SHOULD TAKE OUR LEAVE, RIGEN.
THE SOUNDS OF REVELRY NEXT DOOR HAVE DIED DOWN. MY LORD, PERHAPS YOU SHOULD TURN IN AS WELL.
MY LORD...
MASTER NIKKAI, ALLOW ME TO SHOW YOU TO YOUR ROOM.

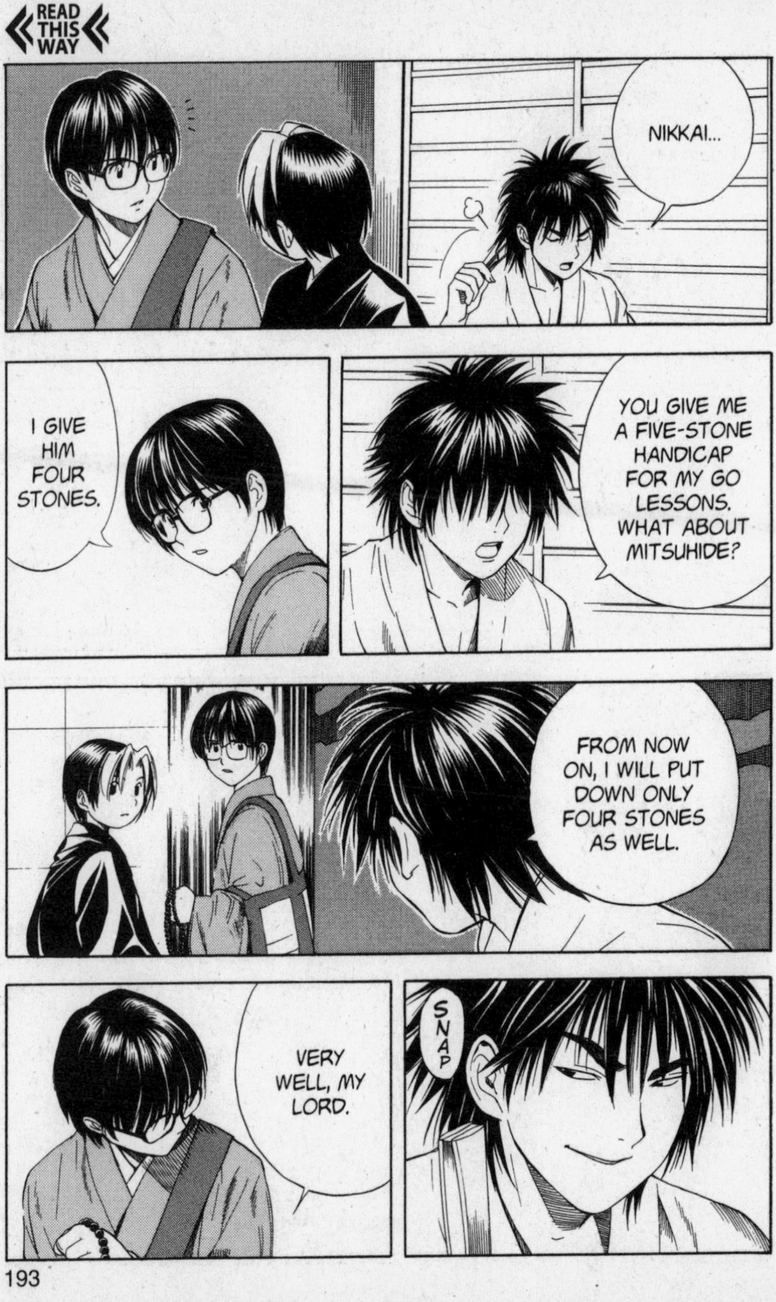
READ THIS WAY
NIKKAI...
YOU GIVE ME A FIVE-STONE HANDICAP FOR MY GO LESSONS. WHAT ABOUT MITSUHIDE?
I GIVE HIM FOUR STONES.
FROM NOW ON, I WILL PUT DOWN ONLY FOUR STONES AS WELL.
SNAP
VERY WELL, MY LORD.

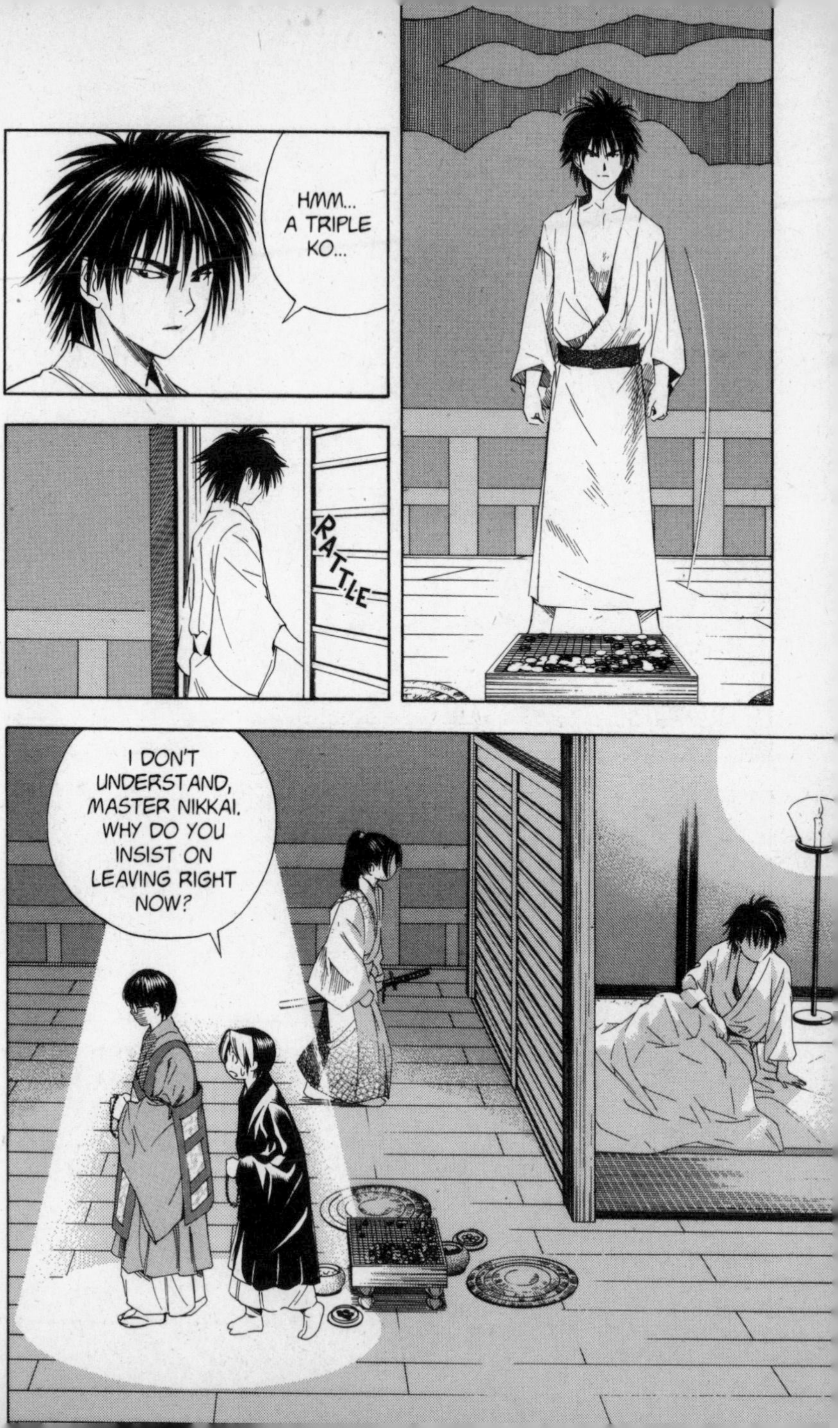
HMM... A TRIPLE KO...
RATTLE
I DON'T UNDERSTAND, MASTER NIKKAI. WHY DO YOU INSIST ON LEAVING RIGHT NOW?

READ THIS WAY

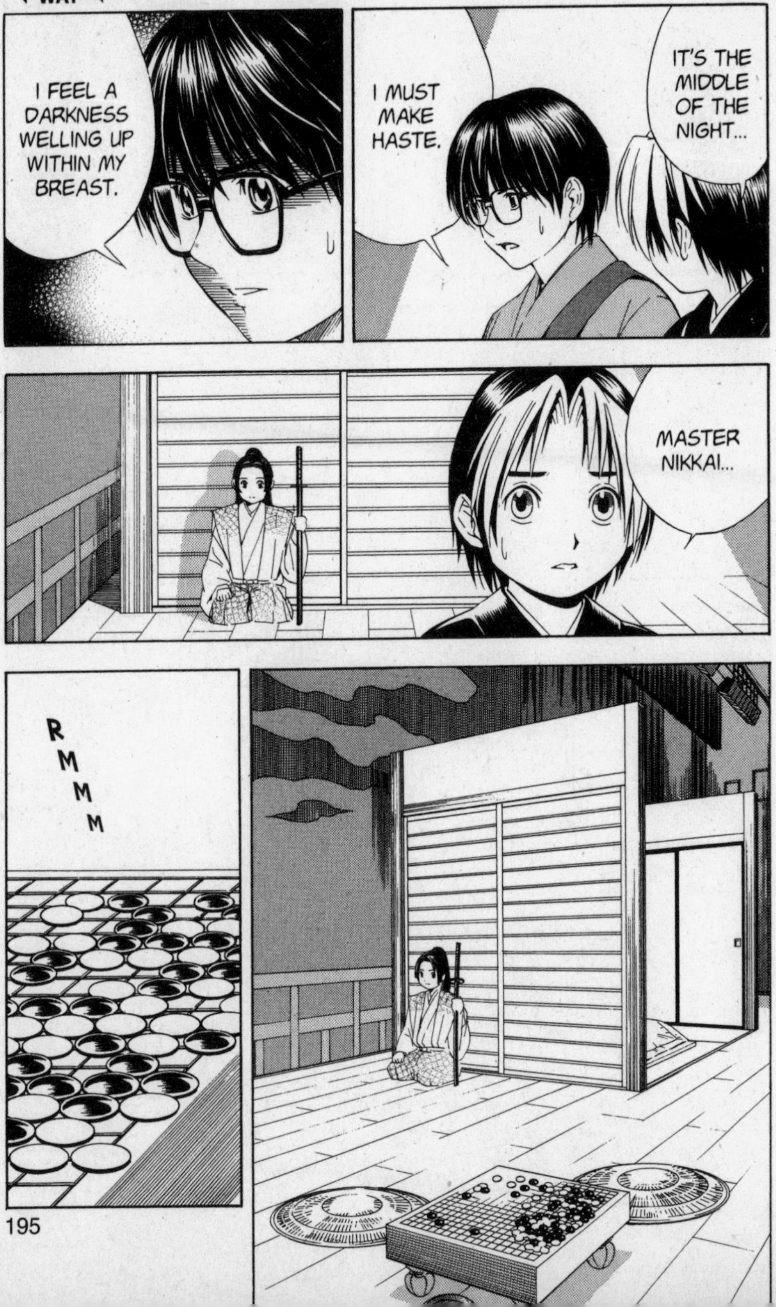
IT'S THE MIDDLE OF THE NIGHT...
I MUST MAKE HASTE.
I FEEL A DARKNESS WELLING UP WITHIN MY BREAST.
MASTER NIKKAI...
RMMM

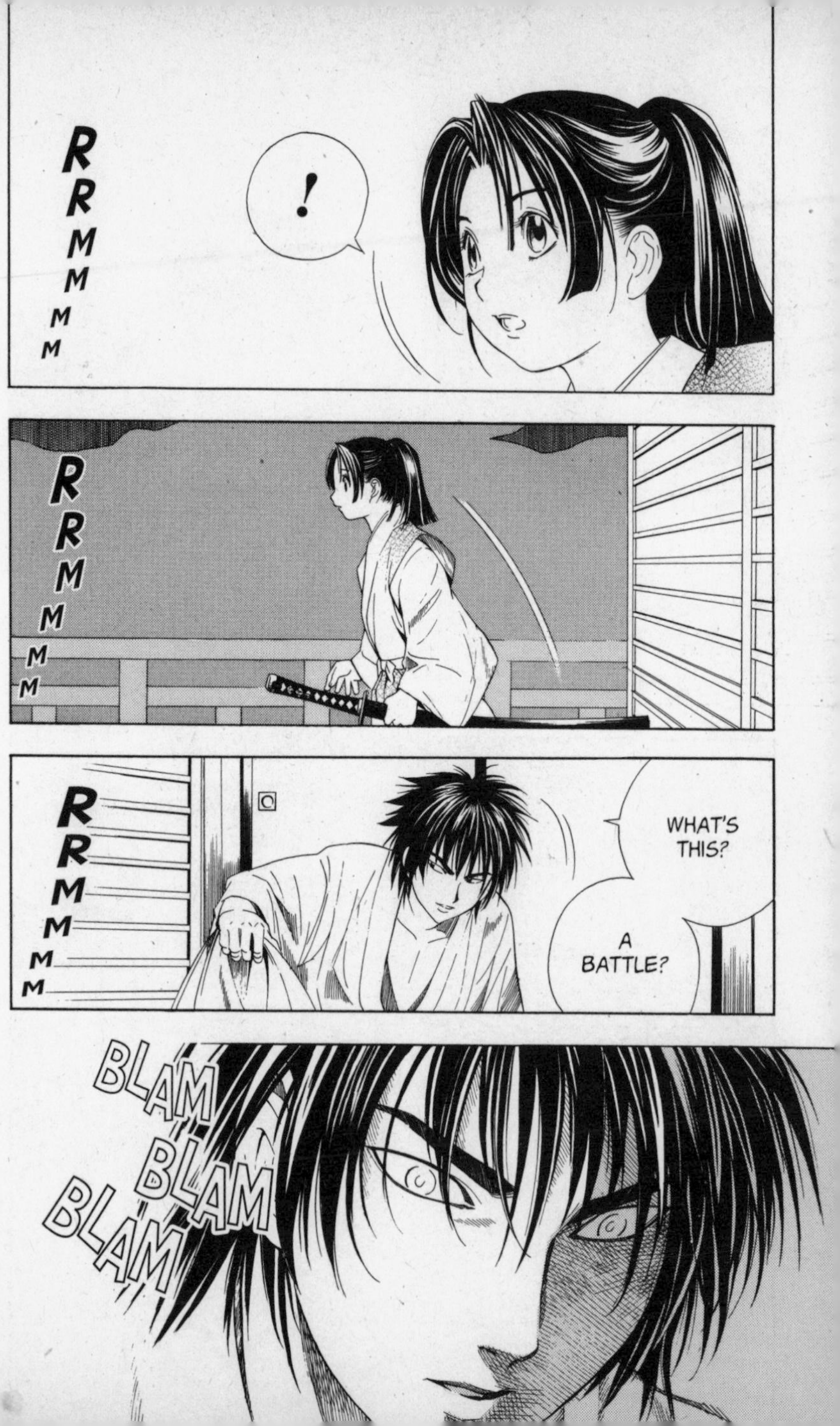
!
RRMMMM
RRMMMM
WHAT'S THIS?
A BATTLE?
RRMMMM
BLAM BLAM BLAM

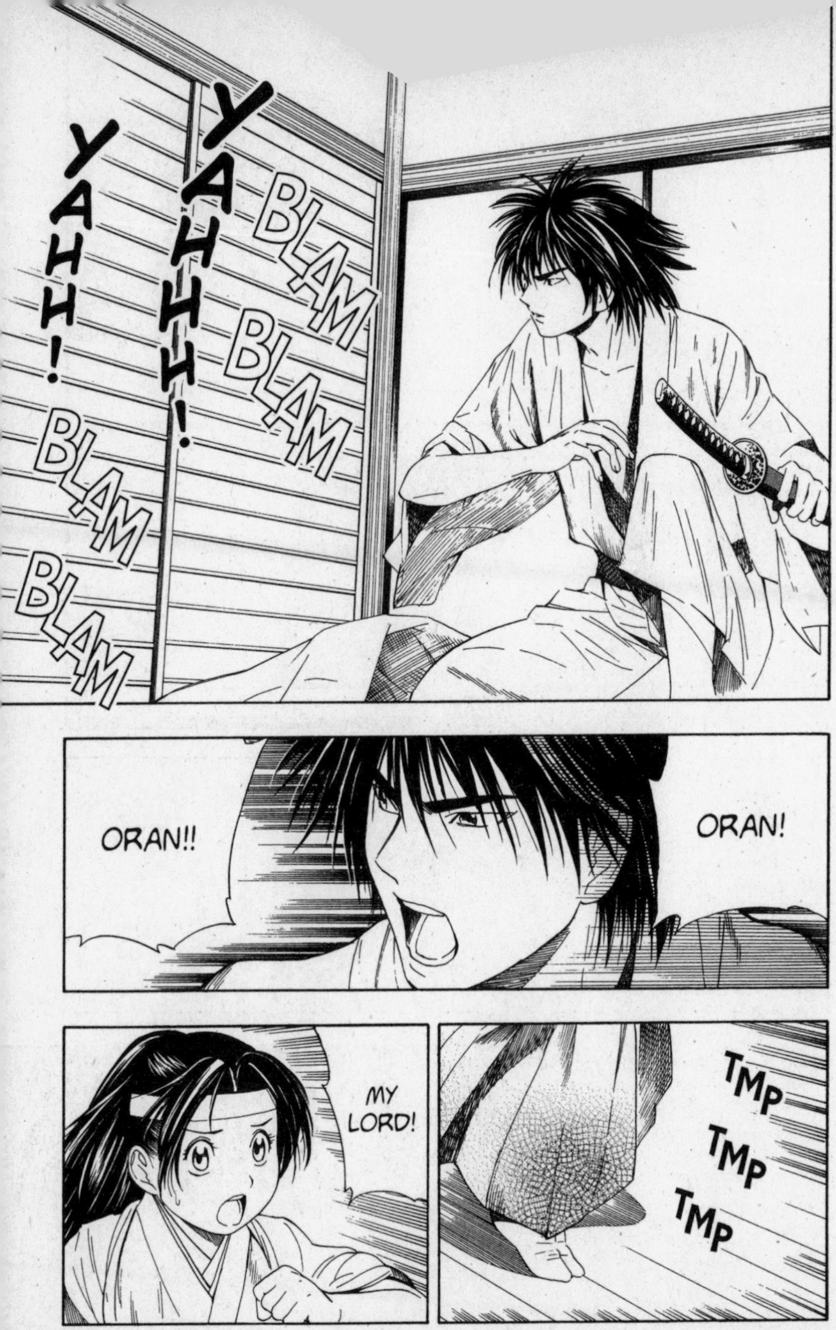
BLAM
BLAM
YAHHHH!
YAHH!
BLAM
BLAM
ORAN!
ORAN!!
TMP
TMP
TMP
MY LORD!

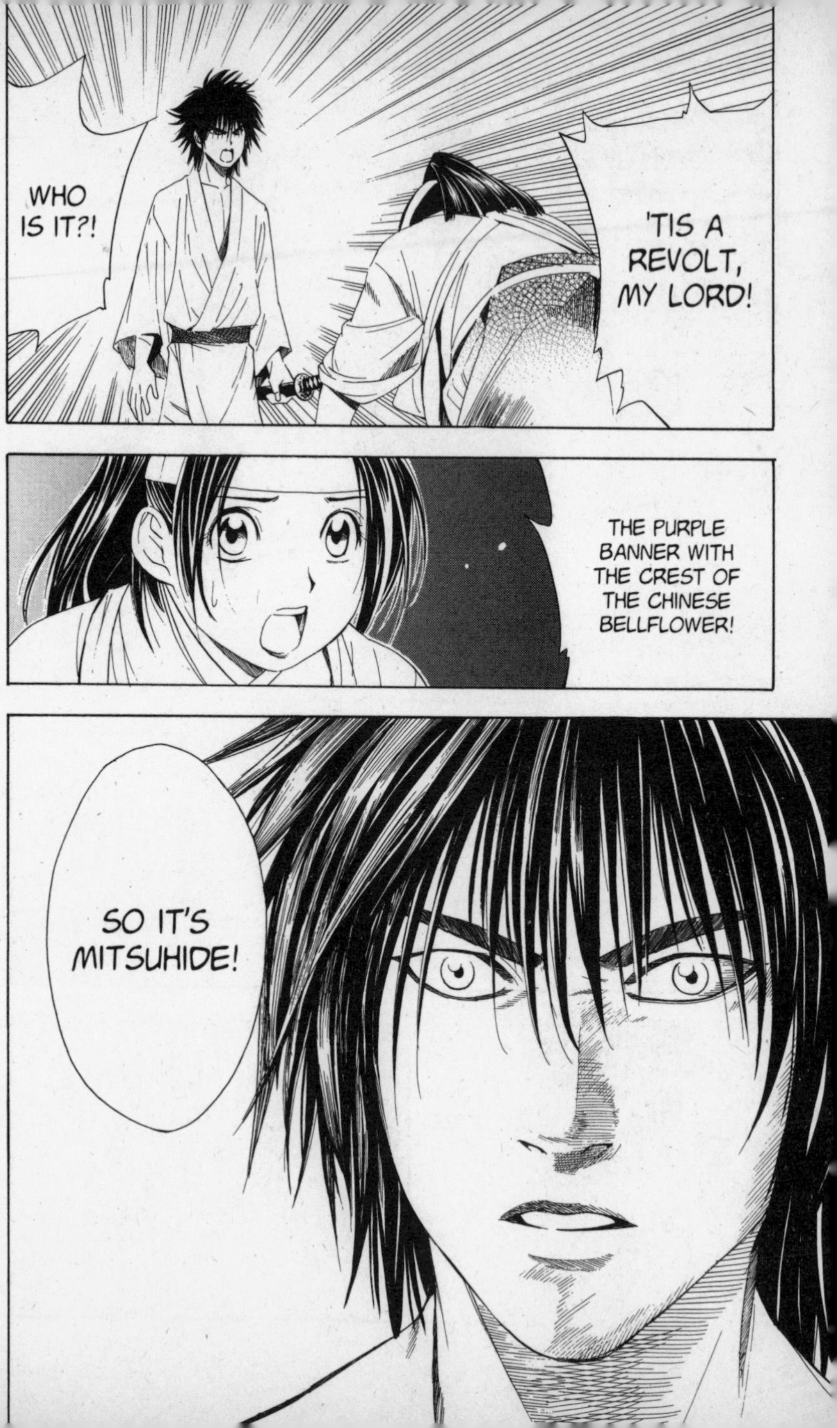
WHO IS IT?!
'TIS A REVOLT, MY LORD!
THE PURPLE BANNER WITH THE CREST OF THE CHINESE BELLFLOWER!
SO IT'S MITSUHIDE!

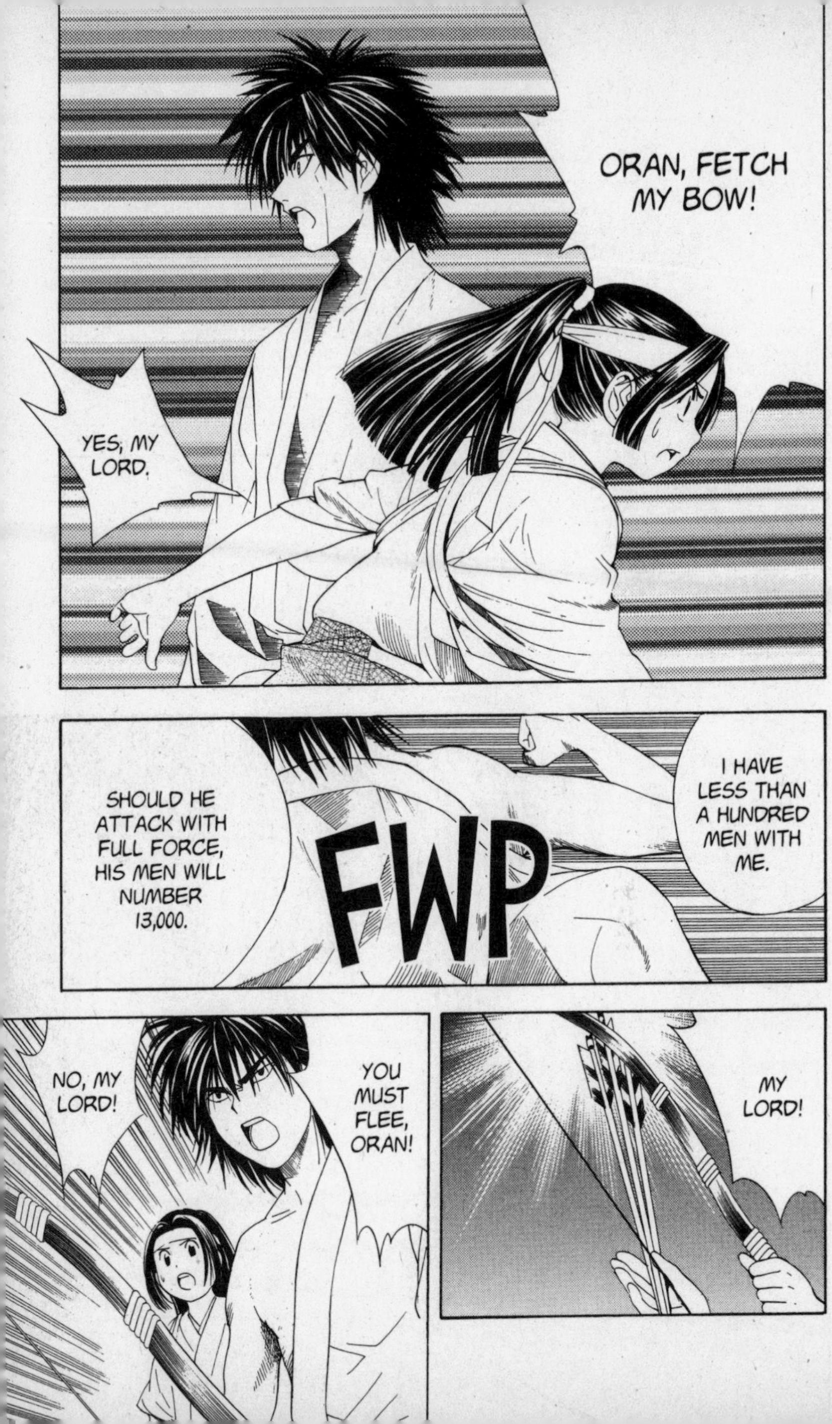
ORAN, FETCH MY BOW!
YES, MY LORD.
I HAVE LESS THAN A HUNDRED MEN WITH ME.
FWP
SHOULD HE ATTACK WITH FULL FORCE, HIS MEN WILL NUMBER 13,000.
MY LORD!
YOU MUST FLEE, ORAN!
NO, MY LORD!

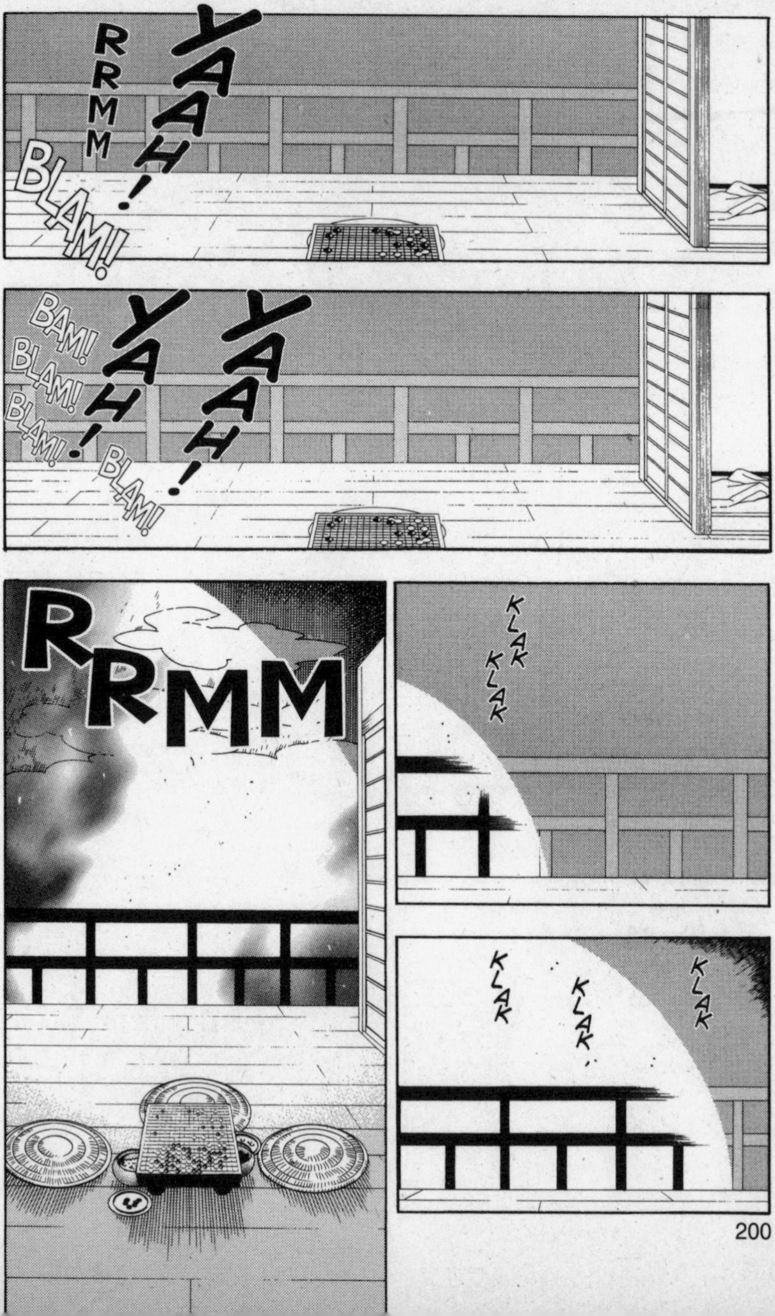
YAAH!
RRMM
BLAM!
YAAH!
BLAM!
YAH!
BAM!
BLAM!
BLAM!
KLAK KLAK
KLAK
KLAK
KLAK
RRMM

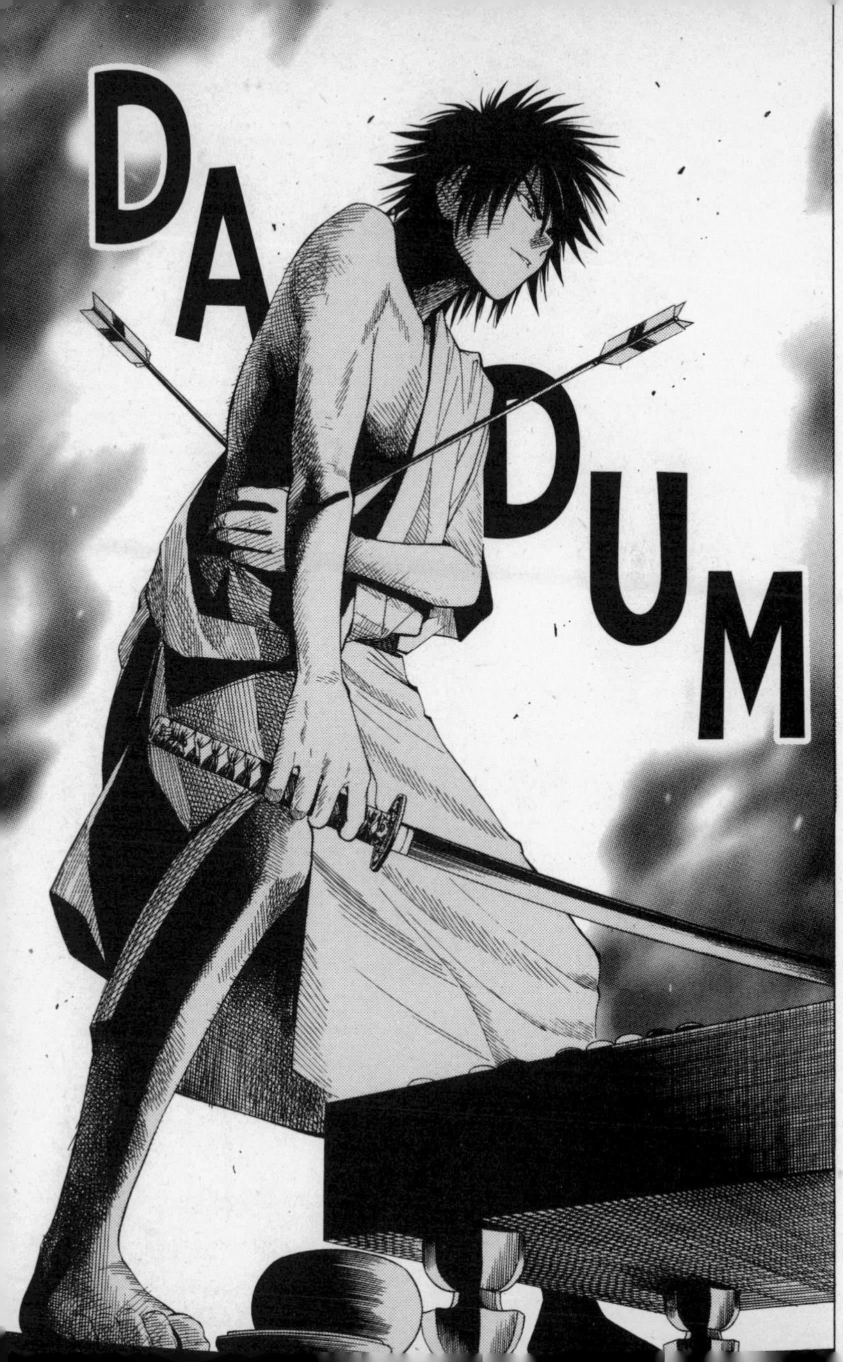
DA
DUM

YAHH!

HMPH!

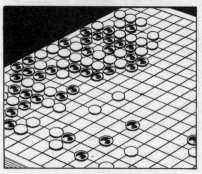

I WILL NOT YIELD TO YOU, MITSUHIDE!

RRRMMM

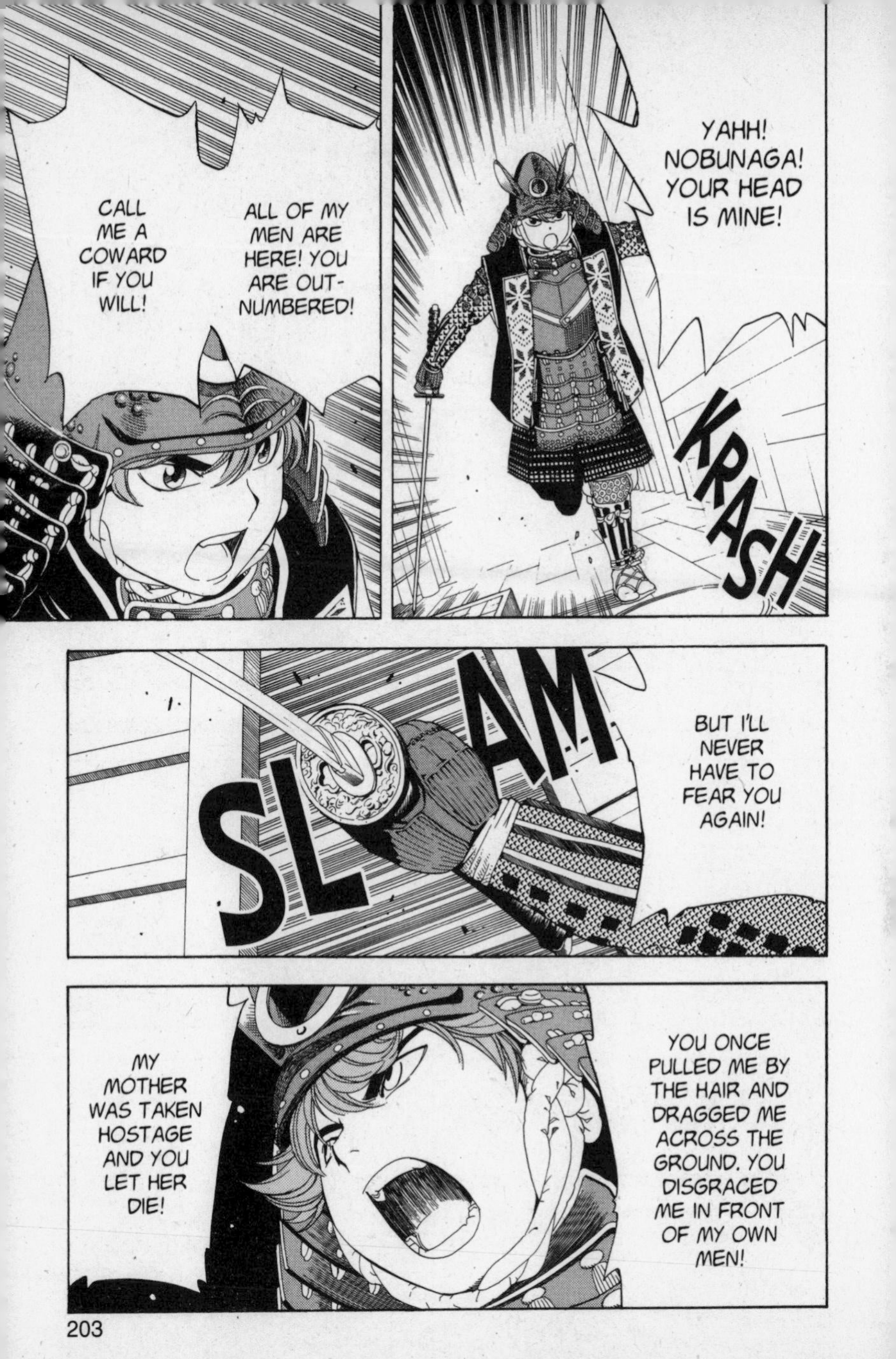
YAHH! NOBUNAGA! YOUR HEAD IS MINE!
KRASH
ALL OF MY MEN ARE HERE! YOU ARE OUT-NUMBERED!
CALL ME A COWARD IF YOU WILL!
BUT I'LL NEVER HAVE TO FEAR YOU AGAIN!
SLAM
YOU ONCE PULLED ME BY THE HAIR AND DRAGGED ME ACROSS THE GROUND. YOU DISGRACED ME IN FRONT OF MY OWN MEN!
MY MOTHER WAS TAKEN HOSTAGE AND YOU LET HER DIE!

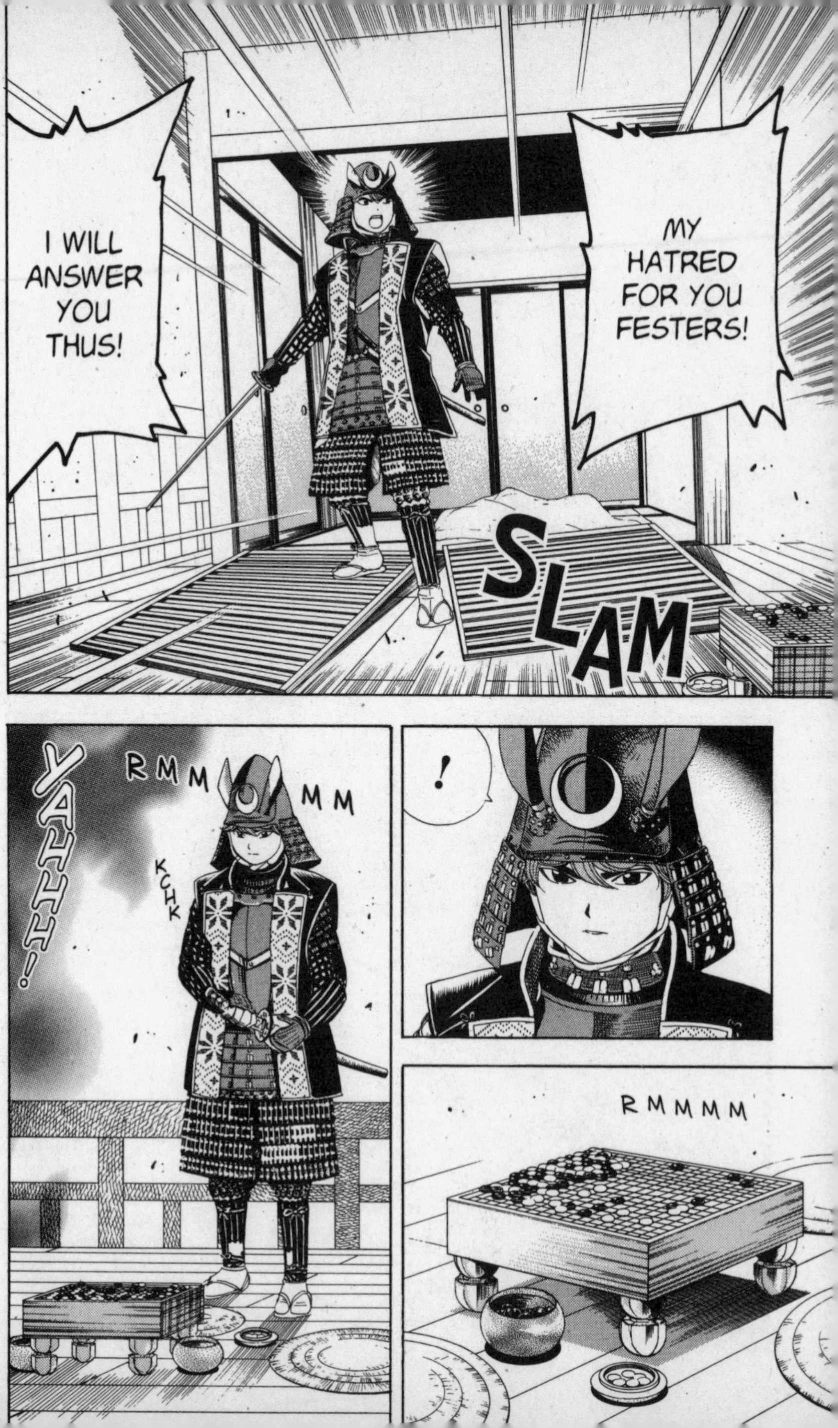
MY HATRED FOR YOU FESTERS!
I WILL ANSWER YOU THUS!
SLAM
!
RMMMM
YAHHHH!
RMM MM
KCHK

RRM M

THE TRIPLE KO...

THEY SAY THE TRIPLE KO IS AN ILL OMEN.

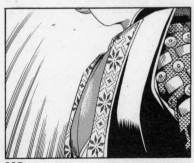

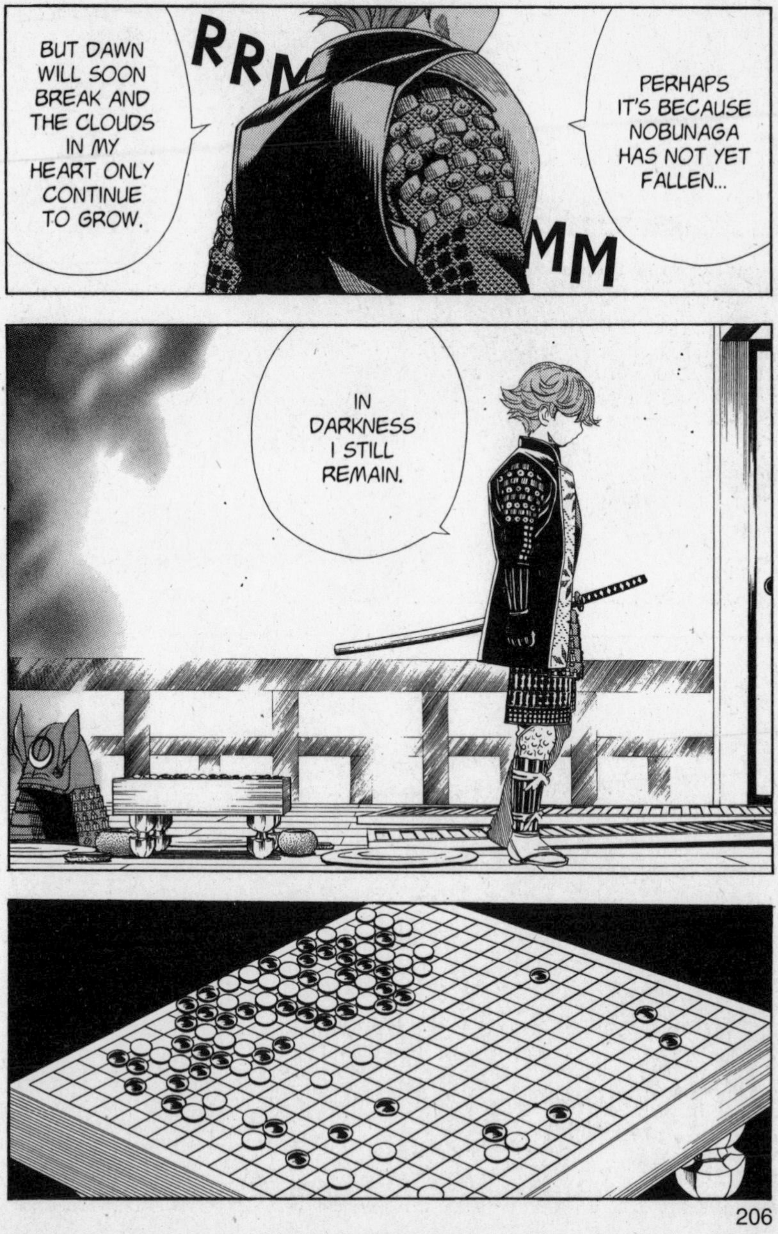
PERHAPS IT'S BECAUSE NOBUNAGA HAS NOT YET FALLEN...
RRM MM
BUT DAWN WILL SOON BREAK AND THE CLOUDS IN MY HEART ONLY CONTINUE TO GROW.
IN DARKNESS I STILL REMAIN.

THE TRIPLE KO...

HMPH

AMAZING...

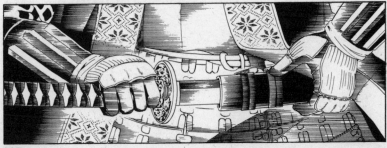

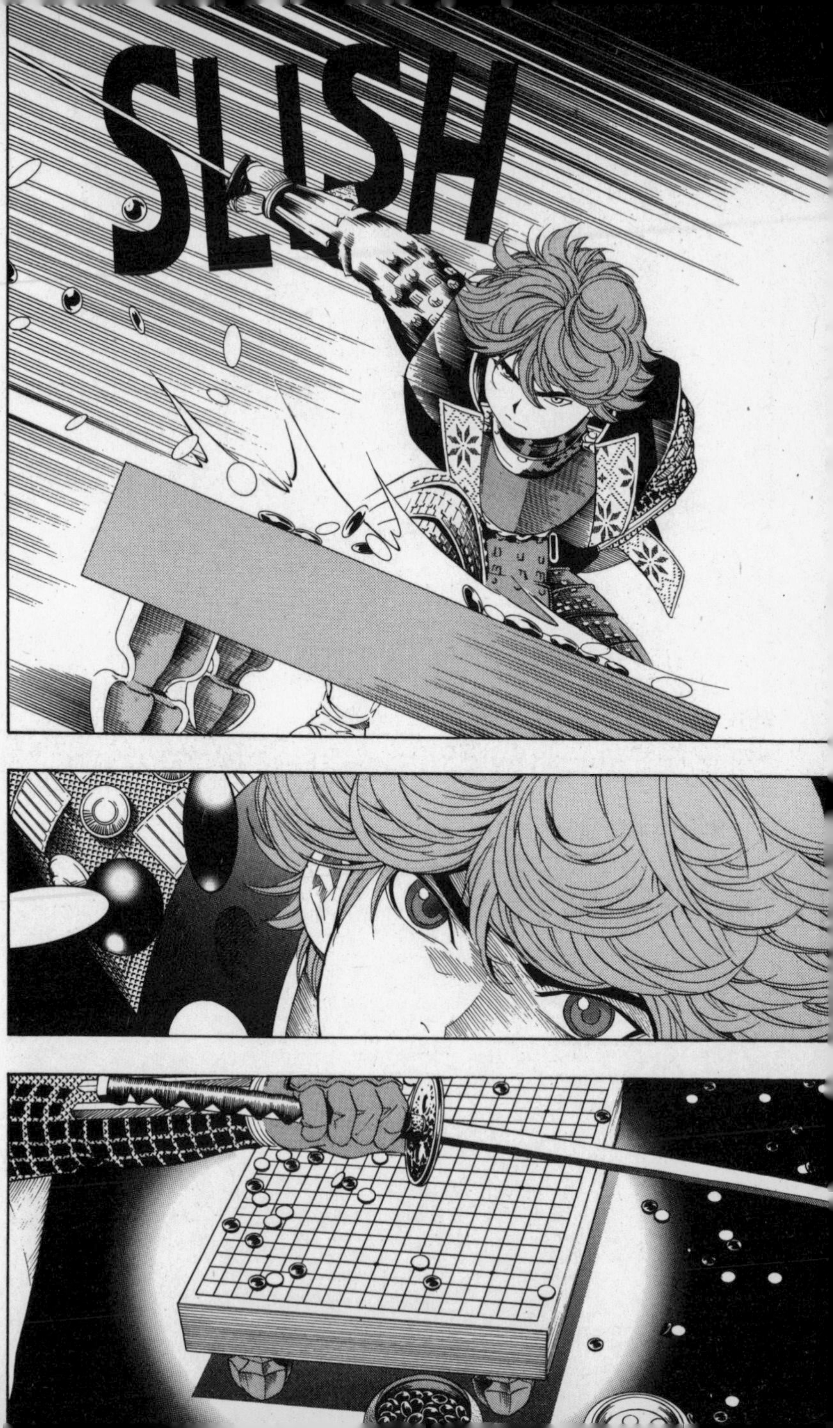
SLISH

READ THIS WAY

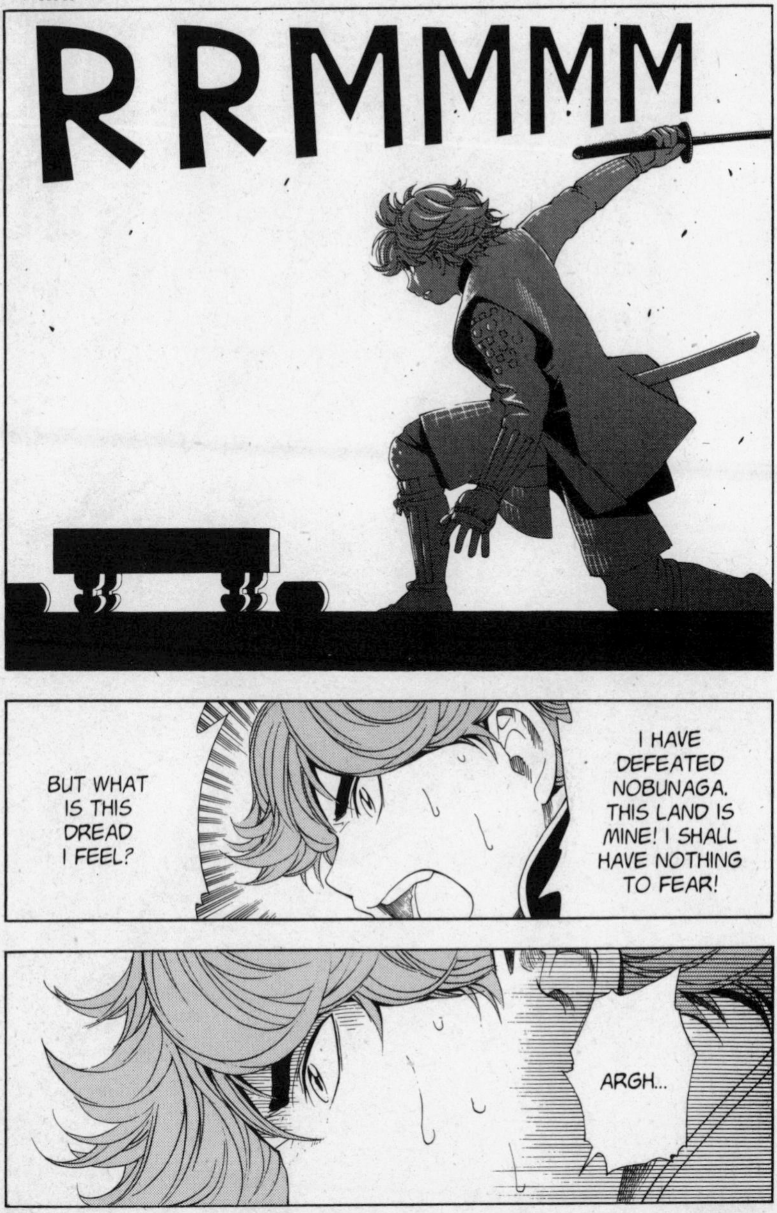
RRMMMM
I HAVE DEFEATED NOBUNAGA. THIS LAND IS MINE! I SHALL HAVE NOTHING TO FEAR!
BUT WHAT IS THIS DREAD I FEEL?
ARGH...

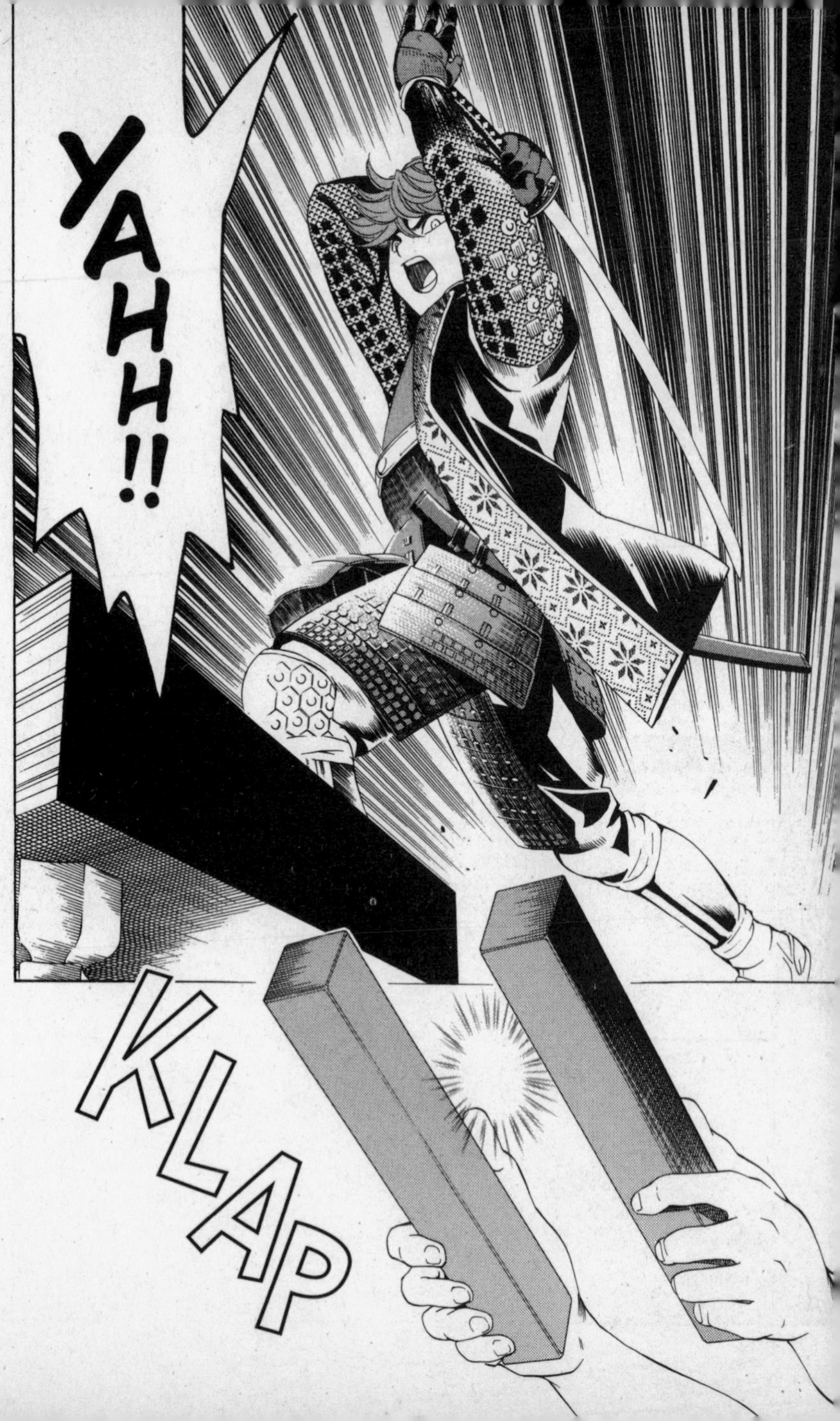
YAHH!!
KLAP

READ THIS WAY

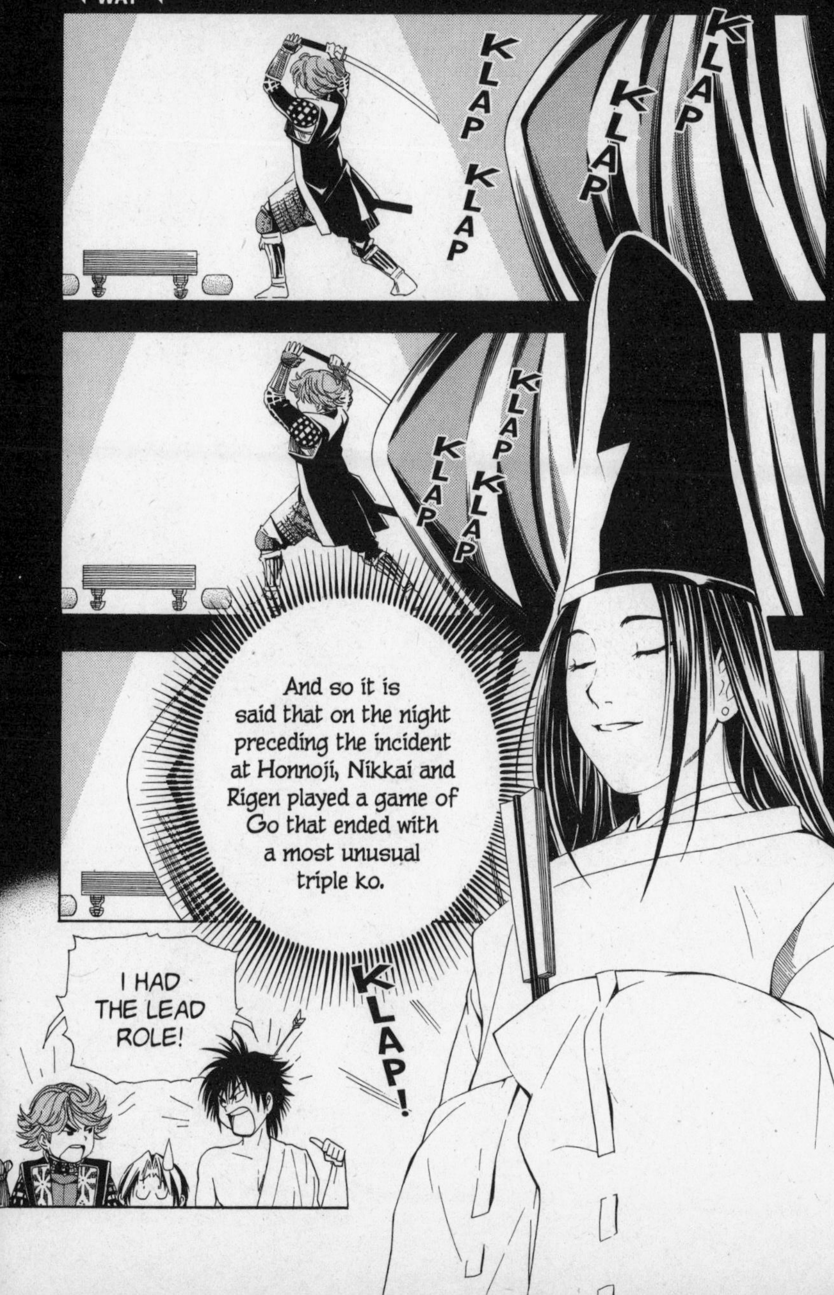
KLAP KLAP
KLAP KLAP
KLAP KLAP
KLAP KLAP
And so it is said that on the night preceding the incident at Honnoji, Nikkai and Rigen played a game of Go that ended with a most unusual triple ko.
KLAP!
I HAD THE LEAD ROLE!

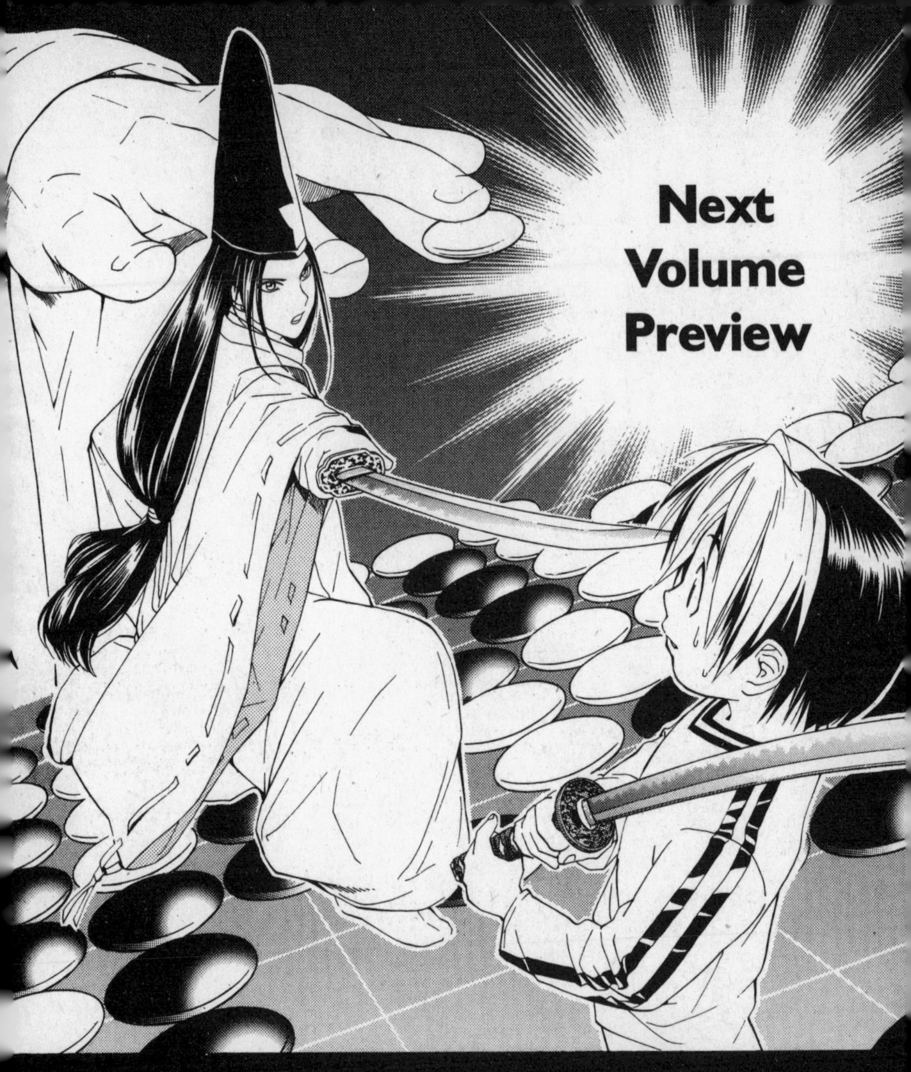
Next Volume Preview

Hikaru may be an insei now, but he's losing to just about everyone in his class. Meanwhile, the Young Lions Tournament is fast approaching, and Akira Toya will be playing in it. Does Hikaru stand a chance of qualifying? Will he even make it out of B League? Only Sai seems to sense the real cause of Hikaru's jitters...

COMING JULY 2006

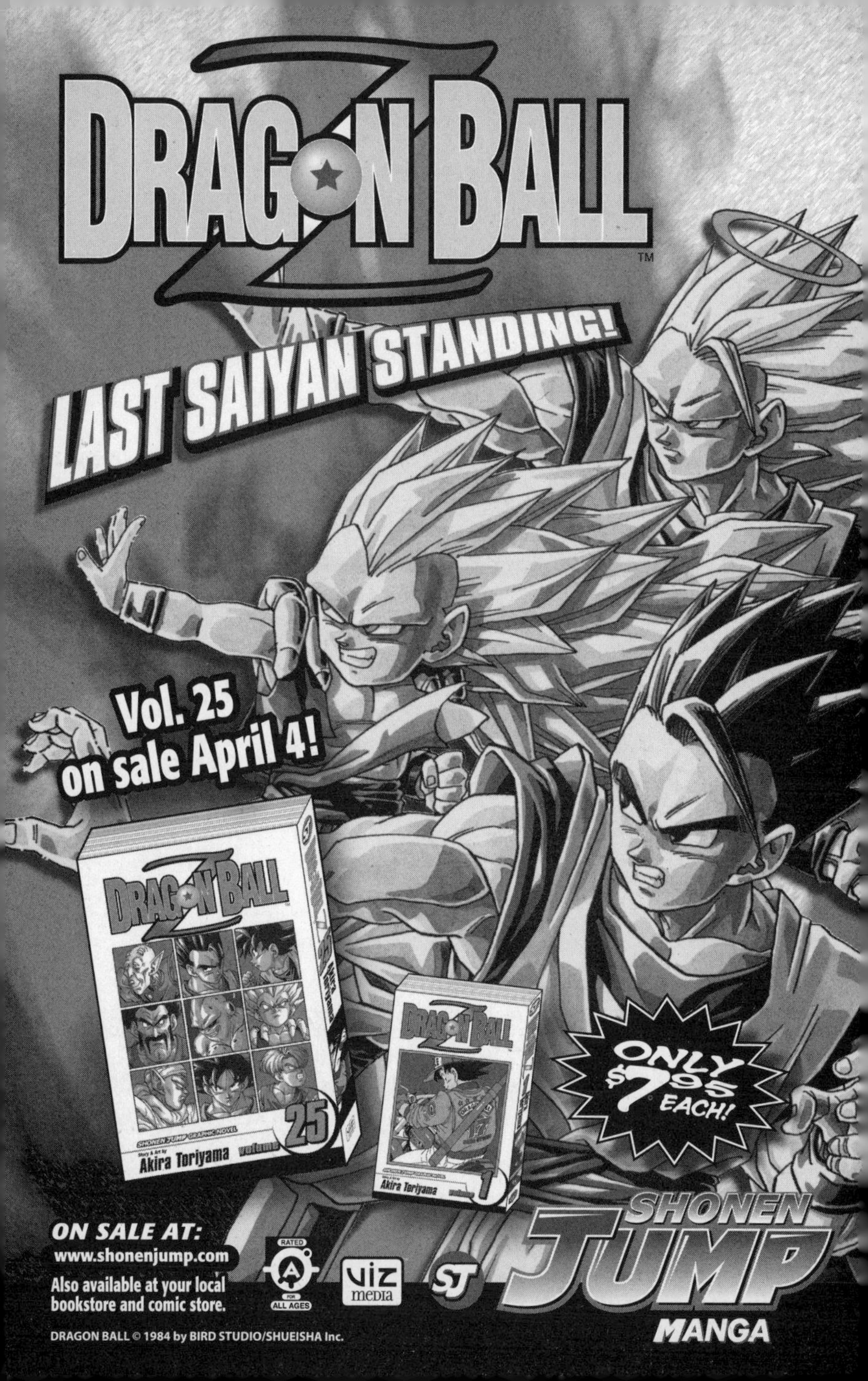

DRAGON BALL Z™
LAST SAIYAN STANDING!
Vol. 25 on sale April 4!
ONLY $7.95 EACH!
ON SALE AT:
www.shonenjump.com
Also available at your local bookstore and comic store.
RATED A FOR ALL AGES
VIZ media
SJ SHONEN JUMP MANGA
DRAGON BALL © 1984 by BIRD STUDIO/SHUEISHA Inc.

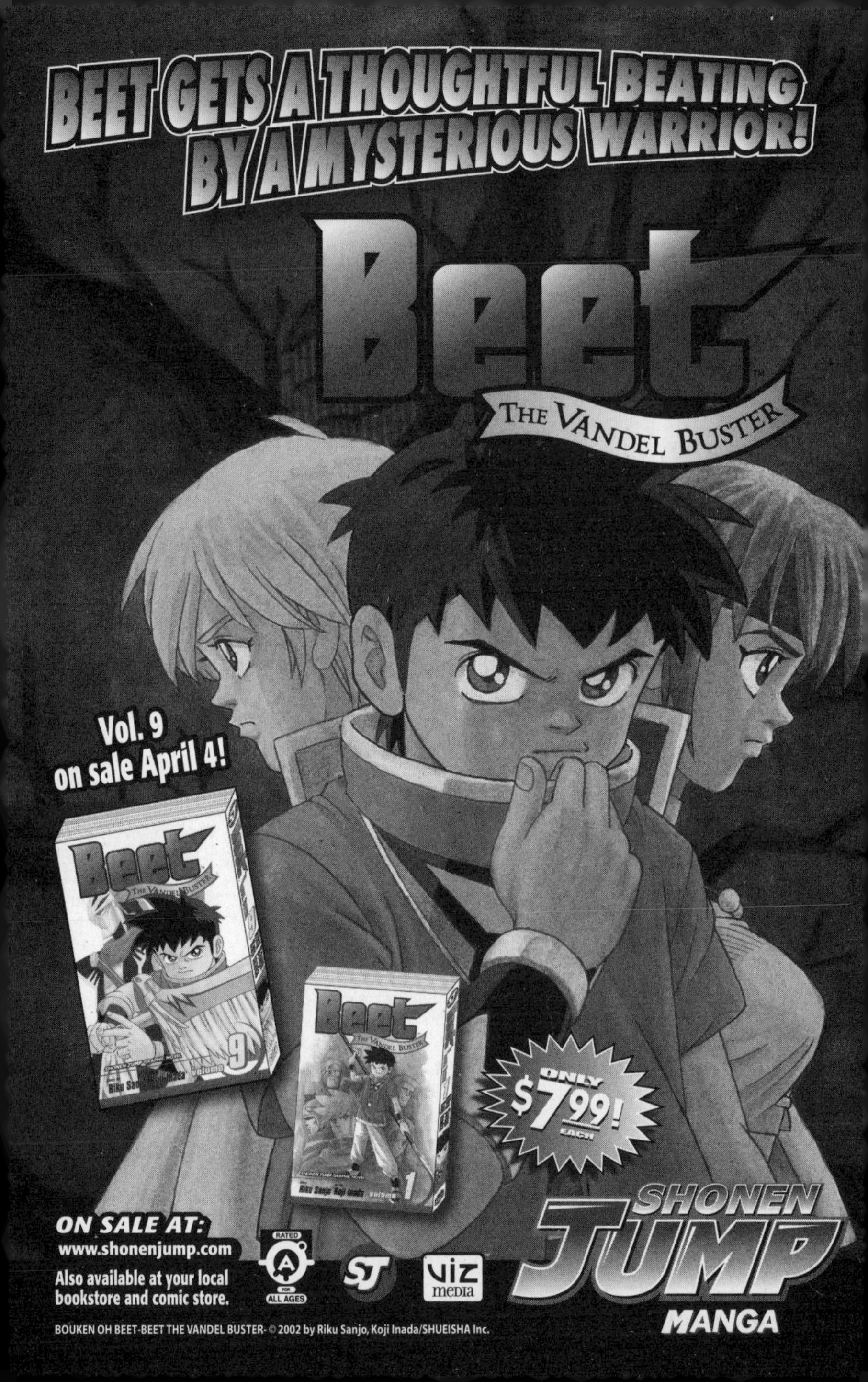
BEET GETS A THOUGHTFUL BEATING BY A MYSTERIOUS WARRIOR!
Beet
THE VANDEL BUSTER
Vol. 9 on sale April 4!
ONLY $7.99! EACH
ON SALE AT:
www.shonenjump.com
Also available at your local bookstore and comic store.
RATED A FOR ALL AGES
SJ
viz media
SHONEN JUMP MANGA
BOUKEN OH BEET-BEET THE VANDEL BUSTER- © 2002 by Riku Sanjo, Koji Inada/SHUEISHA Inc.

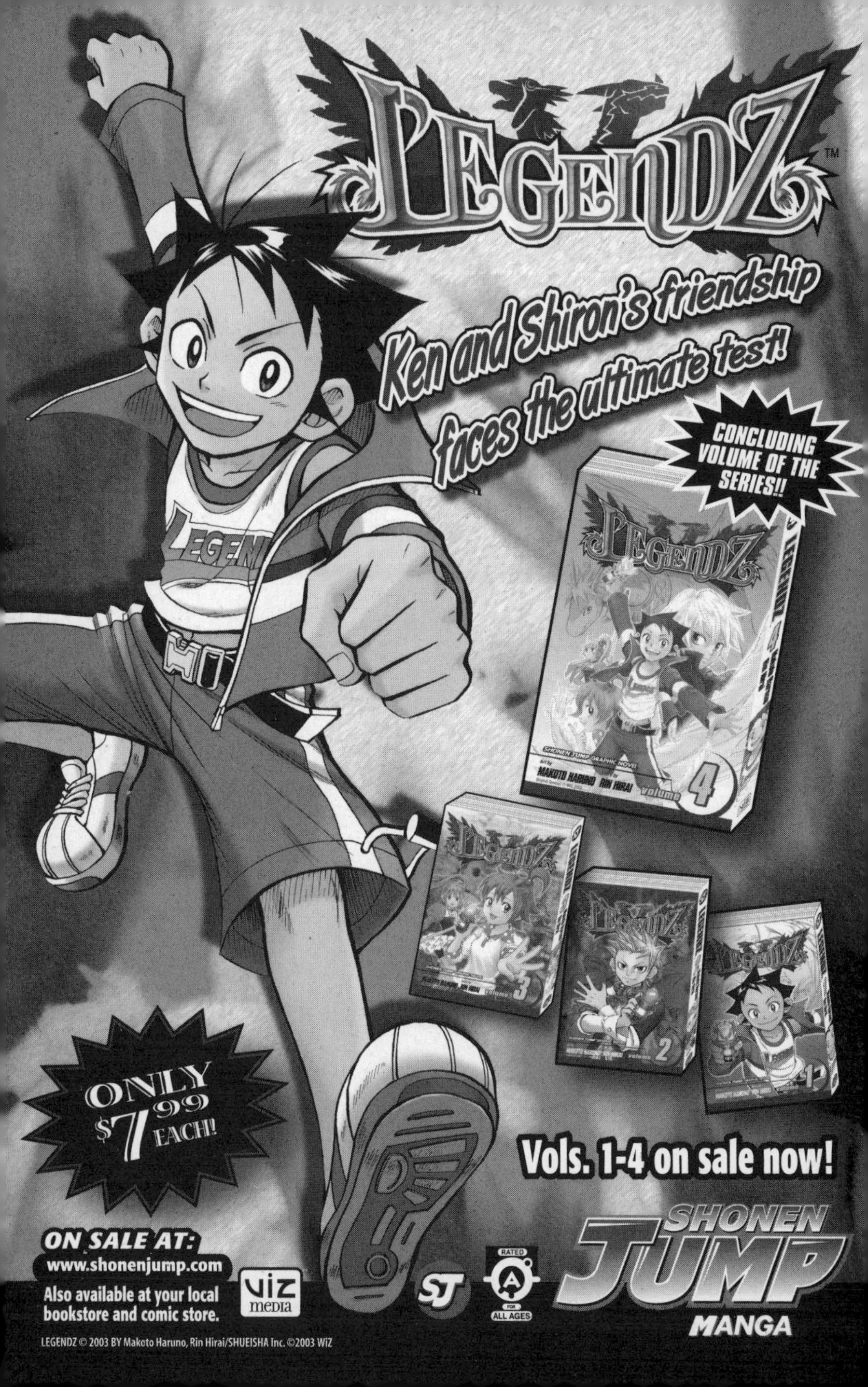

LEGENDZ™
Ken and Shiron's friendship faces the ultimate test!
CONCLUDING VOLUME OF THE SERIES!!
ONLY $7.99 EACH!
Vols. 1-4 on sale now!
ON SALE AT:
www.shonenjump.com
Also available at your local bookstore and comic store.
SHONEN JUMP MANGA
RATED A FOR ALL AGES
LEGENDZ © 2003 BY Makoto Haruno, Rin Hirai/SHUEISHA Inc. ©2003 WIZ

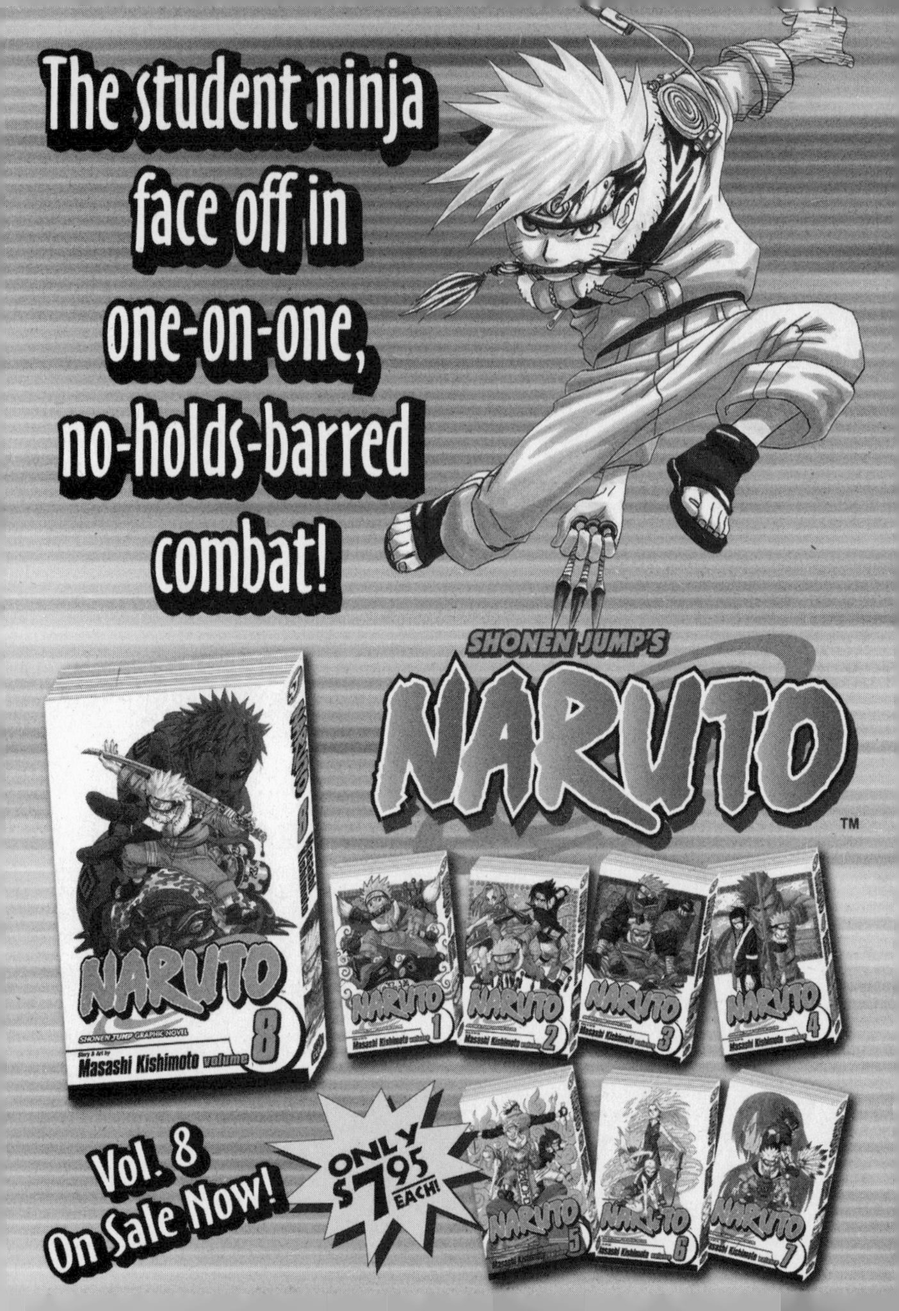
The student ninja face off in one-on-one, no-holds-barred combat!
SHONEN JUMP'S
NARUTO™
NARUTO 8
SHONEN JUMP GRAPHIC NOVEL
Story & Art by
Masashi Kishimoto volume
NARUTO 1
NARUTO 2
NARUTO 3
NARUTO 4
NARUTO 5
NARUTO 6
NARUTO 7
Vol. 8 On Sale Now!
ONLY $7.95 EACH!